CAMBRIDGE ASIA–PACIFIC STUDIES

Cambridge Asia–Pacific Studies aims to provide a focus and forum for scholarly work on the Asia-Pacific region as a whole, and its component sub-regions, namely Northeast Asia, Southeast Asia and the Pacific Islands. The series is produced in association with the Research School of Pacific and Asian Studies at the Australian National University and the Australian Institute of International Affairs.

Editor: John Ravenhill

JM dedicates this book to Linda Weiss
Fellow enthusiast for life, love and learning

DSC dedicates this book to his family
Dae-Whan, Jeong-Whan, A-Young and In-Sook
The source of his inspiration

TIGER TECHNOLOGY

The Creation of a Semiconductor Industry in East Asia

JOHN A. MATHEWS
Macquarie University

DONG-SUNG CHO
Seoul National University

CAMBRIDGE
UNIVERSITY PRESS

PUBLISHED BY THE PRESS SYNDICATE OF THE UNIVERSITY OF CAMBRIDGE
The Pitt Building, Trumpington Street, Cambridge, United Kingdom

CAMBRIDGE UNIVERSITY PRESS
The Edinburgh Building, Cambridge CB2 2RU, UK   http://www.cup.cam.ac.uk
40 West 20th Street, New York, NY 10011–4211, USA   http://www.cup.org
10 Stamford Road, Oakleigh, 3166, Australia   http://www.cup.edu.au
Ruiz de Alarcón 13, 28014, Madrid, Spain

First published 2000

Printed in Singapore by Green Giant Press Pte Ltd

Typeface New Baskerville (*Adobe*) 10/12 pt.   *System* PageMaker® [ER]

A catalogue record for this book is available from the British Library

National Library of Australia Cataloguing in Publication data
Mathews, John A., 1946–
Tiger technology : the creation of a semiconductor industry
in East Asia.
Bibliography.
Includes index.
ISBN 0 521 66269 9.
1. Industrial management – East Asia. 2. Semiconductor
industry – East Asia. 3. Organizational change – East Asia.
4. Technological innovations – East Asia. 5. East Asia –
Economic policy. I. Cho, Tong-sŏng. II. Title. (series:
Cambridge Asia-Pacific studies).
338.4562138152

Library of Congress Cataloguing in Publication data
Mathews, John A. (John Alwyn), 1946–
Tiger technology : the creation of a semiconductor industry in
East Asia / John A. Mathews and Dong-Sung Cho.
p.   cm. — (Cambridge Asia–Pacific studies)
Includes bibliographical references and index.
ISBN 0-521-66269-9
1. Semiconductor industry—East Asia. 2. High technology
industries—East Asia. I. Cho, Tong-sŏng. II. Title
III. Series.
HD9696.S4E185   1999
338.4'762138152'095—dc21   99-35365

ISBN 0 521 66269 9 hardback

Contents

Note

Chinese and Korean names in the book are given according to local custom, with the family name preceding the given name. Japanese names are in accordance with Western practice.

All dollars are US unless otherwise stated.

Figures

Tables

Preface

As this book goes to press, the newly created semiconductor industries of East Asia are emerging from an extraordinarily demanding series of tests. They have been forced to endure the damaging effects of a world semiconductor industry downturn, which has seen prices and output for chip products, and in particular for memory chips, drop precipitately in 1996 and 1997. Leading firms in Europe and the US were forced to withdraw from the memory chips industry as a result of this downturn. In addition to this, the East Asian semiconductor firms have been subjected to the trials of the Asian financial crisis of 1997 and 1998, which saw some of the more indebted firms in the region topple. Each crisis on its own would have been a severe test for firms newly established in one of the most fast-moving and competitive industries in the world. Coming together, they subjected the semiconductor industries in Korea, Taiwan, Singapore and Malaysia to an unprecedented trial of their organisational strength. That they have survived at all, let alone come through this process without major bankruptcies or exits (albeit with some industry consolidation), is a testament to their sustainability.

Now, in mid-1999, the signs are clear that the world semiconductor industry is growing again, and looks set for sustained growth in the twenty-first century. The semiconductor firms established in East Asia over the course of the past two decades, which have been investing heavily even during the depths of this recent industry downturn and Asian financial crisis, have every opportunity to ride a new wave of prosperity. The model of industry creation which they have fashioned therefore becomes of even sharper relevance at the opening of the twenty-first century.

The creation of new knowledge-intensive, high-technology industries in East Asia, of which the semiconductor industry is the most prominent, and the contribution they make to the generation of wealth in these countries, is surely one of the most interesting and significant features of recent East Asian development. It is indeed what we call the 'real' East Asian miracle, as opposed to the largely macroeconomic concerns of the World Bank's use of that term. But it has not always been met by acclamation in the West or in Japan. There is a lingering sense that these industries have been founded using 'unfair' techniques, from piracy of intellectual property, to savage labour practices, to government handouts, to endless imitation of others. No doubt all these have been elements in the appearance and survival of companies which were determined to take a place in the world's most demanding industries. No-one invited these latecomers to join the party. They had to use extraordinary organisational and strategic innovations in order to seize a share of these lucrative markets. That they succeeded at all is a small miracle. Once scholars and policy makers have managed to get over their sense of 'unfairness' then there are abundant lessons to be learnt in the successes these East Asian firms have had.

This book results from our curiosity to discover how latecomer firms could establish themselves in the most technologically demanding industries. Ever since our initial collaboration in Korea in 1994, we have worked individually, and together, to develop a conceptual framework adequate to the task, and conducted a continuous series of investigations in the firms themselves, asking what we call 'genesis' questions – how firms got their start, how they acquired their technological capabilities, how they improved and enhanced these capabilities, and the strategies they have pursued in order to stay alive in such competitive and technologically demanding environments. To our surprise and satisfaction, the firms in the East Asian countries where we have conducted these investigations have been open in discussing their strategies and operations. It is through their candour that we have been able to build in this book an original account of latecomer industry creation that is based firmly on the firms' own efforts, through organisational innovation and learning – rather than on external factors and the calculations of others.

We have constructed a story of policy-guided industry creation that is founded on knowledge and technology leverage by firms and institutions in the countries concerned. We have come to regard the achievements of these firms and institutions not only as remarkable in themselves, but as models of what can be done wherever firms are looking to upgrade their capabilities and extend their business involvement in new markets. This is what we see as the 'real' East Asian miracle, and it provides a legacy that is available to all other countries in the twenty-first century, provided there is the political will to create the institutions and institutional capacities needed to drive the catch-up process. We could not be sure of this conclusion until the most advanced of the East Asian semiconductor firms had shown that they could survive the double-crisis of the world industry downturn combined with the regional financial crisis.

We have worked together and individually on the cases and industry analysis that feed into this book. Dong-Sung Cho started research on the Korean semiconductor industry in 1993, when the Ministry of Science and Technology commissioned him to explore the strategies available to Korean chip makers who were making their mark as leading DRAM producers at the time. His interest goes back further, to the year spent in 1992 as a visiting professor at Hitotsubashi University in Japan, where he was exposed to the scrupulous and rigorous industry researches undertaken there. These researches were undertaken in part by scholarly interests and in part by the concerns of government, which was looking for ways of extending the strong position secured by Japanese semiconductor firms at the time. This kind of collaborative, mutually reinforcing research process made a deep impression on him, and became a model of research that he took back to Korea. The research commissioned from the Ministry in Korea enabled Cho to compare the strategies of the Korean firms with their competitors in Japan, Europe and the US, taking an historical perspective on the industrial dynamics that drove the industry globally. In particular, the study focused on the strategies that Japanese firms had used to catch-up with the American innovators, and the strategies that Korean firms had used subsequently to catch-up with the Japanese. Much of this work was reported in the study 'Latecomer advantages: The experience of Japanese and Korean semiconductor industries' published in the journal *Organization Science* in 1998.

John Mathews took a sabbatical break in Korea in 1994, at Seoul National University, in order to initiate a research program on the strategies of technology leverage of latecomer firms. A fruitful collaboration ensued with Dong-Sung Cho, enabling the two of us to conduct memorable visits to semiconductor plants which resulted in the collection of data and in long discussions as to its meaning. The underlying purpose of Mathews' research program was to build a conceptual model of how latecomer firms acquire capabilities and enhance them through their own organisational processes, as part of a wider concern with understanding the world not as it is, but as it is created. So much of the management and organisational literature is concerned to explain why rich firms are rich, or why leaders lead, without asking the more obvious questions as to how rich firms acquired their wealth in the first place. Mathews saw the emerging East Asian region as a source of data to shed light on these most fundamental questions of firms' and industries' growth and development. The Korean experience served as platform for his own field researches in Taiwan, Singapore, Malaysia and China, all of which have been repeatedly visited in the five years 1994 to 1999, including several visits to Japan, which set the benchmarks for new industry creation. Much of this work has been reported by Mathews in studies on the Taiwan and Singaporean semiconductor industries published in *California Management Review*, in 1997 and in 1999, and in papers delivered to scholarly gatherings such as the Academy of Management and the Academy of International Business. The two of us are pleased to see our joint work finally reach publication in 1999 in the *Journal of World Business*, as well as in this book.

Through this lengthy research program, we have accumulated many debts and obligations as well as acts of kindness and friendship that are a pleasure to acknowledge. Dong-Sung Cho wishes to acknowledge, in particular, Dr Won-Jong Lee, former Planning and Management Officer at the Korean Ministry of Science and Technology, who demonstrated deep trust in Cho's ability to mount a major industry research project. Dr Wi-Sik Min, former Managing Director of Hyundai Electronics Co. and currently Vice-President of Dongbu Electronics, provided both of us with insights and data to which few outsiders would have access. Cho also wishes to acknowledge the efforts of the members of his research team, including Professors Dong-Kee Rhee of Seoul National University, Jeong-Hae Seo of Kyungbook National University, Ki-Chul of Tohoku University, Yoon-Chul Lee of Korea Aviation University, and Dong-Hyun Lee of the Korean Catholic University, and research assistants Dr Jin-A Choi, Dr Byung-Jin Koo and Dr Jin-Young Sirh.

John Mathews wishes to acknowledge the insights that scholars of technological learning and development have shared with him in the course of this project. In particular, thanks are due to Professors Magnus Blomstrom, Mark Dodgson, Martin Fransman, Bob Hayes, Mike Hobday, Hiroyuki Itami, Chalmers Johnson, Ron Johnson, Jomo J. S., Linsu Kim, Sanjaya Lall, Otto Lin, Chi Schive, Jon Sigurdson, Robert Wade, Linda Weiss, John Zysman and Drs Wan-wen Chu, Rajah Rasiah and Poh-Kam Wong. The editor of the Cambridge Asia-Pacific Studies, Professor John Ravenhill, provided much encouragement and stimulus. So many people in East Asian companies provided unstinting help and encouragement, as well as their stories; it would be onerous to name them all, and in any case some must remain anonymous. But special mention should certainly be made of Dr Chintay Shih, the President of ITRI in Taiwan; Dr Otto Lin, now Deputy Vice Chancellor (Research) of the Hong Kong University of Science and Technology, and a former President of ITRI; Professor Mai and Dr Joseph Lee, current and former heads of the invaluable Chung-Hua Institution for Economic Research in Taiwan; Chi-Rak Kim, indefatigable head of the Korean Semiconductor Industry Association; Goh Keng-Swee, former Cabinet member and architect of Singapore's economic development program; Dr Wang Shih-Chien, Minister of State in the Taiwan government and technology strategist; Mr Lai Yeow-Hin, head of the Electronics industry development section of the Economic Development Board, Singapore; Dr Bill Chen, head of the Institute of Microelectronics in Singapore; as well as many others. Entrepreneurs were especially helpful in explaining how they started their firms and spin-offs: special thanks are due to Dr Morris Chang, founding Chairman of TSMC, VISC and WaferTech; Dr Yang Ding-Yuan, founding president of Winbond; Vincent Khee-Lian Low, head of LKTE and SEM; Michael Ng, founder of Globetronics and SGt Industries; Ku Hong-Hai, founder of Unisem; and in Singapore, C.H. Kwok (ASA); Tony Kwong (MIT); and Tan Bock-Seng (CSM and STATS). Welcome collegial support for JM was provided by Professors Dexter Dunphy and Steven Frenkel (UNSW); Bruce Stening (ANU); and Elizabeth More (MGSM), as well as by the other members of the 'Gang of Four' who had so much fun in China: John Merson, Peter Burns and Tim Turpin. Administrative support for the project was ably provided by Marie Kwok at the IRRC (UNSW). Valuable research assistance was provided for JM at different stages of the project by Elizabeth Thurbon, Hye-jin Lee, Teresa Poon, Cathy Xu and Tianbiao Zhu. At Cambridge, excellent advice and editorial assistance was provided by Foong Ling Kong and Paul Watt. And the most pleasant and important acknowledgment of all: Linda Weiss was a scholarly and loving companion and source of strength and ideas for JM at all stages of the project.

Abbreviations

Semiconductor Technology

ASIC	application-specific integrated circuit
BGA	ball grid array
BiCMOS	bipolar CMOS
CISC	complex instruction set computing
CMOS	complementary metal oxide on silicon
CODEC	coding-decoding integrated circuit (for multimedia)
CSIC	customer-specific integrated circuit
DRAM	dynamic random access memory
DSP	digital signal processor
eDRAM	embedded DRAM
EPAC	electrically programmable analog circuit
EEPROM	electrically erasable programmable ROM
EPROM	erasable programmable ROM
Fab	IC fabrication facility
FPD	flat panel display
FPGA	field programmable gate array
IC	integrated circuit
LCD	liquid crystal display
LSI	large-scale integration
MCM	multi-chip module
MOS	metal oxide on silicon
MPEG	motion picture experts group (for video data compression)
MPU	microprocessor unit
NMOS	N-metal oxide on silicon
PGA	pin grid array
PLC/PLD	programmable logic circuit/device
RISC	reduced instruction set computing
ROM	read-only memory
SDRAM	synchronous DRAM
SLI/SoS	system level integration/system on silicon
SMIF	standard mechanical inter-face

SRAM	static random access memory
VLSI	very large scale integration
ULSI	ultra large scale integration (submicron)

Semiconductor Industry

ASET	Association of Super-Advanced Electronic Technologies (Japan)
EIAJ	Electronic Industry Association of Japan
EUV LLC	Extreme Ultra Violet Limited Liability Company (US consortium)
GJGA 97	Global Joint Guidance Agreement (300 mm initiatives; 1997)
I300I	International 300 mm Initiative
J300I	Japanese 300 mm Initiative
JEIDA	Japan Electronic Industry Development Association
KSIA	Korean Semiconductor Industry Association
SELETE	Semiconductor Leading Edge Technologies (Japanese consortium)
SEMATECH	Semiconductor Manufacturing Technology (US R&D consortium)
SEMI	Semiconductor Equipment Manufacturers International
SIA	Semiconductor Industry Association (US)
SIRIJ	Semiconductor Industry Research Institute Japan
STA	US–Japan Semiconductor Trade Agreement (1986; 1991)
TEEMA	Taiwan Electrical and Electronic Manufacturers Association
TSIA	Taiwan Semiconductor Industry Association (formed 1996)
USDC	US Display Consortium
WSC	World Semiconductor Council (formed 1997)
WSTS	World Semiconductor Trade Statistics

Strategic/Conceptual

DRL	developmental resource leverage (authors)
EOI	export-oriented industrialisation
FDI	foreign direct investment
GLC	global logistics contracting
HCI	heavy and chemical industrialisation (Japan 1960s; Korea 1970s)
HTI	high-technology industrialisation
ISI	import-substitution industrialisation
ITD	industrial technology development

LCF	latecomer firm
MNC	multinational corporation
NIC	newly industrialising country
NSEL	national system of economic learning (authors)
NSI	national system of innovation
OBM	own-brand manufacture
ODM	own design and manufacture
OEM	original equipment manufacture

Korea

ABST	Advanced Basic Semiconductor Technology program (1993)
EIAK	Electronics Industry Association Korea
EPB	Economic Planning Board (until 1996)
ESC	Economic and Scientific Council
ETRI	Electronic Technology Research Institute
HEI	Hyundai Electronics Inc.
IDF	Industry Development Fund
IPS	Institute of Industrial Policy Studies
ISRC	Inter-University Semiconductor Research Centre (SNU)
KAIST	Korea Advanced Institute of Science and Technology
KDB	Korea Development Bank
KDI	Korea Development Institute
KEIC	Korean Electronics Industry Cooperative
KETI	Korea Electronics Technology Institute (1991)
KETRI	Korea Electronics and Telecommunications Research Institute (integrated within ETRI in 1985)
KIEP	Korean Institute for International Economic Policy
KIET	Korea Institute of Electronics Technology (integrated within ETRI in 1985)
KIET	Korea Institute of Economics and Technology
KIST	Korea Institute of Science and Technology (1966)
KOTRA	Korea Overseas Trade Association (later: Korea Trade-Investment Promotion Agency)
KTA	Korea Telecommunications Authority
KTC	Korea Telecommunications Company (1977–80)
LG Semicon	Lucky-Goldstar group's semiconductor firm (1995)
MCI	Ministry of Commerce and Industry (changed to MoTIE in 1996)
MoST	Ministry of Science and Technology
MoTIE	Ministry of Trade, Industry and Energy
NIF	National Investment Fund

SEC	Samsung Electronics Corporation
SNU	Seoul National University
STePI	Science and Technology Policy Institute

Taiwan

ASE	Advanced Semiconductor Engineering Inc.
CCL	Computing and Communications Laboratory (a part of ITRI)
CEPD	Council for Economic Planning and Development
EIDP	Electronic Industry Development Program
ERSO	Electronics Research Service Organization (a part of ITRI)
HMC	Hualon Microelectronics Corporation
IDB	Industrial Development Bureau
III	Institute for Information Industry
ITE	Integrated Technology Express
ITIC	Industrial Technology Investment Corporation
ITRI	Industrial Technology Research Institute
MoC	Ministry of Communications
MoEA	Ministry of Economic Affairs
MXIC	Macronix International
NSC	National Science Council
OESL	Opto-Electronics Systems Laboratory
OSE	Orient Semiconductor Electronics
PSC	Powerchip Semiconductor Corporation
STAG	Science and Technology Advisory Group
TEAMA	Taiwan Electrical Appliances Manufacturers Association (1995: TEEMA)
TEEMA	Taiwan Electrical and Electronic Manufacturers Association
TEMC	Taisil Electronic Materials Corporation (silicon wafers)
TKEM	Taiwan Komatsu Electronic Materials (silicon wafers)
TMC	Taiwan Mask Corporation
TSMC	Taiwan Semiconductor Manufacturing Corporation
UMC	United Microelectronics Corporation
USC	United Semiconductor Corporation (UMC joint venture 1995)
VISC	Vanguard International Semiconductor Corporation
WAE	Walsin Advanced Electronics
WEC	Winbond Electronics Corporation
WSMC	Worldwide Semiconductor Manufacturing Corporation

Singapore

ASA	Advanced Systems Automation Ltd
CSM	Chartered Semiconductor Manufacturing
DBS	Development Bank of Singapore
EDB	Economic Development Board (formed 1961)
EPRC	Electronic Packaging Research Consortium
IDS	Innovation Development Scheme
ILC	International Logistics Center
IME	Institute of Microelectronics (formed 1991)
ITI	Information Technology Institute
LIUP	Local Industry Upgrading Program
MIT	Manufacturing Integration Technology Pte Ltd
MTI	Ministry of Trade and Industry (formed 1979)
NCB	National Computer Board
NSTB	National Science and Technology Board
NTP	National Technology Plan (1991)
NUS	National University of Singapore
PAP	People's Action Party (governed since 1959)
SISIR	Singapore Institute for Standards and Industrial Research
STATS	Singapore Technology Assembly and Test Services
STG	Singapore Technologies Group
TECH Semi	DRAM Consortium: Texas Instruments, EDB, Canon, HP

Malaysia

AICS	AIC Semiconductor
BIM	Bank Industri Malaysia (Industrial Bank of Malaysia)
FTZ	Free Trade Zone (former term)
FIZ	Free Industrial Zone (revised term)
IMP	Industrial Master Plan 1986
ISIS	Institute of Strategic and International Studies
KTPC	Kulim Technology Park Corporation
KHTP	Kulim High-technology Park
KNB	Khazana Nasional Berhad (National Treasury investment bank)
LMW	Licensed Manufacturing Warehouse
MIDA	Malaysian Industrial Development Authority
MIMOS	Malaysian Institute of Microelectronic Systems
MITI	Ministry of International Trade and Industry
NDP	National Development Policy 1991
NEP	New Economic Policy 1972
PDC	Penang Development Corporation

SIRIM	Standards and Industrial Research Institute Malaysia
WTM	Wafer Technology (Malaysia) (joint venture between BIM, KNB and VLSI Technology)

China/Hong Kong

ASMC	Advanced Semiconductor Manufacturing Corporation (Shanghai)
HKASTRI	Hong Kong Applied Science and Technology Research Institute (proposed 1998)
HKCIT	Hong Kong Commission on Innovation and Technology (1997)
HKITF	Hong Kong Innovation and Technology Fund (1998)
HKUST	Hong Kong University of Science and Technology
MEI	Ministry of Electronics Industry
SSIP	Singapore–Suzhou Industrial Park

Japan

ECL	Electrical Communication Laboratories (NTT)
EPA	Economic Planning Agency
ERA	Engineering Research Association (for joint projects)
ETL	Electrotechnical Laboratory (MITI)
ISC	Industrial Structure Council
JEIDA	Japan Electronic Industry Development Association
JETRO	Japan External Trade Organization
MITI	Ministry of International Trade and Industry
NTT	Nippon Telegraph and Telephone (formed 1952)

Introduction

The rise of East Asia as a global economic power has been one of the great transformation processes of our time. Countries such as Korea, Taiwan and Singapore, which a generation ago had lain in poverty, have lifted themselves up to become generators of wealth through manufacturing and trade. Their success has overturned earlier approaches to economic development, in that the East Asian countries were outward rather than inward-oriented; their success was based on integration into the world economy through exports, technology transfer and access to foreign capital. This success was also founded on innovations in political economy, such as savings mechanisms for the accumulation of capital, the formation of developmental consortia for the rapid deployment of technological upgrading, and 'pilot' or steering agencies of government to coordinate investment, which have no counterpart in the developmental traditions of Western countries.

The sources of what the World Bank came to call the 'East Asian miracle' (1993) have been the subject of prolonged scholarly debate. Early attempts to come to grips with the magnitude of these countries' achievements tended to be polarised. On the one hand there were strong proponents of the view that the 'miracle' was the outcome of unfettered market forces and responsible, minimalist government intervention to 'get prices right'. On the other hand, there were scholars who saw in the 'miracle' the guiding hand of strong developmental states whose agencies intervened in the economy to 'get prices wrong' (Amsden 1989) – that is, to steer the economies towards investment and development targets which would otherwise lie beyond their capacities. The landmark World Bank report (1993) took the debate to a new level by arguing that the East Asian successes were the outcome of guided markets, where market forces were used as the primary tools of development, but subject to the guiding hand

1

of government institutions and agencies, which ensured that capital was channelled to productive activities.

These accounts apply on the macroeconomic level, and only rarely do they engage with the sectoral level. But it is at the technological level that the real dimensions of the East Asian success are revealed – and it is through the lens of technology that the microprocesses of strategic development may best be viewed. Any visitor to East Asia is struck by the advanced technological prowess of countries such as Korea, Taiwan or Singapore. (Japan has moved beyond 'catch-up' to become a technological giant in its own right.) This expertise, won through intense efforts at acquiring advanced technologies and becoming integrated into the world technological mainstream (rather than being content to compete at the margin), has generated remarkable achievements in economic growth and productivity enhancement that lie at the core of the 'East Asian miracle'.

The technological achievements of the East Asian economies go beyond the familiar labour-intensive and capital-intensive forms of industrialisation, which were the subject of the World Bank analysis, and have penetrated deep into advanced technologies and industries such as electronics, information technology and the semiconductors or 'chips' that feed into these sectors.

In the space of a decade, Korea, Taiwan, Singapore, China and Malaysia have all entered the high-technology world of chip fabrication. They follow in Japan's footsteps, a country that had inserted itself into the mainstream of chip fabrication in the 1970s, and became the world's dominant producer of memory chips (DRAMs) in the 1980s. Japan lost its leading role in DRAMs production in the 1990s not to the US, but to Korea. The Korean firm Samsung took the world lead in chip production in 1993, only a decade after launching its first memory chip product. Samsung's entry into the industry, like that of the other Korean firms, Hyundai and LG, was accomplished through its own internal efforts supplemented by leveraging the most advanced product and process technologies available in Japan, Europe and the US, which were fitted together quickly and efficiently into formidable production systems.

In Taiwan, where a semiconductor industry was created in the 1980s, public-sector laboratories such as the Industrial Technology Research Institute (ITRI) played the role of conduit of the technology required, leveraging the technology through transfer agreements with source firms in the US. It then devised various means for the rapid dissemination of the technological capabilities to the private sector, even creating firms where they did not already exist (such as in the case of TSMC and UMC, Taiwan's two leading semiconductor firms in the late 1990s). In the 1990s the firms themselves have taken the initiative to upgrade to more sophisticated semiconductor technologies such as DRAMs and communications ICs, again through technology leverage from American and Japanese partners.

In Singapore a semiconductor industry has been created largely through the investment of multinationals from the US, Europe and Japan, and in the 1990s from other East Asian countries. Singapore has successfully raised its local skill and technological levels from these multinational activities so that there is now a flourishing cluster of small and medium-sized service firms, as well as indigenous Singapore wafer fabricators such as Chartered Semiconductor, part of the state-owned Singapore Technologies Group.

By the late 1990s these non-Japanese East Asian industries are well established as leading players in this most sophisticated of knowledge-intensive industries, accounting for 30 per cent of world investment in new semiconductor wafer-fabrication facilities.

There is a puzzling aspect to these achievements that forms the starting point for our inquiry and analysis. The entry by Korea, Taiwan and other countries into advanced sectors like semiconductors was achieved without any apparent reliance on conventional sources of high-technology support, such as high levels of R&D expenditure and innovation activity within firms. The firms which have come to prominence, such as Samsung, Taiwan Semiconductor Manufacturing or Singapore Technologies initially lacked all but the most basic resources. They acquired technological capabilities by engineering various kinds of linkages with advanced firms, through contract manufacturing, licensing, joint ventures and other forms of inter-firm collaboration, while maintaining a fiercely competitive approach to winning markets and rapidly developing copies of products introduced by leading firms elsewhere such as in Silicon Valley. Such actions have been the tools of diffusion or dissemination of technologies historically but the process usually spans decades. In East Asian 'latecomer' firms, the transformation has been wrought in under ten years, an unprecedented result that demands analysis.

Such technological achievements simply cannot be explained in terms of the general macroeconomic frameworks used in the debates over the East Asian 'miracle'. The technological transformation of East Asia calls for an account that can shed light on processes specific to the *acquisition of technological competences*. We aim to establish that the key to East Asian success in high-technology or knowledge-intensive industrialisation cannot be found in standard labour and capital-efficiency accounts. It lies instead in the mechanisms for acquiring and enhancing 'technological capability' through various contractual forms of leverage such as engaging in original equipment manufacturing, licensing of technologies and joint ventures.

Rather than pursue a conventional R&D-led innovation strategy, firms in East Asia appear instead to have perfected a strategy of *leveraging* advanced technology as the principal resource for participation in high-technology industries. The strategy is based on the creation in these countries of an institutional framework, involving both public and private sectors, that provides a capacity not just to 'receive' the imported technology and knowledge associated with it, but to *absorb, adapt, diffuse* or *disseminate* and ultimately *improve* it through the efforts of indigenous technologists and engineers (Kim 1997a). It is this emphasis on 'active' technology leverage – as opposed to the notion of 'passive' technology transfer – that seems to characterise Korea's and Taiwan's approaches, which were modelled initially on Japan's success (Fransman 1995). Korea and Taiwan are now being emulated, with different emphases again, and with different institutional frameworks by other countries such as Singapore, Malaysia, China and Thailand (Hobday 1995a).

The 1997–98 Asian financial crisis subjected the new industries to the most demanding of tests, which they survived. While firms in other sectors in East Asia suffered catastrophic losses or were forced into bankruptcy, such outcomes were conspicuous by their absence in semiconductors. And while they had to withstand severe losses, they did not collapse or withdraw from the industry. Their technological capabilities remained intact and were extended during the crisis.

Given the potential significance of such an approach to accelerated uptake of high-technology capabilities, and its apparent robustness in the face of the most severe tests, this study will use the experience in semiconductors to shed light on the following kinds of questions:

- What are the distinctive forms of international technology leverage, and to what extent are they governed by technology and product life cycles?
- What are the distinctive national institutional frameworks which govern the leveraging process, and are some frameworks more effective than others?
- To what extent do firms act as vehicles of technological leverage and learning, and how do they do so?
- Are there specific technological and industrial characteristics of the semiconductor sector that have favoured technology leverage by latecomers, and if so, do these limit the wider applicability of the methods used?
- Are there limitations to such a leverage and learning strategy, such as creating permanent dependencies or inhibiting the development of marketing and product development capabilities in favour of manufacturing capabilities?

- To what extent are the methods used by East Asian firms and countries to engineer their entry into the semiconductor industry applicable in other countries within East Asia and beyond?

In seeking answers to these questions, we draw on a substantial and fast-growing stream of literature which addresses the processes of rapid technological development in East Asia from the perspectives of economics, political economy, industrial dynamics, technology transfer and organisational learning. We draw on all of these and add to them our own conclusions based on our study of the trajectory of a newly created industry. Our emphasis lies always on the processes of technological leverage and learning.

Development of East Asia

Much has been written on the sources of rapid development of East Asia, which culminated in the World Bank report of 1993. This literature has burgeoned, and the insights it has generated into the workings of an alternative political economy have been rich and stimulating. The Asian financial crises of 1997 and 1998 subjected not just the economies of the region to severe stress, but also the accounts of this success couched in general macroeconomic terms. By the late 1990s a less rosy picture was being painted of East Asian economic success, albeit still concerned to highlight the institutional distinctiveness of the processes, as in Aoki *et al.*'s notion of 'market-enhancing' development (Aoki *et al.* 1997). From our perspective, the story of the creation of the semiconductor industry in East Asia is one of 'market-enhancing' interventions by governments concerned to create industries which did not previously exist, and which survived the financial traumas of 1997–98. We provide the technological details which are missing in the more general macro-oriented and finance-oriented accounts.

Institutional Frameworks

Within political economy there is an insistence on the importance of *institutions* in economic development, and in particular the institutions which bring government agencies and private firms into productive relationships. Wade (1990) coined the term 'governing the market' for this process, and amply illustrated its workings in the context of Taiwan and Korea's development experience. Evans (1995) introduced a similar term, 'embedded autonomy', to describe the role that institutions play in guiding and coordinating economic activities, particularly investment, in developmental states. Weiss (1998) discussed a related concept she termed 'governed interdependence', where the emphasis is on industry associations acting as 'bridging' institutions between government agencies and free markets. We apply these general concepts in the particular context of the semiconductor industry in East Asia, focusing on the role that specific institutions such as ITRI in Taiwan or the Institute of Microelectronics in Singapore play in facilitating and disciplining the process of seeding and propagating advanced technologies.

Evolutionary Technological Pathways

Our study of the processes of high-technology industrialisation also has its roots in analyses of Schumpeterian competition, evolutionary economic pathways, technological trajectories, and the rise and fall of industries as driven by forces of innovation, exemplified in the work of Nelson and Winter (1982), Rosenberg (1994) and Dosi *et al.* (1988). Our contribution is to emphasise the specificity of the institutional frameworks needed to drive the process of management of technology diffusion in the East Asian context, where the evolutionary pathway taken is the outcome of political choice.

National Competitiveness

We also take into account studies on the rise and fall of industries and the forces that governments and firms exert to fashion the *competitiveness* of these industries. The sources of competitiveness can be discussed from the perspective of structural characteristics (Porter 1990) or from the perspective of the resources which the firms themselves acquire and use (Barney 1997) or from the public policy issues raised in national contexts (Berger and Lester 1997). Our study extends such treatments by taking an entire industry – encompassing steps in a value-adding chain that spans continents – and examining its dynamics over the course of its lifetime, from the industry's founding in the East Asian countries in the 1970s to its approaching conditions of sustainability in countries such as Korea and Taiwan in the late 1990s.

Organisational Capabilities

Finally, we draw on studies of organisational learning and the development of 'dynamic capabilities' within the firm. These studies may not have addressed the East Asian experience specifically, but they consider cases where firms are consciously acquiring and adapting *organisational dynamic capabilities* as a means of securing strategic advantages. Teece, Pisano and Shuen (1997), for example, have developed a theory of firms' acquisition and deployment of knowledge as a competitive strategy. This theory provides a very apt description of the 'latecomer firms' from East Asia which have implemented various 'knowledge-engineering' techniques to acquire and internalise the advanced technological processes needed for semiconductor production. Other related studies draw on the organisational notions of a firm's 'core competencies' needed for strategic differentiation, and its 'resource leverage' practices for building such competencies (Prahalad and Hamel 1990). We adopt and adapt these concepts to the special case of the East Asian 'latecomer firm' which we describe as using knowledge leverage to acquire and internalise the most advanced technologies.

Our study draws on all these literatures and more. It emphasises the institutional frameworks needed for industry creation in latecomer countries through processes of technology leverage. It aspires to distinctiveness in its analysis of the entire trajectory of a newly created industry from its seeding to its propagation and sustainability. This statement bears elaboration, so let us clarify the central intellectual concern that has governed our choice of topic for study and our approach to analysing and explicating the experiences we examine.

The fundamental thesis of *Tiger Technology* is that the East Asians have been extremely innovative in creating successful high-technology (knowledge-intensive) industries based on the most advanced technologies available in the US, Europe and Japan. No-one welcomed them into this exclusive club. They inserted themselves, not by following conventional strategies which are concerned with exploiting firms' existing advantages and resources. As latecomers they had few resources to exploit, and initially could benefit only from the advantage of low costs – an advantage that was rapidly diminishing by the time that these countries were ready to make their break into knowledge-intensive industries.

So these countries' 'innovativeness' was not of the conventional kind where a firm conducts R&D and develops new technological products and processes. Rather, they have been innovative in the sense that they developed an institutional system for the rapid transmission and propagation of technological knowledge from the advanced countries to themselves, and from firm to firm within their own countries. Their innovations have consisted in the creation of an organisational system for the management of technology leverage and diffusion. We intend to establish the validity of this proposition in the case of the semiconductor industry created by East Asian countries over the course of the past two decades, with a view to gauging its applicability to other industries and countries within the region and beyond.

Conventional accounts of industry evolution tend to fixate on the role played by technological innovation and diffusion through the efforts of the innovating firms (for example, in transferring their new processes abroad in accordance with product-cycle considerations). Such a framework, however, fails to fit the reality of the achievements of East Asian latecomer firms which have taken the steps needed to integrate themselves into high-technology industries such as semiconductors, computing, communications and various IT component sectors. It fails to fit for three fundamental reasons. First, most of the successful firms have not been innovators in the usual sense of the word, nor have they been 'recipients' of diffusion or technology transfer, but rather are the instigators of the process. Second, the successful latecomer firms in East Asia have fashioned sophisticated leverage devices for the acquisition and internalisation of technology, which in themselves have become a source of competitive advantage. Third, institutional structures have been created in East Asian countries to accelerate the process of 'diffusion' and, in the process, taken over many of the functions of the market.

Diffusion as a Process

Technological diffusion is actively managed by East Asians. For them, 'diffusion' is not a passive process, driven solely by strategic decisions and calculations taken by the originators of the phenomenon. Instead it is treated as a complex process where technological leverage and strategic management play critical roles. Diffusion is triggered as much by decisions of the adopters, who assimilate, accommodate, adapt and improve, as by the adoptees or sources of the novelty.

'Diffusion', with its connotations of passive transfer, is thus a misnomer; what we are talking about is a multipolar process of active dissemination and leverage of resources where the adoption and adaptation decisions are primary, and account for the extent to which 'diffusion' (that is, penetration) occurs. In our view this is best described as a process of *technology diffusion management* (TDM).

Diffusion Management as a Source of Competitive Advantage

The strategic calculations of the latecomer firm engaging in leveraging practices are quite different from those normally depicted in discussions of strategy and the enhancement of 'sustainable competitive advantages' by firms.[1] Whereas the conventional discussion is couched in terms of the firm identifying its sources of competitive advantage and then framing strategy to enhance and defend them, this makes no sense at all from the perspective of the latecomer firm. For the latecomer who lacks resources and advantages other than temporary cost advantages, the approach to strategy is to identify the resources which are most available and most susceptible to leverage, and then to implement a framework for actually tapping and incorporating these resources, and then improving on them. This is resource leverage in a developmental context – or what we shall call *developmental resource leverage* (DRL).

Institutions of Diffusion Management

East Asian companies have found that the management of diffusion calls for quite different institutions to those which have been developed in the West to support R&D-led innovation and its market-mediated propagation. The institutions of diffusion management are concerned with accelerating the uptake of technologies by firms, spreading the dissemination of new techniques, and hastening the processes of enhancing organisational capabilities (organisational learning) through such devices as engineering research associations – as in the case of Japan – and developmental consortia. The creation of such an institutional framework means that firms do not have to leverage and learn on their own. The results of earlier experiences with collaborative dissemination can be used to improve the outcomes, in a process which can best be described as 'economic learning'. Such a process is conducted in an institutional framework that we choose to characterise as a *national system of economic learning* (NSEL), in contrast with the more conventional notion of a national system of innovation.

Taken together, these three 'organisational innovations' – which are real innovations in the East Asian context whatever the labels we may attach to them – represent a major departure in the understanding of innovation and its propagation, away from knowledge generation in individual firms towards the management of technological diffusion as a strategic process of national economic upgrading.

The shift in theoretical perspective involved here is profound. What is being created is an 'industry', not just a cluster of firms. The focus is on the value-adding steps that need to be put in place, as well as their upstream and downstream linkages. This in itself is a major shift away from much industrial economics analysis.[2] The firms being created or encouraged seek sources of competitive advantage appropriate to their 'latecomer' status instead of embarking on the conventional quest for new products or processes. A conventional view of industry evolution is concerned with patterns of innovation and their supporting institutional structures. By contrast, the approach pioneered in East Asia is one where the process of technological transformation is seen in terms of the patterns and dynamics of technology diffusion and its management. The emphasis is on how innovations can be leveraged and turned into technological capabilities and competitive products as rapidly as possible by firms which are sometimes created for this very purpose.

It is this achievement that we see as the 'real' East Asian miracle, the one underpinning the miracle processes discussed in the 1993 World Bank report and elsewhere. In many ways, the conventional macro-economic construct of the miracle unravelled during the 1997–98 financial crises. But the 'real' underpinning technological transformation remained intact, and as potent a source of competitive advantage as ever.[3]

Tiger Technology is concerned with this 'real' East Asian miracle: we seek to characterise it, to explicate it, to understand it. We use the rise of the semiconductor industry as our 'laboratory' to test certain arguments and propositions about the character and dynamics of this 'miracle'. Our goal is to present an account of the accelerated management of technology diffusion within the semiconductor industry, where latecomer firms use various forms of technology leverage as a competitive strategy to provide themselves with a practical alternative to the conventional approaches to sustaining competitive advantages based on product and process innovation. We seek to shift the perspective of strategic management literature from seeing imitation by firms as a threat to incumbent advantages to seeing it instead as a viable strategy for latecomers, and one which has the socially desirable effect of accelerating the propagation of innovations from one economy to another.

To sharpen the focus of this alternative perspective, the differences between the three approaches discussed – the basing of competitive advantages on product innovation, process innovation or on diffusion management – are highlighted in Table 1.

The point being made in Table 1, and in the book generally, is that the management of technology diffusion, through the creation and management of various forms of leverage, constitutes a viable alternative as a source of competitive advantage. Moreover, the skills involved in mounting an attack on incumbents through various forms of leverage are every bit as demanding and sophisticated as the better studied skills involved in maintaining competitive advantages through innovation.

Our argument does not look to belittle the significance of innovation, nor is it seeking to justify endless 'free riding' as a viable national strategy. Rather, we seek to demonstrate the significance of diffusion management in the high-technology industrialisation experience of countries where other explanations are lacking, and its even more widespread significance as advanced firms in advanced countries start to take up the leverage techniques for themselves. Thus although industry creation through technology leverage is undoubtedly an East Asian innovation, its applicability is not confined to East Asia. Its replication elsewhere calls

Table 1 Propagation of innovations: competitive postures

Basis of competitive posture

	Product innovation	Process innovation	Diffusion management
Competitive focus	Product	Process	Access to technologies; diffusion
Competitive tools	Intellectual property rights; first-mover advantages	Cost; quality	Resource leverage
Competitive vehicles	Firms	Firms	Firms; government research institutes; consortia
Dynamic capabilities	Product enhancement; R&D	Process enhancement; quality/time improvement	Combinative capabilities; organisational learning
Strategic goals	Sustainable · competitive advantage	Temporary competitive advantage	Transient competitive parity
Sources of competitive advantage	First-mover advantages	Quality/time enhancement	Fast followership
Institutional framework	Atomistic competition	Limited competition	Accelerated diffusion within consortia; linkages with MNCs
Lead countries	US	Japan	Korea, Taiwan, Singapore

not for the familiar elements of technological innovation, but for the organisational innovations involved in countries building institutional capacities in managing the process of technological diffusion.

In these cases, the institutional guidance of the leverage processes that form the core of technology diffusion management can be contrasted with its absence elsewhere in East Asia. In Hong Kong, for example, a flourishing electronics industry was established, but there has been little success in moving beyond this to more knowledge-intensive IT and semiconductor sectors.[4] This is an important counter-case; it enhances the significance of the institutional features documented in the technologically successful East Asian cases. There have also been several failed attempts to leverage high-technology industries in Korea, Taiwan and Singapore, indications that the process is not failsafe, and that it probably has a greater success rate under certain conditions than others.

The principal task of our study is to account for these conditions and their prevalence.

Explanations and Approaches

The methods and assumptions of our study, with its focus on techno-logical transformation through knowledge leverage by indigenous firms and institutions, can be contrasted with those of several major lines of inquiry in the literature on East Asia. For our purposes, we classify these existing approaches as being inspired by neoclassical economic analysis, public policy analysis and production network analysis.

Neoclassical Economic Analysis

For many mainstream economists, the East Asian miracle was nothing but the effect of market forces inducing countries in the region to exploit their comparative advantages of low costs. From this perspective, presumably the 'real' miracle of technological transformation is merely a continuation of the same process, but with more sophisticated capital and labour inputs. This would be Krugman's position, for example, if he ventured to look at sectoral data beyond the very general setting within which he makes his pronouncements about the 'myth' of the Asian miracle.[5] The efforts by neoclassical economists to explain the East Asian industrial upgrading process as reflecting nothing but extended capital and labour inputs are, in our view, both highly illuminating and misleading.

Illuminating because, in spite of themselves, they capture the limits of a process built on the foundations of capital imported from the West combined with intensive labour inputs. Hence, they succeed in sharply demarcating this process from the 'real' technological miracle which is based on the acquisition and harnessing of knowledge inputs. These knowledge inputs, embodied in advanced technology and in processes of organisational learning, are not captured in total factor productivity equations, which are formulated for a static, equilibrium, two-factor world of perfect markets and perfect information, and costless trans-mission systems.[6]

If enhanced capital and labour inputs were all there were to the story, then there would be no differentiating the performance of East Asia from that of other regions with similar inputs such as Latin America. Nor would there be grounds for differentiating between the knowledge-intensive sectors created in Korea, Taiwan and Singapore, as compared with the absence of such sectors in Hong Kong, even with enhanced inputs of capital and labour. It is the special achievements of East Asian countries such as Korea, Taiwan and Singapore in knowledge-intensive sectors which cannot be accounted for in terms of simple capital and labour inputs that call for a more sophisticated explanatory framework.

Public Policy and Accounts based on Transient Advantage

Another line of argument seems intent on accounting for East Asian success in terms of factors such as low costs, government support, unsustainable levels of investments or just plain luck – the implication being that once these transient factors fade away, as they must, the East Asian technological transformation would be seen to be equally transient. These accounts are all focused on factors which are extraneous to the efforts made by firms and public institutions to enhance their technological capabilities. It is these arguments which turn out to be unsustainable, not the East Asian semiconductor industries.

Take the issue of costs. At its crudest, the 'labour intensification' argument holds that East Asian advantages lie solely in lower labour costs and exploitation of labour; its implication is that as the excess labour dries up or if people are no longer prepared to work long hours, the 'miracle' will come to a halt. While cheap labour was one of the advantages enjoyed by East Asian countries in the early 'labour-intensive' phase of industrialisation, it has little validity in the high-technology phase, when labour accounts for so little of the costs. Certainly, firms get their start in the industry through lower costs, including lower labour costs, but these are not the reason for the firms' ability to sustain their presence in the industry.[7]

Likewise a focus on high levels of investment as providing, in itself, an explanation for East Asian success in high-technology industries misses the mark. The implication is that capital availability is the major factor accounting for success rather than anything intrinsic to East Asian firms' internal learning practices. There is no doubt that high levels of investment were of great significance in the creation of the East Asian semiconductor industry, first in the case of Japan, which overtook US investment levels in memory chip production in the mid-1980s, and then in the case of Korea, whose investment levels exceeded those of Japan by the mid-1990s.[8] We will present evidence that levels of investment by firms in Japan, Korea and Taiwan between 1985 and 1995 were very high. These levels were needed to establish the countries' semiconductor industries. Our argument, however, is that these investment levels – particularly the high levels by Korea – represented not a 'success factor' so much as the price of entry into the semiconductor sector.[9] From our perspective the high levels of investment constituted the necessary, but not sufficient, condition for entry into a high-technology sector like DRAMs. They cannot account for success by themselves. Rather, they represent the price of quickly building market share.

We also explore other public policy factors to account for East Asia's catch-up success. A common line of argument is that the East Asian phenomenon was essentially a product of government financial support through hand-outs, subsidies and protection.[10] We discuss the subtleties of the relations between the government and the private sector later in some detail; suffice to say here that the investments in major semi-conductor fabrication activities by East Asian firms were financed almost entirely by the companies themselves from external loans, government credit agencies or, in the case of business groups in Korea and Taiwan, from cross-investment by one part of the business group in another. The evidence on this point is incontrovertible. Certainly in some cases government credit agencies played an important role, particularly in the early seeding phases.[11] But to imagine that government 'hand-outs' constituted the core of East Asian investment in semiconductors or underpinned its success is to misunderstand the facts of the matter. By the stage of high-technology industrialisation, companies are sufficiently sophisticated to be able to arrange most of their financing for them-selves.

Production Network Accounts

The arguments discussed so far address the external features of East Asian success in creating high-technology industries, without generating much insight into the internal dynamics of the transformation process. There is another group of scholars, whom we may call for the purposes of this discussion 'neo-dependency theorists', whose analyses are rather more sophisticated and cognisant of East Asian achievements, but for whom the source of the 'real' East Asian miracle lies not so much in the efforts of the countries concerned in leveraging technologies for their own purposes as in their fortunate location in industry networks created for their own strategic reasons by multinational interests. One version of this story sees the East Asian high-technology achievement as the outcome of the creation by the Japanese of region-wide production net-works involving vertical tiers of suppliers and assemblers and horizontal *keiretsu*, as more or less a replica of what was created domestically in Japan in the 1960s and 1970s. According to this line of reasoning, exemplified in the work of Yamamura and Hatch, the impressive output of high-technology industries in East Asia is simply a veneer that masks a fundamental technological dependence on Japan and likewise a depend-ence on wider Japanese multinational trade and investment strategies. Yamamura and Hatch are quite explicit about this, calling East Asian high-technology industry creation a form of 'captive development' in which Japan's aim is to seal off the entire East Asian region from open competition, as it earlier succeeded in doing for the domestic Japanese economy.[12]

An alternative version of the story sees the same processes of East Asian high-technology creation as the outcome of the strategic calculations of US multinational interests. One of the most sophisticated exponents of this view, Gereffi (1996), argues that East Asian producers have been caught up in production networks initiated from the US, in the form of 'global commodity chains'. Likewise Borrus (1994) characterises the resurgence of global competitiveness in the 1990s of US high-technology firms such as Intel, Motorola and TI as attributable, at least in part, to their creation of an open, global system of production (termed 'Cross-national Production Networks', CPNs) in which operations in East Asia are especially important. It is in East Asia that these firms can build production and logistics operations of equal (or superior) sophistication to those at home, drawing on the high levels of skills in the region, and the high quality of suppliers of components and equipment to keep their costs to competitive levels without sacrificing quality or flexibility. Borrus argues that US firms have 'left for dead' their Japanese competitors because of such open-ended global production strategies.[13]

From both perspectives – that of Japanese international networks or US-sponsored international networks – the role assigned to the East Asian firms is to be part of this drama, but in supportive roles, servicing the main protagonists.[14] For us whether these international production networks are the work of Japanese or US capital – or for that matter, European or other capital – is not the issue. We would be the last to deny the importance of both Japanese and US investments in East Asia, or their importance as sources of sophisticated capital equipment. Indeed it is US and Japanese multinational interests which are central to our account as sources of technology leverage by the East Asian firms. But the existence of such networks provides at best a set of opportunities for local technological upgrading; it offers no guarantee that such opportunities will be exploited or harnessed effectively. The critical issue is *where* the impulse for the upgrading effort comes from. Having the capability to connect with production networks in the first place through local firms acquiring OEM contracts, for example, or servicing contracts for equipment supply and maintenance, represents the beginning of a long and arduous process of capability enhancement on the part of indigenous firms – a process we shall demonstrate in detail for the semiconductor industry. The ability of state agencies such as Singapore's Economic Development Board to regulate and control the flow of investment that builds the networks is also critical to the region's ability to advance to higher and higher levels of technological capability and value-adding activity, as opposed to being stuck at one technological level in a permanent state of dependence, as implied by much of the 'international networks' and 'commodity chains' school of thought. So we are in agreement on the centrality of the emergent high-technology production networks in East Asia. Where we differ is in our seeing such networks as tools of industrial upgrading used by the countries themselves. This contrasts with the view that currently prevails in much of the production network literature, which sees networks in more static terms, as tools of exploitation or market closure by the advanced countries.[15]

Economic Learning and Technological Capability Enhancement

This brings us to the final analytical framework in which we locate our own work. This is the school of thought that sees East Asian success, firstly in medium-technology sectors and most recently in high-technology sectors such as electronics, IT and semiconductors, as being driven by the acquisition of technological competences by firms and public institutions in the countries concerned. Technology and its management – particularly of its import and diffusion – is perhaps the most important and challenging aspect of understanding East Asia's success. The relative paucity of technological upgrading capacity in other development experiences (in Latin America, for example, but also in other parts of East Asia) merely serves to emphasise this point.

Our study, then, draws on a well-developed body of research which elaborates the notions of 'technological learning' by scholars such as Kim, Amsden, Bell and Pavitt, and 'technological competence' (or technological mastery, capability, effort) as developed by Fransman, Hobday and Lall.[16] This tradition includes works on the uptake and the absorption of technology by countries in catch-up mode in specific sectors by such scholars as Anchordoguy, Park and Enos, Lynn, Samuels, and Wong, and, in more general terms, by Dahlman, Westphal, Peck and Tamura, Odagiri and Goto.[17] In their different ways, these scholars have studied the creation of new industries in East Asia from the perspective of the acquisition of technological competencies and the institutional frameworks within which these competencies were acquired and disseminated. Institutions and institutional capacities make the difference between success and failure, but it is the latecomer firms which ultimately have to embody the technological capabilities and act as vehicles for these national technological upgrading efforts.

Key features of the creation of new knowledge-intensive industries through leverage and learning make it very different from the conventional view of knowledge generation within the individual firm, or from the view of technological 'diffusion' as instigated by the innovators that lead to 'transfer' to the recipients. As a prelude to our exposition of how the process worked in the semiconductor sector, let us sketch out the principles of high-technology industrialisation (HTI) as we deduce them from the generalisation of the semiconductor experience. Five such principles seem to be of central relevance in accounting for the success of this process of high-technology industrialisation and industrial upgrading.

First, new high-technology industries are created in East Asia not through the spontaneous diffusion of industries or production systems from advanced countries, but as a deliberate act of policy designed and implemented by the countries themselves, working within the technological dynamics of the industries concerned. This involves creating institutions of technology leverage, a process that remains almost completely unexplored in the existing organisational literature. Industry creation is largely seen in terms of firms taking decisions to pursue, adopt or adapt innovations; it is seen as the unintended outcome of firms pursuing strategies of product leadership or imitation, creating new industries through product leadership.[18] There is a sparser literature on creation of the full institutional 'ecosystem' where the industry is seen as a social system consisting of public-sector institutions, private firms, industry associations and standards-setting and regulatory agencies, all co-evolving as the industry develops.[19]

But as yet there is hardly any discussion of industry creation as a deliberate act of public policy, even though this is clearly what is at stake with the emergence of high-technology industries in East Asia. The process of industry creation starts with the creation not of firms or technology agencies but of an *institutional framework* which provides a pattern or template for subsequent industry growth. The process of high-technology industrial upgrading is concerned not with individual products or even individual technologies, but with the development of a capability to handle an expanding range of increasingly sophisticated products and technologies that are 'knowledge intensive'.

Second, the process of high-technology industry creation in East Asia is achieved through the management of technological diffusion, via imitation, leverage and learning, rather than through R&D-led knowledge generation by individual firms. The generation and diffusion of knowledge is equivalent conceptually to the notion of 'innovation' – except that the Western literature on innovation has an overwhelming bias towards knowledge generation. It was the genius of Japan and the other East Asian countries to realise that the emphasis should really be placed on *diffusion* since this is where national wealth (as opposed to the wealth of an individual person or firm) could be generated. Thus the processes of HTI are concerned with the establishment of institutional frameworks designed to accelerate diffusion of technical knowledge and its uptake by sophisticated firms.

All the East Asian countries recognised that their prior investments in skills and technical training, and in R&D capabilities within public research institutions were essential prerequisites to developing and sustaining knowledge-intensive industries such as semiconductors. The first act of the Korean firm Samsung, for example, when entering the mainstream semiconductor sector in 1982–83 was to hire skilled engineers and technicians, for they were seen, correctly, as carriers of the knowledge needed to enter the knowledge-intensive sector.

Likewise, one of Singapore's first acts when it decided to attract multinational corporations (MNCs) as vehicles of its own high-technology industrial upgrading was to lay the foundations in terms of a solid national core or cadre of 'knowledge workers'. This is where public investment was focused initially.

The emphasis on the diffusion of technology (knowledge) carries with it a commitment to develop an institutional framework that is concerned not with the generation of knowledge within firms, but with the management and acceleration of the process of diffusion itself. This is the perspective that has informed the establishment of public-sector research institutes and the formation of technology consortia in East Asia, all of which constitute various institutional forms for the management of diffusion of technological capabilities.

Third, technological capability is enhanced through resource leverage, by harnessing collaborative networks and competition between sophisticated firms in a developmental, 'catch-up' institutional setting. In high-technology industries, technological upgrading is fundamentally a process of resource leverage – of skills, technology, knowledge – from the advanced to the relatively less advanced. The leverage is conceived and executed by firms and agencies within the relatively less advanced countries themselves – in this sense, its emphasis and focus is quite the reverse of the usual description in Western literature of 'technology transfer', which takes the perspective of the technology-exporting nation. While labour and capital can be 'hired' – labour exacting a fee in the form of wages, and capital in the form of interest or dividends – knowledge can only be generated internally, or leveraged from outside. External leverage is the defining feature of HTI. The contractual forms within which knowledge is leveraged range from simple licensing arrangements to much more complex collaborative arrangements and joint ventures.

The creation of the semiconductor industry provides numerous insights into the workings of this basic approach. In all the instances to be discussed, the focus of activity by public and private institutions was the acquisition of the most advanced semiconductor technology available, either immediately, as in the case of Samsung *et al.* importing 64K DRAM technology in 1983–84, or in the medium-term, as was the case with Taiwan importing then-obsolete 7-micron IC fabrication technology from RCA, with a view to quickly upgrading and diffusing it to the private sector through collaborative networks.

The vehicles of HTI are sophisticated firms. However large and significant may be the role of public-sector agencies in the preparatory stages of the process, the goal is the creation of sophisticated firms capable of engaging with real technologies producing real products in real markets as quickly as possible. These firms are the primary vehicles of HTI, and need to be sophisticated enough to attract capital investments for high-technology activities, and to act as leveraging vehicles, such as in securing licences to advanced technologies and products, or in managing intellectual-property portfolios.[20]

Fourth, the process is effected through industry 'nurturing' rather than 'protection', with industry policy evolving as the industries themselves take root and diffuse via a 'governed interdependence' between state agencies and industries. Industries being created through leverage call for 'nurturing' by public agencies to assist firms and induce them to enter new high-technology sectors by reducing the risks and entry costs. The 'nurturing' can consist of provision to firms of infrastructure support (for instance, technology parks, high-quality power and water supplies); low-cost loans and tax breaks to stimulate investment and R&D; and technology leverage services such as development assistance through public-sector research labs.

Japan used the full gamut of 'infant industry' protective measures, such as excluding foreigners from the domestic market, tariffs and so on. (Japan was the first country in Asia to penetrate to the core of advanced technologies.) Korea used such measures to a lesser degree; it took measures to protect the home market and exercised pressure on foreign joint-venture partners in the 1970s to withdraw, leaving the field to Korean firms. It insisted on technology transfer arrangements as *quid pro quo* for allowing foreign firms access to its domestic market, particularly in the case of telecommunications. It employed tariffs on semiconductor products but had liberalised its trade and capital regimes for this sector by the mid-1980s.

Taiwan pursued a more liberal strategy. It never imposed a tariff on semiconductor products, nor did it exercise preferential purchasing of Taiwanese products. The role played by the state was very much one of 'collective entrepreneur'.

Singapore, in keeping with its reliance on direct foreign investment

(DFI) by MNCs, pursued the most liberal of all strategies – no tariffs, no currency restrictions. But Singapore was not 'open slather' in its approach; government agencies such as the EDB were very active in 'guiding' investment into Singapore, and in leveraging skills from potential and existing investing firms. Malaysia, on the other hand, has vacillated between protectionist and liberal regimes; for example, federally there has been strong promotion of DFI by MNCs only since 1986.

It was the sophistication of the 'nurturing' devices used by the East Asian countries in the seeding and diffusion phases of developmental resource leverage of the semiconductor industry that accounts for its successful creation. But such nurturing strategies call for levels of 'institutional capacity' that far exceed the capacities exercised in simpler matters such as setting tariff levels or enforcing competition. Earlier debates between neoclassical economic accounts and state-centred accounts of East Asian industrialisation have now been superseded by more nuanced understanding of the roles played by both state agencies and industry actors.[21]

Fifth, the process of high-technology industry creation is iterative, with each cycle leading to the enhancement of technological capabilities and ultimately to industrial sustainability, accomplished within national systems of economic learning. In all the cases of industrial upgrading in East Asia that we examine, transition to high-technology industry was an over-riding goal of public policy, to which other issues were subordinate. In Japan, the effort was conducted under quasi-military conditions of focused effort by a single-minded system of state agencies. In Korea and Taiwan, state agencies went to extraordinary lengths to coax the private sector into eventually exposing itself to the risks of high-technology industry activity. In Singapore and Malaysia, the governments' role was critical in determining the opening to the MNCs, and in fashioning the opening itself.

One of the lessons from the creation of a semiconductor industry in East Asia is surely that HTI is effected more efficiently when there are public-sector coordination and risk-reduction processes and mechanisms available. This calls into play the institutional setting in which HTI is effected – which, at bottom, rests on the country's *institutional capacity* in an economic sense, and the level of sophistication of 'governed inter-dependence' between the players involved. The more sophisticated this network of institutions, the faster the economic learning. The less sophisticated, then correspondingly slower is the rate of economic learning, and less certain the HTI outcome. The more sophisticated the firms, the more they are able to leverage themselves abreast of the technological frontier through collaborative alliances and technology development consortia.

While some authors have discussed such issues using the notion of a national system of innovation, we choose not to use this term since our emphasis is on knowledge diffusion rather than generation.[22] Hence we prefer a new term, *national system of economic learning* (NSEL). The point is that economic learning is accomplished not by firms working individually or even in isolated collaborative networks such as private consortia but in 'industrial systems' that provide structure and process between firms and the market, or between firms and the state. Economic learning takes place at a level 'higher' in aggregate than that of organisational learning. While the latter is essential to successful economic learning, it is only a part of the story. The point about economic learning is that there are structures (institutions) that operate between firms and the market, or *between* firms and the state, which enable their activities to be coordinated or orchestrated in a manner that approximates the capacity of a company management to coordinate the operations of the different divisions of a company.[23]

The process of technological upgrading as we depict it is one without end. There will never come a time when a country can state that it has attained a degree of technological sophistication that requires no further advancement. This would contradict our basic Schumpeterian view of the workings of the capitalist economy, let alone our basic sense of reality. Yet there is a goal to the process of HTI, that is, to achieve a state of 'sustainable innovation' in a particular technological field. In such a state, a country's firms will have become so sophisticated that they can enter into collaborative technological alliances with other sophisticated firms around the world. Far from indicating a state of 'weakness' or 'dependence' such alliances in fact represent an advanced state in which foreign firms are prepared to collaborate with the newcomer in the pursuit of common technological goals.

It was the attainment of this state by semiconductor firms in Korea and Taiwan in the 1990s that can be used as a criterion to indicate that they had acquired a degree of 'sustainable innovation' and hence had come close to completing the process of industry creation through leverage in the semiconductor industry. But the process of HTI is never-ending. No sooner has a country acquired a capability in one technology than the field moves on to the next. Capabilities in ICs in the semiconductor industry have been succeeded by capabilities in liquid crystal displays and, in the mid-1990s, by capabilities in multimedia and HDTV, and so the sequence continues.[24] The point is that leveraging, once learnt, can become a permanent way of life for a company and for a country. It is practised initially to gain access to technologies or skills that are beyond reach. Once the firm (or country) becomes a player, collaboration within networks is practised as a way of staying abreast of activities which,

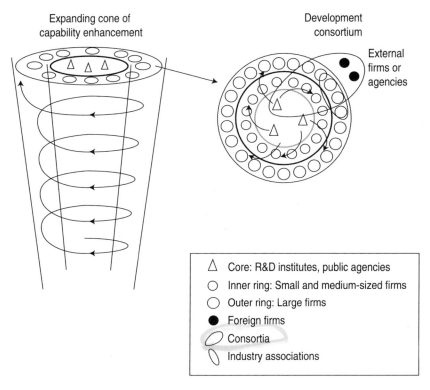

Figure 1   Latecomer capability enhancement and inter-organisational relations

individually, would lie beyond the reach of even a large and advanced player.

The process of leverage and learning is an iterative process of expanding technological capabilities. Each iteration broadens and deepens the technological capabilities which serve as foundation for further iteration. This process is depicted in Figure 1: the left diagram shows the upward spiral of capability enhancement by firms and agencies in latecomer nations and the right diagram is a cross-section of this spiral, showing the complex patterns of inter-organisational institutional relations involved.

The process we describe is thus an endless upward spiral of expanding technological capabilities, nurtured and disciplined through complex and sophisticated institutional frameworks involving public institutions, private firms, consortia, industry associations and government departments. This is the complex that we choose to describe as a 'national system of economic learning'. In our study we seek to develop a more nuanced understanding of the relations between public and private agencies, and of their co-evolution over time as the industry develops, and to generalise from the evidence of the semiconductor industry in East Asia. We are looking for the pattern of 'supra-organisational' structures and processes that have been created in East Asian countries – supra-organisational patterns such as inter-firm networks, industry and trade associations, product development consortia, cross-subsidising integrated firms and clusters. We seek confirmation that it is these structures which provide the framework that facilitates, encourages, disciplines – in a word, *accelerates* – the processes of organisational learning undertaken within individual firms.

It needs to be emphasised that catch-up is different from leadership. Insofar as Japan has established itself as a world technological leader that is on a par with US firms and, in many instances, in advance of them, its institutional frameworks have necessarily evolved to take into account this new situation. (Many would argue that they have evolved much too slowly.) The same process will no doubt emerge in Korea, Taiwan and Singapore as they close the gap between their own technological levels and those of the best firms in the world, or even assume leadership themselves, as Samsung has done in the case of DRAMs.

Our exposition will proceed as follows. In Chapter 1 we sketch out the basic dynamics of the global semiconductor industry and the insertion of firms from East Asia in the production networks of the industry. This chapter provides the essential empirical data with which our argument will engage. Chapter 2 introduces the concepts of 'latecomer firms' and their strategies of technological leverage and learning, tracing out a conceptual and theoretical framework that we use in our exposition of the national efforts to create semiconductor industries in East Asia. This is the framework we dub 'developmental resource leverage'.

Part II consists of country-specific chapters that look at the experiences of Korea, Taiwan, Singapore and Malaysia in creating a semiconductor industry. The chapters on these countries are based on our own fieldwork, discussing the industries' creation and their prospects with company managers, government officials and scholars.[25] Our concern lies in exploring the institutional frameworks within which firms and public agencies were able to leverage the required knowledge and technologies in order to gain access to the exclusive club of firms and countries that make up the global semiconductor industry.

In Part III we turn to the general and comparative issues that arise from these in-depth country-level studies. Chapter 6 develops a comparative analysis of the different East Asian experiences in creating semiconductor industries by looking at the commonalities in terms of technology leverage, and at the differences in terms of strategies and institutional frameworks involved. Chapter 7 examines the effectiveness of leverage strategies in general for creating new industries, drawing on the evidence from the semiconductor industry. The key issue of this chapter is how effective the strategies of leverage have been, and what the evidence is of their spreading beyond the core experiences of semiconductor industry creation. Chapter 8 broadens the focus to look at the systemic features of the industry upgrading processes – what we are calling the national systems of economic learning – and their generalisability.

We conclude by proposing that the organisational innovations developed by East Asian countries to facilitate their acquisition of advanced technologies may now be adopted, with suitable modifications, by advanced firms in advanced countries, as they seek to keep up with an ever-expanding technological frontier. We raise the possibility that in conditions of hypercompetition, techniques of resource leverage pioneered by East Asian firms and agencies may also become sources of competitive advantage for firms in advanced countries.

Notes

1 Porter (1990) takes it as axiomatic that competitive advantages are built on a foundation of innovation.
2 Van de Ven and Garud (1989; 1993) insist that industries are not just collections of firms, but encompass a range of supporting institutions and infrastructure. It is in the provision of such infrastructure that East Asian industry creation initiatives distinguish themselves.
3 The 1997–98 financial crises in Asia, while severely testing the region's economies, and putting many of the earlier accounts of the East Asian 'miracle' to the test, does not damage our account of the use of institutions of technology diffusion management in creating industries like semi-conductors. We are concerned with the creation of new industries, and the institutional frameworks within which this is accomplished, and less so with the fate of the industries once they are established. It is of interest, however, that during the 1997–98 financial crises in Asia, the high-technology industries fared best. The Taiwanese semiconductor industry continued to grow rapidly, even during the crisis. In Korea, even though the downturn in memory chip prices during 1996–97 had severe consequences – major companies had to pare back their investments and their plans for overseas expansion – their technological capabilities remained intact.
4 On Hong Kong's attempts to introduce high-technology industries, and the difficulties encountered, see, for example, Berger and Lester (1997).
5 On the 'myth' of the Asian miracle, see Krugman (1994). For the work on which Krugman's polemic was based, see Young (1994) and Kim and Lau (1994). For a Singaporean perspective, see Goh and Low (1996).

6 It is the disjunction between such assumptions and economic reality that restrains us from debating with these economists on their own data and methods, which tend to omit the most interesting and important processes.

7 Take the case of Korean semiconductor firms. Labour costs in a Korean firm at less than 5 per cent are dwarfed by leveraging costs (interest and royalties) of around 27 per cent. Thus if 'labour intensification' were practised at all, it would account for very little of Korean success. It would not matter whether people worked 24 hours or even 30 hours a day; improvements in this factor alone would have only a minor impact on the total cost structure. Thus 'labour intensification' cannot account for the success of East Asian countries in the high technology field.

8 Itami (1995) presents a fascinating insight into this process through his analysis of the reversals suffered by the Japanese memory chip industry. This Japanese study awaits translation into English.

9 Korea had to pay a high price because its entry was so rapid and highly leveraged, and hence risky. The risks were borne by the major companies and in every case, it was virtually the entire company that was being bet in the early and mid-1980s, with little prospect of immediate return. In Korea high levels of investment could be mobilised because of the institutional framework favouring 'policy loans' and the strong entrepreneurial drive of the founders of the major companies who took advantage of such loans. Investment levels in Taiwan have been much more modest, in keeping with the gradual and more balanced build-up of the semiconductor sector. Here it was public-sector entrepreneurship that led the way, with private capital waiting until the late 1980s before making any significant investments.

10 See the report of the US Office of Technology Assessment (OTA 1991).

11 In Taiwan this included initial investment in DRAMs by Acer (through the joint venture with TI) in 1990, when the China Development Corporation stepped in to save the project, or in Singapore when the EDB invested S$100 million in the TECH DRAM venture, and another S$100 million in the second wafer fabrication facility built by Chartered.

12 See Hatch and Yamamura (1996) and their more recent exposition, Yamamura and Hatch (1997). The originality of their exposition is that they focus not so much on the emerging trading bloc in South East Asia centred on Japan, but on an emerging production bloc built through an extension of Japan's domestic horizontal and vertical production alliances.

13 See Borrus (1994), as well as Borrus and Zysman (1997), where the argument is generalised to encompass a new global relationship between countries competing within components and final systems that the authors call 'Wintelism'.

14 We hasten to point out that Borrus in particular, and to some extent Gereffi, are not specifically concerned with East Asia itself, but more with an analysis of trends in the US and how they are affected by global developments. It is we who are placing the emphasis on East Asia.

15 Bernard and Ravenhill (1995) provide a sophisticated overview of many of these issues connected with the emergence of production networks. Like us, they do not characterise East Asian technological successes as the mere effect of others' calculations.

16 See Kim (1997a; 1997b) and earlier references, particularly Kim (1993); Amsden (1989) and Hikino and Amsden (1993); Bell and Pavitt (1993); Lall (1990; 1992; 1997); Fransman (1995); and Hobday (1995a; 1995b).

17   See, for example, Anchordoguy (1989); Park and Enos (1991); Lynn
      (1982); Samuels (1994); Wong (1995); Dahlman (1993); Dahlman and
      Westphal (1981; 1983); Dahlman, Ross-Larson and Westphal (1987); Peck
      and Goto (1981); Peck and Tamura (1976); Odagiri and Goto (1996).

18   For a review, see Cusumano and Elenkov 1994. They make the point that
      there is still a divide between the literature on technology transfer and
      strategic management of technology, something we attempt to overcome in
      this study.

19   An example would be the study by Van de Ven and Garud of the cochlear-
      implant industry over a thirty-five-year period, and the general framework
      they developed for such studies (1989; 1993).

20   Hobday (1995a; 1995b) discusses such firms using the suggestive termin-
      ology of 'latecomer firm' with its Gerschenkronian overtones. This is a
      fruitful approach that could be developed in the organisation and manage-
      ment literature; for an initial attempt to do so, see Mathews (1997a; 1998b).

21   As in the model of 'governed markets' (Wade 1990) or that of 'embedded
      autonomy' (Evans 1995). The model of 'governed interdependence' (Weiss
      1995; 1998) offers a flexible conceptual framework that captures the fruitful
      interchange between state agencies and industry actors involved in high-
      technology industry creation in East Asia, and the mix of support, facil-
      itation and discipline that characterises the evolving set of 'industry policies'
      and, more importantly, the implementation capacities of countries in the
      region.

22   See Lundvall (1992) as well as the studies of different NSIs reported in
      Nelson (1993).

23   For further elaboration on this point, see Mathews 1996b.

24   These developments are discussed in Chapter 6.

25   References to the Japanese experience in creating a semiconductor industry
      are made in Chapters 2, 6 and 7.

PART I

The 'Real' East Asian Miracle

CHAPTER 1

Tiger Chips: The Rise of East Asia in the Global Semiconductor Industry

Rarely has a technological device so dominated an era. The transistor, only invented in 1947, and then the silicon chip, now feed into a vast array of products and processes, investing them with powers of intelligence that were unthinkable just a few years ago. These tiny slivers of silicon, etched with layers of metal and polymers to spin high-technology webs of unbelievably complex circuitry are the critical technological drivers of our time, creating new products like digital watches, personal computers, high-definition television – and new industries to manufacture them.

Integrated circuits (ICs) have grown in complexity so that what started as a single device – the transistor – now encompasses millions of devices embedded in a single piece of silicon. These are the 'megabit' chips like dynamic random access memories (DRAMs) which, by the year 2000, are reaching the one-gigabyte level: one chip with a thousand million devices embedded in it. This complexity feeds into a multitude of new uses, blending sound, image, text and data in cunning worldwide webs of multimedia information generation and exchange. New worlds of fantasy are spun out of them, a new world of virtual reality.

The world of business that generates wealth from these chips is anything but a 'virtual' reality. The wealth generated on the US West Coast in Silicon Valley, where the chips were designed and, to some extent, fabricated, and Hollywood, where the chips are used to conjure dreams, is all too real. So too is the reality across the Pacific, where great wealth is now created through the fabrication of chips and of the electronic and information technology products that use them. For the countries of the eastern seaboard of the Pacific, beginning with Japan, Korea, Taiwan, and joined now by Singapore, Malaysia and China, the reality of chips is fundamental to their industrial strategies.

29

Semiconductors are Korea's largest export item, and remained so even after the 1997 financial crisis. They are similarly high on the export list for all the other countries of the eastern Pacific rim.

It is the conjunction of chips and East Asian industrialisation that forms the subject matter of this book. While semiconductor chips have been transforming the world through their impact on a vast range of products and processes, they have also been used as vehicles to transform the economies of East Asia. One by one, starting with Japan, these economies have identified semiconductors as a sector of strategic importance, to be mastered at all costs for the wealth it could generate and for the spin-off effects in the rest of the economy. For the Japanese, semiconductors were seen as the 'rice of industry', and no effort was spared to secure the product and process technologies from then-dominant US firms such as Fairchild and Texas Instruments (TI), and to 'nurture' the technological capabilities of Japanese firms to the point where they could sustain the full blast of international competition and emerge triumphant, as they did in the 1980s.

By the mid-1980s, as a result of their concentrated assault on memory chips, the Japanese had seized over 40 per cent of the world semiconductor market, generating a celebrated high-technology trade war with the US which culminated in the 1986 US–Japan Semiconductor Trade Agreement. But by then the US memory chip sector had all but disappeared, with leading firms like Intel and Motorola making strategic exits in the face of the prolonged Japanese assault.

The ink on this agreement was hardly dry before the Koreans arrived. Seemingly out of nowhere, firms such as Samsung and then Hyundai and Goldstar (now LG Semicon) were offering high-quality memory chips at competitive prices to US computer producers, who were keen to find an alternative source of supply from the Japanese. Samsung was already turning a profit from these sales as early as 1987, while the other Korean firms would have to show more patience and resilience in building technology capabilities before they established themselves, which they did by the 1990s. Less spectacularly, but with greater technological breadth and flexibility, the 1990s also heralded the arrival of the Taiwanese as a semiconductor force, led by the world's first exclusive wafer foundry, Taiwan Semiconductor Manufacturing Corporation (TSMC), and such advanced chip suppliers as UMC and Winbond. By the second half of the 1990s the Taiwanese firms had also moved into memory chip fabrication to challenge both the Koreans and Japanese.

Meanwhile Singapore, which had provided a haven for early multinational chip packaging and assembly operations moved rapidly up the value chain, and by the late 1990s boasted several multinational wafer-fabrication plants and its own indigenous wafer foundry, operated by the

Singapore Technologies Group. At the same time Malaysia, Thailand, the Philippines and China were also witnessing major investments in semiconductor activity in both low value-adding IC packaging and, prospectively, in higher value-adding IC wafer fabrication.

We are concerned with the *creation* of semiconductor industries in the East Asian countries, and maintain that the emergence of the industries was not haphazard or the outcome of the blind operation of market forces. On the contrary, we intend to demonstrate that the industries have been quite deliberately planted and nurtured as a deliberate act of public policy. We are interested in accounting for the conditions under which they were successfully seeded and nurtured, and in analysing the strategies that have led to their successful propagation.

Our goal in this chapter is to demonstrate that a substantial semiconductor industry had indeed been created by the late 1990s. Our concern is not to give a report on the latest developments in the industry, but to establish the point that Korea, Taiwan and Singapore and, to some extent, Malaysia had all, by the 1990s, developed a strong presence in this global industry in terms of the production, consumption, trade and investment in ICs and in products based on them such as computers. In other words, we wish to establish that they have become mainstream rather than marginal players, and that they compete at the most advanced levels of technology.[1]

The somewhat euphoric rhetoric that was used to describe East Asian achievements in the mid-1990s was tempered by the 1997–98 Asian financial crisis. How has the crisis affected the semiconductor industry, and how does it affect our arguments in this book? Undoubtedly the crisis has taken its toll on all sectors, including semiconductors. It was combined with a global downturn in the world semiconductor industry, particularly in memory chips, where countries like Korea had concentrated their efforts. Thus the newly established firms like Samsung and LG Semicon were hit by a double downturn. Yet in spite of these difficulties, not one of the newcomer semiconductor firms in the countries we examine – Korea, Taiwan, Singapore and Malaysia – has been forced into bankruptcy. There have been losses, but no company failures. Thus the newly established industries have come through a testing time, intact and ready to invest in the next upturn. Our argument is concerned with the processes through which these industries were established before the financial crisis, and the sustainability of the industries once they were established. The crisis has subjected the industries – and our arguments – to the toughest possible test, and they have shown that they could withstand this test.

The East Asian semiconductor industry has been established within the spaces created by the strategies of the incumbent players in the world

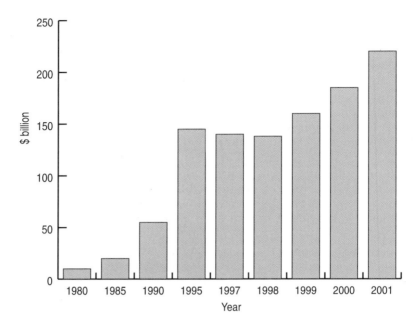

Figure 1.1   Global sales of semiconductors, 1980–2001.
Source: World Semiconductor Trade Statistics (WSTS).

industry. The scale of this global semiconductor industry is shown in Figure 1.1. Sales have grown at a furious pace through the 1980s and 1990s, reaching peaks in the mid-1980s and mid-1990s. Sales were expected to exceed $200 billion in 2001.[2] This would represent a twenty-fold expansion since 1980, making semiconductors by far the fastest growing industry in the world. These were also the years when the East Asian countries made their well-timed entry into a well-targeted industry.

The East Asian Semiconductor Industry in the late 1990s

Our concern is to document the penetration of the global semiconductor industry by firms from East Asian countries. A good starting point for our analysis is to examine three facets of this process: the rise of East Asia as a source of production of integrated circuits (ICs) relative to the rest of the world; as a market for ICs to feed its own electronics and IT sectors; and as a market for semiconductor fabrication equipment.

The data indicate that East Asia had become a significant source of activity in all three areas by the mid-1990s. Take 1995 as a benchmark: East Asian semiconductor activities produced nearly $18 billion worth of

Table 1.1 East Asian semiconductor activities relative to other parts of the world

Region	Semiconductor output		Semiconductor market		Semiconductor equipment	
	$ billion	%	$ billion	%	$ billion	%
Asia-Pacific	17.8	12	32.4	21	5.2	27
Japan	60.6	40	42.2	28	6.4	34
Americas	60.0	39	48.3	32	5.2	27
Europe	12.9	9	28.3	19	2.3	12
Total	151.3	100	151.2	100	19.1	100

Source: Industry sources.

chips, or 12 per cent of the world total of just over $151 billion that year;[3] East Asian countries consumed semiconductors worth $32 billion to feed into their own electronics activities (just over 20 per cent of the world market); and semiconductor producers bought $5.2 billion worth of equipment, amounting to no less than 27 per cent of the world sales of $19 billion.

These changes in the global geography of industrial activity in semiconductors are the product of no more than two decades of accelerated shifts in investment, production and trade, an extraordinary achievement by the countries concerned. The East Asian semiconductor activities relative to those of the other major regions of the world are summarised in Table 1.1.

Production by East Asia

The semiconductor industry has proven to be an extremely good sector for the East Asians to target as their strategic pacesetter. The growth of the sector has been dramatic, as demonstrated in Table 1.1 and Figure 1.2. The latter shows the overall growth of the global semiconductor production system from 1975 to 1995, and the changing proportions of the world's regions in its production activities.

The semiconductor sector experienced almost continuous growth since the mid-1960s – with some blips such as the mini-recessions of 1975, 1981–82, and 1985–86, and then a long boom until the 1996–97 downturn.[4] Japan's output of semiconductor products caught up with that of Europe by the early 1970s, and with the US by 1986. These were highly important milestones for the Japanese. (The US then reversed the position in 1991–92.)

The Koreans and Taiwanese started to make their presence felt in the later 1980s and 1990s, overtaking Europe in terms of output by 1994.

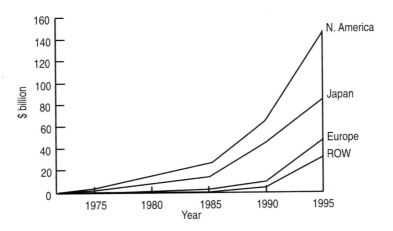

Figure 1.2   Global semiconductor industry, 1975–95.
Source: ICE.

Together, Japanese and Asia-Pacific producers accounted for over half of the world's branded, merchant semiconductor production by the mid-1990s.[5]

Semiconductor Consumption by East Asia

Demand for ICs from electronics industries in East Asia has also shown a dramatic increase, with the Asia-Pacific market overtaking that of Europe in 1995. Figure 1.3 shows how the world share of semiconductor demand has been changing, and reveals where semiconductors are being used in the production of electronics and IT goods. It demonstrates how the centre of electronics activity is shifting eastward. By 1995 just on half of the world's semiconductors were used in East Asia (Japan plus Asia-Pacific).

Equipment Supply in East Asia

Equipment sales constitute a third aspect of the rapid growth of the semiconductor industry in East Asia. Since sales reflect where semiconductor production is actually taking place, it is the most sensitive barometer of shifts in the geography of production. By 1995 the sales of fabrication equipment and materials to East Asian producers had become so significant that they matched sales to US producers, and were more than double the sales to Europe.

Combined sales of equipment to Japanese and Asia-Pacific producers amounted to 60 per cent of total sales in the mid-1990s. Again this shift

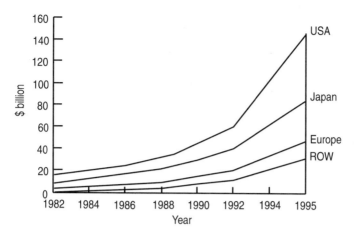

Figure 1.3 World semiconductor market: consumption by region, 1982–95.
Source: ICE.

has taken less than a decade to accomplish.[6] Besides Japan, there is as yet little penetration by the East Asians into the semiconductor equipment supply industry itself, although this industry has been targeted by the Koreans and Taiwanese and there are definite trends towards some degree of indigenisation of the supply industries. This is of a piece with a strategy towards industry creation which is concerned not just with the industry itself, but with its upstream and downstream support linkages.

Investment in East Asia

The contribution by East Asian firms to the global semiconductor industry is brought out even more clearly when we consider investment trends. Through the 1990s, investments by non-Japanese East Asian countries, led by Korea but with Taiwan in hot pursuit, rose relentlessly. They took off from a negligible level at the start of the decade to reach more than $10 billion in 1995 (accounting for 25 per cent of the world total) and, in the depths of recession, to move even higher to $12 billion in 1997, accounting for 30 per cent of the world total. As shown in Figure 1.4, investments by East Asian countries, notably Korea and Taiwan, doubled over the course of the decade, and most significantly, were maintained at high levels through the recession of 1997–98. Japanese firms started the decade as the highest investors, reflecting their rise to dominance in the 1980s, but during the 1990s they slipped back behind the levels of US firms, with European firms trailing the rest of the world.

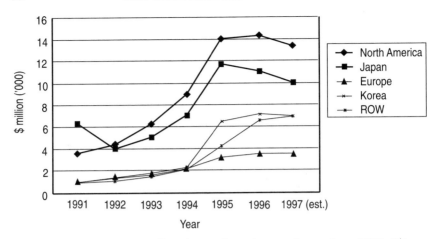

Figure 1.4   Capital spending in semiconductors by region, 1991–97.
Source: ICE *Status 1998.*

By 1997, Japan and the East Asian countries together accounted for 55
per cent of world investment.

East Asian Semiconductor Firms

The semiconductor industry is one of the world's truly global industries,
in that production and trade are conducted according to considerations
of knowledge intensity and value-adding rather than locational advantages, volume or freight charges which dominated earlier industries. The
dynamics of this global industry have set the terms within which East
Asian firms and nations have had to learn to compete.

The firms involved in the global semiconductor industry include some
of the most sophisticated and competitive to be found on the planet.
They include Intel, which overtook Japan's NEC in the early 1990s and
has held the top position ever since; the Japanese giants NEC, Toshiba
and Hitachi; and the US firms Texas Instruments and Motorola. The
most significant of the new East Asian firms is Samsung, which achieved
the distinction of entering the world's top ten semiconductor chart in
1994, rising to seventh place in that year, and sixth place in the peak year
1995, before slipping back to eighth position at the depth of the world
downturn in 1997. These figures are contained in Table 1.2.

The number of firms which had become involved in semiconductor
activities in East Asia by the 1990s exceeded 100. Some of these started
large, as in the case of the Koreans, and grew even larger; some started
very small, and have grown wealthy through judicious targeting of
specific semiconductor sectors. Some have pioneered new business

Table 1.2   Top ten IC firms in the world, 1995–97

	1995			1997	
Rank	Company	Sales	Rank	Company	Sales
1	Intel	13.2	1	Intel	22.8
2	NEC	11.3	2	NEC	11.5
3	Toshiba	10.1	3	Toshiba	9.0
4	Hitachi	9.1	4	Hitachi	8.5
5	Motorola	8.7	5	TI	8.3
6	Samsung	8.3	6	Motorola	8.0
7	TI	7.8	7	IBM Microelectronics	6.0
8	Fujitsu	5.5	8	Samsung	5.7
9	Mitsubishi	5.3	9	Mitsubishi	4.5
10	Philips	4.0	10	SGS Thomson	4.0

Source: Dataquest (1995); ICE (1997).

strategies such as offering 'silicon foundry' services, fabricating chips for the increasing number of firms worldwide which cannot afford to build fabrication facilities of their own.

The major East Asian semiconductor firms by the mid-1990s are displayed in Table 1.3. These are the firms whose efforts created the industry. We shall discuss the operations and strategic profiles of these firms in detail as our story unfolds.

It is clear that East Asian countries have arrived in the global semiconductor industry not as marginal players but as central participants in production, consumption, trade and investment. To find out how the East Asians were able to accomplish so much so quickly we turn to the competitive dynamics of the industry. It is these dynamics that set the terms on which the East Asians had to learn to compete.

The Semiconductor Industry Value Chain

The goal of the East Asian countries, starting with Japan, has been to nurture the creation of activities that span the entire value-adding spectrum of the industry. This spectrum starts with the design of integrated circuits (ICs), performed with sophisticated computer-aided design tools, which results in the production of circuit diagrams in multiple 'layers', each of which is 'etched' onto the silicon substrate of the chip.[7] The value chain then moves through the production of specialised intermediates such as the silicon wafers and the masks (or reticles), which are used to 'etch' the pattern of the circuits on the silicon through a series of highly complex steps known as photolithography. This results in a finished wafer on which are found the ICs, built up through various layers of metal and semiconductor materials in silicon. The value chain then proceeds

Table 1.3   East Asian semiconductor firms, 1995–97

Company	Revenue			Capital expenditure	
	1997	1996 $ million	1995	1997 $ million	1996
Korea					
Samsung	5270	6200	8183	2380	2300
Hyundai	3348	2450	3853	1920	2500
LG Semicon	2640	2400	3600	1600	2300
Taiwan					
TSMC	1534	1416	1092	1015	780
UMC	839	825	900	350	700
Winbond	409	454	676	350	350
TI-Acer	350	400	556	280	675
Macronix	330	373	328	400	250
Mosel-Vitelic	325	461	540	210	200
Vanguard	90	90	—	400	300
Powerchip	n/a	n/a	—	400	500
Singapore					
TECH Semiconductor	425	450	620		
Chartered	410	360	285		
TriTech	80	78	75		

Source: Companies (annual reports); ICE *Status 1997.*

through the testing of the circuits, the cutting (or 'sawing') of the wafer to secure the individual chips, and their packaging onto plastic or resin substrates to form the familiar 'chips' with their multiple leads for insertion into circuit boards. The industrial structure of the semiconductor sector, and the value added at each stage, are shown schematically in Figure 1.5.

Apart from Japan, all the East Asian countries have made their entry into the sector via the last step in the value chain, namely the packaging of chips, since this is (or rather, was) the most labour-intensive, and the step where least value was added. Their goal in every case was to move 'up' the value chain from 'back-end' packaging and testing to 'front-end' wafer fabrication and the associated activities of mask production, wafer production, and supply of specialised materials and equipment. While all the countries of East Asia have moved in this direction, some have moved considerably farther and faster than others; this will provide us with one of the benchmarks of the industry's sustainability in each of the countries concerned.

Semiconductor Market Segments

The semiconductor industry started in the 1950s with transistors and other devices that are now classified as 'discretes'. In the 1960s US firms

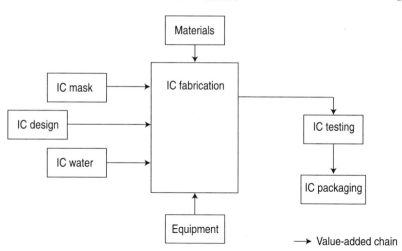

Figure 1.5 Structure of the semiconductor sector.

such as Fairchild and Texas Instruments drove the process of integration of many such devices on a single chip or integrated circuit (IC). In the 1970s new firms like Intel developed entirely new kinds of ICs, such as dynamic random access memories (DRAMs) and general purpose (programmable) microprocessors. In the 1980s the chips available for use in computers, consumer products, communications devices and many more such products exploded, through the process of customisation, producing application-specific ICs (ASICs) and various kinds of logic chips, microcontrollers, digital signal processors and many more such specialisations.

The 1990s witnessed rapid diversification in each of these product areas. By the late 1990s, memory chips, for example, had exploded into traditional standardised memories, plus newer variations like synchronous DRAMs (which could keep pace with the processor in a personal computer), embedded DRAM (linking logic and memory on the same chip) and flash memory (providing non-volatile storage in such devices as cellular phones). Early technologies like bipolar had given way in the 1980s and 1990s to MOS technologies.

These provided the technical and product trends which East Asian firms had to master. Table 1.4 shows the relative significance of these market segments in the late 1990s.

From the perspective of East Asia, there is no more significant market segment than that of memory chips. These chips, particularly DRAMs, have been the focus of protracted dispute between Japan and the US in

Table 1.4 World semiconductor market by market segment, 1997–99 (US$ billion)

Segment	1997	1998 (est.)	1999 (est.)
Discretes	13.2	11.7	11.7
Optoelectronics	4.5	4.6	4.8
Bipolar digital	1.6	1.1	0.9
Analog	19.8	18.9	20.3
MOS Micro	47.8	46.2	50.3
MOS Logic	21.0	17.9	18.8
MOS Memory	29.3	21.8	23.5
Total semiconductors	137.2	122.2	130.3

Source: World Semiconductor Trade Statistics (WSTS).

the 1980s, between Korea and Japan in the 1990s, and by the late 1990s, between Korea, Japan and Taiwan.

DRAMs: Global Competitive Dynamics

East Asians have performed exceptionally well in the memory chips segment, which most closely resembles 'commodified' or standardised products in the semiconductor world. Memory chips have grown as a market segment both absolutely and as a proportion of overall integrated circuits, up from 26 per cent of IC output in 1991 to 41 per cent in 1995 and a projected 49 per cent in 2000.[8] The absolute expansion of the DRAM segment has been remarkable, from the introduction of the first 1K DRAM in the early 1970s to a market valued at $40 billion in 1995. It then plunged into a steep decline in 1996, 1997 and 1998 – a plunge that took its toll on Korean and Taiwanese DRAM producers, and forced European firms like Siemens to abandon the market (see Figure 1.6).

Within this market segment, the shares of East Asians in production have been overwhelming, with the Japanese rising to dominance in the 1980s, and the Koreans in the 1990s. The Taiwanese were starting to make their presence felt by the mid-1990s. These three countries altogether accounted for 82 per cent of world output in 1995. The trends in memory chip production driving the dynamics of high-technology development of the entire region are depicted in Figure 1.7.

The dynamics of competition in the memory chips sector are the most demanding, with ultrashort product cycles that call for expensive investment in new process technology every two to three years (compared with changes that span a decade in the automobile industry, and two to three decades in the steel industry). The East Asian new arrivals, such as the Koreans, had to learn to manage these short product cycles.

Consider the case of DRAMs, the commodity-like, standardised

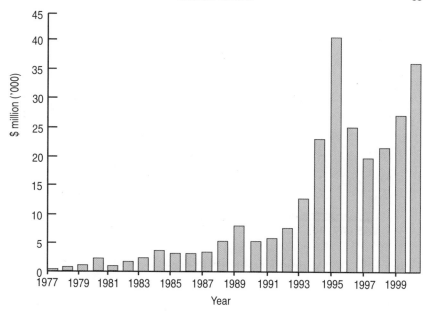

Figure 1.6 World DRAM market, 1977–2000.
Source: ICE *Status 1998.*

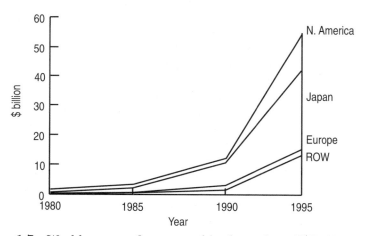

Figure 1.7 World output of memory chips by region, 1975–95.
Source: ICE.

memory chips, which have gone through nine generations since the
Japanese, then the Koreans and now the Taiwanese and many others
have become seriously involved in their production.[9] As Figure 1.8
shows, the size of the market for each generation of DRAM has

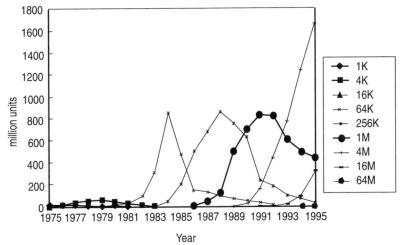

Figure 1.8 DRAM product cycle, 1975–95.
Source: ICE.

expanded from the relatively small markets for the early 1K, 4K and 16K devices to the huge market envisaged for the 64M device which was being introduced commercially with mass production in the mid-1990s, and the even larger markets envisaged for 256M and 1G devices in the early years of the twenty-first century. Once the basic design for DRAMs was introduced by Intel in 1971, these devices have followed a relatively stable trajectory, with new market entry opportunities being generated every two to three years with each new product generation, and the new process technology needed for its production.

It was US firms like Intel which invented DRAMs, and which retained dominance in the early generations when product design flair counted for more than manufacturing ability. Then the Japanese came to the fore in the 1980s as they applied their manufacturing skills and learnt to ride this product life cycle roller-coaster with consummate skill. The Japanese firm Fujitsu startled the semiconductor world in 1979 when it emerged as the first to mass produce a 64K DRAM, a signal that the Japanese had caught up with their US rivals, and had indeed taken the technological lead.

This led to a brutal trade war, in which US firms were forced to beat a strategic retreat. A truce was called in 1986 with the Semiconductor Trade Agreement (STA). Then the Koreans came on board at the fourth and fifth generations (the 64K and 256K DRAMs), rising to world dominance in the 1990s. The Taiwanese entered DRAM production in the 1990s at the sixth generation (1M devices). By the late 1990s the world DRAM market was being contested by the Korean firm Samsung and the US firm Micron (having absorbed Texas Instruments' DRAM operations in 1998) with the Japanese, Koreans (LG Semicon and Hyundai) and Taiwanese contesting in other semiconductor markets.

And so the extremely demanding competitive cycle that shaped the Japanese–US struggle for world leadership of the memory chips sector in the 1980s, and the subsequent rise of Korea in the late 1980s, and Taiwan in the 1990s continues. What counts in this rapid process of product evolution is an ability to translate new designs into real chips using new process technology as quickly as possible, so that profits can be earned early in the product life cycle before competition drives prices down to cost levels, and before the product becomes relatively obsolete.

We turn now to a brief account of the major (non-Japanese) East Asian countries which have staked a claim to be participants in the semiconductor industry, establishing at the outset the major features of their involvement, and the basis of their claim to be major players in this most demanding of global industries.

Korea

One of the poorest countries in the world after the terrible war of the early 1950s, Korea bounced back so that by the 1990s it had achieved a GDP per head of just over $10 000. The symbols of its maturity as an industrial nation were visible everywhere in the 1990s: its hosting of a Science and Technology Expo in 1995; the rise of a 'science city' at Taedok; the looming presence of giant high-technology companies such as Samsung Electronics.

Electronics and semiconductors spearheaded this transition. It is the country's success with semiconductors, and in particular its ousting of Japan as the world's number one supplier of memory chips (such as DRAMs) that is the source of greatest national pride in Korea. Figure 1.9 shows how Korean semiconductor production has grown from less than 1 per cent of the world total in the mid-1980s to reach an output of $16.3 billion in the peak year 1995 – accounting for over 10 per cent of the world 'merchant' (that is, open market) semiconductor output – and moderating in 1997 and 1998. By the late 1990s, Korea was the world's third-largest semiconductor supplier after only the US and Japan. Samsung Electronics, LG Semicon and Hyundai Electronics, each of which spans the operations of IC design, mask production, IC fabrication and testing and assembly dominate the Korean semiconductor industry of the 1990s. (At the end of 1998, LG Semicon and Hyundai Electronics were discussing a merger of their semiconductor operations.) Korea has maintained an active IC test and assembly industry, consisting of many firms beyond the three majors, together with some discretes production (transistors, resistors), amounting to an output of $7.8 billion in the mid-1990s.

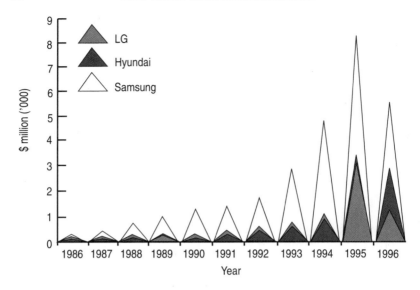

Figure 1.9 Korean semiconductor production: sales to world markets, 1986–96.
Source: Korean Semiconductor Industry Association (KSIA).

The Korean semiconductor industry has grown with an overwhelming focus on exports. In 1995 exports accounted for 91 per cent of production, making semiconductors the largest item in Korea's exports.[10] Exports of chips as a proportion of total output have actually been increasing, from 81 per cent of production in 1991, to 87 per cent in 1993, and 90 per cent in 1994. The 1995 proportion of 91 per cent was the peak, as world competition in DRAMs increased in the latter half of the 1990s and into the twenty-first century.

Export focus is a characteristic feature of high-technology industrialisation in general, and not just in Korea. This is so for at least two reasons. First, the major markets for the products are found in the advanced countries where the IT, communications and electronics industries have traditionally been located. Second, the domestic markets for these products have tended to be small, at least in the initial stages of semiconductor industry creation. The export focus is not just a source of foreign exchange earnings, but a symbol of integration into the world high-technology mainstream.

As Korea's semiconductor industry grew, so its leading firms, led by Samsung, have become global players. Figure 1.9 reveals that the IC revenue figures have been notched up by three integrated firms: Samsung Electronics Corporation (SEC), LG Semicon and Hyundai Electronics

Table 1.5 Production by product category in Korea, 1991–95

Segment	1991	1992	1993	1994	1995
			$ million		
Discrete	163	207	235	308	356
Bipolar	28	26	31	24	42
Analog	170	211	254	329	374
MOS-micro	26	33	60	71	129
MOS-logic	99	122	192	257	395
MOS-memory	1796	2643	4457	7531	14 978
others	8	12	34	45	28
Total	**2290**	**3254**	**5263**	**8565**	**16 300**

Source: KSIA.

Inc. (HEI). Korea's Samsung toppled Japan's Toshiba as the world's number one memory chip supplier, and with its heavy investment levels, looks set to stay as one of the world's top DRAM suppliers for some time to come.

This striking Korean performance has been powered by a relentless concentration on commodity memory chips. In 1995 memory devices accounted for $15 billion of total sales of $16.3 billion, as shown in Table 1.5, giving the Korean industry a highly skewed product structure. Moreover memory chips accounted for 91 per cent of exports of semiconductors in 1995, and this proportion has not shown any tendency to diminish, despite strenuous efforts to diversify on the part of Korean producers.

Export destinations are more balanced. Table 1.6 reveals how Korea's exports of ICs were, by the mid-1990s, quite evenly divided between the world's regions, with 35 per cent going to the US in 1995, 20 per cent to Europe, 29 per cent to the rest of Asia, and no less than 16 per cent also going to Japan. Two years later, the proportion being exported to Japan had risen to 20 per cent, while exports to the depressed Asia-Pacific region fell to 20 per cent. This means that Korea has become the world's most successful country in penetrating the Japanese semiconductor market – based on large DRAM orders being placed with Korean suppliers by Japanese computer firms.[11]

The engine driving these revenue and market share figures is investment. Just as the Japanese employed investment as a weapon against the Americans in the 1980s, so the Koreans wielded the same weapon against the Japanese in the 1990s. Investment levels needed to stay abreast of the game in memory chip production are enormous, and Figure 1.4 shows how the Koreans have been prepared to invest and plough back their profits and constantly seek capital to make investments in new plant and equipment.[12]

Table 1.6 Korean export destinations 1995–97 (%)

	US	EC	Japan	Asia-Pacific
1995	35	20	16	29
1997	36	24	20	20

Source: KSIA.

In the space of a decade, three Korean firms have emerged in semi-conductors: first, as keen followers of trends and efficient producers, then as companies with their own formidable product development and process engineering capacity, to a position where they are world leaders in the DRAM market – and not just in commodity DRAMs, but in higher value-adding devices such as synchronous DRAMs, embedded DRAMs, and flash memory devices. In the late 1990s Samsung is the undisputed Korean leader – moving up to higher value-added DRAM chips, and expanding its production facilities abroad – but LG and Hyundai are not far behind.[13] There is fierce competition, but also a sense of national achievement and economic learning. This is what Porter identifies as a significant source of national competitive advantage, namely strong domestic competition and an outward export orientation.[14]

Taiwan

Taiwan is another East Asian 'miracle' economy which started with simple labour-intensive export-oriented industrial development but over the course of the 1980s and 1990s has driven its industries towards 'knowledge-intensive' activities. Taiwan's involvement in the semi-conductor sector goes back to the 1960s, when packaging and then test operations were started by multinationals, sparking emulation by local companies. High value-adding wafer fabrication was initiated by the Taiwanese themselves as an act of public policy through the public-sector Industrial Technology Research Institute (ITRI). Its electronics labora-tory, the Electronics Research Service Organisation (ERSO), entered into a technology transfer arrangement with RCA in 1976 which, for a royalty fee, made available its then-obsolete 7-micron IC product and process technology, and trained a cadre of Taiwanese engineers. ERSO spun off Taiwan's first mainstream IC company in 1980, the United Microelectronics Corporation (UMC), which was located on the newly established Hsinchu Science-based Industrial Park, near ITRI/ ERSO.

From these modest beginnings a mighty industry has flourished. By the mid-1990s Taiwan had ousted European industrial giants like Germany to become the world's fourth-largest semiconductor producer

Table 1.7 Structure of the Taiwanese semiconductor industry

Industry cluster	No. of companies
IC design	72
Wafer supply	3
Mask making	2
IC fabrication (active and under construction)	20
IC foundry	3
IC packaging	23
IC testing	11
Materials: Specialty chemicals supply	6
Equipment: Lead-frame supply	9

Source: ERSO/Industrial Technology Research Information Service (ITRIS).

behind the US, Japan and Korea. By the late 1990s its IC fabrication industry and related activities notched up sales of nearly $10 billion, or around 7 per cent of the world total. The Taiwan IC industry is expected to continue to grow fast, as major memory chip investments come onstream in the late 1990s.

Unlike its Korean rival, Taiwan has fashioned an exceedingly well-balanced semiconductor industry, shared among several firms which started small and are now growing large (one of them, TSMC, exceeding $1 billion in revenue by the end of the 1990s), and spanning a broad spectrum of IC products, including those at the world technological frontier such as Winbond's digital signal processors. It features two of the world's largest IC foundry operations in TSMC and UMC, and continues to generate considerable revenue from lower value-added IC packaging operations which accounted for around $2 billion in 1998.

More to the point, the industry has been developed so that it spans all phases in the value-adding process, thereby reducing the need for imported vital components, and enhancing the sustainability of the industry. Table 1.7 shows the structure of the Taiwan IC industry.

Figure 1.10 shows output of the Taiwan industry allocated to the various value-adding activities: IC production, packaging, design and foundry work. It reveals that Taiwan's output of IC production exceeded lower value-adding IC packaging activities by 1992. This was an index of the value-adding progression made by the industry.

The Taiwan market for semiconductors, reflecting the island's intense production of electronic and IT systems, is also significant, reaching $8 billion in 1995. Taiwanese IC firms were able to supply just on 39 per cent of this demand – a sign of their sophistication and the openness of the Taiwanese IC market, and room for further domestic supply.

Table 1.8 details the output of the various IC companies in Taiwan in the 1990s. The range of companies involved is impressive, with TSMC,

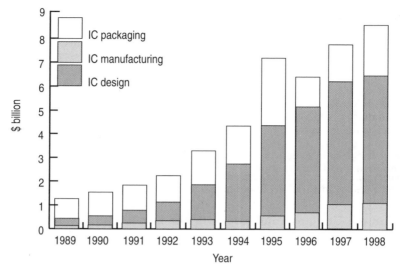

Figure 1.10   Taiwan: IC-related revenue, 1989–98.
Source: ERSO/ITRIS.

UMC and Winbond emerging as the most significant. By the late 1990s, there were fourteen firms involved in IC fabrication alone, with a combined output of $4.4 billion – or 3.3 per cent of world IC output – up from less than 1 per cent in 1988, when the combined output of six firms was worth $240 million. The range in size of these companies is striking, from the large (TSMC, UMC group, Winbond) through to the medium (MXIC, Mosel-Vitelic) to quite small IC producers like a host of fabless chip producers that specialise in certain types of designs for customised chips (ASICs).

In its first decade TSMC grew to become the world's largest 'pure-play' silicon foundry, and as it entered its second decade it was expanding into related businesses through its DRAM affiliate, Vanguard Semiconductor, and internationally through Wafer Tech, a joint venture between TSMC and some of its US customers. Wafer Tech was producing chips from its Camas, Washington fabrication facility ahead of schedule in 1998. In the late 1990s the number of IC fabrication firms was growing, with the new DRAM entrants such as Nan Ya Technology and Powerchip Semiconductor adding their contribution, and spin-offs from UMC adding theirs as well. The process of replenishing the IC industry in Taiwan with new entrants seems to be far from exhausted.

The case of Powerchip is instructive. This new venture, launched in 1996, involved a new and highly successful IT firm, Umax, which made its initial foray into scanners and has since become an important player

Table 1.8 Revenue of Taiwanese IC fabrication companies, 1992–94

	1992	1993 ($ million)	1994
TSMC	262	466	704
UMC	254	379	530
Winbond	119	186	303
Mosel-Vitelic	163	216	288
TI-Acer	67	231	28
Macronix	67	144	22
HMC	91	86	10
Holtek	68	57	6
Total	1091	1765	1891

Table 1.9 Taiwanese DRAM fabrication initiatives, 1993–98

Date of production	Company	Technology transfer source
1993	TI-Acer (ASMI)	Texas Instruments
1994	Mosel-Vitelic	Oki
1995	Vanguard	ERSO
1996	Nan Ya	Oki
1997	Powerchip	Mitsubishi
1998	Winbond	Toshiba
1998	MXIC	Matsushita

Source: ERSO/ITRIS.

in PCs. Umax was looking to enter the semiconductor industry, and scored a coup by becoming the first non-Japanese firm in Asia to enter a joint venture with the giant Mitsubishi Electric to form a new, state-of-the-art DRAM production house. Production was underway by 1997, with yields rapidly increasing and an anticipated range of technology cooperation projects opening up as a result of the agreement.

By the late 1990s the technology infusion process was still underway in Taiwan, but at a very sophisticated level, and with the private sector directing the process. Taiwan's DRAM initiatives from 1993–98, which have made it a major DRAM producer alongside Korea and Japan, are detailed in Table 1.9. At this point, Taiwan's semiconductor industry was in aggressive expansion mode, with several of the leading firms announcing major investment programs for the next ten years despite the semiconductor industry downturn and the Asian financial crisis. Expansion plans worth up to $60 billion in total had been announced, involving the building of new 8-inch and projected 12-inch wafer-fabrication facilities in the existing Hsinchu Science-based Industry Park and in the second such park built at Tainan in southern Taiwan. Even if only a fraction of these plans came to fruition, they would significantly expand the Taiwan industry.

By the late 1990s Taiwan's IC firms were investing nearly 100 per cent of their revenue in capacity expansion (as opposed to an average of 20 to 25 per cent for mature firms), and were accounting for a significant proportion of worldwide sales of semiconductor equipment.[15] These are the signs of an industry investing during a downturn to pick up business on the upturn.

The government in Taiwan has shown exemplary understanding in nurturing a high-technology industry like semiconductors through the creation of public-sector technology leverage agencies such as ITRI and public-sector infrastructure like the Hsinchu and Tainan industrial parks, where virtually the entire Taiwan semiconductor industry is located.

ITRI has grown since its foundation in 1973 to become a technology powerhouse. It operates as a non-profit research institute funded partly through government disbursements to build technological capabilities in strategically significant industries, and partly through industry contracts. By the end of the 1990s, ITRI was a 6000-person research operation with an operating budget exceeding $1 billion. ERSO, ITRI's electronics laboratory established in 1974, was its first specialist arm. By the late 1990s, ITRI had ten of these, covering such areas as optoelectronics, computing and communications, aerospace, energy and resources.[16] ITRI's business is technology leverage rather than fundamental research; that is, it acts as a huge technology filter for Taiwan industry, trawling the world for new technological developments. It sends its staff to technical conferences, trade fairs and on fact-finding missions and they bring back technologies thought to be of strategic significance to Taiwan so that ITRI can build a capability in them. From its first technology transfer agreement with RCA in 1976, which seeded the semiconductor industry in Taiwan, this has become a well-honed leverage strategy at ITRI.[17]

The Hsinchu Park was an initiative of the Taiwanese government, and modelled quite explicitly on the success of the Stanford Research Park in California's Silicon Valley. To many observers, Hsinchu has taken the best features of Silicon Valley and adapted them to the Taiwanese situation.[18] Hsinchu Park offers firms settling there an attractive working environment and living conditions (much better than the crowded conditions of cities like Taipei and Kaohsiung) as well as proximity to technical expertise and design and manufacturing facilities. Because it is government-owned, it also offers a range of special benefits, such as low rents on land, low-interest government loans; R&D matching funds; tax benefits; special exemptions from tariffs, commodity and business taxes; government purchase of technology abroad for transfer to participating companies; government equity investment of up to 49 per cent of enterprise capitalisation; and access to government laboratories and test facilities in the Park.[19] These amount to substantial benefits and make gaining access to the park a high priority for knowledge-intensive firms. By the same token, the Park administration keeps a close watch over the activities of firms to ensure that they remain at the leading technological edge and do not stray into dirty or low value-added activities.

By 1997 the Hsinchu Park held 245 firms, with a combined output of $11.9 billion. Companies in the park were spending between 4 and 5 per cent of their revenues on R&D, compared with around 1 per cent for Taiwan's manufacturing industry overall.[20] The semiconductor industry has consistently been the largest sector in the Park.[21]

Based on the success and rapid filling of available space in Hsinchu and its extension, the National Science Council announced in 1995 the establishment of a second science-based industry park, to be located at Tainan in the south of Taiwan. The two parks, Hsinchu and Tainan, are seen explicitly as being the twin engines driving Taiwan's high-technology development in the twenty-first century.[22]

Tariff protection has never been imposed on semiconductors in Taiwan, which has been a signal factor in the country's ability to avoid (up until the late 1990s) the trade wars which have plagued Japan and exerted material damage on Korea. A trade dispute involving alleged dumping of DRAMs did in fact break out with the US in 1998, but the case was weak.

Government agencies played a continuing but changing role into the 1990s. In 1992 the Ministry of Economic Affairs, through the Industrial Development Bureau (IDB), issued a set of strategies and measures to assist the development of the 'Top Ten Emerging Industries'. Naturally, the semiconductor sector was one of the ten. The IDB stated in 1995 that it expected Taiwan's semiconductor output to reach $17 billion by 2000 – or nearly 6 per cent of the global market. This would appear to be a conservative target – and yet it would represent a growth rate of 34 per cent or twice the expected global average. Ten Taiwanese companies are expected to be in the world's Top 50 semiconductor companies by then.[23]

Singapore

Singapore presents the traveller today with the image of a bustling, confident and wealthy city – a 'tropical city of excellence', as it calls itself. One statistic tells the story: in 1960, Singapore was a struggling Third World economy, with a per capita income of $1300; by 1995 it was classified by the OECD as a 'dynamic Asian economy' with a per capita

Table 1.10   IC fabrication facilities in Singapore, 1985–99

Year	Company	Wafer size
1985	SGS	6 inch
1987	Hewlett Packard	6 inch
1989	Chartered I	6 inch
1993	TECH Semi I	8 inch*
1996	Chartered II	8 inch**
1997	TECH Semi II	8 inch
1997	SGS-Thomson	8 inch
1997	Chartered III	8 inch
1998	Chartered Silicon Partners	8 inch
1998	Hitachi/Nippon Steel	8 inch
1999	Silicon Mfg Partners	8 inch
1999	Hitachi/Nippon Steel	8 inch
1999	TSMC/Philips	8 inch

Note: * Won *Semiconductor International* fab of the year award in 1993.
** Won *Semiconductor International* fab of the year award in 1996.

income of nearly $25 000.[24] This transformation has been wrought through a single-minded concentration on manufacturing, and particularly electronics and, latterly, semiconductors. By the mid-1990s, after a decade of focused development of the semiconductor sector, Singapore boasted a flourishing chip fabrication, test and assembly industry, employing 20 000 highly skilled people and generating revenues of $8.3 billion in 1996.[25] The semiconductor cluster in Singapore is expanding rapidly, spanning firms in the IC design sector, IC (front-end) fabrication, IC test and assembly, and ancillary services. By 1998, Singapore had no fewer than eleven of the world's most advanced chip fabrication facilities, operated by leading multinationals such as SGS-Thomson, Texas Instruments, Hewlett-Packard, Hitachi, Nippon Steel and the successful indigenous Singapore firm Chartered Semiconductor Manufacturing (CSM), a part of the state-owned Singapore Technologies Group (Table 1.10). CSM has itself been aligned with world leaders such as Toshiba, HP and Lucent to build new, advanced fabrication facilities. But plans for the future are even more ambitious. Singapore's Economic Development Board (EDB) has invested heavily in establishing three 'wafer-fabrication' specialist parks, and publicly committed itself to attracting ten further wafer-fabrication facilities by 2005.

Singapore's industrialisation and modernisation strategy has been focused on manufacturing from the early 1960s, when the island's manufacturing resources and capabilities were meagre, to say the least. Manufacturing output expanded at an annual rate of 21 per cent, reaching just over $80 billion in 1995. This is the 'bedrock foundation' of the

Table 1.11 Semiconductor industry cluster in Singapore, 1997

Industry cluster	No. of firms
IC fabrication	5
IC foundry/OEM	1
IC test and assembly	22
IC masks	1
Silicon wafers	1
IC design	23
IC support (e.g. equipment)	22

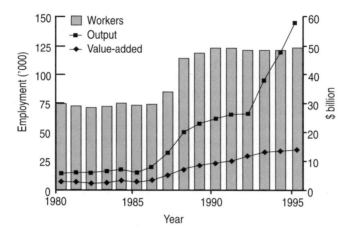

Figure 1.11 Electronics industry in Singapore, 1980–95.
Source: Economic Development Board.

Singaporean economy, and source of its wealth and employment. Much of this manufactured output was exported, so that direct exports grew by 19 per cent a year, to reach $50 billion by 1995. The electronics, petroleum products and fabricated metal products industries have been the mainstay of Singapore's manufacturing, accounting for at least half of output in the 1970s and 1980s. By 1995 the electronics industry cluster was dominant, accounting for over half of manufacturing output.[26]

The electronics industry in Singapore is dominated by two high-tech sectors: semiconductors and data storage for computers (hard disk drives). Output of electronics products reached $43 billion in 1996, up from $41.3 billion in 1995 – and value-added in Singapore (net output of material inputs) reached $11 billion, contributed by a workforce of 128 700 (Figure 1.11).

Singapore's electronics and semiconductor industries are made up almost entirely of the activities of multinational corporations. They came in the 1960s for cheap labour and stable working conditions; they stayed on and steadily upgraded the scope and depth of their activities. Wave after wave of multinationals arrived, from the US, Japan, and later, Korea and Taiwan.[27] Singapore has turned the practice of leveraging skills and technological knowledge from these companies into a high art. Its core semiconductor industrial cluster now encompasses a number of IC wafer-fabrication facilities and test and assembly facilities, but alongside them have grown indigenous silicon foundries and test and assembly operations, and indigenous specialist materials and equipment suppliers. The latter are linked to the multinationals through targeted vendor development and 'supplier upgrading' programs. Such practices have allowed indigenous small and medium-sized enterprises to play an important role in the industrialisation process, particularly in such manufacturing sectors as electronics contract work, fabricated metal products and precision machinery – the clusters that support the development of a semiconductor sector and other advanced IT sectors such as hard disk drives.[28]

The Semiconductor Industry Cluster in Singapore in the Mid-1990s

By the late 1990s the EDB counted over 50 Singaporean companies as being involved in the semiconductor sector. These companies employ more than 20 000 staff, many of whom are highly skilled. Output reached $9 billion in 1995, falling to $8.3 billion in 1996 – most of which is accounted for by multinational assembly, testing and packaging operations, as well as wafer-fabrication and foundry activity. The value-added in Singapore in 1995 reached $2.8 billion. All of this is value-added within multinationals or under contract to multinationals; there is as yet no branded semiconductor product produced by an indigenous firm.[29] The range of chips produced is impressive, from DRAMs (TECH), logic chips and ASICs to mainstream logic and memory products (SGS-Thomson).

Of the companies involved in the semiconductor sector, the major players are all multinationals, including Hewlett-Packard, AMD, Lucent (formerly AT&T), Chartered Semiconductor, Linear Technology, Matsushita, National Semiconductor, NEC, SGS-Thomson, Siemens, Silicon Systems, TECH Semiconductor and Texas Instruments. Only Chartered is an indigenous entity. Singapore has followed the strategy of attracting multinational offshoots and then inducing internal transfer of skills and technologies across to local training and R&D institutes, as well as to home-grown operations. The latter now include semiconductor service provision firms, such as Advanced Systems Automation and Manufacturing

Table 1.12 Firms making up the IC industry cluster in Singapore, 1998

IC design	
MNEs	AMD, Fujitsu, Harris, HP, Hitachi, Linear, Lucent, Motorola, NEC, Philips, SGS-Thomson, Sharp, Siemens, Silicon Systems, Sony, Temic
Local firms	Azfin, Serial Systems, TriTech
IC fabrication	
MNEs	SGS-Thomson, TI-HP-Canon (TECH Semiconductor), HP, Hitachi/Nippon Steel (1998)
Local firms	Chartered Semiconductor Manufacturing (CSM), Chartered Silicon Partners (CSM-HP); Silicon Manufacturing Partners (CSM-Lucent)
IC test and assembly	
MNEs	AMD, Adaptec, Brooktree, Delco, Fujitsu, HP, Linear, Lucent, Matsushita, NS, NEC, Philips, Seiko-Epson, SGS-Thomson, Siemens, Silicon Systems
Local firms	KES-Rood Technologies, Singapore Epson Industrial, STATS (STG), Unitrode
IC support and ancillary services	
MNEs	Photronics (IC masks), Wacker–Siltronics, and others
Local firms	M&M, MBE Technology, and others

Source: Economic Development Board.

Integration Technology, but also specialist firms like MBE Technology, which produces gallium–arsenide epitaxial wafers for the merchant market. Testing, assembly and packaging operations, which started off the industry in the 1960s and 1970s, continue to be important, and are themselves being upgraded so that they now represent a source of high-technology development in their own right. The companies involved – 22 by the end of 1995 – are introducing sophisticated IC packages and becoming centres of package development themselves, as shown in Table 1.12.[30]

The development has been carefully overseen and coordinated by the EDB, the city-state's prime industrialisation agency.[31] The EDB also plays an active role in promoting investment in wafer fabs by becoming an equity partner itself.[32] To support such investments, in 1994 Singapore established a S$1 billion Cluster Development Fund, managed by the EDB. The fund's aims are to facilitate investments in strategic projects in Singapore to enhance core capabilities of local industry clusters (as in the case of CSM's foundry operations); to accelerate the development of local enterprises; and to undertake strategic investments with local and multinational companies which will strengthen Singapore's links with the South East Asian region.

R&D and training infrastructure to support and reproduce these operations in Singapore are also being developed. The Institute of

Microelectronics (IME) was established as a centre of excellence in 1991, with funding largely from the National Science and Technology Board (NSTB). It is expected to work with firms in pre-competitive R&D in highly focused consortia.[33] Supporting industries have been or are being established to provide specialised materials and equipment for the semiconductor industry.[34] The major inputs that had hitherto been lacking in Singapore were masks (reticles) and wafers. By the late 1990s both were covered by multinational operations Photronics (masks) and Wacker-Siltronics (wafers). These supporting and ancillary activities add to the depth of the semiconductor cluster in Singapore, thereby making it even more favoured as a location for high-technology semiconductor and IT industry development. This is the power of 'increasing returns' at work.

The EDB supports semiconductor investment with specially constructed and serviced wafer-fabrication 'parks'. One such park was established in 1995 at Woodlands, on the northern perimeter of Singapore across from Malaysia. The Woodlands park houses the TECH DRAM facility and Chartered's new fabs, and provides each company with room for expansion. In 1995 a second park was announced for Tampines, an area just five minutes from the Changi International Airport. In 1998 a third was constructed at Pasir Ris to house the TSMC/Philips wafer fab. Each park is designed to hold at least seven to ten fabs each – making an anticipated total of around twenty fabs by the early years of the twenty-first century. If even a fraction of these plans come to fruition, Singapore would indeed be counted as the 'Silicon Island' of South East Asia.[35]

Malaysia

Malaysia has followed a somewhat wayward course in its industrialisation, but manufacturing has been central to its development, and electronics central to its manufacturing. After its independence from Britain, Malaysia initially followed a conventional import substitution strategy in the 1960s, but with meagre results. When Singapore showed success in opening up to multinationals by pursuing an export-led strategy, Malaysia followed, but lagged behind by a few years, particularly in the island state of Penang off the northwest coast, which pursued Singapore-style strategies actively from 1970.

Malaysia was preoccupied with communal issues, and only swung behind all-out export-oriented strategies, with full openness to multinational investment, after 1986, when a severe recession knocked out a good proportion of its electronics industry. Since then, growth has been extremely buoyant, led by recovery in electronics and semiconductors.

Production of semiconductors and electronic components generally

grew from $3 billion in 1987 to $18.3 billion in 1995. Virtually all of
this output is packaged and assembled chips, produced by multinationals
or by contract firms working to multinationals (such as Unisem and
Carsem), and almost all is exported ($15 billion in 1995).[36] The elec-
tronics industry is already the largest manufacturing sector of the
Malaysian economy, and is still growing rapidly: output of electrical and
electronics products tripled in size between 1988 and 1995, while
manufacturing output overall doubled over the same period.[37]

While the scale and scope of the semiconductor industry in Malaysia
were not as impressive as Singapore's by the mid-1990s, it was moving in
the same overall direction. The site of most of Malaysia's electronics and
semiconductor activity over the past twenty years has been the small
island of Penang, and the Klang Valley region around the capital, Kuala
Lumpur. Regular announcements of production expansion and technological upgrades are made by such multinationals as Intel, SGS-
Thomson, NEC, Hitachi, Motorola, AMD and many others. However
neither Penang nor the Klang Valley has yet made the breakthrough to
IC wafer fabrication, which is the central goal of all the East Asian
semiconductor industries.[38]

So, despite its impressive scale and scope of activity by the world's
leading multinationals, the Malaysian semiconductor industry is not yet
at the same level of maturity as its counterparts in Singapore, Taiwan and
Korea. The most likely location for the breakthrough into IC wafer
fabrication in Malaysia is the high-technology park established in Kulim
in the state of Kedah, adjacent to Penang. The Malaysian government
and Kedah state government have combined to form the Kulim Hi-Tech
Industrial Park (KHTP) which promises to be the focus for Malaysia's
semiconductor and IT development in the twenty-first century. It has
been designed to act as a natural extension of Penang's development,
providing the land and labour that is now in short supply on the island.[39]
The KHTP is a long-term venture that will not be completed (in its
present conception) until the year 2003. It is inspired by the Taiwanese
success with the Hsinchu Science-based Industry Park and Japan's high-
technology centre, Tsukuba. By 2003 it is expected to cover a massive
1500 hectares and encompass six zones – industrial, urban, research and
development, housing, amenity and institutional – in other words, to
become a 'technopolis'. It is anticipated that this high-technology park
will be the site for a number of important wafer-fabrication ventures, and
support infrastructure and materials supply activities. By the late 1990s,
many such firms had announced their intentions of making major wafer-
fabrication investments in Kulim – among them the US semiconductor
firms VLSI Technology and Atmel Corporation.[40]

By the late 1990s Malaysia was also witnessing the emergence of local companies servicing the needs of advanced semiconductor firms. These include automated equipment suppliers such as Eng Technology and LKT in Penang, which have become suppliers with their own expanding export markets through their close links with the MNCs operating in the state. Other locals include contract test and assembly firms such as Globetronics in Penang and Malaysian ventures Carsem and Unisem, state-of-the-art contract IC test and assembly operations in Perak state.[41] The emergence of such firms is the real index of the enhancement of a country's absorptive capacity sufficient to support local indigenous firms.

As in Singapore, the state agencies in Malaysia have played an important role in shaping the overall trajectory of the semiconductor industry, and in building up the capabilities needed to catalyse an indigenous industry. The Kulim Park is the most impressive venture yet from the federal government, and some of the state governments have put in place development agencies such as the Penang Development Corporation. In this way Malaysia has been seeking to fashion an institutional framework within which MNCs are induced to act as the engines of the country's high-technology industrialisation, export growth and the formation of small service and components firms that leverage skills and business from the MNCs.

Developments Elsewhere in South East Asia

Singapore and Malaysia were far from alone in seeking to establish the roots of a semiconductor industry. By the late 1990s Thailand, the Philippines and Indonesia had made progress towards semiconductor involvement, taking advantage of their low labour costs to encourage investment by multinationals in IC assembly and test operations.

Thailand

Before the 1997–98 financial crisis Thailand seemed on course towards the development of a strong 'back-end' IC packaging industry, and also towards front-end wafer fabrication through the activities of its Alphatec Group. Founded in 1988 as Alphatec Electronics by entrepreneur Charn Uswachoke, the company got its start in semiconductors after buying out the interests of Philips/Signetics in its IC packaging plant. After operating this plant for five years and building up absorptive capacity, Uswachoke executed a number of deals, purchasing the Thailand packaging operations of US multinational National Semiconductor, and gained a foothold in Silicon Valley through the purchase of Indy

Electronics (part of the Olin Group). Thus emboldened, Uswachoke pushed ahead into joint ventures with Texas Instruments and Taiwan's TI-Acer to build an advanced wafer-fabrication foundry, to be called Alphafab, and another DRAM fabricating facility, to be called Alpha Memory.

Unfortunately Uswachoke ran out of finance, the deals collapsed in 1997, and by 1998 Alphatec was struggling to keep from going under altogether. Other indigenous Thai ventures have fared better. The Hana Group, for example, followed a rather more cautious expansion path. It was founded as an electronics contract manufacturing firm in 1978, and moved into IC packaging in the 1990s. By the late 1990s it was operating several IC test and assembly plants, in Bangkok, northern Thailand, Hong Kong, Shanghai and Silicon Valley. The Hong Kong operations were bought from the Hong Kong-based Swire Technologies in 1996 (making an interesting case of reverse takeover of a Hong Kong firm by a developing country group) while the Silicon Valley operations were acquired from Olin.

The Philippines

After the disastrous political situation of the 1980s, the Philippines was making great strides in the 1990s, attracting high-quality foreign invest-ment and rapidly upgrading its technological capabilities. Even during the world semiconductor downturn and Asian financial crisis, the IC packaging industry in the Philippines was growing by more than 30 per cent per year. Much of the activity was concentrated in the former US naval base at Subic Bay, which has been transformed into a high-tech-nology manufacturing zone modelled on Penang in Malaysia. Indeed, the Taiwanese government has built a technology park at Subic Bay largely to house Taiwanese firms establishing operations there (a case of Taiwan exporting its Hsinchu model).

Employment in IC packaging and related activities in the Philippines passed 100 000 by the mid-1990s, and multinationals like Philips, Intel and Cypress were all making major investments. The Philippines is also home to a large IC packaging operation owned by the Korean Anam group, which by the 1990s had become the largest contract IC packaging firm in the world.

Indonesia

Some progress has been made to establish IC packaging operations in Indonesia, largely concentrated on the island of Batam, which was being jointly developed in the 1990s with Singapore as a manufacturing zone.

Siemens, for example, established a major test and assembly plant on the island. The ruin of Indonesia's economy in the crisis of 1997–98 called a halt to any further expansion. Indigenous initiatives like those of PT Astra Microelectronics ended up being sold to US investors.

Some idea of the progress made in South East Asia in IC packaging can be gleaned from the sale of semiconductor fabricating equipment to firms operating in the region. In 1997, sales amounted to $1.4 billion, with Singapore accounting for $740 million, the Philippines $300 million, Malaysia $250 million and Thailand $150 million. Much of the expenditure by Singapore-based firms was for front-end fabrication equipment, while back-end test and assembly equipment sales were directed towards the Philippines, Malaysia and Thailand. These sales provide an index of the level of activities in the countries concerned.

Finally, it is of interest to look at semiconductor developments in Hong Kong and China – for two very different reasons. Hong Kong represents the most important counter-case to the general thesis of industrial upgrading through leverage in East Asia; it appears to have practised *none* of the leverage techniques mastered elsewhere in East Asia. China, on the other hand, looks set to become a semiconductor powerhouse in the twenty-first century, by applying the lessons learned in *all* the previous East Asian experiences: in the 1990s it was using a Korean–Japanese model, a Taiwan model and a Singapore model, all at the same time.[42]

Hong Kong

The Hong Kong 'city state' is an extraordinarily successful economy, a wealth-generating machine of prodigious proportions. Yet most of this wealth is created through trade and financial services, and through the management of an increasingly broad-based manufacturing network that spans the Pearl River Delta in China and South East Asia. These manufacturing activities tend, however, to be in the most cost-competitive sectors, not the most advanced knowledge-intensive sectors. What is conspicuously lacking in Hong Kong is a semiconductor industry or, indeed, any advanced technology industry in the electronics and IT sectors – no CD-ROM industry, no HDD industry, not even a real PC industry. Yet Hong Kong was one of the first of the East Asian countries to become involved in electronics in the 1960s and 1970s, when its firms and its products were the equal of anything produced in Taiwan, Korea or Singapore.[43] Why, then, did Hong Kong not go on to the more demanding levels of technological capabilities that were tackled through leverage by other East Asian economies?

In short, Hong Kong lacked the institutional means to upgrade technologically. Its state structures were a marvel of clean and responsible government, which provided maximum discretion for entrepreneurial activity, but no one would ever have accused the colonial administration of pursuing an interventionist strategy in the manner of Japan or the other East Asians. Hong Kong instead cultivated a stance of 'positive non-interventionism' – *positive* in the sense of being 'business friendly', favouring entrepreneurs and providing maximally efficient social infrastructure, and *non-interventionist* in the sense of refusing to target any specific kind of industry or sector. After being at the same level of technological sophistication as their East Asian competitors in the 1970s, Hong Kong's entrepreneurs preferred to invest in lower-risk expansions of activity towards low-cost regions of China, rather than seek to compete in the more technically demanding and higher risk categories like semiconductors. In the absence of any state involvement to force the pace, there was little inducement for them to do so.[44]

The really interesting development in Hong Kong is that, around the time of the transition or 'handover' to China in 1997, there appeared to be a mounting recognition that a more activist approach from public agencies was needed if Hong Kong were to become a player in knowledge-intensive industries in the twenty-first century. One of us was involved in a discussion in Hong Kong in September 1997, just after the 'handover', and at the very beginnings of the financial crisis that beset East Asia. The discussion concerned the potential role to be played by government agencies and the public sector more generally in the creation of some high-technology industries in Hong Kong.[45] The new government had just made its first policy speech and announced the formation of a new government agency to coordinate the development of an IT industry in Hong Kong – the first 'targeted' state agency in Hong Kong's history. The discussion was notable in that the speakers explicitly recognised that Korea, Taiwan and Singapore presented 'models' of high-technology upgrading that were relevant and important for Hong Kong in the context of catch-up. Once catch-up has been achieved, perhaps at some time early in the twenty-first century, the institutional strategy would change.

Although Hong Kong had little to show in the way of advanced technology export firms at the end of the 1990s, it was moving in a new direction towards some involvement in knowledge-intensive manufacturing. The post-1997 Hong Kong administration has shown itself determined to take a new direction in the technological development of the Hong Kong economy. The chief executive appointed a Commission on Innovation and Technology that in late 1998 recommended the formation of an Innovation and Technology Fund (HKITF) and a new R&D institute, an Applied Science and Technology Research Institute (HKASTRI). The Fund was actually established late in 1998, with an initial contribution from the government of HK$5 billion (US$6 million). The most tangible expression of a new direction being taken in Hong Kong towards the acquisition and enhancement of technological capabilities in the public sector is the creation of the Hong Kong University of Science and Technology, founded in 1990 with the explicit intent of providing Hong Kong's industries with a higher level of technical sophistication.[46] By the mid-1990s the university was promoting the rapid technological upgrading of Hong Kong's industries through collaborative R&D programs and the training of high-calibre scientific and technical staff.[47]

Hong Kong in the twenty-first century is likely to play the role of stimulator of advanced technology development in China, arranging for financial and technological leverage through its superb business institutions. For its part, China was making enormous progress in its bid to become a semiconductor and electronics powerhouse in the twenty-first century.

China

Of all the countries in East Asia beyond those explicitly covered in this text, China shows the greatest potential to become a major semiconductor power. Combined with the financial and investment capabilities of Hong Kong, the Chinese semiconductor industry looks set for steady expansion, both to feed China's own burgeoning electronics and IT industries and for exports. By the end of the 1990s China still benefited from enormous cost advantages, giving it the window to rapid development that was used so successfully by its East Asian predecessors. Since 1979 China has been open to foreign investment, and this has made an enormous difference to the country's technological capabilities and future prospects.

China's growth in electronics has been spectacular through the 1990s, with output reaching $45 billion in 1997, and imports and exports amounting to $48 billion. China sees electronics and IT as driving industries for the country's development, and has created a Ministry of Electronics Industry (MEI) to guide this development and to regulate the foreign direct investment that is pouring into the industry. In semiconductors proper, China early on developed a capability in discretes and simple ICs through its own state-owned enterprises like the

nics Group (SEG) or the Huajing Electronics and luctor Devices at Wuxi, currently the 'Silicon Valley'

China reached around $3.6 billion in 1997, while output exceeded $1 billion by the mid-1990s. Rapid ity and technological level promised to drive this

Table 1.13 Semiconductor fabs planned for China, 1995

Name	Location	MNC partner	Wafer
Front-end wafer fabs			
Wuxi Huajing Semiconductor	Wuxi	Toshiba	6 inch
Shanghai Belling			
Microelectronics Mfg	Shanghai	Alcatel (Fr)	8 inch
Advanced Semiconductor			
Manufacturing Corp	Shanghai	Philips, Nortel	6 inch
Shougang NEC	Beijing	NEC	6 inch
Hua Yue Microelectronics	Shaoxing	Fujitsu	6 inch
Motorola (China) Electronics	Tianjin	Motorola	8 inch
Intel	Shanghai	Intel	8-inch flash memory
IC assembly facilities (back end)			
STM-SEG	Shenzhen	SGS-Thomson (Eur)	
Hyundai	Shanghai	Hyundai (Kor)	
Samsung	Suzhou	Samsung (Kor)	
Stone Computer	Suzhou	Mitsubishi	
Harris Semiconductor	Suzhou	AMD (US)	
Hitachi Semiconductor	Suzhou	Hitachi	
HuXu Microelectronics	Shanghai	Matsushita	

Source: ICE *Status 1996*; industry sources.

output figure higher. The MEI upgraded its foreign direct investment efforts in advanced IC operations in the 1990s, not only in back-end IC assembly and test operations, but in front-end wafer-fabrication activities as well. The result has been a surge of new investment. Projects commissioned since 1995 are shown in Table 1.13: these included no less than six planned wafer-fabrication facilities, along with nine IC packaging, assembly and testing facilities.

By the mid-1990s, many of the world's leading multinationals had announced plans to establish or upgrade semiconductor activities in China.[48] Advanced Semiconductor Manufacturing Corporation (ASMC) of Shanghai is a typical example of these developments. It began as a joint venture between Chinese firms and the Dutch multinational Philips in 1993, which resulted in the building of a small 5-inch IC fabrication line. The Canadian multinational Nortel was then invited to join the venture in 1995, and its scope was enlarged considerably, with a new 6-inch IC fabrication line being constructed. ASMC has emerged as China's most successful IC 'foundry' on the model of TSMC in Taiwan, another Philips joint venture. Output of 6-inch wafers started in 1996, and was due to overtake those of the earlier fab by 1999. Meanwhile ASMC was improving its yields and its 'absorptive capacity' so that it could make the transition to 8-inch and then 12-inch wafers. By 1998 it was employing nearly 500 workers, and training programs provided by

Philips and Nortel were one of the principal avenues for raising the company's absorptive capacity. Of the US multinationals, Motorola was making the most substantial investments in the Chinese semiconductor sector, building a submicron wafer fab in Tianjin, and a huge new China and East Asia headquarters, while Intel was committed to building a flash memory fab near Shanghai.

The Singapore government, through the Economic Development Board (EDB), has created a huge high-technology park and associated city at Suzhou, where much of China's future semiconductor industry is likely to be located. Multinationals which have already committed to building IC fabrication or packaging facilities there include Samsung, AMD and Hitachi. This development is one which was conceived as creating a 'second Singapore' in China, and it has been driven by Singapore's Senior Minister, Lee Kwan Yew.[49]

The MEI late in the 1990s launched a further technological upgrading effort focused on the Pudong microelectronics complex near Shanghai called Project 909. The Ninth Five-Year Plan (1996–2000) highlighted four key areas for further development: ICs, new types of electronic components (such as flat panel displays and silicon-based sensors), computers and software, and telecommunications. The Plan called for China to develop large-scale production volumes of 6-inch wafers for ICs designed to 0.8 micron geometry, and to begin production of 8-inch wafers at 0.5 micron geometry in selected areas such as Pudong. New institutions of technology leverage have been created, such as the Shanghai Science and Technology Development and Exchange Centre. By the late 1990s there was no doubt about the expansion in scale and technological depth of China's semiconductor activities. It has studied the lessons of East Asian success closely, and applied them.

An East Asian Semiconductor Industry

From this brief survey, it is clear that the process of creating a semiconductor industry had by the mid-1990s taken root in the core East Asian countries of Korea, Taiwan and Singapore, and the same process was spreading to Malaysia as well as Thailand, the Philippines and above all to China. Hong Kong was the only one of the 'Four Tigers' of East Asia not to develop a semiconductor industry – for reasons that are highly relevant to our story – but it too was making impressive efforts by the late 1990s.

We wrap up this discussion of the achievements of East Asian countries and their firms in creating a semiconductor industry by looking comparatively at the scale of operations in the region. Figure 1.12 indicates the IC output in various countries of the region, as well as their

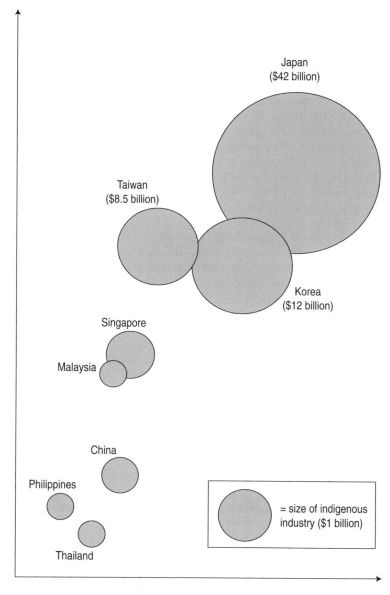

Figure 1.12 East Asian semiconductor production, 1997.

evolution along the dimensions of industrial capability and experience. Japan is by far the dominant producer and exporter, while Korea is a major producer in its own right, followed by Taiwan, while Singapore is just establishing itself as an indigenous producer.

In Singapore and Malaysia the production volumes reflect the value-adding activities of multinationals. There is also significant semiconductor activity in the Philippines, Thailand and particularly China, reflecting the fact that these countries were, by the late 1990s, offering cost-competitive alternatives for such activities as chip testing and packaging.

The fact of success of these East Asian countries is mirrored in the fact of failure in other parts of the world. Nowhere else in the developing world has an attempt been made on the commanding technological heights of the semiconductor sector. Even in otherwise advanced countries such as Canada and Australia, earlier efforts to establish semiconductor industries have met with scant success. There is therefore something critical in the approach taken by the East Asian success cases to the acquisition and diffusion of advanced technology. How the countries of East Asia were able to acquire these advanced technologies and, even more significantly, how they were able to adapt and improve them, indigenise and diffuse them, is the heart of our story. We turn now to establish the conceptual framework needed to understand these processes, as a prelude to analysing them in detail in the core countries of East Asia.

Notes

1   For a useful discussion of the strategic options available, see the 1993 World Bank symposium on 'Developing the electronics industry', in particular Steinmueller (1993) and Simon (1993). Likewise the World Bank discussion paper on the East Asian Miracle and IT by Hanna, Boyson and Gunaratne (1996) provides a useful analytical framework and country case studies on Japan, Korea, Taiwan, Hong Kong and Singapore.

2   Wherever possible we have used official sources for data on the semiconductor industry, or well-recognised market research sources such as Dataquest (now part of the Gartner group) and Integrated Circuit Engineering Corporation (ICE). Official sources that we have used include: World Semiconductor Trade Statistics (WSTS) – a consortium of national industry associations; Korean Semiconductor Industry Association; Economic Development Board (for Singapore); ERSO/Industrial Technology Research Information Service (ITRIS) for Taiwan; and Semiconductor Equipment

Manufacturers International (SEMI). Dataquest materials are published widely in the semiconductor trade literature, and ICE data has been taken from the annual report on the semiconductor industry, Status 199x. Figures 1.2, 1.3, 1.7 and 1.8 were commissioned from ICE specifically for inclusion in this book.

3   Note that this does not include foundry and OEM activities, which are counted by Western market research firms such as Dataquest as being attributed to the commissioning firms in North America, Europe or Japan.

4   These recessions were of major strategic significance since they provided the opportunity for counter-cyclical investment on the part of the Japanese in 1975 and 1981–82, taking them to world leadership, and on the part of the Koreans in 1985–86, which helped to get them established.

5   Own use production by firms such as NEC, Toshiba and Fujitsu is much more significant in Japan than in the US, while Asia-Pacific producers also fabricated much of the production that is attributed to others in Europe, Japan or the US. Thus the 52 per cent actually understates the real proportion of production activity undertaken in East Asia.

6   The trend continued strongly in 1996, when total sales of equipment amounted to $26.3 billion. By then, Asia as a whole accounted for 60 per cent of world sales; Japan $7.9 billion; Korea and 'Rest of World' $7.6 billion; North America $7.5 billion; and Europe $3.4 billion. (Data courtesy of Semiconductor Equipment and Materials International, SEMI.)

7   A succinct overview of the technology of integrated circuits and semiconductors, and processes used to produce them is provided in the glossary.

8   ICE Status (1996), p. 7-1.

9   The nine generations started with the 1K device in 1971, then proceeded through 4K, 16K, 64K, 256K, 1M, 4M, 16M and 64M generations.

10   Korea's trade balance swung into deficit in 1996, reflecting the downturn in memory chip prices. The downturn was certainly a factor in the severity of the subsequent 1997 financial crisis.

11   This is a highly significant finding in the context of the discussions of 'market access' to the Japanese semiconductor market, and the continuing difficulty on the part of US semiconductor firms to raise their share of the Japanese market. Flamm (1996) discusses the issues at length.

12   The estimated 1996 investment levels in Korean currency are 7.63 trillion *won*. This makes the semiconductor industry in Korea the country's highest investment spender – higher even than the automotive industry, which had plans to spend 4.5 trillion *won*.

13   As an indication of the growing sophistication of the Korean IC industry, patent applications for IC-related technologies by Korean firms leapt to 4889 in 1994, up 25 per cent on the previous year.

14   See Porter (1985) for the basic exposition of sustainable competitive advantage, and his 1990 book on sustainable national competitive advantage for an analysis of Korea's performance. One of us (DSC) has developed a critique of the Porter framework from the perspective of East Asia: see Cho (1994b).

15   In 1997, Taiwan's purchases of semiconductor equipment amounted to $3.8 billion, or 14 per cent of the world total. Compare this with Taiwan's share of world IC output in the same year of about 5 per cent.

16   ITRI's ten divisions cover: electronics (ERSO); optoelectronics (OESL); computing and communications (CCL); chemicals (UCL); energy and

resources (ERL); mechanics and machinery (MIRL); materials research (MRL); measurement and standards (CMS); industrial safety and health (CISH); and aviation and space technology (CAST).

17   ITRI's president, Chintay Shih, was head of the IC pilot fabrication plant in the late 1970s. His connections with Taiwan's IC industry go back to the very beginning.

18   The US Semiconductor Industry Association is one of Hsinchu's admirers; see Howell, Bartlett and Davis (1992).

19   Many of these conditions are spelt out in the founding legislation for the park; see Statute for the Establishment and Administration of a Science-based Industrial Park, September 1979.

20   In 1995, for example, the R&D budget for firms in HSIP was $310 million, which was 20 per cent of Taiwan industry's total R&D budget.

21   All twelve IC fabrication firms and supporting firms were actually located on the Park; their combined output in 1997 was just short of $6 billion. Between 1995 and 1998, eleven new IC fabrication plants were built in the park: ten of these at the most advanced 8-inch wafers.

22   Aggregate production in the two parks is expected to reach NT$1 trillion by the year 2003, or one-eighth of Taiwan's total production.

23   The ten are: TSMC, UMC, Winbond, TI-Acer, VIS, Powerchip Semiconductor, Nan Ya Technology, Mosel-Vitelic, MXIC and ASMC.

24   The equivalent in Singapore dollars was S$34 459. In 1996 the OECD upgraded the classification to count Singapore as a 'developed country'.

25   The output moderated slightly in 1997 due to the effects of the financial crisis and the global downturn in the semiconductor industry.

26   The electronics sector itself has seen sustained growth in Singapore, at a rate of nearly 40 per cent a year in the 1970s, moderating to 19 per cent average in the 1980s, and to 16 per cent in 1990–95.

27   See Natarajan and Miang (1992) for an excellent analysis of the arrival and impact of MNE investments in South East Asia, particularly in Singapore, Malaysia and Thailand.

28   See Chew (1988) and the Singapore chapter of the World Bank study of SMEs and their role in development by S. T. Wong in Meyanathan (1994). The latter study states explicitly: 'the presence of large MNEs in the disk drive industry [in Singapore] depends on the availability of high quality ancillary supporting services that are provided by SMEs in the precision engineering industries' (1994: 69).

29   This means that none of the value-added in Singapore is recorded as such by the world's leading market research firms such as Dataquest or ICE, who allocate production figures according to the originating firm.

30   These new package technologies are designed to accommodate chips with leadcounts of 100 to 300 pins (compared with 6 to 12 pins in the early days) and include major technical innovations in packaging.

31   For discussions of the EDB, see the studies by Low et al. (1993) and Schein (1996).

32   It has invested in both the TI joint venture TECH (taking a 24 per cent stake in this venture) and in the expansion of CSM (granting S$100 million to CSM for its second fab), and it was expected to put a substantial amount into the proposed Hitachi/Nippon Steel 64M DRAM venture.

33   It has signed research partnerships with several of the major companies already operating in Singapore such as AT&T, Siemens, SGS-Thomson, Toshiba and NEC, as well as Chartered, thereby leveraging the skills of these

companies across to Singapore technicians and engineers. In 1995 it formed eleven Singapore-based MNCs and local firms into an Electronic Packaging Research Consortium to conduct further leading-edge collaborative research and development work on the model of the product development consortia that are formed in Taiwan.

34 These include masks, lead frames, burn-in and testing services, bonding wires, automated equipment, ceramic packages, epoxy resin manufacturing, gas and chemical supplies, wafer fab equipment and clean-room design and installation.

35 The Tampines development is in two parts, with Phase 1 being ready for tenant firms to start construction in mid-1996, and Phase 2 in 1998. Both parks are being supplied with dedicated power substations and reliable water supply, as well as another park reserved for semiconductor support and ancillary activities (such as supply of specialty chemicals). The EDB is guarding against wafer fab overcapacity by seeking to attract a portfolio of IC fabrication activities. For example, TECH is producing DRAMs, while CSM is producing to contract (as a 'silicon foundry'), while SGS-Thomson is producing logic and non-DRAM memory chips.

36 Value-added is very much lower than these figures suggest, because most of the activity is at the end of the chip producing process, concerned with testing and packaging.

37 The electronics industry now accounts for around 25 per cent of Malaysian GDP. Semiconductor activity makes up 40 per cent of electronics, and is growing at three times the overall rate of GDP.

38 There were announcements of plans to establish DRAM fabrication plants by Hitachi and by LG Semicon but these were placed on hold in 1996 due to the downturn in the memory chip market.

39 The KHTP is owned and managed by the Kulim Technology Park Corporation (KTPC), which is 100 per cent owned by the Kedah state government.

40 VLSI Technology and Atmel Corporation announced joint venture fabrication facilities for Kulim Park in October 1997. Both were structured as joint ventures with the Malaysian financial institutions Bank Industri Malaysia Berhad (Industrial Bank of Malaysia) and Khazana Nasional Berhad (National Treasury), the investment arm of the Ministry of Finance. In 1998 the proposed investments were on hold pending resolution of the financial crisis.

41 These latecomer firms are described in greater detail in Chapter 5.

42 We develop this argument in Chapter 7.

43 On the origins of the electronics industry in Hong Kong and the role of foreign investment, see Hobday (1995a; 1995b).

44 This assessment is in accordance with the study of Hong Kong's technological competence and business future commissioned from the MIT Industrial Performance Centre: see Berger and Lester (1997). Earlier discussions of Hong Kong's technological direction were developed in the 1979 Diversification Report and the 1991 Technology Road Map, and recommendations made, but they were ignored by the 'hands-off' British administration.

45 It was taken as a starting point that Hong Kong has missed out on the high-technology revolution enjoyed in Taiwan, Korea and Singapore largely because of the absence of state sponsorship of systematic leverage strategies.

46 Interestingly, the university's initial endowment of over HK\$2 billion came from the Hong Kong Jockey Club, which represents the cream of the island's business establishment.

47   Dr Otto Lin, former Director of ITRI in Taiwan, was appointed Pro Vice
      Chancellor of R&D, with responsibility for directing these collaborative
      programs in 1996. His appointment signalled a new direction being taken
      towards technological enhancement in Hong Kong.

48   Some of the high-tech latecomer firms emerging in China through these
      forms of leverage include the following.

      • Shenzhen/SEG-SGS Thomson: The state-owned Shenzhen Electronics
        Group (SEG) was looking to become involved in wafer fabrication and
        IC assembly activities for some time. Earlier ventures fell through, but a
        joint venture with SGS-Thomson Microelectronics (STM) to build an IC
        assembly and packaging plant was agreed to in 1995. This was followed
        by a joint IC Design Centre in Shenzhen.

      • Stone/Mitsubishi: The huge Mitsubishi Corporation established a $2
        billion semiconductor joint venture with one of China's leading PC firms,
        Stone Computers, which holds a 30 per cent stake in the venture. An ini-
        tial investment of $100 million was agreed in 1996, with production
        beginning in 1997.

      • Huajing Semiconductor: The Japanese giant Toshiba joined with Huajing
        Electronics group to create a joint venture, Wuxi Huajing Semiconductor
        Co. An initial plant was established at Wuxi to produce bipolar chips for
        TV sets and audio equipment. In 1995, Toshiba licensed its 1M DRAM
        technology to the joint venture, and a new DRAM wafer facility was built
        by 1998. Cooperation between Toshiba and Huajing Electronics goes
        back more than fifteen years.

      • Shougang NEC: Japan's NEC entered a joint venture with China's Shodu
        Iron and Steel Co. to create Shougang–NEC Electronics, with plans to
        build the largest chip fabrication plant in China, at Shi Jing Shan, near
        Beijing. The involvement of Shodu indicates the preparedness of China's
        steel industry to move up to semiconductor technology involvements on
        the pattern of its counterparts in Japan, Korea and Taiwan.

      • HuaYue Microelectronics: In 1995 this well-established Chinese firm
        negotiated a comprehensive technology transfer agreement with Fujitsu
        covering bipolar IC technology for chips used in consumer electronics
        products. Fujitsu was to have access to a share of the output, for second-
        sourcing of its own products.

49   This development is also discussed in Chapters 5 and 6, in connection with
      the international expansion of Singapore's industries. See Yeung (1998) for
      an insightful critical discussion.

CHAPTER 2

Technology Leverage as Latecomer Strategy

Attempts to understand the phenomenon of high-technology indus-trialisation in East Asia have foundered on the apparent contradictions involved when viewed from the dominant Western perspective. It appeared that Japan, and then Korea and Taiwan, were creating high-technology companies and industries with minimal research and development expenditures, with little evidence of skilled engineering talent, and with minimal investment in brands and marketing outlets. All this contributed to a view that their efforts were superficial at best or 'cheating' at worst.

The problem was that these perspectives were not attuned to the special characteristics of industrialisation by catch-up. Such a process clearly involves a very different set of strategies from those developed in the nineteenth and twentieth centuries by Western industrialising countries.[1] Alice Amsden captured the essence of the shift in her phrase 'industrialisation by learning', using it to contrast the experience of new industries in NIEs such as Korea and Taiwan in such sectors as steel, shipbuilding or electronics, with previous phases of industrialisation by 'invention' (the case of Britain in the eighteenth century) and by 'innov-ation' (the cases of Germany and the US in the nineteenth century).[2] Amsden argues that the East Asian industrialisation experience is essentially a process of catch-up, in which replication of industrial techniques is achieved through 'learning', that is, through accelerated acquisition and adaptation of product and process technologies. Thus it is the institutions of 'economic learning' which turn out to be the pass-port to success in these endeavours, rather than the institutions of con-ventional R&D.

From a theoretical perspective, the problem is to account for the fact that latecomer firms like Samsung in Korea, Winbond in Taiwan and

71

STG in Singapore, which are now operating at the technological frontier, have not pursued a conventional R&D-led approach to technological capability enhancement. In the conventional sense, they are not 'innovators', and so their experience does not sit easily with conventional accounts of innovation seen as the generation of new knowledge within individual firms. The process in East Asia has instead witnessed a rapid uptake of existing technological opportunities – recombining, absorbing, adapting and ultimately improving them.[3] Thus the focus has been on *diffusion* rather than knowledge generation; on institutions of diffusion rather than individual firms; and on the acceleration and management of diffusion as a source of competitive advantage rather than on innovation.[4]

In this chapter we provide a 'map' of the process of technological learning in terms of the patterns and dynamics of induced technological diffusion.[5] The purpose is to apply such a map to the processes involved in the creation of a semiconductor industry in East Asia. We might call this diffusion-oriented process *industrialisation by technology acquisition and adaptation*, which in many ways is a more neutral term than 'learning' in that it does not imply that nations have to regard their 'teachers' as superior. On the contrary, an essential feature of the catch-up process is that the 'learners' have full and absolute confidence in their ability to acquire and adapt the technology developed by Western firms and to apply and diffuse it within their own institutional settings in an effective fashion. It was this confidence which drove Japan to the state of technological parity it achieved in the 1980s rather than followership, and which more recently has driven the technological transformation of Korea, Taiwan and now Singapore (and to a much lesser extent, Malaysia). Elements of the process have been picked up and emulated by the advanced countries themselves.[6] For reasons which will become clear, we choose to call the catch-up process 'industrialisation by technology leverage'.

Industrialisation by Technology Leverage

If the world economy were one of stable products, markets and technologies (that is, the static world depicted by conventional neoclassical economic analysis) then industrialisation by leverage could not possibly work. There would be no 'point of leverage' or entry point which new firms in new nations could use to their own advantage. Once firms had established themselves with a certain set of products or processes, they would be very difficult to dislodge; they would be able to keep competitors at bay through their superior access to information, research results, scale economies, and through the credible threats they would be able to exercise to keep marketing outlets 'loyal' to the existing firms. These are the advantages of 'incumbency': they are very real, and would effectively keep out new firms unless they were launched with comparable capital and technological endowments – which would, by definition, be beyond a developing nation.

But industrialisation by leverage demonstrably *does* work. The economy is anything but a world of 'stable products, markets and technologies'; on the contrary, in any realistic description, the economy is the site of seething and churning upheavals in products, technologies, firms and markets. Firms which ride one wave of innovation oust the old and establish themselves; they in turn are threatened with destruction as new firms rise by riding new waves of innovation. This is the restless, dynamic feature of the capitalist economic system that underpins, in the most fundamental sense, the success of industrialisation by leverage.

It was the Austrian economist Joseph Schumpeter who best captured this sense of the restlessness of the economic system by drawing attention to the 'creative gales of destruction' that sweep away the incumbents and create opportunities for the new, in ever-repeating cycles of creation and destruction. As Schumpeter put it:

> [The] capitalist economy is not and cannot be stationary. Nor is it merely expanding in a steady manner. It is incessantly being revolutionised *from within* by new enterprise, such as by the intrusion of new commodities or new methods of production or the opening up of new commercial opportunities. Any existing structures and all the conditions of doing business are always in a process of change. Economic progress, in capitalist society, means turmoil . . . Possibilities of gains to be reaped by producing new things or by producing old things more cheaply are constantly materialising and calling for new investments. (1942–50: 31–2)

Competition from this perspective was not the self-equilibrating process mediated by the price system beloved of neoclassical analysis but the *dynamic competition* introduced into the economy by novelty. What counts, according to Schumpeter, is not price competition,

> but the competition from the new commodity, the new technology, the new source of supply, the new type of organisation (the largest-scale unit of control for instance) – competition which commands a decisive cost or quality advantage and which strikes not at the margins of the profits and the outputs of the existing firms but at their foundations and their very lives. This kind of competition is as much more effective than the other as a bombardment is in comparison with forcing a door. (1942–50: 84)

The process described in such graphic terms has been witnessed over and over again. When Schumpeter was writing, he had in mind such upheavals in the nineteenth century as the ousting of canal transport by rail or the replacement of cast iron by steel (none of the old casting firms survived the transition) or the substitution of natural dyes by artificial dyestuffs based on new chemical processes.[7] Since his studies, the same process has been observed – such as in the origins of the semiconductor industry, where new firms pioneered the introduction of solid state devices, while most incumbent firms, whose business was based on valve technology, failed to make the transition.[8] It is the fundamental dynamics of capitalism, the very engine of growth and development, that create the opportunities for newcomers. Schumpeter himself insisted that 'this process of creative destruction is the essential fact about capitalism' (1942–50: 83).

The semiconductor industry provides dramatic illustrations of this process. It is the exemplar of the restless, technology-driven capitalist enterprise where competition is intense, product life cycles are short and there is relentless downward pressure on price within each cycle. The sequence of DRAM generations – displayed in Figure 1.8 – provides a starting point for our discussion. While each product generation lasts only three years or less, the whole sequence forms part of a larger pattern that we can identify as a technology trajectory. Since Schumpeter was writing in the early decades of the twentieth century, scholarly understanding of technological change and dynamics has improved somewhat. The character of technological change is now understood as being 'lumpy', confined through a process of path-dependent evolution to certain 'trajectories' or 'technological regimes' which become dominant in management and engineering over lengthy periods. Such regimes or trajectories define the problems to be solved, the design limits that are accepted, the tools used for intervening and the materials and processes used in a given technical field.[9]

In the case of DRAMs, once the basic technology was invented by Intel in 1971, it has remained locked within a certain set of design parameters and operational principles that constitute a technological 'trajectory'. The Japanese were the first ones able to read this trajectory and target DRAMs for their entry into US semiconductor markets in the late 1970s and 1980s. Then the Koreans were able to do so, targeting the same markets in the late 1980s and 1990s. But the difficulties involved in making these technological judgements should not be underestimated. When Samsung settled on the 64K DRAM as its point of entry into mainstream semiconductors in 1983, it was done partly in response to engineering and technical analyses, but also in the context of an owner–entrepreneur driving the engineers to strive for the technological frontier, no matter what the cost.

Likewise in the case of Taiwan, there was considerable agonising over which technological trajectory to 'attach' to in ERSO's first program of semiconductor technology leverage. The trajectory chosen, of CMOS general logic chip technology, turned out to be prescient, placing Taiwanese efforts on a rapid learning curve. Thus it is the capacity to 'read' technological trajectories that provides one of the critical points of leverage that latecomers need in order to effect entry.

Technological Diffusion and Product Life Cycles

Diffusion of technologies is a process driven by product life cycles and the patterns of investment in products at the earlier, middle and later stages of those cycles. There is a rich literature on the movement of products from their inception, to an early stage of experimentation in new forms, to the point where a 'dominant' model or technological regime is established, after which the emergent model is rapidly diffused as late entrants adopt it and seek to make their presence felt through minor product adaptations and process improvements.[10]

In the context of East Asia, the most popular account of industrialisation patterns is that of the movement of production and trade through 'product life cycles'. Production moves through phases beginning with innovation and early product development in more advanced countries, while mass production of standardised commodities shifts to less developed countries with lower labour costs.[11] In a celebrated paper Cumings (1984) argued strongly that the secret to Japan's, Korea's and Taiwan's industrial success lay in their ability to identify and navigate their way along the 'product life cycle' trajectories with 'virtuosity', and that the three were linked, by pre-war colonial ties, into a coherent economic region in which patterns of production and trade followed closely the predictions of the 'flying geese' model.

From our perspective, these product cycles provide the 'limits' within which leverage activities can hope to succeed. But they do not necessarily determine how the leverage process will proceed; as we shall see, there is scope for a great deal of strategic choice in pursuing industry creation within the framework of industry life cycles.

Industry Creation in Accordance with Life Cycles

Japan was the first East Asian nation to create new industries through active technology leverage, and its success remains the benchmark for the rest of East Asia. Through the 1950s, the Japanese economy went through wrenching structural change, as older industries based on coal-mining, foodstuffs and textiles were phased out, and newer 'heavy and chemical industries' – steel, petrochemicals, cement and machinery – were phased in. This process continued through the 1960s, with industries such as synthetic textiles, plastics, automobiles and electronics being introduced and 'nurtured'. The agency that developed this process into a fine art was MITI.[12] When the business was considered too risky or expensive for the private sector, a joint public–private corporation could be created.[13] A replica of this approach was taken by Taiwan in establishing the first companies involved in the semiconductor industry in the 1980s.

During the first half of the 1950s, MITI concentrated on 'nurturing' the steel, electric power, shipbuilding and chemical fertilisers industries. In 1953 it moved on to create and 'feed into the economy' new industries concerned with synthetic textiles, plastics and petrochemicals (1955), automobiles (1956) and electronics (1957). The electronics industry was created according to a variation in the MITI pattern, in the form of a 'temporary measures law', passed in 1957. MITI acted as the orchestrator and coordinator, in cooperation with other economic structures such as the 'enterprise groups'; the latter were of fundamental importance in enabling Japan to phase out coalmining in the 1950s and phase in cement production as a replacement business.

The heart of this Japanese model of industry creation is *technology leverage*. There is no assumption that technology must be created 'from scratch' as it were – a process which would have Japan pursuing the West for centuries before it might hope to achieve parity. The central assumption is that the technology needed is available and can be accessed through one means or another. The steps are all couched in terms of preparing firms for their decisive technology leverage encounters.

The 1950s Japanese 'MITI-model' of industry creation had to adjust to changes in the international economic order. The model was essentially framed in 'infant industry' protective terms, and calls for exclusion of foreign companies and foreign capital on any terms other than those extremely favourable to Japanese firms. As the years passed, and Japan's success became all too evident, these practices were increasingly difficult to get away with – although Korea and Taiwan (the latter in more liberal mode) were quite successful in replicating many of them. Japan was forced by external pressure – and by local industry pressure – to 'liberalise', which involved dismantling many of the government controls over its economy and opening it to international competition. First there was relaxation of direct controls over the currency; then there was phased 'liberalisation' of capital, providing the means for Japanese firms to access foreign capital, and for foreign firms to invest in Japanese enterprises or found new firms. This was accompanied by the phased opening up of the Japanese market itself through reductions in tariffs and through painfully slow dismantling of non-tariff barriers. All along, the aim of Japanese industrial policy has been not to perpetuate protection, but to create strong companies capable of withstanding international competition.

The most important element of the new approach was the continuous *upgrading* of the technological capabilities of an established industry. This is exemplified in MITI's approach to the steel industry, which upgraded to the newly invented Basic Oxygen Furnace (BOF) method in the late 1950s. By the early 1960s, the entire industry had been transformed, as a prelude to its becoming the strongest steel industry in the world.[14]

This approach to industry nurturing (*ikusei*) was further evolved in the case of high-technology industries. As described by Imai (1986) MITI's approach in the 1970s and 1980s was to select a field with high innovative and spin-off potential, using a network of advisers, and then to prepare scenarios and 'vision statements' which play a role analogous to 'business strategy' scenarios for private firms. At this point a decision was made as to whether the sector should be targeted or not. If so, MITI provided pump-priming subsidies, mainly to get some generic technology developed and commercially available to encourage private firms to follow up the possibilities created. If necessary, sources of foreign technology would be located and acquisition strategies formulated and implemented. This 'MITI' model has been highly influential in East Asia, particularly in the period of 'catch-up' that characterises attempts to create advanced industries such as semiconductors.

The Latecomer Firm: Turning Disability into Advantage

The puzzle at the heart of latecomers such as Korea's and Taiwan's achievement in high-technology industries is this: how were they able to overcome such severe disadvantages in terms of knowledge, technologies and access to advanced markets so completely and so quickly, in the face of such overwhelming competitive pressures from incumbent firms?

The key to a plausible solution lies in explicating the term 'latecomer'. While latecomer countries, and indeed the latecomer firms they generate, have extreme initial disadvantages linked to their poverty of technological resources, they also have some potential advantages if they know how to use them. They are starting with a 'clean slate', without commitments to any particular technology or approach, whereas incumbents have such ties and all the institutional inertia that goes with them. This clean slate concept means they can purchase the very latest technology and capture its improved efficiencies, whereas incumbents are looking to depreciate earlier investments. They have the advantage of having a very clear strategic goal to guide their efforts – the goal of 'catching up' with their advanced competitors.

But all of these potential advantages would be worthless if latecomers could not also count on some advantage due to their own state of development – something intrinsic to their status as latecomer. In the earlier years of industrialisation in East Asia, this advantage was clear: it was low wages and low costs generally. In the 1980s, with knowledge-intensive industrial upgrading, this advantage was less clear cut but still there. Furthermore the latecomer firm could offer its incumbent rivals advantages by subcontracting some operations such as the more labour-intensive testing and packaging of computer chips, and leverage knowledge from the contractee in the process. The latecomer firm views the world through very different strategic lenses, seeing incumbents not only as competitors but also as sources of knowledge to be leveraged through appropriate business arrangements such as subcontracting.

It was the Russian historian Alexander Gerschenkron who coined the term 'latecomer'. He pointed to the possibilities for latecomer nations to catch up with early starters through the creation of appropriate institutional arrangements.[15] Writing in the 1950s, he recognised the peculiar character of nineteenth-century European latecomer industrialisation in Germany, Italy and Russia, namely the opportunities it offered the latecomer to leverage advantages from others' success, and to be able to do so with institutional arrangements quite different from those in first-comer nations. He saw the advantages accruing to latecomer industrialising nations in terms of their capacity to develop a set of *new* institutions designed more explicitly to coordinate and facilitate the industrialisation process. The role of the state in effecting the transition by such latecomer nations was crucial.[16]

Gerschenkron's focus enabled him to show how relatively backward countries would be able to turn their *disabilities* into *advantages*. In discussing the relative paucity of skilled and disciplined labour in most underdeveloped countries, he argued that this would induce the coordinating agencies in such countries to seek out 'the most modern and efficient techniques' whose application could bypass the demands for conventional skills, whereas in advanced countries, it would be the very existence of such skills that would act as a social drag on the introduction of new techniques that would render them obsolete.[17] He cites the example of German blast furnaces, which in the mid-nineteenth century very rapidly exceeded the scale and productivity of British furnaces, despite the fact that Germany did not at first possess a workforce skilled in steelmaking. This example is very similar to the case of Japanese steelmaking in the 1960s and Korean steelmaking in the 1970s.

Gerschenkron theorised the process of latecomer industrialisation in the form of seven propositions or hypotheses. For him, the more backward the country, the more rapid will be its industrialisation in terms of its rate of growth of industrial production; the greater will be its stress on producer (capital) goods compared with consumer goods; the larger will be the typical scale of plant and firm, and the greater the emphasis on latest, up-to-date technology; the greater will be the pressure on the consumption levels of the population – consumption levels will be squeezed to promote a high rate of capital formation; the less will be the role of the agricultural sector as a market for industrial goods and as a source of rising productivity in its own right; the more active will be the role of special institutional factors – great banks as in Germany, the government ministry of finance in Russia – in supplying capital and promoting industrialisation; and the more important will be ideologies of industrialisation in the shaping of policies and events.

Gerschenkron's emphasis on the institutional underpinnings of late industrialisation in nineteenth-century European industrialisation finds its counterpart in late twentieth-century high-technology industrial upgrading in East Asia. This is the significance of his contribution for our study: the characteristic institutional framework and setting for the process of latecomer high-technology industrialisation.

Technology Transfer and Resource Leverage

The business and management literature, with its Western conceptions, sees the world as full of competitors, both actual and potential. This is the core of Porter's influential account of competitiveness of the firm and the country. But the East Asian perspective is to see the world as full of *resources*, particularly of knowledge and technology resources. These are resources which can be tapped in order to kick-start the process of capability enhancement within East Asian firms. The resources are held by firms in the advanced countries. Consequently these firms are not seen as *competitors*, as much as potential *collaborators* who can be used as a source of technological knowledge and skills. The object of the East Asian approach is to devise strategies and practices that will align the interests of these firms with those of firms or agencies in East Asia, so that these resources can be tapped.[18] Once acquired, the resources can be adopted, adapted, improved and given new twists by being embodied in new products that will command a market.

This is what we mean by resource leverage – the tapping of resources and their use to build up capabilities that can be used to develop products and markets much more sophisticated and extensive than would have been feasible without such a process. It is leverage in the sense that a small investment of capabilities is made to secure a return of greater levels of capabilities. The process results in 'technological learning', that is, the acquisition of ever-expanding and deepening technological capabilities.[19]

Leverage implies getting more out of a process than is put in. This is its original meaning in mechanics, and is the sense in which it is used in financial analysis. In management and business strategy literature it has been extended to the concept of 'resource leverage' – the capacity of firms to tap into financial, technological and other resources to accelerate their entry into new product markets or to enhance their capacity to upgrade their process technology.[20] This is precisely what East Asian firms have been able to do in the case of the semiconductor industry, and many other industries. They have been exemplary 'resource leveragers', in particular, leveragers of technologies from abroad through multinational import, licensing, OEM production and eventually, joint collaborative development efforts.

The change of perspective here is profound. It involves a switch to seeing the world in terms of resources, and fashioning strategy to secure them, rather than in terms of maintaining or sustaining some 'inherited' competitive advantage. It is essential to grasp what an *activist* conception of the world this implies; it takes the world as it is given, but devises ways to intercept developments and take advantage of opportunities. Our concept is far removed from a traditional notion of 'technology transfer' with its overtones of technology being 'granted' to an underdeveloped part of the world by a technology donor in the advanced world.[21] Rather, it is closer to a notion of 'capability transfer' and capability leverage.[22] Technology leverage is a form of active transfer, in which there is a dynamic of capability enhancement through an upward learning spiral that drives the process of technological upgrading.

Firms engaging in these processes have not had to do their 'leveraging' entirely on their own. In the case of the East Asian catch-up processes, firms have operated within a framework of institutions, consisting of public agencies, government departments and their organisational infrastructure, trade associations, *keiretsu* and *chaebol* interfirm linkages, and novel structures such as the collaborative engineering research associations developed by the Japanese. Institutional settings have accelerated and facilitated the process of economic learning, acting as an accelerating national system of innovation, where the emphasis again is on technology capture and diffusion.

Resource leverage takes place through well-defined channels that refer to various forms of investment and contractual relations, as elaborated in Table 2.1. These are the 'channels of diffusion' that scholars such as

Table 2.1   Mechanisms of technology leverage

Firm A in Korea or Taiwan (say) enters a relationship with firm B in a more advanced country through:

Sub-contracting	This requires firm A to execute an order for the contractor firm B, without necessarily sharing any technical knowledge other than the instructions and specifications needed to complete the order.
OEM original equipment manufacture	This entails the contracting firm A providing goods or components to a purchaser firm B, normally a well-established producer, which are sold under the purchaser's brand name, or go into final assembly of a product by the the purchaser.
ODM own design and manufacture	This is an extension and development of OEM arrangements where the contracting firm A also performs the design and scheduling of production of the components or (normally) the finished goods for firm B. Thus firm A brings a high level of capability to the contractual arrangement.
Licensing	In this case, firm A acquires the right to produce a product using a design or pattern developed by firm B, by paying a licence fee or royalty. Normally such an arrangement would also provide some technical support from firm B to the licensing firm A.
Technology transfer agreement	This is a more comprehensive arrangement than licensing. In this case firm A purchases all the know-how connected with a product or process technology, and is normally given substantial technical support by the originating firm B. The benefit gained by the originator is that firm A can act as a 'second source' for a product or range of products, providing extra capacity without firm B having to invest in that capacity itself.
Joint development agreement	This is an arrangement where two firms collaborate in a product or process development project, where they have a more equal contribution. Such an agreement exists between firms A and B, and does not require any other corporate identity.
Purchase of a company	This is an arrangement where the leverager has the financial resources to buy a stake in an advanced company, for the purpose of securing access to its technological resources. The strategy usually fails if the company is completely taken over – but if it is allowed to run as an independent business, then this can prove to be an extremely effective channel for resource leverage.
Joint venture	This is an arrangement where the joint development is actually housed in a separate corporate identity, to which both firms (or all firms if there are more than two) may contribute different amounts, and thereby have different claims to the joint product.

Pavitt (1985) speak of. Mastery of these contractual arrangements is the 'business' of resource leverage and catch-up industrialisation; mastery that is just as central to the success of firms as their grasp of the technologies themselves. This is where an institutional arrangement – for example, the existence of a public sector research institute like ITRI in Taiwan that negotiates technology licences on behalf of Taiwanese firms generally – could make all the difference between success and failure in industrialisation by leverage.

The point about these institutional forms is that they entail different levels of risk for both the originator of the technology, and for the adopter firm or country. OEM arrangements, for example, call for little investment by the adopter, but they must be able to provide high-quality manufacturing services at competitive prices and delivery schedules. Multinational corporations constitute a significant channel of transfer, usually favouring direct foreign investment in wholly owned facilities – but they may be induced to enter joint ventures, or pass on their expertise in other institutional forms. There is room for strategic judgement in choosing what kind of contractual framework best suits firms or agencies at their level of development – and such judgements reflect the prior learning and capabilities developed within these firms and public agencies.

Leverage and Organisational Learning

The core process of resource leverage is the learning undertaken by latecomer firms. It is firms which ultimately must be the repositories of enhanced technological and organisational capabilities. As latecomers, they must seek to translate their initial disabilities into advantages, through their strategies of resource identification and acquisition. Central to this process is organisational learning.

Organisational learning is the subject of intense discussion and research in management and organisational literature; the sense of how firms learn and use their learning to competitive advantage is improving rapidly.[23] The learning by a firm is organisational in the sense that it transcends the acquisition of knowledge by individuals; it is a process that is embodied in the development of organisational routines and procedures that are generally accessed by members.[24] The recent literature on the sources of firms' competitive advantage has sought to highlight the significance of organisational competencies as underpinning the competitive position of firms – in contrast to the traditional strategic analysis, which focused on the characteristics of products and markets and the firm's chosen position within them.[25]

The acquisition of competencies by a latecomer firm such as Samsung is as much an organisational as a personnel issue. While Samsung and other Korean firms had to recruit skilled engineers to make their entry into semiconductors feasible, on its own this would have been no guarantee of success. The critical factor was an ability to acquire and internalise technical competencies rapidly, and to apply them in the setting up and improvement of chip fabrication systems.

We draw on three conceptual innovations which seem to be most relevant to comprehending the organisational learning by a latecomer such as Samsung or Winbond. The first is the notion that 'core competencies' underpin the strategic success of firms and that these are acquired through processes of 'resource leverage' from external sources.[26] This perspective shifts analysis from the 'external' industry focus associated with scholars such as Porter to an 'internal' focus on firms themselves and their inner resources. It thus fits neatly with the conception of the latecomer, whose over-riding objective is to enhance its 'inner resources' and capabilities. This perspective also provides a welcome 'business' content to the notion of organisational learning, in the sense that it sets improvement in business performance as the clear outcome to be expected of organisational learning processes.

The second concept is the notion that firms need a basic platform of competence in order to build further competencies. They need to be able to master the mass production of simple products before tackling more complex products, for example. This straightforward idea is captured by the notion of absorptive capacity (Cohen and Levinthal 1990) or combinative capability (Kogut and Zander 1992). While derived separately and for different purposes, both concepts refer to the 'receptivity' of a firm to external sources of knowledge or technique.[27] The concept is central to understanding the long period of organisational 'apprenticeship' frequently undertaken by East Asian firms in the mass production and contract manufacturing of electronic products, before launching themselves into the semiconductor mainstream.

The third conceptual innovation we propose to use is the distinction between single-loop and double-loop organisational learning, introduced by Argyris and Schon in 1978.[28] Single-loop learning involves a feedback loop so that errors in the organisation's operation are detected and corrected; it results in performance stability or improvements as described by the idea of the 'learning curve' or 'experience curve'.[29] Double-loop learning on the other hand engages with the learning loop itself, subjecting the goals of learning to critical inquiry; it has been described aptly as 'learning how to learn'. Although the impression created in the literature is that double-loop learning is relatively rare, we maintain that it is in fact exceedingly common, and underpins the business success of firms which are able to adjust their operating structures and processes as circumstances change. This is the principal characteristic of the latecomer firm, which is engaging in accelerated adjustment and creation of capabilities in its quest to catch-up.

While all firms when faced with competitive markets must adapt their approaches and acquire – that is, learn – new competencies, the imperative for latecomer firms is to do this rapidly and acquire competencies at the same time. Using a strategy of resource leverage, the catch-up firm acquires knowledge and technological competencies from a variety of sources (for example, through technology licensing, purchase of equipment, hiring of competent engineers) and faces the challenge of rapidly assembling or combining these disparate elements into a coherent production and marketing system.[30] The 'core capability' needed by the firm to make a success of such an enterprise is a 'combinative capability' that enables the firm to put together, for example, equipment bought from Japanese and US manufacturers and 'tweak' it to provide superior performance. This rapid 'learning by doing' or single-loop learning needs to be accomplished within each product generation. The faster the firm is able to improve its performance (in productivity, yield and quality) the more quickly it can secure a return on investment.

There is nothing particularly special about single-loop learning; it is widely observed as 'learning by doing'. Single-loop learning on its own will never provide sufficient leverage for a latecomer firm. Where its real 'combinative capability' is called for is in moving rapidly from one product generation to another, internalising the competencies acquired in one generation in the assembling of process technology for the next, and moving into mass production at higher and higher levels of performance with each generation. In our view this is best understood as a form of 'double-loop' organisational learning, since it entails a capability of assembling the pieces of process technology more and more effectively and efficiently with each product generation.

Kogut and Zander (1992) introduced the term 'combinative capabilities' without reference to latecomer firms. For them, such capabilities explain how firms are able to move quickly into new business areas if they are able to 'combine' skills and technologies from different areas. This is indeed how most innovation is accomplished – not by radical breakthroughs, but by adaptations and novel combinations. The term is so evocative, and so good at capturing what the latecomer firm does, that we adapt it for our purpose, and signal its use as 'developmental combinative capability'. We do so to identify such a capability as the necessary 'core competency' of the latecomer firm.

Thus the conceptual foundations for an explication of the firms' success in breaking into high-technology industries are provided by four categories: the concept of the latecomer firm which turns initial disadvantages into sources of advantage; the process of resource leverage, which captures how latecomer firms acquire the knowledge and technology needed; the quality of absorptive capacity, which is what the latecomer firms need to build if they are to internalise the leveraged resources; and combinative capability, which is the 'core' capability needed by latecomer firms to leverage resources from a variety of sources and meld them into an integrated and efficient production system.

In the same spirit of 'combination' we propose as a shorthand the use of the term 'developmental resource leverage' (DRL) to mean the processes through which latecomer firms exercise resource leverage based on their absorptive capacity, using their combinative capabilities to enhance and deepen their technical and marketing capabilities. These are the latecomer firm's 'intangible assets', and their use should be demonstrable in terms of significant capability enhancement or organisational learning. It is possible to demonstrate the features of organisational learning in latecomer firms' acquisition and mastery of advanced technologies, as we show below.

The approach we outline here constitutes a potentially fruitful research program. Empirical work on organisational learning, such as it is, has focused mainly on single-loop learning or 'learning by doing'. Our approach would indicate that the focus of empirical work should instead be directed towards measures of double-loop learning, as exemplified in improvements in performance over successive product generations. This is precisely the kind of evidence we shall seek in the East Asian semiconductor industry.

Specifically we shall look for evidence of East Asian firms being able to improve their yields of ICs within each product generation (single-loop learning). More fundamentally, we expect that successful entry should be associated with successive improvement of learning from one product generation to another. An example of such an effect could be linked to yields of good chips per silicon wafer. In this case, evidence of double-loop learning or improvements in 'combinative capabilities' would be found if initial yields – as firms moved from pilot production to mass production – improved with each product generation. We reveal in Chapter 7 our success at gathering data to support our contention that it is the efforts of firms themselves that underpin the creation of the semiconductor industry in East Asia.

Developmental Resource Leverage

Following Gerschenkron, we argue that the set of institutions and procedures created by latecomer nations to facilitate resource leverage is best described as 'developmental'. It is developmental in that the goal of public policy is not just to create firms or capture technologies, but to do so in a process of accelerated national development. This is the over-riding feature of East Asian high-technology development in sectors such as semiconductors; it is not just an economic goal to create a high-technology industry, but a national political goal. Thus firms are created by entrepreneurs with explicit national development goals and normal profit-making goals, while programs of accelerated organisational learning (such as the various VLSI programs) are formulated and implemented to meet explicit national goals of economic and technological development.

Our use of the term 'developmental resource leverage' (DRL) can be defined as firms engaging in 'resource leverage', but in conditions created and shaped by a wider 'industry policy' framework and insti-tutional setting that has 'development' as its explicit goal.[31] Thus it is meaningful to talk of the 'developmental resource leverage' strategy pursued at an industry level, and not just at the level of the firm, in all the East Asian high-technology-creating nations.

The point is worth stressing. Business literature emphasises the challenge facing firms in forming 'core competences' or long-term sources of competitive advantage (Hamel and Prahalad 1994). They form these competences through the leveraging of resources, including technologies from partners and collaborators. This is what firms in a new industry have to learn to do if the industry is to become established. Generally speaking, business literature discusses resource leverage as if firms operate entirely on their own. But in latecomer nations like Japan, Korea and Taiwan, they do not operate on their own. On the contrary, they are given every assistance and discipline to ensure that they acquire core competencies.[32] The point of 'developmental' resource leverage is that public agencies create an institutional framework within which firms can successfully leverage the resources they need to become players in an advanced industry.[33] The demands of diffusion management are such that the conventional language for describing the processes – technology life cycles, stages of imitation, reverse life cycles – are not in our view sufficiently tuned to the specific needs of the technology leverage process. We intend to develop an account of East Asian industry creation and diffusion management strategies which will serve as the template for our description of the actual experiences of East Asian countries.

DRL can be described according to its four different processes. These are the patterns of resource leverage in terms of relations between markets and technology; the dynamics of the process, that is, its evolutionary stages; the forms the process takes, that is, the different national institutional models pursued in East Asian countries; and the strategic goals of the process with the emphasis on indigenisation of technology, diffusion and nurturing of new firms and capabilities. DRL results in the acquisition of new competencies and the enhancement of existing competencies – a process of technological learning.

Pathways of Diffusion

Scholarly treatments of technological learning by latecomer firms and countries tend to look at the enhancement of technological capabilities or at marketing and contracting issues in detail, without necessarily tying the two together.[34] Alternatively, these issues of customer linkage and technological capability enhancement are framed in an evolutionary manner, as a pathway along which latecomer firms develop (Hobday 1995). While each approach has its merits the danger in adopting a 'stages' approach to diffusion is that it becomes a conceptual 'mould' that imprisons analysis. The fact is, while some firms evolve along the pathways described by Hobday, many others do not. A general account should seek to provide support for all the phenomena observed.

An integrating perspective is called for so that the different strategic options and actions taken by firms and agencies in the process of leveraging themselves abreast of advanced technologies may be given some coherence and plausibility. What is needed is a framework that does for 'management of technological diffusion' what Abernathy and Clark's transilience framework (1985) did for 'management of techno-logical innovation'. The key to their account lay in their capacity to integrate or synthesise the issue of innovation in terms of technology with the question of market impact. They captured this synthesis in their notion of the 'transilience map' for any particular innovation – a 'map-ping' of the effect of an innovation measured along the twin dimensions of depth of technological impact and market effect. We aim to develop a comparable synthesis for the case of DRL, where the object of analysis is not 'effect of an innovation' but 'leverage of an advanced technology' – and where the twin dimensions for measuring the process of such managed diffusion will have to be those appropriate to diffusion rather than innovation.

Taking our cue from Abernathy and Clark, we characterise the pathways along which technological diffusion is managed in terms of two dimensions: enhancement of technological capabilities (deepening, broadening)[35] and enhancement of access to or linkage with customers in advanced markets.[36]

These are not the same as Abernathy and Clark's twin dimensions. Rather, they reflect the latecomer firms' urge to leverage more and more advanced capabilities, and to do so through more and more advanced

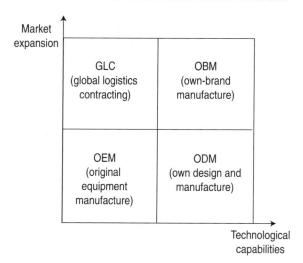

OEM: At the simplest level of market access and technological capability, latecomer firms can secure contract manufacturing jobs from either final producers in advanced countries (original equipment manufacture) or from retail outlets in those countries (private brand manufacture). The technology is supplied to a large extent by the contractor, while the market access is provided likewise by the contract arrangement. What the latecomer contractee firm has to supply is low-cost, reliable products. It needs to have accumulated sufficient production capability and technological capability to be able to absorb the new standards being demanded.

ODM: Moving upwards in terms of technological capability, the firm is able to handle more and more of the functional aspects of the job itself, to the point where it can execute own design and manufacture orders. It no longer needs to receive exact specifications, but can produce these itself from vague orders like 'we need 10 000 copies of a computer game that captures the essence of Gameboy but costs half as much'. The design, product development, product engineering and process engineering are all taken care of by the contractee latecomer. But its marketing capabilities are still quite undeveloped; it has access to advanced markets only via its contracts with producers or retailers.

GLC: Moving upwards in terms of market access and management of industry costs, firms are increasingly involved in securing 'global logistics contracting', where they are required not only to produce the goods to certain specifications, but to deliver them to specified points around the world, within specified times, as well. Thus the contracting firm is required to carry a proportion of the inventory costs, and is forced to manage its logistics flow if it is to succeed in such a business.

OBM: Innovative R, D and PE and brand support: The culmination of this dual development of capabilities on the part of the latecomer firm is full innovative potential in terms of research, development and process engineering (Pavitt 1985) and development of marketing channels, brand development and customer support (e.g. through after-sales service and customer support). This can be called 'Own Brand Manufacturing'.

Figure 2.1 Diffusion map: leverage strategies.

market linkages. It is not the impact of innovation that we are concerned with (which is the subject of their 'transilience map'), so much as the acceleration of diffusion via leverage, and the *degrees* of leverage involved.

The actual pathways of diffusion may be characterised by various contractual linkages, as shown in Figure 2.1. Thus we may characterise the management of technological diffusion in terms of four degrees of leverage involving more and more complex relations between the initiatives of the firm doing the leveraging and its contractual partners, and between technological competences. They are, in sequence: OEM, ODM, GLC and OBM.[37]

The actor in this diffusion map is not specified, but in most cases it is a latecomer firm. But in the absence of such firms, it might be a public agency, as in Taiwan before firms entered the nascent semiconductor industry, or a government economic development authority (say, Singapore's EDB). The cells indicate states desired to be reached as fast as possible by leveraging agents in order to accelerate the diffusion process. In each case, the strategic goal of the process is to move upward and outward, towards greater levels of technological capability and more advanced market access. While the map captures diffusion patterns, the emphasis is on leveraging the activities of the firms or agencies in the latecomer nation rather than on the originating actions of the advanced firms, which is the usual perspective in discussion of technology transfer.

Some scholars have sought to combine these developments in a 'stages theory' of technological and marketing capabilities acquisition.[38] Such a stages theory has been found to fit quite closely the development of many firms from latecomer countries such as Korea, Taiwan and Singapore, as they move from simple contract assembly to enhanced production and design capabilities, to full product and process development capabilities. Anam from Korea is a typical case. From our perspective, the problem with such a stages account is that it fits only a fairly narrow class of firms who move through the entire sequence. Other latecomer firms that enter at higher levels of technological and marketing capabilities may practise leverage of a different degree. Thus we prefer a more general depiction of trends and degrees of leverage in our diffusion map.

The Dynamics of Capability Enhancement

Industries are now widely seen to evolve through multiple stages. They start in any one of a number of initial fluid states and move to states where technologies become more standardised, and competition de-volves on cost factors more than on innovation and performance. They reach a stage of maturity where few players remain in the industry as consolidation takes place. For example, Van de Ven and Garud (1989;

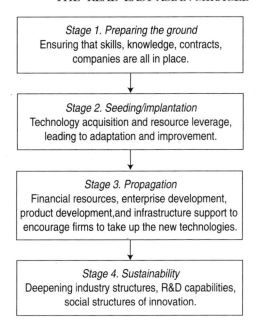

The process is then extended through a new round of seeding, propagation, sustainability, with the newly created technological capabilities serving as platform for the next.

Figure 2.2   Steps in developmental resource leverage.

1993), in their discussion of the emergence of high-technology industries, see the process unfolding over four distinct phases.[39] Likewise Mueller and Tilton (1969), in their discussion of barriers to entry, construct a model of industry creation that moves through four stages.[40] There are overlaps between these two models, which may be taken as representative of the technology development cycle literature.

While any industry created as a matter of public policy will have to pass through evolutionary stages which approximate those outlined by Mueller and Tilton and Van de Ven and Garud, for us these models do not capture the essential technology diffusion management features found in East Asian industry creation. East Asian newly created industries will mimic the first three phases of these models, yet in terms of these models, be confined to the 'industry consolidation' phase. This is not very satisfactory either in theoretical terms or in terms of public policy implications.

The dynamics of diffusion may be modelled in a manner which overcomes such theoretical difficulties. The model focuses on the sequence of steps associated with a resource leverage approach. This process of resource leverage proceeds logically through four steps:

preparation, seeding, propagation and sustainability. This will be the case for each technology targeted for industry creation. The general sequence, which is followed by all high-technology industries successfully created in East Asia, is shown in Figure 2.2.

Preparation

East Asian countries have appeared to pay careful attention to establishing preliminaries, such as an adequate skills base and adequate financial resources prior to embarking on major technological upgrades. These preliminaries include establishing a skills base of engineers and technologists through domestic education, education abroad, recruitment of specialists and import of advanced training materials and methods; establishing a research base by setting up R&D institutes that can form links with advanced centres of technology development; and encouraging companies to form subsidiaries in advanced technology sectors, and create 'listening posts' in centres of excellence where these companies may become acquainted with advanced product and process technologies.

The importance of this preparatory step lies in the creation of preconditions for successful take-up and development of an advanced technology; without the build-up of such 'absorptive capacity', technology 'transfer' initiatives will wither and die.

Seeding

This entails activation of the channels of technology transfer through technology licensing and associated training; OEM contracting (and associated technology transfer); technology consortia, collaborative R&D and other networks; joint ventures; and acquisition of technology-based small firms. In one form or another, these involve securing access to an advanced technology by an organisation that is competent to develop it. The *quid pro quo* for the donor organisation or co-developer apart from licensing fees and royalties (sometimes attractive enough in themselves), is frequently market access in the importing country.

Propagation

The key to successful industry propagation is the emergence of a group of firms, together with all the associated institutional infrastructure and support, that can compete internationally. Van de Ven and Garud (1989; 1993) emphasise that an 'industry' is more than just a group of firms arbitrarily assigned to a group of products; it is a constellation of actors – the firms themselves, but also the public sector research agencies, the trade associations, the regulatory authorities, perhaps the consumer associations and supplier groups – whose complex interactions and forms of collective behaviour make up an industry with real dynamics. This is certainly a point understood by East Asian latecomers.[41] The goal of industry creation is not narrowly confined to the launch of a few firms or the provision of finance for the firms' formation and ensuring that they have access to technology but, more strategically, involves the creation of 'preparation' institutions such as KIET in Korea, ITRI in Taiwan and the IME in Singapore.

Sustainability

The goal of industry creation in East Asia is not the formation of groups of firms which are dependent on subsidies or other forms of perpetual assistance, but of clusters of firms which can compete successfully in world markets. This entails attention being paid by public agencies as well as by the new firms to such issues as: sustaining product development cycles; forming joint development consortia; underwriting of R&D activities; firms moving into own-brand manufacture (OBM); and deepening and broadening of industry ('moving up the food chain' as in creation of an equipment supply industry). This stage calls on firms to develop all the associated skills to underpin capabilities in manufacturing, such as new product development and marketing products through independent channels under their own brands. We discuss what we mean by 'sustainability' in greater detail later.

What is depicted in this framework is a sequence of activities in which one level of activity depends on a prior build-up of competence, with the whole process moving through iterative cycles. Seeding is logically prior to diffusion, and preparing the ground is logically prior to seeding. It is in distinguishing between these phases, and tailoring policies for each of them, that industry policy in East Asia has achieved its successes so far.[42] Thus the dynamics of the process can be defined in terms of a number of necessary 'stages' in a manner that parallels the evolutionary description of industry life cycles – with the very important distinction that these are acts taken by agents in order to deliberately create a new industry or upgrade an existing one.

From the perspective of DRL, the actions taken to prepare, seed and nurture new industries are deliberate acts of public policy undertaken by public agencies in a spirit of national development. It is in this sense that one can speak meaningfully of 'industry creation' initiatives in East Asia, and can describe the institutional structures created for this purpose.

Institutional Vehicles of Leverage

The institutions (agencies, firms) through which technology diffuses in East Asia are chosen explicitly to be tools of leverage rather than instruments of innovation. In the conventional literature on innovation, two principal vehicles of R&D activities are generally recognised, namely the private firm and the public laboratory. The interactions between them have varied strongly between countries and historical periods. Likewise the institutions of leverage discovered so far (and which appear to exhaust the possibilities) are threefold: large, already established, firms in the industrially upgrading country; public sector laboratories and institutions linked to a consortia of small firms; and external leverage via linkage with multinational corporations.

While there are obvious country identifications with these approaches, we prefer to label them neutrally as Model A, Model B and Model C to inquire into the prevalence of their use, and the limitations that are intrinsic to each.

Model A

The Korean approach, very much modelled on Korea's perception of what Japan did (especially in Japan's industrial colony of Manchuria developed in the 1930s), was to use as vehicles of leverage the existing large firms that had been created in the early years of industrialisation. The Korean policy approach in the semiconductor industry was to prod the existing large firms, which had honed their leverage and export skills through earlier phases of industrialisation, to enter the high-investment, high-risk area of VLSI semiconductors in the 1980s.

Model B

In the absence of such large firms, or where there is a preponderance of small and medium-sized firms, as in Taiwan, there is an alternative vehicle of leverage in the form of public sector agencies. This is the role that ITRI and its laboratories, such as ERSO and CCL, have played for the semiconductor sector. These agencies acquire the technology in the first place, then build up expertise in the products and processes and improve and adapt the technologies and then diffuse the capabilities as rapidly as possible to the private sector, in some cases even creating the companies for the purpose (as in the case of UMC).

Model C

A third variant is to recognise that multinational corporations constitute the world's most abundant source of technological competencies, and use them to secure access to these competencies. The approach, pioneered by Singapore, is to offer multinationals favourable conditions for location of their activities in the host country, with a view to raising overall skill and technological capabilities, and to set in train a process of upgrading through inducing the multinationals to enhance their own operations and pass on (indigenise) more and more of their own internal capabilities. Quinn (1969) foresaw the significance of multi-nationals for technology transfer and forewarned of all the potential dangers that might be met in the process, and proposed policy remedies for them. Singapore appears to be one of the few countries that has pursued a strategy closely in keeping with Quinn's remarkable analysis. Since then, many others have followed Singapore's example, and now many regions of the advanced countries, in North America and Europe, also compete vigorously for multinational investment.[43]

There is a point in generalising these vehicle-specific processes; they may be replicated. Indeed, countries may find ways to create new industries using one or more of these leverage vehicles. China offers perhaps the most striking example in its use of all three vehicles simultaneously, as we discuss in Chapter 7.

The 1997–98 Asian financial crisis subjected the three forms to further rigorous testing. Model A, with its high debt levels, has been shown to be most vulnerable, while Model B, with its more modest capital require-ments, has been shown to be remarkably robust. Model C remains the pathway of choice for almost all countries that lack sophisticated firms of their own, and even for those which do, but are not at the forefront of manufacturing innovation (such as Canada or Australia).[44]

Strategic Goals of Leverage Processes

The overarching strategic goal of the latecomer firm, and of the country which generates it, is to catch up with industrially advanced firms in industrially advanced countries. It is catch-up that creates the critical strategic framework, and justifies practices and perspectives that may have to be abandoned or modified once catch-up has been accomplished – practices such as targeting, government-induced collaboration and collective risk reduction through public facilitation.

Samuels (1994) captured the essence of the strategic goal of catch-up in his description of Japanese efforts to become integrated in aerospace technology – efforts which have now borne fruit, with Japanese firms at the forefront of aerospace technological developments. Samuels describes this overarching goal as 'techno-nationalism', that is, the quest to acquire and master technologies as a national goal or effort. It has subsidiary goals which are identified in Japanese policy documents as indigenisation (adoption), diffusion and self-sufficiency.

Indigenisation is the quest to establish domestic sources of the tech-nology as well as an ability to adapt it and transform it, that is, to innovate within the limits of the technological trajectory.

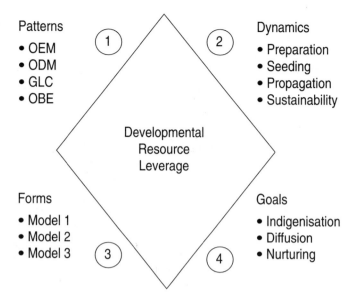

Figure 2.3   Developmental resource leverage – an integrated perspective.

Diffusion is the conscious public goal of propagating the technology to as many firms in the industry as can use it for productive, export-oriented activities, without creating unwanted conditions of 'excess competition'.

Nurturing refers to the battery of measures taken by Japan during its catch-up phase to ensure that fledgling companies or new business arms of existing companies are able to adopt and adapt the technologies for their own purposes, thus internalising them.

These are goals of 'catch-up' everywhere, and they drive the process as observed in all its variants in the wider East Asian region beyond Japan. It is because the goals of catch-up differ strategically from the goals of sustaining technological leadership once it is acquired that so much confusion is generated in technological policy discussions.[45] But the East Asian countries seeking to integrate themselves in advanced technological activities appear never to have confounded the two.

Capability Enhancement through Developmental Resource Leverage

The four facets of developmental resource leverage, are captured in Figure 2.3. In practice, these work together to reinforce each other. Thus, the progression from, say, OEM to ODM and OBM is dependent on the process of technology acquisition moving through seeding to propagation, as firms are founded which provide a cluster of support and ancillary activities. The various vehicles of the process all take their place as constituents of the leveraged industry as it approaches sustainability. Such an industry can be said to have reached the strategic goals associated with catch-up.

Industry creation is a complex process of multiple interaction sub-processes and feedback loops, driven in East Asia by highly sophisticated techniques for identifying dominant technological trends and 'locking' on to them through leverage techniques.

A biological analogy is in order. In ecology, it is understood that the deliberate creation of, say, a grassland (or prairie), with its mix of grasses, cannot be achieved simply by seeding the grasses desired. They wither and die for lack of support. Rather, successful grassland recreation (as a deliberate act in, say, run-down urban areas) requires a clear understanding of the 'ecological dynamics' of the process of establishment of grassland, and in particular of the stages that a successful prairie goes through in order to create the right balance of competing and cooperating organisms. Thus early grasses provide a certain kind of organic mix in the soil; they attract birds which find habitats, and these provide an environment which then becomes favourable for the 'final' grasses to be seeded and survive, given that the environment has been adequately prepared through earlier stages of development. Likewise there is discussion of the 'ecological dynamics' of successful industries or clusters of industries, as in the case of California's Silicon Valley.[46]

The process of leveraged industry creation can be pictured as a spiralling, iterative sequence of technological enhancement and improving market access, with each stage of the process – or each round of DRL – providing the platform for the next. Each such iteration creates an expanding 'cone' of capabilities, as depicted in Figure 2.4. This then provides the platform for the next round of leverage and capability enhancement at a new technological frontier. Thus, Korea, Taiwan and Singapore have all built on their success with semiconductors to move into more advanced and high value-adding activities such as logic chips, microprocessors and associated ancillary activities.

Resource leverage is widely practised by firms in all countries, being one of the principal mechanisms involved in organisational learning. Industries emerge all around the world as a result of technological innovation in a constantly self-renewing cycle of growth and decline. What we see as special in East Asia is that resource leverage is practised quite consciously as a matter of public policy, with the intent of creating industrial ecologies or industrial systems/clusters that did not previously exist. The resource leverage practised in catch-up industrialisation is developmental in spirit and form.

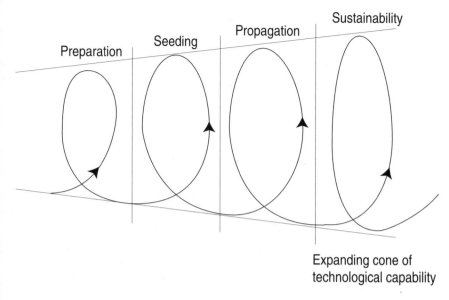

Figure 2.4   Technology resource leverage and the cone of capabilities.

The analytical framework proposed here is consistent with the perspective identified with 'technological learning' and, even more generally, with evolutionary economic perspectives (Nelson and Winter 1982). At the level of the firm, the framework is consistent with the perspective of 'dynamic capabilities and strategic management' introduced by Teece, Pisano and Shuen (1997). For them, the critical issue in strategic management is less how firms sustain competitive advantage as how they build them in the first place:

> The essence of (the firm's) competencies and capabilities is embedded in organisational processes of one kind or another. But the content of these processes and the opportunities they afford for developing competitive advantage at any point in time are shaped significantly by the assets the firm possesses (internal and market) and by the evolutionary path it has adopted/ inherited. Hence organisational processes, shaped by the firm's asset positions and moulded by its evolutionary and co-evolutionary paths, explain the essence of the firm's dynamic capabilities and its competitive advantage. (1997: 518)

Our aim is to demonstrate how strategic advantages are achieved in the special case of a latecomer firm catching up with incumbent rivals in high-technology industries such as semiconductors.

Notes

1 On the industrialising experiences of the nineteenth century, and the role played in them by technology, see the classic accounts by Rosenberg (1994) and Rosenburg, Landau and Mowery (1992).

2 See Amsden (1989) for an exposition of her argument, and Kim Linsu (1995) for an elaboration.

3 See Bell and Pavitt (1993) for an account of the critical differences between innovation in advanced countries and in 'catch up' countries.

4 Of course the literature on innovation also recognises the significance of diffusion, as in Rogers (1995).

5 In so doing we adapt the approaches that scholars such as Abernathy and Clark (1985), Rosenberg (1994) and Van de Ven and Garud (1989; 1993) have taken for the case of innovation.

6 Chiang (1991) discusses the trend to what he calls 'diffusion-oriented' technological development in the US, in place of the previous emphasis on 'mission-oriented' strategies. Using this terminology, the East Asian approach is essentially 'diffusion-oriented'.

8 It was new firms in the US such as Fairchild and Texas Instruments which had no background in radio valve technology that made the running in the semiconductor industry; incumbent firms based on valve technology such as Sylvania failed to make the transition for the reasons adumbrated by Schumpeter. Interestingly, Japanese firms like NEC did manage to make the transition.

9 For a useful overview of the concept of technological trajectory, see Dosi (1982). On technological regimes, see Nelson and Winter (1982) as well as Burgelman (1995).

10 Abernathy and Utterback (1979) introduced the notion of the 'dominant product design' and suggested that its appearance brings a new competitive dynamic to an industry. The notion was elaborated by Utterback and Suarez (1993) who locate the 'standardisation' of a product as the point where process technological capabilities count for more than product design capabilities. It is at this point that there arise competitive possibilities for firms in East Asia.

11 Two influential versions of this story have been given by the US economist Raymond Vernon (1961) and earlier by the Japanese economist Kaname Akamatsu (1962). Akamatsu is originator of the notion that industrial dynamics works through successive waves of product import, import substitution and eventually export, taking on the appearance of overlapping 'V' formations that reminded Akamatsu of flying geese in formation; hence the so-called 'flying geese' pattern of industrial development and trade.

12 Johnson (1982) specified a series of steps that industry creation goes through in what we may call the 'MITI model'. There are seven steps: a basic policy statement is drafted on the need for the industry and its prospects; foreign currency allocations are authorised by MITI and funding is provided for the industry by the Development Bank; licences are issued to Japanese firms for the importation of technology; the nascent industry is designated as 'strategic' in order to give it special and accelerated depreciation allowances on its investments; nascent industry is provided with improved land on which to build its installations, either free of charge or at nominal cost; the industry is given tax breaks such as exemption from

import duties to assist import of capital goods, refund of duties paid on imported components and exemption from export duties; MITI creates through 'administrative guidance' a cartel of firms to regulate competition and coordinate investment among the firms in the industry (1982: 236). Johnson illustrated the process using the creation of the petrochemical industry, which was effected in the mid-1950s.

13   An example was the Japan Synthetic Rubber Corporation, established in 1957.

14   The new BOF technology was developed in Austria in the early 1950s. The Japanese became aware of it through their technology scanning mechanisms, and licence agreements for its transfer to Japan were signed, under MITI supervision, in 1956. The first BOF mills were built in 1957, and within five years the entire industry had been transformed – a decade ahead of the changeover in the US. Lynn (1982) provides a comprehensive discussion of the experience. Lest MITI's powers be exaggerated, Lynn points out MITI failed to persuade Kawasaki Steel to use BOF in its expansion plans, a decision the company came to regret; and MITI failed to dissuade another company from using the ill-fated Kaldo technology, which rapidly declined in the face of the superior BOF process.

15   See Gerschenkron 1952; 1962.

16   See Weiss and Hobson (1995) for a discussion of historical examples, such as Germany and Russia in the nineteenth century, as well as cases from East Asia in the twentieth century.

17   Gerschenkron 1952: 7.

18   This is the significance of contract (OEM) manufacturing, for example; it is an alignment of interests between the firm outsourcing the manufacturing, and of the firm in East Asia which accepts the sub-contracted work as a stepping stone towards competence enhancement.

19   In the 1980s, the notion of 'technological capabilities' was introduced and discussed variously by Dahlman and Westphal (1983), Dahlman, Ross-Larson and Westphal (1987) in their World Bank series of studies and by Lall (1990). According to the OECD's 1992 study the notion of technological capabilities (in general, East and West) is a concept that:

> attempts to capture the great variety of knowledge and skills needed to acquire, assimilate, use, adapt, change and create technology. It goes well beyond engineering and technical know-how to include knowledge of organisational structures and procedures as much as knowledge of the behavioural patterns of workers and customers. Firms need certain complementary assets and capabilities in order to create, mobilise and improve their technological capabilities. (1992: 262)

In Korea, Kim has translated these ideas into a stages theory of technological capabilities acquisition by latecomer firms, as outlined in Kim (1997a). Bell and Pavitt (1993), in their exposition of developed and developing countries patterns of innovation, emphasised the distinction between 'technological capabilities' and 'production capacities'.

20   For a discussion of 'resource leverage' see Prahalad and Hamel (1990); for an exposition of much of the research behind this article, see Hamel (1990). For a more recent exposition of their views, see Hamel and Prahalad (1994).

21   This is a stylised view of the technology transfer literature; see Rosenberg and Frischtak (1985) or Bell and Pavitt (1993) for approaches that are closer in spirit to the perspective developed here. From the perspective of South East Asia, see Koh (1995).

22   Baba and Hatashima (1995) discuss 'capability transfer' in the context of the diffusion of the Japanese electronics industry into the wider East Asian region by making the point that the diffusion is driven as much by the quest for enhancement of capabilities by firms in countries such as Malaysia and Thailand as it is by the calculations of the Japanese principals.

23   For the original statement of organisational learning, see Argyris and Schon (1978/1995).

24   On the development of organisational routines as a form of 'organisational memory' see Nelson and Winter (1982).

25   Grant (1991) provides succinct accounts of the resource-based theory of competitive advantage and draws its implications for strategy.

26   See Prahalad and Hamel (1990).

27   Cohen and Levinthal (1990) introduced the notion of 'absorptive capacity' to make the point that firms need to make strategic investments in 'capabilities' not immediately related to current activities in order to be able to take account of unforeseen technological turnings. For them, absorptive capacity is a kind of organisational learning buffer or insurance against unforeseen events. Mascitelli (1999: 100–3) uses the concept in the same way to help explain the rise of high-technology firms in Silicon Valley. Kogut and Zander (1992) introduced their notion of 'combinative capabilities' to capture a similar idea, namely that successful firms need to be able to access resources (products, technologies, markets) from a variety of sources, and develop a competitive advantage based on new 'combinations' of existing products and technologies, rather than always seeking something totally new. The term evokes the process of 'genetic combination' as underpinning biological diversity and adaptation.

28   See Argyris and Schon (1978) for their discussion of the question what is an organisation that it may learn.

29   The 'experience curve' has been much discussed and demonstrated in a wide variety of industries; see for example the review by Lieberman (1987).

30   Early accounts of this process in the context of Korea's industrial development, can be found in Amsden (1989) and Kim (1993; 1995) and in elaborated form in Kim (1997a).

31   This term was introduced by one of us in his study of Korea and Taiwan; see Mathews (1995a).

32   Dahlman and Westphal make a similar point in their comment that firms on their own might not find it in their interest to introduce advanced technologies 'unless influenced by some form of public intervention' to do so (1982: 123).

33   In the case of industry creation strategies in Japan, the state agency MITI oversaw every facet of the technology leverage process. As Johnson (1982) describes it:

   The importation of technology was one of the central components of postwar Japanese industrial policy . . . Before the capital liberalisation of the late 1960s and 1970s, no technology entered the country without MITI's approval; no joint venture was ever agreed to without MITI's scrutiny and frequent alteration of the terms; no patent rights were ever bought without MITI's pressuring the seller to lower the royalties or to make other changes advantageous to Japanese industry as a whole; and no program for the importation of foreign technology was ever approved until MITI and its various advisory committees had agreed that the time was right and that the industry involved was scheduled for 'nurturing' (*ikusei*). (17)

This control by government over technology transfer to Japan, and its subsequent nurturing, was exercised under the Foreign Capital Law, which remained in force from 1950 to 1980. Just how the government, and MITI in particular, exercised this control, is at the heart of what came to be called in Japan 'industry policy' (*sangyo seisaku*) – meaning public policy over which industries should be promoted and at which stages in the economic development process. The capacity to exercise 'industry policy' rested, in turn, on the creation of an institutional framework within which the strategic decisions of firms might be influenced and coordinated to reflect the goals of public policy. These concepts were very influential in East Asia.

34   See treatments on technological capability enhancement by Dahlman and Westphal (1982) and scholars associated with the World Bank's 'Technological capability enhancement' project. See also Enos (1991), and Park and Enos (1991).

35   This topic is treated in the literature under the rubric 'industrial technology development'; see, for example, Najmabadi and Lall (1995). Baranson and Roark (1985) drew strong distinctions between 'duplicative' (early stage) and 'innovative' (late stage) capabilities, just as Kim (1997a) refers to the transition from 'imitation' to 'innovation'. Dahlman and Westphal (1982) drew distinctions between four capabilities as aspects of what we call 'leveraging': production engineering, project execution, capital goods manufacturing and R&D. They later refined this to three distinct capabilities: operational (for running productive facilities); investment (for expanding capacity, making modifications and establishing new productive facilities); and innovation (Westphal, Kim and Dahlman 1985).

36   Wortzel and Wortzel (1981) discussed the expansion of marketing functional capabilities as proceeding through five stages: passive importing and low-cost labour assembly; active seeking of contracts for manufacturing through foreign buyers; marketing of own designs and establishment of marketing outlets abroad; active expansion of product marketing, expansion of range of products, and beginnings of brand development; and own brand production and marketing through various channels.

37   On contractual linkages, see Wong (1991).

38   Hobday (1995) adapted Wortzel and Wortzel (1981) by adding complementary stages of development of technological capabilities to their five-stage sequence: assembly skills applied to mature, low-cost products; incremental process improvements and reverse engineering; full production skills, process innovation and product design capabilities; product innovation capabilities and process engineering; and competitive R&D and PE capabilities, with product development linked to market needs.

39   The phases in the Van de Ven and Garud model are: creation of resource endowment, for example, by basic R&D in public sector research institutes; appropriation of public knowledge by private firms, formation of new firms

or diversification by existing firms; industry expansion, technical and economic activities of firms, institutional regulation, financial structuring and reimbursement, development of industry standards, and formation of pools of competencies; industry stabilisation, emergence of a 'dominant design', ushering in a period of consolidation.

40   The stages of the Mueller and Tilton model are: innovation – invention, development, pioneer firms; imitation – imitative firms, adaptations and improvements to the technology; technological competition – intensive R&D undertaken, advantage shifts to large firms; standardisation – patents expire and barriers to entry based on initial R&D fall, competition shifts to manufacturing efficiency.

41   Tang and Yeo (1995) provide a telling description of the process in the context of the shift towards higher value-adding technological activities in Singapore. They emphasise that successful propagation involves a balancing of different priorities at different stages, as between leveraged start-up activities, competence building and selective pioneering by indigenous firms.

42   Of course there have been failures too – as in the case of Korea's attempts to enter the PC industry, or Taiwan's bid to become a player in software – but these can be attributed to poor judgement or bad luck rather than to a flaw in the general resource leverage approach. See Chapter 7.

43   The literature on this topic is immense; for a review, see Battat, Frank and Shen (1996).

44   See Mathews (1998a; 1998c) for a discussion of the impact of the Asian financial crisis on East Asian institutional structures, particularly the Korean model. Weiss (1998) treats the same issue from the perspective of the 'institutional capacity' of the countries concerned.

45   The issue of 'targeting' for example is frequently treated as something best left to individual firms, which is appropriate in a setting of technological leadership, but not in one of strategic catch-up.

46   The constituents of the Silicon Valley industrial ecosystem are venture capitalists, a talent pool of knowledge professionals, universities and research institutes, a sophisticated service infrastructure, as well as customers and lead users of innovative technologies. Scholars such as Saxenian (1996) locate the dynamism of Silicon Valley as stemming from close collaboration between systems houses and various forms of specialised suppliers of such items as application-specific integrated circuits.

PART II

National Institutional Pathways

CHAPTER 3

The Tangun Boom and the Chaebol: *How Korea Did it*

In February 1983, Korea's most famous businessman, Lee Byung-Chull, founder and chairman of Samsung, made his most famous statement in a long and distinguished career. Samsung intended, he said, to become a world player in memory chip production. He was prepared to put up 100 billion *won* – an astonishing $133 million – to back his assertion for a company as small as Samsung. In effect he was betting the future of the company on semiconductors. Less than two years later, Samsung astonished the world with its 64K DRAM, produced at its gleaming new wafer-fabrication plant at Kiheung. Within another two years, it was making profits from its 256K DRAM, produced only months after Japanese industry leaders were scaling up their own production. Within less than ten years, Samsung had emerged as the world's number one producer of DRAMs, generating enormous wealth for itself and Korea in the process.

Lee was no stranger to challenges, having navigated Samsung from one industry to another, always noting where Japan had been successful and seeking to emulate the Japanese strategy, but with lower costs. He grew up under the Japanese occupation of Korea, studied for a time at Waseda University in Japan, and in 1936 founded a small rice mill in Taegu, southern Korea, with inherited funds. Over the next few years Lee traded in commodities, expanding into Japanese-occupied Manchuria. In 1938 he incorporated his small venture as Samsung Commercial Company (Samsung means 'three stars' in Korean), modelled on the triple diamond of Japan's Mitsubishi. He profited from trade in foodstuffs during World War II and again during the Korean War, emerging in the 1950s with a sizeable fortune. He risked it all in a manufacturing venture to produce sugar. To this end he founded the Cheil Sugar Refinery (*cheil* means first in Korean), employing the most

105

advanced refining technology available. Everything, from machinery to process skills, was imported. It was a great success, and was followed up quickly by Lee's expansion into textiles, again using advanced imported equipment for woollen textiles production. German engineers were employed to get the plant going, and Korean engineers despatched to Germany to absorb as much technical knowledge as possible. Lee even hired a Japanese textiles technologist to draw up a master plan for the company's navigation through successive anticipated technology shifts – and this before the company sold even its first bolt of cloth!

With the coming to power of the military regime in 1961, Lee was arrested, along with other 'profiteer' entrepreneurs, and put in jail. He was released in 1963, pledging his skills to the future development of Korea. This was how the new military strongman, President Park Chung Hee, secured the compliance of Korea's leading businessmen. Lee lost no time in picking up the reins at Samsung again. Cheil Wool was put through further rounds of technology leverage, while new businesses were established in strategic areas such as fertilisers (the Hankuk Fertiliser Company, established in 1964), food companies, a daily newspaper, a paper company (to supply the newspaper), a department store, a land development company, a construction company (to build on the land developed), an insurance company and so the list goes on.

In 1969 Lee took Samsung into its most demanding manufacturing business, namely electronics. This was effected using techniques that by now Lee understood very well – by leveraging the skills and technology from incumbents. In this case he found joint-venture partners in Japanese firms NEC and Sanyo, firms keen to invest in Korea following 'normalisation' of relations between the two countries in the mid-1960s. Samsung emerged with total control over these enterprises after leveraging the required technology and expanding through the 1970s into consumer and industrial electronics, largely through 'own-brand' manufacturing contracts with US retailers like Sears, J. C. Penney and K-Mart.

The 1970s saw Samsung acquire some experience in LSI semiconductors, but only enough to convince its managers that this was a field beyond even a latecomer firm as brash as Samsung. Hence the shock, not least among Samsung's own managers, when the 72-year-old Lee announced in 1983 that he was 'betting the firm' on Samsung's ability to become a player in VLSI memory chips. The Japanese had shown that their firms could best the dominant US players when Fujitsu emerged as the world's first producer of a 64K DRAM at the beginning of the 1980s. Lee assumed his impeccable Japanese contacts would enable him to license DRAM technology from one of the Japanese firms, but they gave him the cold shoulder, as did the US majors like Intel, TI and Motorola. But there was a way into the industry, opened up for Lee by his listening post in Silicon Valley. The US fledgling DRAM producer, Micron, was short of cash and prepared to license its 64K DRAM design to this upstart Korean. Samsung seized this chance, and hired semiconductor engineers by the dozen from leading US firms, paying them up to three times the chairman's salary! Working around the clock, these engineers produced Samsung's own version of the 64K device, and assembled a fabrication plant at Kiheung using equipment bought from a variety of suppliers and with the help of moonlighting Japanese engineers and the assistance of Sharp, then an outsider in the Japanese semiconductor hierarchy.

But just as Samsung unveiled its fabricated 64K DRAM in 1985, the bottom fell out of the market. It was the beginning of one of the worst cyclical downturns in the world semiconductor industry. Undeterred, Lee ordered his engineers to press on with the next-generation 256K DRAM and invested in a whole new generation of equipment. By relentlessly driving up their yields, by mid-1986 Lee's engineers were ready to mass produce their own 256K DRAM, just as the industry was starting to pick up again. And here Lee and Samsung had a stroke of luck. The Japanese and US giants called a truce in their semiconductor trade war, signing the 1986 Semiconductor Trade Agreement, which restrained Japanese exports to the US, and set a floor price for the memory chips sold there. US memory chip producers had been devastated by the confrontation with Japan, and were unable to respond in time to the new opportunities. With PC makers like IBM and Hewlett-Packard clamouring for memory chips, Samsung was able to offer them its new 256K device, and business boomed. It was turning a profit on this product far earlier than Lee, or anyone else in Korea, had anticipated. Lee died shortly after, in 1987, a national hero in Korea.

Lee's fellow *chaebol* chairmen were not far behind. In April 1983, barely a month after Lee's announcement that Samsung would enter the VLSI memory chips business, Jung Ju-Young, chairman of Hyundai, made a similar commitment on behalf of his company. By the early 1980s Hyundai had emerged as Korea's largest conglomerate, pioneering the country's entry into construction and heavy engineering, as well as automotive production. But in 1983, when Jung made his announcement that Hyundai would become a player in semiconductors and industrial electronics, the firm had no experience in either. To enter the industry, Jung would have to call on his well-honed business development, investment and mass-production skills – but in a completely new technical field.

Jung upped the ante with Samsung by announcing that Hyundai would invest 300 billion *won* ($400 million) in the new venture. There followed feverish activity at Hyundai to implement the chairman's goals.

For Hyundai, a double latecomer in semiconductors and starting from ground zero, everything was more difficult. It too established a listening post in Silicon Valley, and hired dozens of US-trained Korean engineers to build its first product and first fabrication plant at Icheon. Hyundai was late with its 256K DRAM, licensed from a Silicon Valley startup Vitelic (which would subsequently become a major player in Taiwan's industry) and late again with a 1M product, partly licensed from the same source. It was given a reprieve when Texas Instruments approached Hyundai to act as OEM producer ('second source') for its 256K DRAM. This provided the fledgling company with much-needed technical expertise, but also relieved its over-capacity problem. By the 1990s, Hyundai had suffered nearly ten years of losses in semiconductors, and was desperate for a breakthrough.

At this point Hyundai hired Dr Min Wi-Sik to head up their development efforts. Dr Min proved to be a master technical strategist and leader, the kind of unsung hero who makes the difference in latecomer successes. He had been working at Intel for the previous six years, and had wide experience of semiconductor technology. His first job at Hyundai was to develop a sense of technical direction that would guide production of a 4M DRAM. Worldwide, the planar process for laying down 'sandwich' layers on silicon to form transistors and circuits, which had been in force for over a decade, was being improved in two quite different directions. American firms, led by IBM, were expanding the surface area of the chip by drilling 'trenches' in the silicon. Japanese firms like NEC were pursuing a different strategy of constructing corrugated 'stacks' of metal and polymer on the silicon surface. Dr Min was aware of them and set up two parallel development teams: one to work on a 'trench' solution and the other on a 'stack' solution – in competition with each other![1]

His approach paid handsome dividends. The two teams worked around the clock to produce their own experimental devices and to improve their yields on the pilot fabrication line. Dr Min instituted regular morning meetings for all his senior engineering staff, where the problems encountered the day before were discussed in an atmosphere of frankness and tolerant mutual criticism. By early 1991 it was clear that the stack solution could be produced with fewer and simpler processing steps – an important factor when there are between 90 and 100 processing steps involved – and this was the solution adopted.

Through Dr Min's leadership, Hyundai was able to bring a 4M DRAM to market in time to catch the wave, and the company actually started to make a profit on its semiconductor business. But in Dr Min's R&D labs, the pace never slackened. He had R&D teams working simultaneously on three generations of DRAM. While the 4M chip was being 'shrunk' (to squeeze more ICs out of a given 8-inch die) a new team was working frantically on the next-generation 16M DRAM, again using parallel teams to test different technical options. Then a development team for a 64K DRAM was formed in 1991 to look for a way to produce a chip which was then at the very frontier of semiconductor technology. In this way, Hyundai was able to reduce the development time between generations and their 'shrunk' versions to a year and a half.

Hyundai broke through to profitable DRAM production by the early 1990s, a decade after Jung's announcement. It was able to secure a substantial proportion of the world 4M DRAM market after Samsung, but ahead of many of the Japanese firms. This paved the way for a technology transfer agreement with Fujitsu, thus anchoring Hyundai's technology development towards the 16M and 64M DRAMs. Dr Min continued his efforts with Hyundai into the 1990s, guiding the company towards 'system on a chip' and other diversifications away from commodity DRAMs.

In 1997 Dr Min was ready to establish his own semiconductor wafer-fabrication company. He found a backer in the form of Dongbu Corporation (one of Korea's middle-level *chaebol*) and a technology source in no less a company than IBM. He finalised agreements with Dongbu and IBM by the end of 1997 – just as the Korean financial crisis broke in full force. His efforts had to be put on hold.

Such setbacks have fuelled the determination of Koreans to become major players in the most advanced technological sectors. The story of Korea's entry into high-technology industries like semiconductors is one of ardent entrepreneurs taking extraordinary risks, and ardent engineers like Dr Min making extraordinary efforts beyond what would normally be expected. This is how latecomers overcome the odds stacked against them.

The roots of Korea's success in semiconductors went back many years to the earlier preparatory and seeding phases of its development of knowledge-intensive industries. In this chapter, we trace these steps, focusing on the institutional details of leverage and their effectiveness.

The Creation of a Semiconductor Industry: Development Stages

Although the Korean semiconductor phenomenon only really took off in the mid-1980s and did not achieve world-class status until 1991–92, its roots can be traced back to the 1970s, when the leading *chaebol* established their electronics businesses, and before that to the 1960s, when the *chaebol* themselves were established and the Korean export-led economic boom got underway. In 1965, Korea was the world's thirty-third largest exporter of manufactured goods; by 1986 it had risen to tenth place. Like Japan, the emphasis of industrial policy in Korea has been to

Table 3.1   Stages in the evolution of the Korean semiconductor industry

Stage I Pre-1974 Preparation	Stage II 1974–81 Seeding/ implantation	Stage III 1982–88 Propagation	Stage IV 1989–98 Roots of sustainability
Assembly and test operations established by foreign companies KIST established Expansion of technical education	Indigenous industry established and beginnings of IC fabrication in Korea KIET leads technology leverage	Incursion into mass memory chip production VLSI take-off Joint development of 4M DRAM	Full-fledged memory chip production and diversification/consolidation of a semiconductor industry Ancillary industries established Collaborative R&D programs Science and technology strategy as political priority

effect a relentless catch-up through technological upgrading and acquisition of knowledge and skills. Much more so than in Japan, which had a large domestic market, Korean exports have been used to facilitate the process, but the goal has been to achieve global capabilities, not just export success.

Korea's sights have been set not so much on catching up with the West, important as this may be, but on catching up with – and surpassing – Japan.[2] It would be hard to find an industry where the goal is not more readily apparent and the pride in achievement more fiercely held, than in that of semiconductors.[3] There are four phases of the semiconductor industry evolution in Korea, which took place from the 1970s to the late 1990s.[4]

Stage 1: Pre-1974 – Preparation

Korea began its push into sophisticated industries on the back of its experience of accelerated industrial development. From a conventional import-substitution strategy pursued in the 1950s, in the 1960s it swung decisively behind exports as a 'make or break' development effort. Under the military government of Park Chung-Hee, installed by a coup in 1961, economic development became the central national goal, and indeed the defining source of political legitimation for the regime. Inspired by the Japanese success with export-led growth, and initial

Taiwanese successes with the same strategy, Park switched Korea away from its predilection for import substitution towards an export orientation with a strategic focus on certain high-potential industries, a radical break for Korea.[5]

To anyone familiar with the Korean developmental efforts of the 1960s and 1970s, the idea of neoclassical economists querying whether the government can make a difference in economic development must seem quaint. In Korea the government was everything: it set the goals for companies, rationed the finance, disciplined poor performers with financial stringency and rewarded good performers with financial largesse. It did everything except own and manage the companies. In terms of technological learning the government vetted all technology licensing and capital equipment import transactions in order to ensure that the best deals were secured and that strategic directions were complied with.

Important agencies were established at this time to oversee Korea's rapid developmental efforts. The Economic Planning Board was created in 1962 with the Deputy Prime Minister as its chair. This agency, and the bureaux of the Ministry of Commerce and Industry (MCI) would henceforth play critical roles in targeting strategic industries and overseeing their performance. The central agency was the Presidential Blue House itself, where a 'war room' was maintained to monitor export performance, and monthly meetings were held with the country's most important chief executives and senior government officials to ensure that growth targets were met, investment channelled according to strategic directions, and action was being taken when targets were missed.

The first steps in the development of an electronics and semiconductors industry can be located during this period. In 1965 the MCI selected thirteen industries as strategic targets for export-led growth. Despite its small size then, electronics was chosen as one of the thirteen, largely because it had already been selected as such by Japan. The government sought to attract multinational electronics and semiconductor companies to invest in assembly and testing operations in Korea, following a similar strategy pioneered by Taiwan. At this stage, relations with Japan had not yet been 'normalised' (following Korea's bitter colonial experience) and so approaches were limited to US and European firms. The terms of investment were to be set by the EPB, under the overall guidance of the Foreign Capital Inducement Law passed in 1963.

Initial Semiconductor Investments

Korea's major competitive advantage at this point was abundant, low-cost labour, something it wasn't slow to exploit. The US was the world centre of semiconductor production, with companies such as Fairchild, Motorola and Texas Instruments leading the way. Feeling the first waves of competitive pressure from Japan, these companies were looking to invest in low-cost assembly operations abroad, initially in Hong Kong, and then in Taiwan and Korea.[6] Fairchild had invested in such facilities in Hong Kong in 1963, and it was interested in establishing similar operations in Korea and Taiwan.

A lead was provided by a small American company, Komi, which invested in transistor/diode production facilities in Korea in 1965, thereby providing the founding date for the country's semiconductor industry.[7] While this was a minor investment in itself, it had a useful demonstration effect.

The real beginning can be traced to the interest exhibited by Fairchild, then the third-largest semiconductor company in the world and technologically the most advanced. Fairchild proposed an extensive plan for manufacturing and assembling semiconductor devices to the Korean government in 1966. The conditions Fairchild imposed were fairly onerous – they insisted on retaining exclusive ownership of the facility, and on having access to the Korean domestic market for the products manufactured in Korea – and went against the nationalist grain of the Korean government. After some anxious consideration, permission was granted, and Semikor was set up as a wholly owned Fairchild subsidiary.

As anticipated by the Korean authorities, other companies were not slow to follow suit. Signetics and KMI followed in the same year, and Motorola in 1967. By 1974, there were nine such US-owned facilities in Korea.[8]

The US investments were driven by three main factors. First, the IC production process now had a major labour-intensive phase of chip assembly and packaging (to be followed shortly by chip testing) which could be carried out competitively in a low-cost country.[9] Secondly, the Korean government relaxed its controls over foreign investment in the case of Fairchild, and subsequently codified the conditions in a re-vamped Foreign Capital Inducement Law. The US government also provided incentives in the form of exemption from US tariffs for goods assembled abroad, and encouragement for local investment in Korea in recognition of the military assistance rendered in Vietnam.

After relations between Korea and Japan were 'normalised' in the mid-1960s, Japanese electronics multinationals also established assembly and test facilities, starting with Toshiba and Sanyo in 1969. By 1973 there were at least seven Japanese facilities, operated by such firms as Toko, Rohm and Sanken. The Toshiba investment was critical, being the first. Initial discussions to establish a germanium transistor plant had been aborted in 1967 (germanium was becoming an obsolete technology), but a joint venture to establish a silicon transistor plant in 1969 bore fruit. The plant was established at Kumi, then a farming area – but it was rapidly provided with all essential infrastructure under personal orders from the President.[10] Kumi would subsequently be established as Korea's first Electronics Industrial Complex, in 1970. As such, it would provide the base for the country's rapidly expanding industry.

For its part, the Korean government favoured these multinational investments because of the contribution made by exported chip assemblies to foreign exchange earnings, which could then be ploughed back into further development efforts. The chip assembly operations provided useful employment, contributing to the labour-intensive phase of industrialisation. They also provided some limited exposure on the part of Korean companies to sophisticated international capitalist procedures.

Foreign investment by US and Japanese multinationals was one aspect of the preparatory stages of high-technology industrialisation. Of equal significance were the efforts which the Koreans themselves poured into technical training and the establishment of technical and engineering institutes. A start was made in 1966 with the founding of the Korea Institute of Science and Technology (KIST).[11] This institute in turn provided the focus for advanced technical training and for the build-up of the country's 'absorptive capacity' for advanced technologies. It was KIST leaders who first formulated a Korean strategy of technology import, adaptation and assimilation as a passport to industrial development – a strategy which has been consistently maintained over the subsequent three decades.[12]

The Korean government put in place legislation to build capabilities in the electronics industry as early as 1969. In this year, the Electronics Industry Promotion Law, which empowered the MCI to devise and implement discriminatory industry development measures, was enacted.[13] Under this law, modelled closely on its Japanese equivalent which had been adopted in 1957, the MCI drew up an Eight-Year Plan for the promotion of the electronics industry.[14] Central to it was the establishment of the Kumi Electronics Industrial Complex, promulgated in 1970. In the same year, the Korean government promulgated a Free Export Zone at the port city of Masan, modelled on the Taiwanese initiative; this too proved to be a magnet for Japanese capital, and three Japanese semiconductor firms – Toko, Sanyo and Sanken – had established plants there by 1973. The Japanese investments were driven by factors similar to those driving the Americans – namely the assembly of labour-intensive semiconductor and electronic devices in low-cost locations.

The point of all this activity was to attract Korean domestic investment into the semiconductor and electronics industries. Several of the emerging large firms, or *chaebol*, became involved in electronics at this time, in accordance with government strategic directives. A pioneer was Goldstar, part of the Lucky-Goldstar group. The firm had been involved in radio production as early as 1958, and expanded these activities through the 1960s. Samsung was in fact a relatively late starter; it fashioned its entry into the industry only in 1969, through two joint ventures with Japanese firms, Sanyo and NEC. Samsung's entry actually provoked a furious row in Korea. It was a move strongly supported by the Korean government (it had been one of the recommendations of MCI in 1967), but it was bitterly opposed by the Korean electronics industry at the time, which saw Samsung as likely to become dominant and push smaller firms out of the industry. These fears were well-founded, for this is exactly what happened. But arguably this was to Korea's advantage, in that Samsung raised the technical standards of the industry, forcing incumbent firms to raise their technical levels or perish. Samsung had ambitious plans for vertical integration between its two joint venture operations to become a major player in electronics – ambitions which have been amply realised.[15]

Other Korean firms made efforts to enter the industry in this early stage as contractors to the multinationals. Anam Industrial was established in 1967 as the first semiconductor contract assembly operation, financed entirely by Korean capital. Foreign currency loans were allocated to this project by the MCI to induce Korean involvement. Anam has since gone on to become a major semiconductor company, and by the mid-1990s the largest contract IC packaging and assembly operation in the world.

Technology and financial leverage at this first, preparatory stage was entirely through foreign investment, initially from the US, and after normalisation, from Japan. This investment was very much under the control of the Korean government, which set the terms and maintained a close watch. The extent of foreign investment and the companies involved is shown in Table 3.2.

In terms of resource leverage, these semiconductor beginnings did not transfer substantial technology, but they did create the foundations for an ongoing industry of chip assembly and testing, and created a pool of experienced staff with some knowledge of the semiconductor industry. Some (limited) diffusion of this expertise occurred, with the setting up of Korean-financed assembly contract operations such as Anam. The electronics manufacturers were grouped by the MCI into a single organisation, the Korea Electronics Industry Cooperative (KEIC), as early as 1967. This was modelled on Japan's EIAJ, through which MITI was able to coordinate industry policy effectively through an industry association rather than deal with individual firms.

Table 3.2 Foreign investment in Korean semiconductor operations, 1965–73

Year	Firm	Foreign investor	Amount $m	Degree of foreign ownership (per cent)
1965	Komi	Komi (US)	0.01	25
1966	Fairchild Korea	Fairchild (US)	2.25	100
1966	Signetics	Signetics (US)	1.75	100
1966	Korea Micro	KMI (US)	0.22	49†
1967	Motorola	Motorola (US)	8.00	100
1968	IMEC	Komi (US)	1.21	100
1969	Korea Electronics	Toshiba (Jpn)	1.40	70*
1969	Samsung Electronics	Sanyo (Jpn)	1.50	40**
1970	Taehan Micro	AMI (US)	2.26	100
1971	Toko Korea	Toko (Jpn)	0.39	100
1972	Rohm Korea	Rohm (Jpn)		95
1972	Tokyo Silicon	Sanyo (Jpn)	1.62	100
1973	Korean Sanken	Sanken (Jpn)	0.70	100

Note: † Closed in 1969.
* Named Korea Electronics Corp (KEC) in 1974.
** Named Samsung Electronics in 1972 when Sanyo withdrew; likewise with Samsung Semiconductor and NEC.
Source: KSIA; Yoon (1989); industry sources.

The first phase of Korea's accelerated industrialisation, which was highly leveraged in terms of technology and finance, came to an abrupt temporary halt in 1971 when major firms defaulted on debts, and the IMF was called in to stabilise the market. This led to a period of consolidation, as leading *chaebol* absorbed lesser players. The stage was now set for the next leap forward. In his annual State of the Nation address in 1973, President Park announced that 'heavy and chemical industrialisation' was to be the new direction of industrial development in Korea (emulating the same strategy pursued in Japan a decade earlier). This would entail a substantial shift towards more capital and technology-intensive industries, with consequent upheavals in the less-favoured industries. Again, one of the six 'strategic sectors' chosen was electronics and semiconductors despite the fact that these industries were neither 'heavy' nor 'chemical'. The seeding of a national semiconductor industry could now begin in earnest.

Stage II: 1974–81 – Seeding/Implantation

The 1970s saw a rapid deepening of the industrialisation process in Korea, and dramatic export successes notched up by the electronics industries. At the same time, Korean electronics firms were coming up against their technical limitations and dependence on foreign suppliers (particularly the Japanese) for basic components such as the chips that operated electronics products. This provided the policy agenda within which semiconductor manufacturing in Korea was viewed, and underscored the need to seriously engage in the 'seeding' of more advanced semiconductor technological capabilities.

Strenuous efforts were made by the Korean government to foster these capabilities. In 1973 the National Council for Science and Technology, chaired by the Prime Minister, was established to develop plans for the formation of high-technology sectors such as electronics. The Ministry of Commerce and Industry (MCI) announced a further six-year plan to indigenise the production of electronic components, including semiconductors.[16] Under this plan, formulated in 1974, a national focus was to be achieved through the creation of research institutes, tertiary training of electronics engineers and technology acquisition achieved via licences from overseas firms and use of consulting engineers rather than multinational investment. The edifice of Korea's 'absorptive capacity' was thus built, without allowing foreign firms to dominate the nascent industry.[17]

These efforts coincided with massive resource mobilisation for the Heavy and Chemical Industrialisation (HCI) drive, spearheaded by a National Investment Fund (NIF) that was created in 1973 to channel available resources to the six targeted strategic industries. The drive was complemented by tax reduction incentives for these industries, matching those already available for foreign investments. Massive state expenditure was poured into the construction of industrial complexes to support the strategic industries, including Kumi for electronics.[18]

These efforts were complemented by more specific technological upgrading instruments. In 1973, the Law for the Promotion of Technology Development was enacted, requiring new firms in the electronics industry to conduct development activities aimed at bringing new products to export standard.[19] This was a conscious technology leverage device. In response, there were some indigenous Korean efforts to enter semiconductor production, but on a very small scale that hardly matched the prodigious successes in consumer electronics. One early response to the government's plans had been Goldstar's initiative to enter a joint venture with the US multinational, National Semiconductor, to produce transistors. Launched in 1972, this venture was soon mothballed – the difficulties were too great. In 1974 a Korean chip production operation called Korea Semiconductor was founded, as was Samsung Semiconductor, which took over the assets of the discontinued joint venture with NEC and then Korea Semiconductor. This milestone signalled the start of the 'seeding' phase of Korea's semiconductor industry development and marked the emergence of a genuine semiconductor industry under Korean control.[20] By the mid-1970s Korean firms were taking their first, tentative steps towards indigenous semiconductor manufacture – at the same time as first steps were being taken in Taiwan, where it was the public sector that provided the vehicle for leverage.

Largely because of the expansionary policies pursued by the government, the Korean economy as a whole experienced a boom from 1976 to 1978.[21] The electronics and semiconductors industries were at the forefront of this boom, and this period saw a spate of further investments and announcements of impending involvement in semiconductors by the Korean *chaebol* such as from Daewoo, Taihan and Goldstar. By the late 1970s there were at least four private companies developing a stake in LSI chip fabrication: Samsung (via Korea Shipbuilding and Engineering Corporation, KSEC), Goldstar, Daewoo and Taihan. Investments were still on a relatively small scale; Goldstar was at this stage the lead firm, having built the most advanced facility on the Kumi complex.

An important element in the Korean entry into semiconductors was the use of the public-sector telecommunications system. In the early 1980s the telecom sector was re-organised, with some less efficient firms being forced out and major *chaebol* such as Samsung, Goldstar and Daewoo being allocated profitable segments. All existing technology-transfer agreements with foreign firms were subject to renegotiation. Thus through public agency intervention the major semiconductor firms were provided with profitable telecom sectors in which to build up specialised chip businesses, and introduced to leading foreign telecom firms (such as ITT, AT&T, Nortel) who were 'persuaded' to enter joint ventures as the price of continuing involvement in Korea.[22] This is another demonstration of the 'developmental' feature of resource leverage at work in Korea, where companies leverage their resources, but in circumstances fashioned for them by the public agencies.

Progress was also being achieved in the 'back end' of the industry, in chip assembly, packaging and testing. The first all-Korean semiconductor assembly operation, Anam, expanded its operations at this time, and diversified into electronics production. It operated exclusively as a sub-contracting firm, providing OEM services to US and other IC firms, saving them the trouble of having to establish their own assembly plants in off-shore locations, an inspired strategic move on Anam's part.

Another assembler, Korea Electronics (KEC, which had taken over the operations of Toshiba in Korea) entered into a technology-licensing agreement with Toshiba in 1979 for production of silicon transistors. Anam and KEC remained active and prosperous in Korea in the late 1990s.

Seeding Phase – Achievements

By the start of the 1980s, four firms had a presence in the semiconductor wafer-fabrication industry. The level of technology and the scale of activities were, however, still at LSI capability. Initiatives were driven by government prodding, and by the rapidly increasing demand for semiconductors by Korea's electronics industry.[23] Korea was following Japan in seeing its consumer and industrial electronics industries provide first, an industrial boost through their exports, and then a secondary boost through their articulation with components production. Semiconductors were the most significant components, and it appeared as if the early leveraging efforts were paying off. There was some advanced VLSI technological capability in Korea at this time, but not yet in any of the *chaebol*. It was the public-sector telecommunications research centre KIET, established on the Kumi complex in 1976, which first acquired VLSI capabilities. It had three research divisions for semiconductors – semiconductor design, processes and systems – each headed by a Korean with research experience in the US semiconductor industry. The institute opened Korea's first VLSI pilot wafer-fabrication facility in 1978 through a joint venture with a Silicon Valley high-technology firm, VLSI Technology. By 1979 it had built a fully operational wafer-fabrication facility capable of producing 16K DRAMs.[24]

Technology Leverage during Stage II

The technology needed for semiconductors had been secured from US and Japanese sources throughout the 1970s. The technology transfer agreements listed in Table 3.3 provided the technical foundation for Korea's push into microelectronics and semiconductors.

By the beginning of the 1980s the foundations had been established for a major push into VLSI semiconductors. The targeted sector was identified by government agencies who developed a workable strategy; financing and infrastructure instruments were put in place; and sophisticated, export-oriented companies were already producing advanced electronics products, having moved rapidly along the 'industrialisation by learning' curve, and were now honing their technology importing skills in the field of semiconductors. A thriving assembly and testing industry had been established for over a decade, and provided a training ground for numerous Korean engineers. KIET was assembling skilled engineers and scientists, and taking the first steps towards mastering the technology of VLSI semiconductor fabrication. The industry had been organised into a coherent entity with a single voice, the industry association EIAK. Government ministries such as MCI (henceforth MTI) were vigorously

Table 3.3   Korean technology transfer agreements, 1972–80

Year	Korean organisation	Partner	Technology
1972	Goldstar	Nat Sem. (US)	Transistor prod[†]
1975	KESEC	ICII (US)	LSI IC fabrication[*]
1976	Taihan	Fujitsu (Jpn)	LSI IC fab[**]
1977	KTC	ITT (US)	Telecom ICs fab[***]
1978	Korea Explosives	Nat Sem. (US)	Transistor/IC fab[††]
1978	KIET	VLSI Tech (US)	VLSI IC fab: pilot
1979	KEC	Toshiba (Jpn)	Transistor prod
1980	Goldstar	Western Electric (AT&T)(US)	Telecom ICs fab

Note: [†] Collapsed in 1974.
[*] Taken over by Samsung in 1977–78.
[**] Taken over by Goldstar in 1979.
[***] Taken over by Samsung in 1980.
[††] Collapsed 1979.
Source: KSIA; Yoon (1989); industry sources.

promoting both 'catch-up' and 'self-sufficiency' strategies. The missing ingredient was private sector investment in major production facilities. This was to come, finally, in a big way, in the early 1980s.

Stage III: 1982–88 – Propagation/VLSI Capability

At the beginning of the 1980s, after the tumultuous decade of 'heavy and chemical industrialisation' the Korean economy plunged into another financial crisis with threatened default on external debts, and was rescued and stabilised once again by the IMF.[25] This ushered in a further economic consolidation phase, while politically the country was forced to endure another military government under General Chun Doo Hwan, after Park's assassination in 1979. The Chun government was keen to see Korean electronics companies take the plunge into VLSI semiconductor production, in head-to-head competition with the Japanese and the Americans. It recognised that such a move would need a far greater commitment of resources by both companies and state agencies than had been available hitherto. Numerous state agencies coordinated by the Presidential office (Blue House) were involved in drafting a Comprehensive Industry Development Plan for the semiconductor sector, adopted in 1981 as part of the Fifth Five-Year Plan (1981–86).

   The highlight of this period was a yet more detailed Long-Term Plan for the Promotion of the Semiconductor Industry (1982–86), which brought together a range of industry promotion measures and really put pressure on the *chaebol* to make serious commitments. It called for total public investment of $400 million, of which 40 per cent would be financed by the National Investment Fund and the remainder by the Electronics Industry Promotion Fund (then not yet created). It was a level of envisaged promotion ten times larger than anything attempted up to then, and also marked a quite different style of intervention. The heavy-handed state guidance of the HCI phase had been wound back, and stabilisation in place of expansion was now given greater priority.[26] In this context, promotion of the semiconductor industry was seen as part of a new emphasis on coordination by public agencies of Korea's transition to a knowledge-intensive economy. Japan's recent experience with MITI-coordinated projects as the VLSI Project, which ran from 1976 to 1979, is very much in evidence in Korean promotion plans of the 1980s. The watchword now was coordination rather than state domination and control.

The 1981 Plan was formulated by a working group chaired by the head of the Bureau of Electric and Electronics Industry within Korea's MTI.[27] Their Plan identified four specific sectors to be promoted: VLSI semiconductors, computers, communications equipment and electronic components (such as monitors and keyboards). In the semiconductor field, the plan favoured wafer fabrication over 'back end' test and assembly, and identified the mass production of memory chips for export as the most viable strategy, not domestic demand.[28] This was based on the argument that there was a large and growing world market for such products (computers, telecom devices, consumer products); they were standardised and thus suitable for mass production; chip designs could probably be licensed from US firms; and the fabrication technology could be bought on the open market (mainly from US and Japanese firms). But very large capital investments would be needed, in the order of hundreds of millions of dollars. For the companies involved the decision to enter this market was a huge risk. The government's role was perceived to be one of spreading and reducing this risk as much as possible, by arranging finance and guaranteeing loans, providing infrastructure and other supports, and in some cases by ensuring a baseload market for output via public procurement (for example, through telecoms chip purchases).

Bolstered by direct government prodding and promised support, Samsung, Hyundai and Goldstar all announced in 1982 major involvement in the mass-production of chips at the VLSI technology level, particularly of MOS memory chips such as DRAMs. Samsung chairman and founder, Lee Byung-Chull, announced in early 1982 that 100 billion *won* (around $133 million) would be invested up to 1986 to drastically upgrade Samsung's involvement in the semiconductor industry – an extremely large and risky investment, quite uncharacteristic of Lee or Samsung. But a Korea equipped with VLSI semiconductor capabilities had become a national goal that over-rode normal commercial caution. Goldstar followed with a similar announcement. Other firms were not far behind – Daewoo (a *chaebol* that had rapidly diversified from construction into machinery, automotive and electronics), Taihan Electric Wire Industries (having a second shot, after the winding-up of its 1970s initiative), and others, though not all were able to realise their aspirations.

Then came Hyundai's announcement that it too intended to enter the semiconductor field and industrial electronics generally, backed by an investment commitment of 300 billion *won* ($400 million) over the next five years, the largest commitment to date. Hyundai's move jolted Samsung and Goldstar into yet larger investment announcements of their own. (Such bidding wars are characteristic of the hypercompetition between the Korean *chaebol*.) The business strategy of these companies was the government-formulated one: to emulate Japanese production of standardised commodity products such as memory chips, but at lower costs. The means they intended to follow was the tried and tested one of importing the product and process technology and know-how needed to get started, as practised already in the electronics and IT ventures entered during the 1970s. Taking the longer-term option of building up indigenous expertise through strengthening the existing VLSI pilot IC fabrication plant at KIET was not considered realistic. The push into VLSI activities was to be led by the private sector, using the leverage of advanced technologies from abroad.

Technology Resource Leverage in Stage III

Acquiring the product and process technology needed to implement the Korean DRAM 'crash through' strategy did not prove to be easy. Neither US nor Japanese major firms were likely candidates as sources. Bruised and battered by their early 1980s encounter with the Japanese in 64K DRAMs, US majors like Motorola, Texas Instruments, National or Intel would not entertain the possibility of setting loose 'another Japan' by licensing technology to the Koreans.[29] For their part the Japanese understood only too clearly what the Korean aspirations were, and for the most part – with the important exception of Sharp – declined to assist.

The way into the world of mainstream chip production came through Silicon Valley. The restless culture of Silicon Valley in California was the location of many world-class semiconductor firms, which employed US-trained Korean–American engineers who could be lured to work for the Korean *chaebol* at attractive salaries by appealing to their nationalist pride.

They brought with them high levels of expertise and knowledge of the internal workings of the US semiconductor multinationals. All three *chaebol*, particularly Samsung, pursued this route as a means of rapidly acquiring VLSI capability by establishing listening-post companies and engaging in active recruitment.

Silicon Valley was also the source of many capital-starved start-up firms, some with excellent chip design know-how but no manufacturing capacity. Korean firms offered these small US design houses good terms for the manufacture of their chips in return for the right to license their designs. To many, this was an offer too good to refuse, and so it was that small firms like Mosel, Vitelic and Micron (not located in Silicon Valley, but sharing its mentality) and others became the source of what the US Commerce Department regarded as 'technology leakage' to the Koreans.

But chip designers were not the only source of technological leverage. US majors like IBM, TI and Intel were also pleased to use new Korean DRAM facilities as foundries for their memory chips, transferring vital fabrication technological know-how in the process. Moreover, US chip users such as personal computer manufacturers were keen to find alternatives to Japanese DRAM suppliers. They represented a potentially lucrative market for Korean-produced chips. In this process, Korean firms were able to use the networks already established through KIET's Silicon Valley liaison centre.

How Samsung Put Together its 64K DRAM Samsung shocked Korea, if not the world, when it announced on 1 December 1983 that it had produced a good working version of a 64K DRAM, then a state-of-the-art product in the semiconductor industry. It was a symbolic moment, an affirmation that this once-impoverished country could make it in a high-technology world.

Samsung was Korea's premier company at the beginning of the 1980s, already achieving success as a mass manufacturer of electronic goods and a formidable producer of heavy equipment and engines, electric power machinery, petrochemical products, textiles, construction materials, food products such as sugar and so on. This wide-ranging industrial experience meant that Samsung already had strong capabilities in managing mass-manufacturing plants and in exporting goods to foreign markets, particularly the US. By then Samsung was also engaged in semiconductor fabrication, producing low-level (LSI) chips for consumer goods such as watches and calculators, partly for its own internal consumption but mainly for export. But this business was a poor performer with persistent quality problems – hardly the base for a major leap into advanced semiconductor production.

Samsung's founder, Lee Byung-Chull, was nearly seventy by now and a legend in Korea. He longed to transform his company into one of the great enterprises in the world. After a 1982 visit to the US, and a return visit to Japan, he came to see semiconductors as the core business of the future where Samsung could make its mark. He called together a task-force that drew on all the existing businesses within the Samsung group, as well as outside experts, particularly Korean engineers working in the semiconductor industry in the US, and charged them with the development of a comprehensive plan for entering the new business. The team developed their plan, revising it considerably after a study tour to the US in January 1983, which opened their eyes to the pace of technological change in the industry. The elements of a business strategy were put together, which Lee announced to the world in February 1983 (in a statement issued, oddly enough, in Tokyo).

The plan called for Samsung to assemble at breakneck speed the elements of an advanced VLSI semiconductor operation, bypassing or 'leapfrogging' all previous LSI technological steps, and focusing on the standardised memory chips where Japanese firms had already made their mark. Frontier product and process technologies were to be sought through licensing, and internalised within Samsung's own capabilities as quickly as possible through massive recruitment drives for specialist engineers. The chips would be mass produced almost exclusively for export, using the most advanced equipment available. The plan called for the then unheard of investment of $300 million to get the business up and running.

Samsung spared no effort in launching its new enterprise. Engineers were recruited, and paid up to three times the salary of the company president. Outpost offices and labs were established in both Silicon Valley and Tokyo, then the twin capitals of the semiconductor world. Japanese companies were approached for assistance with DRAM product designs, but none complied; eventually Samsung secured a design for a 64K DRAM from the US firm, Micron.[30] DRAM-process technology was acquired from the Japanese company, Sharp, an outsider that had been excluded from the MITI-organised semiconductor 'club' in Japan.[31] Samsung established two parallel development teams, one to produce a working version of the Micron design, and the other to assemble the process technology at a new plant being built at breakneck speed at Kiheung, south of Seoul. The development teams responded to the internally generated crisis atmosphere, working day and night. The teams developed both the product and the process for producing it within six months, by November 1983 – without prior experience of VLSI technology. The public announcement followed a month later. Chips were being mass produced and sold in the US market within a year.[32]

This was the resource leverage strategy: to secure access to new product and process technologies and internalise them as core capabilities. These could then be applied to the development of the next-generation product. Even before the 64K DRAM chips were ready for sale, Lee had ordered development teams to start on the next-generation 256K DRAM. In this case, two parallel development teams were set to work, one in Korea working with a new product design licensed again from Micron, and the other in Silicon Valley working to produce their own product. This was a highly innovative way of tackling product development. It was used by Japanese firms such as Toshiba, and would be used by Korean competitors such as Hyundai.

The Korean team produced a working 256K DRAM die by July 1985, matched with the then best-process technology of 5-inch wafers, which allowed the firm to get mass-produced 256K DRAM chips into the US market by 1986. Around the same time, Samsung was attracting foundry (OEM) production contracts from such US majors as Intel and IBM, which acted as a further channel for technology leverage. By the mid-1980s, Samsung had already leveraged the basic technologies and was now embarked on its own internal processes of capability enhancement.

The other Korean *chaebol* were not far behind Samsung. Goldstar was able to secure chip designs from Advanced Micro Devices (AMD), another Silicon Valley firm, while it made substantial investments (approaching $60 million) in a design centre in Sunnyvale, developed in conjunction with its joint venture partner AT&T. Goldstar attempted to jump ahead of Samsung with the purchase of technology for a 256K DRAM from AT&T. But its success in this strategy was limited until it struck a deal with Hitachi much later. The Goldstar case reveals how formidable were the obstacles standing in the way of these *chaebol* ventures, and the limits to their effectiveness at this stage of development.

Hyundai, too, was in the market for product technology. It was able to purchase advanced 64K DRAM designs from Vitelic, and 64K SRAM designs from Mosel, both start-ups founded in Silicon Valley by Chinese–Americans. It was much more dependent than its Korean rivals on a US 'listening post' and product development facility in Silicon Valley, established in 1984 at great expense.

Daewoo initially established its own design house, IDFocus, in Santa Clara, as a means of developing non-standard ICs for its internal use. When it shifted to DRAMs, it bought a controlling stake in a Silicon Valley firm, Zymos Corporation, thus securing access to its chip design portfolio.[33]

The common elements to the leverage strategy are apparent: a focus on the soaking up of expertise through the hiring of engineers, the licensing of product designs and the purchase of process technology from advanced firms, offering in exchange either cash (for cash-starved but technology rich start-ups), or fabrication capacity (for firms without it), or second sourcing and OEM contracts for the established players. This was an acceptable *quid pro quo*; it meant that the leverage strategy was feasible. Whether it worked or not depended on the corporate strategies and implementation capabilities of the individual companies.

In fact, the corporate strategies chosen by the four semiconductor *chaebol* to secure a place in VLSI activities were quite different. Samsung led with a clear focus on memory chips, as the most standardised of semiconductor products, backed by its existing expertise in linear LSI chips and logic products. Samsung's corporate models were the leading integrated Japanese firms such as Mitsubishi (always Samsung's model), NEC, Hitachi and Toshiba. Goldstar followed a more cautious 'wait and see' strategy, electing to follow Samsung when it seemed that no other options were available. It reserved a considerable part of its VLSI output for its own use. This would prove to be a very weak strategy, and by the end of the decade, Goldstar was desperate for a new start. The newcomer Hyundai focused entirely on advanced memory chips to the exclusion of all other semiconductor products. Its strategy was one of 'leapfrogging' over intermediate technological stages (discretes, LSI chips) straight to advanced VLSI MOS memory chips. This was a logical, albeit very bold, strategy for a 'late' late developer.[34] Daewoo pursued a strategy somewhat similar to Goldstar, but with higher technological aspirations – it sought to enter microprocessor production instead of memory chips at this early stage. This strategy would prove to be quite unrealistic, and Daewoo soon dropped out of the running in VLSI semiconductors, and pursued other aspects of electronics and semiconductors instead.

Thus the private-sector-led push into VLSI semiconductors in Korea provided the occasion for a kind of semi-controlled 'experiment' in viable product and market strategy. When Samsung's approach proved to be superior, Goldstar fell into line through a major technology transfer agreement with Hitachi in 1989. By the early 1990s, the strategies of the Big Three in semiconductors had more or less converged.[35]

Financial Resources Leverage

Apart from the manufacturing and marketing competencies which the Koreans brought to the semiconductor industry, the huge capital demands of the industry called for considerable financial resources. How were these to be raised? Much against their will, the government-controlled banks in Korea were dragooned by senior political circles into providing the bulk of the finance for this big push into semiconductors. In all, the government provided as much as $350 million in low-interest credit, under the terms of the promotion plan announced in 1982. This was at a time when targeted credit was being pared back for the rest of Korean industry. Access to foreign capital was also exploited, such as through the floating of Eurodollar bonds by Korean companies (executed first by Samsung in 1983).[36] Foreign capital and internal funds (that is, internal to the *chaebol*) gradually emerged as the major sources for financing the VLSI expansion, taking over from domestic credit.[37] The scale of the investment was huge by any standards. The four major players at this time – Samsung, Goldstar, Hyundai and Daewoo – committed more than $1.2 billion between 1983 and 1986, ten times the scale of investment in Taiwan's semiconductor industry over the same period.

Over the longer period 1983 to 1989, the firms are estimated to have invested approximately $4 billion. The push into VLSI semiconductors took the companies not just to a new level of technological sophistication, but to new heights of financial leverage as well. This spelt the end of close state control over the financing of Korea's industrial expansion; the investment initiative now lay firmly with the firms themselves, that is, with the private sector. Financial leverage has been a source of strength for the Korean system, giving firms great flexibility in arranging the financing of their investment programs, but it has also been exploited by weaker *chaebol*, leading to the disastrous bankruptcies of 1997 (such as Hanbo Steel) and the subsequent financial crisis.

Technological Resources Leverage

The initial breakthrough by Samsung and the others in the 64K DRAM was a significant effort, but by the time production was underway, the Americans and Japanese were already producing the next-generation 256K DRAM. At Lee's insistence, Samsung poured resources into its development, even as the lines for 64K devices were being cranked up. Hyundai was not far behind.

The manufacturing efforts with the 256K devices focused not just on synthesising the product and process technology acquired from others, but in developing indigenous improvements acquired through experience.[38] Initial product designs were acquired, but Samsung and later Hyundai engineers were able to develop their own second-generation versions of these products, which were the ones that went into mass production. Samsung and Hyundai had twin teams working on these development efforts, in their Silicon Valley affiliates and in Korea. The competition between these teams was intense, and added to the crisis atmosphere in which the development was pursued.

Herculean efforts were thus made by these *chaebol* to establish their new VLSI chip fabrication plants in 1983 and 1984, and to perfect the designs of the memory chips that they intended to produce. By the time the Korean firms had actually produced marketable products, in the mid-1980s (led by Samsung), the world semiconductor industry was heading into a cyclical recession, and the US–Japan trade war in semi-conductors was at its height. This was far from a favourable commercial environment for Korean chips, and early sales in the US market were dismal.

These setbacks prompted a furious debate in government and business ranks in Korea. The Economic Planning Board (EPB), backed by the banks, argued that Korea had no future in this risky business, and that the huge investments being made were simply throwing good money after bad; moreover they were starving other industrial sectors in Korea of much-needed capital. The MTI, on the other hand, maintained that the difficulties were due simply to a cyclical downturn and that demand would pick up; Korean firms would benefit from such an upturn if they hung in and kept up the pace of development of new and better products. The MTI argued that Korea's involvement in semiconductors would carry spin-offs for the rest of the economy.

The Ministry of Science and Technology (MoST) emerged in these debates as a major proponent of state support for Korea's long-term transition to a knowledge-intensive economy, perhaps even more forcefully than the MTI. There was no resolution to this debate, meaning that there was no decision to pull out of the industry. The impact was that no further finance was to be made available on easy terms to the private semiconductor firms. This was a storm they had to weather themselves.

Thanks to long-term planning horizons, deep pockets and cross-subsidisation from profitable sectors such as telecommunications and consumer electronics, and a favourable commercial environment for semiconductors, the industry survived. In 1985, the Plaza Agreement of the Group of Five resulted in currency realignments that greatly favoured Korea (and Taiwan) against the Japanese, which gave Korean exports across the board a boost.[39] In 1986 Japan and the US settled their trade differences in the Semiconductor Trade Agreement, limiting Japanese access to the US market and setting a floor price for semiconductor products. Both aspects of the agreement favoured Korean producers who were ready with new products: they had greater access to US markets, and prices were higher than anticipated. The boom in personal computers fuelled the demand for chips in 1987 and Korean firms were able to sell all the chips they could produce. Samsung in particular turned a handy profit in 1987, and a substantial profit in 1988, surprising itself and its harshest critics in government policy circles. It looked as if Korea might be able to make a go of advanced semiconductors after all.

VLSI Research Consortium: 1M DRAM In the mid-1980s the world semiconductor industry witnessed a frantic race to produce the next-generation 1M DRAM, a race which would be won by Toshiba, with its revolutionary CMOS product. The challenge for Samsung and Hyundai was to produce the 1M DRAM without the benefit of any licensing of product or process technology from abroad. At this early stage, even if a full Japanese-style VLSI project were beyond them, some form of collaborative next-generation product development was desirable. The chairman of Samsung Electronics and Telecommunications (then the company's semiconductor producer), Kang Jin-Ku, who was also then head of the EIAK, approached President Chun in 1986 with a plan for a Korean 1M DRAM development consortium to be coordinated by the industry research body, ETRI. The plan was rapidly acted on, with the government outlining a modest development budget, to be matched by contributions from the companies concerned – mainly Samsung, Goldstar and Hyundai. This was to prove a timely initiative, resulting in a basic product design being fashioned in the companies' laboratories by 1987, when it was handed over for scale-up to pilot operation and then mass production. The consortium was subsequently extended to encompass the development of a 4M DRAM, which was set to be world market leader by the beginning of the 1990s.

While modelled on the Japanese VLSI project of 1976–79, the Korean collaborative effort differed from its Japanese counterpart in very significant ways. As with Japan, the Korean project was coordinated by the Ministry of Trade, Industry and Energy (MoTIE), backed by (relatively modest) government funds, expended in the government research labs (ETRI) and in company research facilities, and involved only the existing large firms. But there the similarities end. The essential goal of the Japanese project had been to develop the processing equipment needed for VLSI chip production. Ten years on, Korea's goal was to develop product designs and manufacturing processes needed to produce the chips, on the understanding that the necessary equipment could be bought on the open market.[40]

A joint government–business research fund was established for the Korean VLSI project, and a board of ETRI-sponsored experts was made responsible for allocating funds to support projects nominated by company-based research teams.[41] ETRI's role was to specify engineering standards for the chip designs and processing steps being worked on. Company-based teams whose samples met these specifications were rewarded with preferential loan repayment rates.[42] But even the most sanguine observer would have to admit that the Korean collaborative project played only a minor role in the companies' efforts; in the end, they had to develop their 1M DRAMs themselves.

Likewise KIET's role was declining, as the individual companies gained technological capabilities. KIET made no attempt to move its pilot production facility from 16K to 64K memory chip capacity – this was left to the companies themselves, henceforth to be the pattern in Korea.[43] The leading role played by government in securing Korean foundations in the semiconductor industry was very significant but limited in time to the seeding and propagation phases, lasting for around a decade from the mid-1970s to the late 1980s.

Corporate Strategies As Samsung soared into profit, and Hyundai continued to battle to make its DRAM catch-up strategy work, Goldstar was falling rapidly behind. Its alternative strategy of focusing on application-specific ICs (ASICs), logic chips and telecom products had not generated the business it anticipated. In the meantime the consumer and industrial electronics arms of Goldstar were clamouring for memory chips. Only then did the company execute a policy U-turn and seek DRAM technological capabilities at the then-frontier level of 1M DRAM.[44] In this it was greatly assisted by an unlikely ally.

Goldstar's 1M DRAM The emergence of LG Semicon as a world-class player in the mid-1990s is the result of a series of resource leverage initiatives going back to the early 1970s and involving links with many firms, including AT&T, NS and Hitachi. Goldstar became a 'late' late-starter in memory chip production in Korea. It took advantage of this position to enter a comprehensive technology transfer agreement with Hitachi, with whom the LG group had enjoyed close relations for many years.[45] A new company, Goldstar Electron (GSE), was formed in December 1989, bringing together all of Goldstar's existing semiconductor activities (including the AT&T joint venture) and establishing a new fabrication facility for memory chips at Chungju.

The agreement with Hitachi was the most comprehensive technology transfer agreement yet entered into by a Korean with a Japanese company. Hitachi transferred technology, know-how, equipment suppliers and technical assistance, offering virtually a 'turn-key' system for the production of 1M DRAMs. Indeed Don Chun, head of GSE's semiconductor memory division, stated that 'We are virtually duplicating the Hitachi wafer fab'.[46] The agreement did not come cheaply: GSE had to agree to pay several million dollars upfront as an initial licensing fee, plus royalties on sales of between 1 and 3 per cent of revenue over a period of three years. GSE was thus able to enter the 1M DRAM market in 1990 as a mass producer, a lag of eighteen months after Samsung, and level with Hyundai. What Hitachi gained from this arrangement was the financial flow of royalty fees, and a secure second source for its DRAM products. GSE co-produced a 4M DRAM with Hitachi in 1991–92, and a 16M DRAM in late 1993. By 1995 the two companies were jointly developing the 64M and 256M DRAMs, but no longer under the stringent terms of the original technology transfer agreement.

How Hyundai Broke Through Hyundai (HEI), meanwhile, was struggling. The company had spent freely to establish its own fabrication facility in Korea to produce the items in its first memory chip product portfolio. But the road to semiconductor success was not easy for this Korean *chaebol*. It would be ten years before Hyundai could turn a profit on its semiconductor investments. How Hyundai was able to soldier on and eventually break through to successful production with the 4M DRAM in the early 1990s is a story as dramatic and as instructive as anything in Korea's remarkable high-technology experiences. It is a story that illustrates in the clearest possible terms how corporate organisational learning efforts were needed to underpin the acquisition of semiconductor capabilities.

Hyundai started its semiconductor journey by drawing on resources from around the world and establishing its own state-of-the-art facility. A first fabrication facility was constructed at Ichon in only ten months, between October 1983 and July 1984. By October 1984 it was equipped with an advanced clean-room and pilot production technology. An assembly and test facility was completed by March 1985, again in only nine months.[47] Saleable products were being produced by late 1985. Early sales efforts, however, were disappointing, due partly to the 1985–86 recession, and partly because HEI's products were compared unfavourably with those of Samsung. Sales in 1986 returned only $7.9 million, and $28.5 million in 1987; the company was operating at a severe loss during these first three years.

Early on, HEI was able to secure an OEM contract with Texas Instruments, which was hurting from the 1986 squeeze and looking to spread its manufacturing activities. This contract came in the nick of time for HEI, providing major work for the Ichon fabrication lines, and giving HEI engineers access to TI expertise. TI sent up to twenty engineers at any one time to fine-tune Hyundai's fabrication lines, creating in the process a section of the facility that was adapted exclusively to TI's needs. This acted also as a forcing mechanism to upgrade HEI's skills and efficiency. HEI was able to absorb the fundamental lessons of DRAM manufacturing, creating a foundation that it has built on ever since.[48] Due largely to the TI contract, HEI's sales rose to $205 million in 1988, the first year that HEI actually recorded revenue in excess of costs.[49] But product development remained slow, and Hyundai was facing a crisis by the end of the decade.

The development of the 4M DRAM in 1990 was a make-or-break issue for Hyundai, which had purchased product and process technology for its first efforts, the 64K and 256K DRAMs, from US start-ups such as Vitelic, but was having trouble internalising these technical capabilities. Hyundai was late again with the 1M DRAM, which it developed along parallel pathways to the Samsung model, with one development team working with a design acquired once again from Vitelic, and another seeking to build on earlier experiences to produce their own product. Impatient to catch the market, Hyundai put the Vitelic design into production in 1988. This chip turned out very low yields and its production was abandoned after a year. By then the internally developed product was ready, and it proved to be more stable in production. But again precious time was lost, so Hyundai caught very little of the 1M DRAM market. The company was still a distant second to Samsung and even further behind the Japanese. Things had to improve with the 4M DRAM or the company would in all likelihood be forced out of the semiconductor business.

Hyundai's 4M DRAM 1990–91 Senior management were looking for yet another product licensing source, desperate for a product to bring into the market in time to catch the wave of innovation. Hyundai hired Dr Min Wi-Sik to head up their development efforts, who immediately got down to business at Hyundai's sprawling Ichon complex in the cramped R&D lab. To choose a technical direction between a 'stack' or 'trench' design, Dr Min set up two development teams and let them work in parallel on two versions of the 4M DRAM, to see which could be produced most efficiently. The two teams of around ten engineers each scoured the world for information and produced designs that they then put through their paces. By early 1991, the stack solution was adopted. Samsung had already adopted this solution in its own development efforts.

The parallel teams concept was simply one of a number of important organisational innovations which enabled Hyundai R&D to sustain a punishing pace of development. Process technology was developed alongside product development, as at Samsung, thus squeezing the overall development time. Another of Dr Min's innovations was to stage regular morning briefings, attended by up to twenty of the lab's hundred or so engineers. The meeting would go over the previous day's results and plan the next day's work. The group would invite junior engineers

to present their results, providing them with much needed acknow-
ledgement – or with punishing criticism. But the emphasis of the meetings was not on personalities, but on results and action.

For instance, earlier development efforts had used a scaled-down
version of the chip under development to probe the processing steps and
identify the 'yield killing' defects in the processing steps (such as dust
particles causing shorts, or metal lines edging too close together on the
silicon surface). Hyundai had not been able to use this technique well,
but in the case of the 4M DRAM a 16x smaller version (that is, a 256K
array) was built and turned out to be an efficient predictor of problem
steps. This was a technique borrowed from leading labs and perfected
within Hyundai.

The process lines integrated equipment purchased from several
sources, and in their efforts to integrate the processes (over 100 individual processing steps were needed for the 4M DRAM) engineers were
able to identify some processing steps as redundant. One precautionary
measure, the 'plug implant' step that placed sufficient doping
contaminant in the silicon to ensure electrical contact, was found
through experimental runs and actual wafer runs to be non-essential.
Eliminating it through several repetitions meant that the Hyundai
process could be reduced to around 90 steps of greater simplicity, making for higher yield levels. Such innovations were only possible by
running the product and process development efforts in parallel.

To catch up, HEI had to accelerate the development of next-
generation devices, to reduce the gap in mass production from the
'normal' level of three years to one-and-a-half years in the case of 1M to
4M DRAM transition. The 16M DRAM development was proceeding
(again using parallel teams to test different technical options) while the
4M chip was being finalised. Then a 64M DRAM development group was
formed in early 1991. So Hyundai had development teams working
simultaneously on three generations of DRAM, and on new 'shrunk'
versions within each generation. This was a technique used by leading
firms such as Intel and Samsung; the experience was internalised by
Hyundai, and used to create a 'hothouse' atmosphere of accelerated
development needed to catch up.

These organisational innovations were born of necessity. The concept
of using competing teams to sort out the 'stack versus trench' decision,
for example, was a kind of insurance against making a major technical
failure which could have catastrophic consequences further down the
line. The earlier Japanese consortium-led development was really a
version of the same kind of thing: the different approaches tried by
consortium members provided all member firms with a kind of

'collective insurance' against serious technical glitches. Because of the lack of cooperation between the Korean firms (even within the 4M DRAM consortium) individual firms had to resort to the 'self-insurance' model identified by Hyundai.

Hyundai ramped its 4M DRAM into full mass production by April 1991, only six months behind arch-rival Samsung. The initial yields were higher than 50 per cent, and were raised successively as production experience was gained. Yields of between 80 and 90 per cent were being achieved within six months, in 1991. Indeed yields were higher than on the lines producing 1M DRAMs for Texas Instruments to TI specifications under an OEM contract, within the same fab! Such was the measure of Hyundai's learning from one product generation to the next.

It was the 4M DRAM that finally launched Hyundai as a serious player in the semiconductor industry. Indeed Hyundai's 4M DRAM technology was considered so good that the Japanese firm Fujitsu licensed it, and produced Hyundai-4M DRAM chips at its US fab in Gresham, Oregon, as a 'second source'. This led to a wider technology alliance between Hyundai and Fujitsu that has benefited both companies. Hyundai is now confidently on the way to becoming one of the world's top ten semiconductor firms by 2000.[50]

Propagation Phase – Achievements

The propagation phase of semiconductor industry development was driven initially by an intensive (and expensive) round of technology leverage, followed by furious efforts on the part of the firms involved to internalise, synthesise and improve these technologies for themselves. It was a feasible strategy for these firms because of several features: their large size, technical sophistication (honed during the 1970s), access to US semiconductor competencies (particularly through the hiring of Korean national engineers) and the availability of product and process technology on the market.

The cost involved – the 'price of entry' – was enormous. There were upfront investment costs, totalling around $4 billion up to the end of 1989; the royalty charges imposed by US firms for their designs and process technologies; and the trade disputes, which exacted a political cost as well as extra royalty charges on patents.[51] These costs – royalties and interest charges – were the major cost items borne by the Korean semiconductor firms (far larger than labour costs, see Table 6.4. These were the costs of accelerated, leverage-led high-technology development. The benefits came from the accelerated creation of a world-class industry operating at the technological frontier.

Table 3.4   Licensing agreements with Korean firms, 1982–86

Company	Year	Technology
Samsung and		
ITT	1982	Telecom ICs
Micron	1983	64K DRAM
Sharp	1983	CMOS process
Zytrex	1983	High-speed CMOS process
Zilog	1984	8-bit MPU
Intergraph	1984	32-bit MPU
Intel	1985	Microprocessors
Exel Microelectronics	1985	16K EEPROM
Goldstar and		
AT&T	1984	Telecommunication chips
Zilog	1985	Z80 microprocessor
AMD	1985	64K DRAM
United Microtek	1985	1M DRAM
Hyundai and		
Western Design Centre	1984	8-bit, 16-bit 6502 MPU
Vitelic	1985	256K DRAM, 1M DRAM
Mosel	1985	64K, 256K, 1M SRAM
LSI Logic	1985	gate arrays
Daewoo and		
Zymos	1985	MOS ICs*
Anam and		
VLSI Technology	1986	ASIC design centre

Note: *Company acquisition.
Source: Industry interviews.

The major source of Korean technological capability had come
through the purchase of equipment from a variety of vendors, American
and Japanese, and the 'tweaking' of this equipment to raise yields and
produce a coherent and integrated production system. Technology
licensing was also an important source.[52] The technology leverage
practised by the Korean firms during the diffusion phase is summarised
in Table 3.4.

By the late 1980s, Korean firms had successfully established themselves
in the US semiconductor market, and were starting to enter the
European market. The Japanese market remained to be conquered.
They had invested an enormous sum in the new industry, and had
developed early strength in mass production of commodity memory
chips, but had yet to demonstrate any sustainable capacity in products
beyond these, such as logic circuits and the ultimate prize, microprocessors. They had shown their capacity to develop their own new
products, such as the 4M DRAM, with little (LG) or no reliance (Samsung, Hyundai) on imported designs or technology. But they were also

still critically dependent on US and Japanese firms for the imports of fabrication equipment and materials. The stage was set for the critical test: could Korean firms develop a sustainable competitive base to remain in and prosper within the semiconductor industry?

Stage IV: 1989–98 – Roots of Sustainability

The 1980s closed in Korea with a tumultuous swing towards democratisation, initiated by the Declaration of 29 June 1987 from President Chun. He stepped down, and announced open presidential elections for December of that year, which were won by Roh Tae Woo. Long-suppressed social unrest that had simmered through the years of breakneck industrialisation broke out in waves of protest. In the midst of all this social revolution, Korean *chaebol* and state agencies attempted to hold course to their chosen high-technology strategy. With the brakes off the long-suppressed labour movement, wages were to rise steeply in Korea, making the shift towards knowledge-intensive industries like semiconductors of even greater strategic significance.

The 1980s saw the creation of a semiconductor industry in Korea at VLSI technology standard, but its impact on the world stage was still modest. It was the 4M DRAM, developed in prototype form in 1988 and launched as a mass market product by Samsung in 1991, and by Hyundai and LG shortly after, that really provided the breakthrough for Korean producers into the US market, establishing them as a strong presence. On the basis of this success, Samsung set up a 'submicron' (ULSI) laboratory in its Kiheung plant to work on the next generation 16M DRAM chip, developed in 1990, neck and neck with Japan.

By 1994 Korean firms had acquired around 40 per cent of the world market for 16M DRAMs, a remarkable result for an industry no more than a decade old. Huge investments in 1994 and 1995 did much to safeguard this hard-won position by the Koreans. They were now recognised as being competitors of the first rank by both the Americans and Japanese.

Behind the spectacular market penetration results achieved by the Koreans in DRAMs were substantial initiatives taken to build the sustainability of the semiconductor industry more generally. These have sometimes gone unnoticed by critics of the Korean model, or their significance has been downplayed. The major developments in the 1990s that have contributed to enhancing the industry's sustainability include the deepening of private-sector commitment to innovation; further technology leverage, particularly through global product development alliances; the broadening of product output; diffusion of wafer-fabrication activities beyond the 'Big Three'; enhancement of supply to

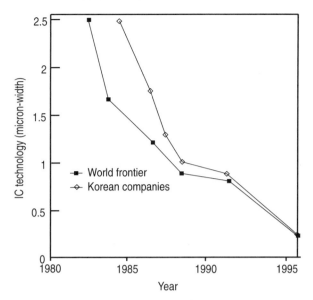

Figure 3.1   Korea closes the technology gap in memory chips.
Source: KSIA.

Korean domestic market; creation of support or ancillary industries; expansion of production facilities abroad; joint R&D; and further evolution of the institutional framework for support of high-technology industrialisation.

   The combined effect of these developments was to close the technological 'gap' that separated Korea from the most advanced countries in semiconductors, as shown in Figure 3.1.

Private-sector R&D Commitment

Throughout the 1980s, the major *chaebol*, led by Samsung, were establishing their own R&D institutes, and raising the proportion of their revenues allocated to new product development. By 1990, Samsung had 26 research centres, while Goldstar had eighteen and Hyundai fourteen. Each of these *chaebol* ran its own advanced institute for semiconductor product development.[53] Samsung poured resources into R&D. By 1995, for example, these expenditures were estimated to be $1.2 billion, or 6 per cent of total sales. Samsung was also investing in small high-technology companies all around the world. These investments gave it a foothold in advancing waves of innovation: it can gear up its investments at any time if the linked company showed signs of developing something significant. Likewise LG and Hyundai were by the mid-1990s pouring profits from their semiconductor operations into R&D centres and into equity positions in small, high-technology companies around the world.

Further Rounds of Technology Leverage: Strategic Alliances and Technology Trade

As the costs of developing new products and putting them into production spiralled upwards (a new product and fab was costing in the order of $500 million in the early 1990s, and by the mid-1990s around $1 billion), so firms were forced into joint ventures and strategic alliances to spread the costs and share the risks. The same pattern was being followed by US, European and Japanese firms. Strategic alliances, linking Samsung to NEC and Toshiba, for example, or Hyundai to Fujitsu and LG to Hitachi, provided another sustainable source of competitiveness for the Korean semiconductor industry. The range of strategic alliances developed in the 1990s is shown in Figure 3.2.

Samsung's Strategic Alliances Samsung's major development and production alliance has been with NEC for the joint development of 256M DRAMs, and development and production of synchronous DRAMs. These efforts brought the two companies into joint leadership of the memory chip world market. Samsung and NEC subsequently agreed to align their development and production of synchronous DRAMs (SDRAMs), beginning with the introduction of a jointly produced 16M SDRAM in mid-1996. SDRAMs in particular were to grow rapidly in importance in the latter half of the 1990s, driven by the high-speed demands of personal computers. In 1996, Samsung clinched an important deal with Intel to supply SDRAMs for Intel's new chipset, thus underpinning Samsung's leadership of the emerging synchronous DRAM market.

At the same time Samsung was also working hard to diversify its output from memory chips to other forms of ICs and semiconductor products. It announced its intention of bringing non-memory products up to 50 per cent of its output by 2000. It was entering further alliances to

Another example of the trend in alliances is that between Samsung and the Japanese firm Oki, in this case, the transfer of 16M SDRAM technology from Samsung to Oki. *This is the first known case of technology transfer from Korea to Japan in semiconductors.* Samsung leveraged itself into the flash memory market through an alliance with Toshiba.[54] Toshiba and Samsung have been jointly developing and producing ICs for liquid crystal displays. In 1995 the technical cooperation was expanded to encompass transfer to Samsung of Toshiba's bipolar IC technology, thus extending Samsung's product range. Samsung was also cooperating with Mitsubishi in the development of 'cache' DRAM devices.

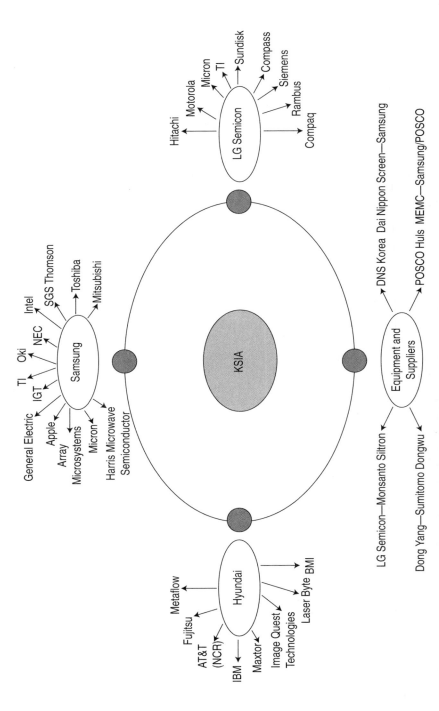

Figure 3.2 Korea's strategic alliances.

secure access to critical technologies, such as with Harris Semiconductor in the US, to gain access to gallium/arsenide chip technology (used in high-performance ICs); with Ixys (US) to gain access to field effect transistor technology; with SGS-Thomson Microelectronics to access 32-bit microcontrollers and 16-bit digital signal processors (both used in fast multimedia products); and with Array Microsystems (US) for multimedia technology. Samsung took a 20 per cent equity stake in Array Microsystems, and teamed with the company to jointly produce chips for video compression and multimedia. In return, Array gained access to Samsung's foundry facilities for production of its own devices.

Samsung formulated a strategy to enter the microprocessor market on the basis of licensing agreements for RISC technology from Advanced RISC Machines Ltd (ARM), and for the Alpha processor from DEC.[55] By the late 1990s Samsung was a global player of substance.

Hyundai's Strategic Alliances With rising costs of product development, HEI was forced in the 1990s to look for strategic alliances, and entered several, the most important of which was a long-term link-up with the Japanese IC and computer company, Fujitsu. Hyundai and Fujitsu announced their pathbreaking general agreement in 1993, following exploratory talks initiated by the Japanese company in 1992. A comprehensive technology cooperation agreement was signed in March 1993 (and made public in October of that year), under which Hyundai and Fujitsu agreed to join forces in developing a range of products. The agreement with Fujitsu also enabled Hyundai to evade the punitive US customs tariff of 11 per cent placed on its chips shipped to the US.[56] Under the agreement, Fujitsu produced Hyundai's 4M and 16M DRAMs at its Oregon plant which it then sold to Hyundai for sale in the US. In this and many other ways the world's trading rules are being complicated by such international alliances. HEI has been actively seeking other alliances in the area of ASICs and non-memory products. The search focused on small, high-technology start-ups in the US, and some alliances along these lines have already been established.[57]

LG Semicon's Strategic Alliances Like Hyundai and Samsung, LG Semicon was actively seeking to broaden its technological capabilities through its own R&D efforts and technology partnerships with small high-technology firms in the US. LG Electronics operated a major research centre, employing 300 technical staff in 1995 with a budget of $45 million, under the leadership of Dr Kim Chang-Soo.[58] The centre undertook original research into the design of algorithms and models for signal compression and decompression, which provided the key to the chips used in high-definition television receivers, for example. In the US, LG Semicon acquired a 5 per cent stake in Zenith Electronics Corp for around $15 million. Goldstar thereby acquired access to Zenith's Flat Tension Mask display technology, used in HDTV applications. It was also actively licensing technological developments such as high-speed memory interface technology from the US firm Rambus Inc, which Goldstar would be able to use in the manufacture of 16M DRAMs. LG Semicon signed an agreement with the German firm Siemens to develop logic chips (8-bit microcontrollers) for use in communications equipment, vehicles and other consumer products. In April 1995, LG Semicon announced that it had taken a minority equity position in the US flash memory device producer SunDisk Corporation. LG Semicon was able to leverage this investment to produce SunDisk's 16M and 32M flash memory chips in 1995; marking LG's initial foray into flash memory.

As part of the expansion of the IC industry in Korea, other *chaebol* like Daewoo were by the late 1990s entering technology alliances. In 1997, for example, Daewoo announced a technology tie-up with the European semiconductor firm, SGS-Thomson, creating a joint venture located in Seoul to develop ICs for electronic application products.

Broadening the Product Range of the Semiconductor Industry

While expertise in DRAMs and their more sophisticated versions such as SDRAMs was the core strength of the Korean industry, reliance and dependence on this group of memory products was also the industry's weakness – as became manifest in the worldwide memory chip downturn of 1997–98. Efforts were made by the three major *chaebol* to enter alternative semiconductor areas, but they had borne little fruit by the time of the downturn. Sales by product for the 1990s were as in Table 3.5.

Clearly memory products continued to dominate Korean output right up to the mid-1990s. The increases in output of MOS-logic chips and analog chips provided some evidence of diversification trends. Further diversification efforts have been mounted collaboratively with government involvement, as discussed below.

Beyond the 'Big Three'

Another weakness of the Korean industry has been the monopolisation of wafer-fabrication activities by Samsung, Hyundai and LG Semicon. By the mid-1990s there were signs of a further diffusion of these activities beyond these founding firms. Daewoo remained intensely interested in becoming a serious semiconductor producer, and had wafer-fabrication plans under review. The contract IC assembly and packaging firm, Anam, was also reported to be entering the wafer assembly business as Korea's

Table 3.5 Production by product category in Korea, 1991–95

Segment	1991	1992	1993	1994	1995
			$ million		
Discrete	163	207	235	308	356
Bipolar	28	26	31	24	42
Analog	170	211	254	329	374
MOS-micro	26	33	60	71	129
MOS-logic	99	122	192	257	395
MOS-memory	1796	2643	4457	7531	14 978
Others	8	12	34	45	28
Total	**2290**	**3254**	**5263**	**8565**	**16 302**

Source: KSIA.

first pure silicon foundry. This would be a logical progression for Anam, to extend its existing contract business from the 'back end' to 'front end' operations.[59] In 1995 it was reported that the medium-scale Il Jin group planned to enter wafer fabrication on the basis of a technology transfer agreement signed with the US firm Integrated Device Technology (IDT).[60] Another major investment announcement was made in 1997, involving the middle-ranking *chaebol*, Dongbu, which announced plans to enter DRAM fabrication at a very advanced level, based on a comprehensive technology transfer and product supply agreement with IBM Microelectronics.[61] These investment initiatives were encouraging for the Korean industry, but must be counted as a slow rate of propagation beyond the initial Big Three, when compared to the rapid propagation in Taiwan.

Enhancement of Supply of Chips to the Local Semiconductor Market

The Korean market for semiconductor devices to be used in the local production of computers, communications systems and other electronic and IT products, was itself growing as an outlet for Korean production. The market size in Korea reached $4.4 billion in 1995. While the level of imports was in excess of 80 per cent in 1991, it had dropped below 70 per cent in 1995, revealing a trend towards greater domestic self-supply. The trends in Korean demand for semiconductors are shown in Table 3.6.

The structure of Korean trade in semiconductors was still somewhat lopsided, with most chips produced being exported (90 per cent) and most chips used in Korea being imported (68 per cent). The demand for imported chips was in the areas under-produced by Korean firms: microprocessors (94 per cent import dependence), logic chips (84 per cent dependent) and analog (79 per cent dependent). It was only in

Table 3.6   Korean semiconductor device market, 1991–95

	1991	1992	1993	1994	1995
			$ billion		
Sales	2.32	2.57	3.08	3.33	4.40
			per cent		
Import ratio	81	82	78	70	69
Domestic supply	19	18	22	30	31

Source: KSIA.

memory chips that Korea had self-sufficiency, supplying 80 per cent of its domestic needs. There was a balance in supply of chips to the Korean market from the US, accounting for 29 per cent of imports in 1995, and Japan, which accounted for 32 per cent.[62] With Japan, Korea still runs a substantial overall trade deficit, taking into account semiconductor materials, equipment and specialised chips. It is a national goal to eliminate this imbalance.

Deepening Korean Industry through Local Supply of Equipment and Materials

The Korean semiconductor industry was established entirely on the foreign supply of manufacturing equipment and materials, largely from the US and Japan.[63] In the 1990s, the Korean government agencies took active steps to encourage the formation of a domestic equipment and materials supply industry, to broaden the base of the Korean industry. This 'local production' strategy has been pursued vigorously, just as the Japanese pursued their national autonomy strategy to avoid 'import dependence' a decade earlier. There has been active encouragement of clustering of supply firms on the Chonan Second Industrial Complex in central Korea so that several emerging supply firms, such as DNS Korea, Mirae and POSCO-Huls are now located there or in its vicinity.

There is still a long way to go until any form of 'self-sufficiency' can be declared. A 1993 study by the Bank of Korea found that only 38 per cent of the value of semiconductors was added locally: imported materials and equipment accounted for 62 per cent.[64] However the trend is towards greater self-reliance.

Manufacturing Equipment Supply

Purchases of semiconductor manufacturing equipment by Korean producers amounted to $2.5 billion in 1995, of which 75 per cent was imported and 25 per cent produced locally. In 1991 and 1992, when purchases were just less than $1 billion, around 90 per cent of equipment

Table 3.7   Korean semiconductor equipment market, 1990–96

	1990	1991	1992	1993	1994	1995	1996
				$ million			
Sales	717	904	874	1392	3081	4170	4722
				per cent			
Import ratio	94	90	89	92	89	92	87
Domestic supply	6	10	11	8	11	8	13

Source: KSIA.

had to be imported. The Korean industry was on target to increase local self-sufficiency to 30 per cent by 1997 and beyond, as shown in Table 3.7.

Equipment was imported by Korean producers from US and Japanese suppliers in roughly equal amounts. In 1995, Japanese suppliers accounted for 47 per cent of imports, while US suppliers accounted for 30 per cent and other non-Korean (European) sources accounted for only 5 per cent. The trend is downwards for the Japanese and upwards for the American supply firms, again a reflection of the Korean IC producers' ability to wean themselves off an initial dependence on Japanese suppliers. The balance between Japan and US as sources of supply was an important point for the Koreans, to keep playing the two off each other.[65]

The Koreans have been assiduous technology leveragers in their efforts to raise the standards and breadth of operations of their local equipment supply industry. Foreign suppliers have been invited to Korea, particularly when they are prepared to set up joint ventures with local firms, or establish local technology centres.[66] A further leverage device is that the Big Three chipmakers actively support (through their purchasing decisions) those equipment makers who are prepared to invest in Korea. Samsung led the way with a joint venture with Japan's Dai Nippon Screen (DNS) to form DNS Korea: this will produce spinners and wet stations from its base at Chonan. Both Samsung and Hyundai are to be customers for its products. Samsung is also the instigator of a joint venture with POSCO Steel and MEMC (US), known as POSCO-Huls, to supply the Korean industry with silicon wafers.[67] In 1994 it was ramping up its plant at Chonan to produce 8-inch wafers for 16M DRAM production. LG Semicon actively encouraged silicon wafer production through various leverage devices by its Siltron operation; this too has scaled up to 8-inch wafer production.[68] There were also numerous joint ventures for the supply of specialist equipment. Three of these local self-sufficiency initiatives are Mirae, DI Corporation and Shinsung, all evidence of the indigenisation of the supply industry.[69]

Table 3.8 Materials supply to Korean producers, 1990–96

	1990	1991	1992	1993	1994	1995	1996
			$ million				
Sales	510	570	713	945	1354	2048	2005
			per cent				
Import ratio	68	66	63	63	59	54	56
Domestic supply	32	34	37	37	41	46	44

Source: KSIA.

Semiconductor Materials Supply

Materials used in semiconductor production in 1995 cost the Koreans $1.9 billion. Of this, 54 per cent were imported, and 46 per cent supplied locally. The trend was towards further local sourcing, up from 34 per cent local supply in 1991, to an expected level of over 50 per cent in 1996. Local supply made a big jump in 1994, due to new facilities coming on stream and further advances in 1994 and 1995.[70] The policy of localisation in materials supply was more advanced and successful at this stage than is the case for equipment (see Table 3.8).

Again the Koreans have been assiduous practitioners of technology leverage in their nurturing of a local materials supply industry. Japanese, US and European firms have been invited to establish operations in partnership with local Korean firms.[71] In addition, there are numerous suppliers of packaging materials, such as bonding wire, from Korean initiatives and joint ventures.

It is the MoTIE which is actively promoting the local production of foreign allied and Korean supply of semiconductor equipment and materials. It has provided financial (bank loans) and other incentives (tax holidays) to allied and Korean suppliers.[72] For our purposes, these developments provide clear evidence of the leveraging strategy moving through another iterative twist of the industry capability enhancement spiral. The pattern of the developments is clear: there is a strong preference for local Korean involvement in a joint venture or other association with a world-class supplier which is prepared to transfer technology and locate operations in Korea.

Expansion of Production Facilities Abroad

Before the Asian financial crisis, Korean semiconductor firms were making good progress in internationalising themselves. By the mid-1990s all three major Korean semiconductor companies were committed to expanding their wafer-fabrication facilities beyond Korea, although the

1997 financial crisis has forced some of these plans to be scaled back. Samsung led the way, focusing initially on Europe.[73] In China, Samsung joined the Singapore government in developing the Souzhou region as a major Chinese semiconductor base. Samsung began construction on a semiconductor assembly and packaging plant at Suzhou in mid-1995, to be known as Samsung Electronics (Suzhou) Semiconductor Ltd (SESS). By 1996 transistors and non-memory ICs were in full production. Samsung has blazed a trail at Suzhou that other semiconductor companies such as AMD from the US and Hitachi from Japan have followed.[74] Samsung then moved to establish a fabrication presence in the US, building a plant at Austin, Texas, for the production of DRAMs. This remained its American platform for ramping up production of DRAMs as the worldwide memory chip crisis was drawing to a close in 1998.

Not to be outdone, Hyundai announced in 1995 a five-year overseas semiconductor fabrication expansion plan worth $6.6 billion, involving the construction of four memory chip plants in the US, Scotland and South East Asia. The first of these, a DRAM fabrication facility at Eugene, Oregon, was approved and production started in 1997. But Hyundai's further expansion plans had to be put on hold in 1997.

By the end of 1995 LG Semicon was likewise committed to establishing at least two memory chip fabrication facilities abroad: one in the UK to service the European market, and one in Malaysia, to service the South East Asian market. The Malaysian venture, due to be built on the Kulim High-technology Park, was to be established in partnership with Hitachi, but abandoned in 1997 because of the uncertain financial climate. The UK plant also had to be put on hold.

While somewhat curtailed by the events of 1997–98, these plans indicated how the Korean 'Big Three' were committed to becoming global players in memory chips, with production facilities in each of the world's major chip markets in the US, Europe and South East Asia. Their international expansion was being carefully monitored and coordinated by government agencies, the MTI's Advisory Committee on the Semiconductor Industry. Local pressure from the countries accepting Korean investment will no doubt lead to the expansion of these new production facilities to encompass product development and customer service activities, thus inducing the Koreans to become more like genuine multinationals.

Joint R&D Projects

One final piece of evidence in support of the longer-term viability of the Korean industry concerns a new commitment towards inter-firm collaboration in joint R&D projects. The highly individualistic and competitive *chaebol* have made collaborative development programs very difficult to establish and operate in Korea. Despite its best endeavours, the Korean government was unable to get the Korean *chaebol* to collaborate effectively in the development of 1M and 4M DRAMs. Further efforts to establish joint R&D arrangements were mounted in the 1990s, after the lessons of earlier efforts. The first appeared to be a 'throw-back' to the days of government directions being given to the industry. A new semiconductor development consortium was announced by MoST in December 1989, with little consultation, to develop the basic technologies associated with 16M and 64M DRAMs.[75] This research program showed how the private sector, which took the initiatives in semiconductor development and undertook the lion's share of research, had run ahead of public agencies such as ETRI, which provided no more than a technically competent secretariat. From this point on, the real research was to be conducted within the *chaebols*' own institutions.

The demonstration of the new direction came in 1993, with a quite different kind of collaborative R&D activity. In order to strengthen Korea's basic science capabilities in semiconductors, the companies through KSIA agreed at the end of 1993 to launch a new, private-sector joint R&D project in Advanced Basic Semiconductor Technology (ABST). A coordinating committee was established, and funds were disbursed for the first time in 1994.[76] The project was given three major aims: to promote joint research on fundamental pre-competitive issues between the major device makers; to promote improved equipment and materials supply in Korea through better collaboration between the suppliers and device manufacturers; and to promote university research in the fundamentals of semiconductor science, and to provide supporting infrastructure grants for this purpose. Each of these aims signalled a recognition of a weakness in the sustainability of the Korean semiconductor industry, and represented a national commitment to do something about the problems.

The bulk of the funds have been allocated to the Big Three to support their development of next-generation process technology.[77] Universities have also been participants in some of the joint projects funded by companies under the government loan scheme. The universities' involvement pointed to a broadening of Korean semiconductor competencies beyond the three major firms. The consortium was focusing on generic technologies at the pre-competitive stage, which would be used by all participant companies as they gear up for the future chip generation challenges.[78] In terms of administration, the ABST joint R&D project is also innovative in that it is being administered by the KSIA, rather than by a government agency. It is very much a private-sector initiative.

Through the KSIA, the Korean firms in 1995 became foundation members of a new international consortium formed to take the industry smoothly towards 300-mm (12-inch) wafers (from the present 8-inch). This consortium, called the International 300 mm Initiative (I300I), involves thirteen companies from the US, Europe, Taiwan and Korea (but not Japan) each contributing $2 million over an eighteen-month period to develop 300-mm wafer technology to pilot stage. It was as good a demonstration as any that the Korean firms were now accepted as equal partners in worldwide coordination of major new technical initiatives such as the shift to a new wafer size for production in the twenty-first century.

Evolving Public Policy: Knowledge-intensive Industrialisation

The early 1980s had seen a distinct bureaucratic cleavage in Korea, with agencies such as the EPB and MoF pursuing the policies of 'stabilisation and adjustment' (which eschewed any hint of targeting) and the MTI and its industrial allies like the EIAK arguing strongly for a 'continuation of industrial policy by other means', very much in the mould of Japan's high-technology policies through the 1970s.[79] The unexpected successes of Samsung and other Korean *chaebol* in the US semiconductor market had silenced the most vociferous critics of long-term industrial promotion. It also paved the way for the Ministry of Science and Technology (MoST), previously a lightweight in the Korean bureaucratic pecking order, to exert more influence.

In 1989, the MTI announced a 'Five-Year Plan for the Development of High Technology Industries' to promote seven carefully targeted industries including microelectronics (and thus, semiconductors). The plan envisaged enactment of 'temporary measures' (a Japanese euphemism for permanent arrangements) to foster the development of the targeted industries, in fairly conventional manner – mostly through adjusting and stimulating levels of demand such as through manipulation of tax rates.[80] At the same time, MoST issued its own plan for the promotion of technology-intensive industries in Korea through 'supply-side' questions of technology development and targeted support. Thus a degree of bureaucratic competition emerged in the Korean promotion of knowledge-intensive industries between MTI and MoST, the former emphasising the stimulus of 'demand', the latter on the promotion of 'supply'. Korean industry was the beneficiary of both approaches. Furthermore, in December 1989 the Ministry of Communications (MoC) announced its own plan to develop the 'information industry' as the linchpin of Korea's high-technology development, calling for total investment of 63 trillion *won* over the next eleven years to 2000; it was envisaged that the government would provide only 5 trillion *won* (8 per cent) with the balance coming from the private sector.

As the culmination of these activities, the Council of Science and Technology, dormant for many years, was reconvened by the Prime Minister to develop an omnibus science and technology promotion program in which fourteen specific S&T goals were announced or endorsed. Released in August 1991, this became known as the 'G7' program, since it called for Korea to become a fully developed country by 2000, and a candidate for membership of the Group of Seven advanced nations.[81] Many of these programs had a tactical goal – to promote Korea's membership of the WTO and the OECD.

The 1990s have seen the Korean industry move from a stage of 'catch-up' to one involved with all the challenges of 'maturing'. Against all the odds a Korean semiconductor industry was established, not in a marginal fashion, but as a mainstream player engaged in intense competitive rivalry and in collaborative international ventures. In the 1990s, determined efforts were made to transfer some of the profits made into investments in deepening the roots of sustainability, through R&D activities, international collaborative ventures, and through globalising production and marketing, to close the technology gap. And it was closed, at least in the memory chips sector. While progress made in this direction is substantial, there remained deep structural problems that were the legacy of the rapid leverage strategy adopted. The industry downturn of 1996–97, followed by the Korean financial crisis, has been a testing time for the Korean semiconductor players. They have come through it diminished but unbowed. How successful and sustainable the industry had become by the late 1990s is a subject of intense debate in Korea as well as in the wider scholarly community, which we will turn to in Chapter 6.

Notes

1   This was how Toshiba had accelerated the pace of development of its revolutionary CMOS 1M DRAM in Japan.
2   This is a goal which burns fiercely in nationalistic Korea, which had been under Japanese rule from 1910–45.
3   General sources for this and following sections include Yoon 1989; Byun and Ahn (1989); Soh (1992); Woo (1991); Choi (1996); Hong (1992; 1997); Kim L. (1993; 1997a; 1997b); Kim Y. S. (1997), Pecht *et al.* (1997) and Kim S. R. (1998). See also Mathews and Cho (1999) and Cho and Rhee (1998).
4   The designation of stages given here corresponds closely to that provided by the KSIA; it is also close to that used by Yoon (1989) and Soh (1992). We

have established our own periodisation based on our DRL model, and events as described in the text.

5   President Park was a great admirer of the Japanese, having served in the Japanese army in the 1930s in Manchuria, where he witnessed first hand Japanese experiments with new forms of political economy. These experiences and influences were put to the test in Korea.

6   Assembly and testing are the labour-intensive, low value-adding phases of chip production after wafer fabrication and circuit printing.

7   In December 1965 the Korean government approved the formation of Komi Industrial Company as a 75:25 joint venture with the small US firm, Komi.

8   Along with eight in Hong Kong, three in Taiwan, nine in Singapore, eleven in Malaysia and six in the rest of Asia (Davis and Hatano 1985: 129).

9   Rumour in the semiconductor industry was that Fairchild recovered its investment in its 1963 Hong Kong facility within six months; this had a powerful demonstration effect.

10 Kumi was the hometown of the Korean partner in the joint venture, and of the Korean President.

11 This institute, the first in Korea devoted to advancing the science and technology capabilities of Korean industry, was established as an autonomous entity with assistance from the US Battelle Institute. Funding was provided by the World Bank.

12 The first president of KIST was Dr Choi Hyung-Sup. The technology assimilation strategy was developed under his leadership. He later went on to become Korea's first Minister of Science and Technology. For an insight into his thinking see Choi (1975).

13 A report to MCI and the President on the possible development of an electronics industry in Korea had been drafted by Professor Kim Wan-Hee, a Korean professor of electrical engineering at Columbia University, New York. This report advocated continued promotion of foreign investment; a strengthening of the export orientation of local firms; and active inducement for the major *chaebol* to enter the electronics industry. Professor Kim was to become head of the EIAK in 1978.

14 Export targets were set at $100 million in 1971, $200 million in 1974 and $400 million in 1976.

15 As things turned out, the joint ventures with Sanyo and NEC were terminated in 1972, after they had served their purpose of technology transfer. The Korean government changed the rules governing joint ventures, insisting that they not be allowed to supply the domestic market, partly to assuage industry protests. This created severe difficulties for Sanyo and NEC, which were making the investments predominantly to secure access to the Korean market. Samsung broke with Sanyo in 1972, and turned the previous joint venture into its own subsidiary, Samsung Electronics. It did the same with NEC in 1974, forming Samsung Semiconductor. Subsequently, the Korean government changed the rules again, allowing joint ventures to supply the domestic market, which was Samsung's intention all along.

16 In practice, this was meant to reduce Korea's dependence on Japanese components, a recurring theme in Korea's industrial policy.

17 Wade (1990: 313) discusses this strategy of technology acquisition.

18 Other complexes established at this time included Okpo (shipbuilding), Changwon (machinery and heavy engineering), Onsan (non-ferrous metals) and Yochon (petrochemicals). Visitors to these complexes in the

1990s would still be overwhelmed by their sheer size and sense of con-centrated industrial strength.

19 Like many of Korea's industrial policy promulgations, this was virtually a translation from the equivalent Japanese statute.

20 Korea Semiconductor Corporation (KSEC) was founded by a Korean–American engineer, Dr Kang Ki-Dong, in 1974, and began operations in 1975. The then-current LSI technology was imported from his US employer, Integrated Circuits International Inc (ICII), to establish an operation to produce ICs used in consumer electronics applications such as electronic watches. After Samsung's takeover of the venture, Kang went on to play an important role in Samsung's development of semiconductor expertise.

21 This was dubbed popularly the Tangun boom – it was unprecedented since the time of Tangun, the legendary founder of Korea.

22 This is how Samsung became involved in a joint venture with ITT (via its takeover of KTC), and Goldstar with AT&T. The profits from telecoms activities also provided a secure source of cash flow while the huge invest-ments in semiconductor fabrication were being undertaken.

23 During the phase of seeding, demand for ICs grew from $17 million in 1974 to over $300 million in 1983. Demand shifted from discrete devices to ICs, which accounted for nearly 70 per cent of demand in 1983.

24 See Wade (1989: 90). This was a process very similar to the Taiwanese initiative that saw ITRI/ERSO establish a pilot IC fabrication plant in 1977–78 through its licensing deal with RCA. However, the diffusion from KIET's operation to the private sector seems to have been less successful in Korea than Taiwan.

25 There had been an earlier IMF intervention in 1971, after Korea's first decade of breakneck development ended in overcapacity and a threatened debt crisis.

26 The new direction was spelt out in the *Comprehensive Measures for Economic Stabilization* (CMES) issued under presidential authority in April 1979.

27 The group brought together representatives of all the bodies and agencies with a stake in the future direction of the electronics industry. There were representatives from five ministries (MTI, EPB, MoC, MoF and MoST); four companies (Samsung, Goldstar, Anam and Sanhwa Condenser); and two research institutes (KIET and KETRI). The KETRI had already commis-sioned two reports in connection with these matters from the Nomura Research Centre in Japan and the Korean think tank, the Korean Develop-ment Institute (KDI).

28 There was at the time considerable Korean activity in back-end assembly operations, and substantial revenues being earned – as in the case of Anam. But these firms were not seen, correctly, as the appropriate launching pad for the new and higher stage of capability involved in VLSI wafer fabrication.

29 The exception was the telecommunications sector, where the 'carrot' offered to firms like AT&T and ITT in return for technology was access to the expanding Korean domestic market.

30 Micron was itself a start-up based outside Silicon Valley in Idaho.

31 Sharp had a plausible reason for licensing CMOS technology to Samsung in 1984. Sharp was the world's leading producer of LCDs, but had not been included by MITI in the Top Six IC manufacturing firms because it was considered a 'consumer electronics' firm.

32 For further details, see Kim (1997a; 1997b) and Choi (1996).

33   See Langlois *et al.* (1988: 82); and the *Wall Street Journal*, 'South Korean firms honing their skills in US's microchip Mecca, Silicon Valley,' 3 October 1984.

34   Hyundai, however, took a detour, via static RAM memory chips, before discovering that the market for these would not be nearly as large as that for DRAMs. This detour lost Hyundai precious time, and illustrates the pitfalls involved in 'leapfrogging'.

35   On the wider East Asian stage, the 'experiment' also included the quite different strategies pursued in Taiwan, which turned out to be more robust than those followed in Korea.

36   Samsung secured a $15 million foreign line of credit, without a domestic Korean bank's repayment guarantee, in March 1983. It followed this with a $35 million syndicated loan in September (Yoon 1989: 134). These were unprecedented initiatives in Korea, and directly responsible for opening the gates to foreign capital for Korean industry in the 1980s.

37   By the end of 1985, the four largest *chaebol* groups had secured $285 million by issuing commercial paper (bonds and debentures) abroad, most of them dedicated to semiconductor investment. In 1984 Samsung raised a total of $190 million in this way without guarantees from the Korean government or domestic banks: $140 million in syndicated foreign loans, $30 million in floating-rate notes in Europe, $20 million in convertible bonds on the Eurodollar market (Yoon 1989: 140).

38   In the context of Japan, Peck and Tamura called this activity 'improvement engineering' (1976: 542–43); Korea was an able exponent of the strategy.

39   The Plaza Agreement, named after the New York hotel where the representatives of the Group of Five (France, Germany, Japan, the UK and the US) met, resulted in a coordinated realignment of currencies, with the US dollar devalued particularly against the *yen*, and less so against the Korean *won* and Taiwanese NT.

40   The rationale for this Korean approach was basically sound. While the sharing of development tasks might have been feasible for the Japanese in the 1970s, it was no longer viable in the 1980s. Advanced semiconductor firms that built their own chips had to be in control of all phases of the fabrication process because of the integration between them. In the intervening ten years, the process of product design had been greatly automated, and the testing of production steps was now a far more significant feature of next-generation product development. The sharing of process development data through a neutral 'arbiter', namely the ETRI, could prove to be a major advantage.

41   The Director of the VLSI Project at ETRI was Dr Kim Jeong-Deok. In 1995 he held a senior position in the government, as Vice-Minister of Science and Technology.

42   By the end of the project, eighteen such collaborative projects had been filtered through the consortium, with total R&D expenses estimated at $250 million (OTA 1991: 320).

43   Indeed, KIET abandoned its R&D capacity in semiconductors, and its fabrication facilities were sold to Goldstar. Its operations were then merged with those of the telecommunications laboratory and the combined entity was called the Electronics and Telecommunications Research Institute (ETRI).

44   Goldstar's early strategy was not concerned with DRAMs at all, and focused on industrial and telecommunications chips, which promised greater added value. Goldstar built a fabrication plant at Kumi in 1984 for production of

computer and telecommunications chips, with technology transferred from AT&T. It also invested around $60 million in a design centre based at Sunnyvale in Silicon Valley to coordinate its joint ventures with US partner firms. In 1986 Goldstar further diversified, taking advantage of the Korean government's decision to phase down its public sector R&D support for the semiconductor industry, and purchased the obsolete semiconductor fabrication line at KIET.

45 On the history of the LG group, including its long-established relations with Hitachi, see Taniura (1993).

46 *Far Eastern Economic Review*, 24 August 1989: 50–1.

47 These fabrication lines produced the 64K DRAM and then a 256K DRAM licensed from Vitelic, and the 64K SRAM and 256K SRAM licensed from Mosel.

48 The OEM contract never matured into a licensing arrangement or strategic alliance; it was discontinued by mutual agreement in 1992.

49 Under the leadership of its CEO, Chung Mong-Hun, Hyundai invested heavily in new equipment to keep itself in sight of the world technological frontier. His attitude is summed up by his comment that: 'The semiconductor is by its very nature a risky business. To make a decision based on 100 per cent confidence means you are too late. A 55 per cent level of confidence is acceptable.' The remark encapsulates the Korean high-risk approach to industry creation.

50 It entered the Dataquest world ranking at number 10 in 1995, on the strength of strong DRAM sales, but dropped back in 1996 and 1997 as DRAM prices slumped and revenue plummeted. In 1998 Hyundai was engaged in protracted talks over the absorption of LG Semicon.

51 In 1986 Texas Instruments filed a suit against Samsung and the eight Japanese chipmakers, while Intel filed against Hyundai. These suits were eventually settled in favour of the American firms, forcing the Koreans to pay millions of dollars in royalties, in addition to the interest charges they were bearing for the substantial loans incurred.

52 Overall, between 1982 and 1986, a total of 53 technology transfer agreements were concluded by Korean firms. Of these, 48 involved wafer-fabrication technologies. The US was the major source, providing 36 such agreements; Japan provided 13 (Hong 1992: 198).

53 In that year, Samsung allocated 240 billion *won* to semiconductor product development efforts, while Goldstar allocated 37 billion *won*, and Hyundai 30 billion *won*. Thus there was in effect created in Korea not one 'national system of innovation' but *three* – one in Samsung, one in Goldstar and one in Hyundai.

54 In 1992 Samsung signed a comprehensive technology cooperation agreement with Toshiba to jointly develop NAND-type flash memory devices in competition with Intel's competing NOR-based standard. The agreement evolved from cooperative development and production of 16M devices to 64M devices in 1995.

55 Under this agreement, Samsung was to embed the ARM6, ARM7 and ARM610 technology in products to be jointly developed from 1995 onwards.

56 A punitive tariff of 11 per cent was placed in response to dumping charges; Hyundai was cleared of these charges in early 1996, and the US Department of Commerce agreed to refund millions of dollars collected by the tariff.

57 They included the following: Metaflow – a small design house producing

high-speed RISC chips, such as advanced workstation CPUs; Maxtor – a leading US producer of hard disks which fell on hard times, and was eventually acquired by HEI; Image Quest Technologies Inc – a start-up firm focusing on technologies needed to produce thin film transistor liquid crystal displays (TFT LCDs); BMI – a small producer of flash memories; HEI became an equity partner in 1994, and produced its first flash memory chips in 1995; Laser Byte – a producer of optical disk drives; ICT – a producer of programmable logic devices (PLDs) based in San Jose, Silicon Valley. HEI held a major equity position. ICT was founded in 1991 after acquiring the business originally established by International CMOS Technology, in 1983.

58   Dr Kim earned his PhD at the University of Florida, then worked in the US semiconductor industry, with Harris Semiconductor, RCA Laboratories, and Digital Equipment Corporation. He was a consulting engineer for DEC when he got the call from Goldstar to return to Korea.

59   Indeed in 1996 it was announced that Anam would construct an ASIC wafer foundry in Korea, in a joint venture with Texas Instruments. This was put on hold in 1997.

60   The conglomerate Il Jin was planning to build a $750 million fab at Hwasung, on the outskirts of Seoul, to come on stream in late 1997. However the project was abandoned as the DRAM market took a downturn in 1996.

61   Again the financial crisis of 1997 forced this proposal to be put on hold.

62   This was frequently pointed out by the KSIA, and used to counter charges from the US that Korea is running an excessive trade surplus with the US on DRAMs.

63   Indeed, it was the entry of Korean firms such as Samsung and Hyundai into chip production, and their eagerness for state-of-the-art equipment, that helped revive the fortunes of some US firms such as Applied Materials Inc and Lam Research. This too was used as a factor in trade disputes over DRAMs.

64   See the study by the Bank of Korea, *List of Import-Inducing Effects of Korea's Major Goods* (Seoul: Bank of Korea, 1993; cited in Bernard and Ravenhill 1995: 191).

65   From the US, Korea imported mainly ion implantation and testing/measurement equipment from companies such as Varian, Applied Materials, and the Silicon Valley Group's Micrascan. From Japan, Korea imported photolithography equipment such as steppers from Nikon and Canon, and photoresist and wafer cleansers and diffusion systems from TEL.

66   As in the case of LAM and Applied Materials Korea.

67   MEMC Electronic Materials was the world's leading supplier of advanced silicon products, with manufacturing facilities in the US, Europe, Japan, Malaysia, Korea (through the POSCO-Samsung joint venture) and, subsequently, in Taiwan. MEMC under its previous Monsanto ownership had been involved in an earlier joint venture with the Korean firm Dongbu Industrial, known as Korsil, which established a wafer polishing plant at Kumi as early as 1986.

68   Initially it entered a technology transfer agreement with the US firm, Siltec Corp in 1985; this operation absorbed the Dongbu joint venture, which had bought out Monsanto's shares, and the combined operations were relaunched in 1991 as Siltron Inc. In this way LG's operation absorbed Monsanto's.

69 The Mirae operation, located on the Chonan complex, manufactured test handlers. In 1994 the company won an export contract from Texas Instruments to supply its Portuguese IC fabrication facility. Mirae was given financial and other encouragement from Samsung to upgrade its efforts from production of simple magazines (chip containers) to sophisticated test handlers. The firm DI Corporation (formerly Dong-Il) was involved in production of test equipment for the semiconductor industry since 1988. Shinsung Engineering was a general industrial systems company that became involved in supply of clean-room facilities for semiconductor fabrication in 1991. Shinsung produced the fan-filter unit which is the core of clean-room facilities, and had already captured 95 per cent of the domestic market in Korea for this highly specialised product; it was exporting its clean-room systems to Taiwan, Malaysia and the Philippines. Shinsung expanded its technological capabilities through a joint venture with Asyst Technologies, the US-based supplier of modular clean-room equipment.

70 The largest supplier of materials (such as gases, silicon and etching materials) was Japan, accounting for 36 per cent of supplies in 1995. The US supplied only 7 per cent (from 21 per cent in 1993). Local supplies were 46 per cent, while other countries accounted for 5 per cent. The US was source of many of the basic chemicals, while Japan was the source for specialised process chemicals and resins.

71 Some of the local production initiatives for semiconductor materials were as follows: POSCO-Huls – a joint venture between POSCO (Korea's steel company), Samsung and MEMC, to produce 6-inch and 8-inch silicon wafers (operational in 1993, providing 6-inch and 8-inch wafers); Siltron – a wafer supply operation sold by Monsanto to Goldstar in 1989; Dupont Korea Photo Mask (a wholly owned subsidiary of the US firm) to produce masks; it became operational in 1992; Hoechst Korea (a joint venture between Hoechst and Handok) to supply photo resist material; Dongwoo Pure Chemical (a joint venture between Dong Yang and Sumitomo of Japan) for the supply of wet chemicals (operational in 1993); Korea Specialty Gases (a joint venture between Hankuk Gas and the Japanese firm Dakachio) for supply of specialty gases; Samyoung Pure Chemicals (joint venture between Youngwoo and Mitsubishi Gas) for supply of wet chemicals such as hydrogen peroxide; and Samsung Aerospace – supply of leadframe packaging material, through a technology alliance with US firms Composite and Vanguard.

72 In 1994, the Korean government announced a joint public–private assistance program, offering 200 billion *won* ($244 million) over the next three years to encourage the development of local suppliers of chip-making equipment and materials. Existing chip makers and suppliers were to provide 60 per cent of the funds, and the government 40 per cent (by arranging long-term bank loans, to be refunded). A joint steering committee was formed to identify the projects that showed most promise.

73 In 1993 an agreement with Texas Instruments was reached, whereby Samsung took over a share of the TI fabrication plant in Oporto, Portugal. The new company, TI-Samsung Electronica Portugal (TISEP) gave Samsung direct access to the European DRAM market.

74 See also Chapter 2 and Chapter 6.

75 The consortium plan called for 28 participants – three from state-run research institutes, three from large companies, five from medium-sized

firms supplying materials, design and equipment, and 17 from universities. The goals announced included developing a 16M DRAM by March 1991 and a 64M DRAM by March 1993, with ETRI as coordinator.

76   Total budget for the joint R&D project over four years (1994–98) was $244 million ($61 million per year). This needs to be contrasted with the total R&D spending of the Big Three each year of $750 million to $1 billion; they were allocating a considerable proportion of this budget to joint research, but maintaining their own individual strength as well.

77   The joint research budget was to be allocated as follows: $130 million to device makers (i.e. the Big Three) at commercial loan rates (with interest charges of 6–7 per cent); $94 million to device makers and equipment and material suppliers, at government loan rates (i.e. no interest charges); $60 million to device makers; $24 million to equipment suppliers; and $10 million to materials suppliers. A further $20 million was allocated to universities and research institutes in the form of grants to projects thought worthy of support.

78   The three major areas of research to be supported under the ABST project were: IC fabrication technology needed for 256M DRAM production; advances in equipment and materials supply technology (e.g. etching, CVD, sputtering, tracking, furnaces, cleaning systems). Some of these projects were to be conducted jointly with overseas companies such as the US firms Varian and Applied Materials, and the Japanese firms Dai Nippon Screen and TEL, indicating a degree of internationalisation of the Korean industry.

79   Such as through provision of R&D-stimulating finance and the promotion of product development collaborative consortia.

80   Based on its five-year plan, the MTI selected a list of 146 technologies to be promoted in Korea, allocating a total of 24.7 billion *won* to this purpose (11.5 billion *won* coming from the government, and 13.2 billion *won* from the private sector). The specific development of next-generation 16M and 64M DRAMs was singled out, with 2 billion *won* being allocated to this goal.

81   In relation to the semiconductor industry, the G7 program called for the development of a 64M DRAM by 1993 (achieved ahead of target), a 256M DRAM by 1996 (achieved ahead of target by Samsung) and a 1G DRAM by 2000. However there were few funds attached to this program, and the targets must be seen as largely symbolic.

CHAPTER 4

A Cat Can Look at a King:
How Taiwan Did it

In the mid-1980s, when Japan and the US were locked in their battle for world supremacy in semiconductors, and Korean firms like Samsung were making their first forays into the DRAM sector, the Taiwanese semiconductor industry did not look much like a threat. There were several foreign-owned and domestic IC packaging and testing companies operating at the 'back end' of the semiconductor value chain and a few IC design houses that took advantage of the favourable conditions at the Hsinchu Science-based Industry Park. But there were only two IC fabrication plants on the island – one operated by the public-sector research institute, ERSO, and one operated by the ERSO spin-off company, UMC. By international standards the latter was a very small company, and its output was limited to simple LSI chips for consumer product applications such as toys, watches and greeting cards. Plans to produce DRAMs or other complex IC products like microprocessors seemed a long way off.

Only ten years later, the Taiwan semiconductor industry had risen to be the fourth largest in the world, and its firms were holding their own in international competition, and entering strategic alliances with the cream of the Japanese, European and American industry players. Like the cat in the fairy story, Taiwan had shown that it could look the industry leaders in the face. Clearly there was a lot more happening in Taiwan in the mid-1980s than was evident to the outside observer.

The roots of Taiwan's semiconductor activities go back to the plans and strategies of some remarkably prescient men. In the early 1970s, Y. S. Sun, a technologist–politician who had headed up Taiwan's electric power utility, and had become the Minister for Economic Affairs, was laying the foundations for Taiwan's technological upgrading at a time when the rest of the world saw the country as a source for plastic toys and

157

low-cost running shoes. The Industrial Technology Research Institute (ITRI) was founded near Hsinchu, south of Taipei, in 1973 under his stewardship of the ministry. ITRI would become the driving force behind Taiwan's industrial upgrading; no sooner was it established than Sun was developing plans for advanced industries like semiconductors to feed into the country's nascent electronics industry and for export.

In August 1974 Sun met with his colleague and friend, Dr Pan Wen-Yuan, in Princeton, New Jersey to discuss how to take Taiwan into the 'knowledge-intensive' industries then being pioneered in the US by companies such as Fairchild, and being emulated by Japan. Pan was a brilliant electrical engineer employed at the David Sarnoff Laboratories, then one of the premier industrial labs in the US, at RCA. They agreed that the electronics industry would be the key to Taiwan's future high-technology development, and that it would need to have a foundation in a semiconductor and IC industry whose elements would have to be leveraged from abroad. They identified Chinese engineers working in US technology companies as their key to launching the new industry. Pan then acted on his initial meeting to form an advisory group at Princeton. It met regularly and came to be known as the Technical Advisory Committee. Specific recommendations for starting a new semiconductor industry were framed by this committee, and taken to Cabinet by Sun. The Taiwanese government agreed to establish a specialist laboratory under the auspices of ITRI to kickstart the industry. This led to the creation of ERSO in 1974, whose head was immediately charged with the task of developing the technological capabilities needed to generate a semiconductor industry.

ERSO scoured the world for knowledge of IC fabrication, emulating Japanese methods of study tours and knowledge leverage, and used the Princeton-based network of advisers meeting with Pan. Under Pan's influence, in 1976 RCA was prevailed upon to transfer its obsolete IC fabrication technology to the fledgling ERSO. RCA was at this point thinking of getting out of semiconductors, and saw no harm in earning some royalties on its 7-micron technology, then severely behind the world LSI best of 2-micron circuit design. From ERSO's perspective, the technology transfer from RCA offered a window into the secret world of advanced technology. A group of young and enthusiastic engineers spent the best part of a year in the US and at ERSO learning the technology of IC fabrication from RCA. It is out of this group that virtually the entire senior echelons of the subsequent semiconductor industry in Taiwan was formed.

ERSO built its pilot IC fabrication plant under RCA guidance, and started producing its own experimental chips. ICs such as those needed in electronic watches were produced first, using RCA designs. Later the

ERSO engineers were able to produce their own designs, and tweak their equipment to improve the yields, so much so that by 1978 or 1979 ERSO was securing better yields than RCA itself. The US firm started buying chips from its erstwhile pupil, albeit on a very small scale.

But Taiwan's leaders were much more ambitious. Principal among these leaders, apart from Sun, who became premier in 1979, was Dr K. T. Li. He served as Minister for Economic Affairs before Sun, and went on from there to the Ministry of Finance. Li had been a brilliant young Chinese physicist, educated at Cambridge, where he performed original research in the Cavendish Laboratory before being caught up in the Sino–Japanese war of the 1930s. His contribution to China's war effort was a radio-based detection system used to provide advance warning of air raids. Subsequently he transferred to business and rose to be head of a shipbuilding company which left the mainland and crossed to Taiwan with the Kuomintang in 1949.

Li soon became involved in government affairs, taking over the Ministry of Economic Affairs in 1965, followed by the Ministry of Finance in 1969, from where he directed the flow of capital into Taiwan's industrialisation programs. His most notable achievement up to this point had been the creation of Taiwan's first Export Processing Zone outside Kaohsiung. It was the world's first example of a duty-free manufacturing enclave, modelled on the duty-free ports established by the British in Singapore and Penang in the nineteenth century.

As ERSO was embarking on its semiconductor venture, Li retired from the Ministry of Finance, and looked around for ways to stimulate the country's high-technology development. His first act was to call together the country's scientific and technical elite to consider the country's future. This conference, staged in 1978 and attended by 400 of the country's best and brightest, proved to be a landmark event. The conference adopted a 'Science and Technology Development Program' which was subsequently endorsed by Cabinet. This document targeted semiconductors and computers, energy, materials and automation as the sectors of most strategic value for Taiwan. It called for the creation of a new permanent advisory body, to be named the Science and Technology Advisory Group, chaired by Li.[1] Most significantly, it called for the creation of specialist infrastructure needed to support advanced industries like semiconductors.

Such a project was championed by Professor S. S. Shu, who had been President of the National Tsinghua University, and served as President of the National Science Council and as Chairman of ITRI. From these influential positions he shepherded the idea of a specialist knowledge-intensive industry park, as a public-sector counterpart in Taiwan to Stanford's Silicon Valley. This became a special project of the National

Science Council (NSC), which overcame considerable opposition and scepticism in the Taiwan Cabinet to have the new park created under its auspices, and secure land near Hsinchu from the Taiwan military for its establishment. The new park, located near the ITRI campus and the Tsinghua University was duly launched in 1980. The Hsinchu/ITRI/Tsinghua complex has been an extremely important element in Taiwan's semiconductor success, housing all the firms founded through the 1980s.

The first of these was not a creation of the private sector, but of ERSO itself. By 1980, while Taiwan had many firms engaged in back-end IC activities such as packaging and testing, there were no LSI front-end activities. So Premier Sun, Dr Li, Dr Hu Ding-Hua, the head of ERSO, and Dr Shih Chintay, head of the IC pilot plant, created a company to do so. ERSO was charged with formulating the plan for the launch, which resulted in the formation of the United Microelectronics Corporation (UMC) in 1980. It was established with around $14 million in capital, 49 per cent of which was provided by state investment vehicles. The founding of UMC marked the beginning of a commercial semiconductor industry in Taiwan. It was the first company to be located in the new Hsinchu Science-based Industry Park and has prospered there ever since, evolving into a group of companies that, by the end of the 1990s, is engaged in a broad range of semiconductor activities and earning over $1 billion a year in revenue.

Taiwan's semiconductor industry took an enormous leap forward in the mid-1980s with the founding of Taiwan Semiconductor Manufacturing Corporation (TSMC) as a joint venture with the Dutch multinational Philips. TSMC was the brainchild of Dr Morris Chang, who joined ITRI as its new president in 1985. He had a long career behind him in the world semiconductor industry, heading up Texas Instruments' global semiconductor operations, before becoming President of General Instruments. From there he was recruited to head up ITRI, a far-sighted move on the part of Taiwan's leaders. Chang brought with him the concept of a silicon foundry, then practised as a sideline by semiconductor firms to use spare capacity in building chips for third parties. Chang saw that the costs of establishing wafer fabs would continue to rise, and that there would be a future market for a full-time silicon foundry. Such a venture could also play a critical role in fabricating ICs for Taiwan's small chip design firms which could not afford to build the chips themselves.

TSMC was launched in 1986 as the world's first 'pure play' silicon foundry, working on contract with IC firms and not producing products of its own. Its operations, thanks to the technology transferred from Philips, brought it abreast of the world technological frontier. Chang became the chairman of TSMC, and in that capacity oversaw its expansion into DRAM fabrication – as major shareholder in the new Vanguard Semiconductor venture in 1995 – and its expansion overseas in the form of WaferTech, which built a wafer plant in Camas, Washington, in a joint venture with US semiconductor firms.[2]

ERSO continued to spin-off new ventures, both officially (like UMC and TSMC) and unofficially, as clever engineers left to start their own firms – usually with ERSO's full blessing, which was in the business of building a viable semiconductor industry in Taiwan. One of these was Dr Yang Ding-Yuan, who left with his staff in 1987 to found a new company. Yang had held various posts in ERSO, most recently as analyst of its various business ventures before making the break in 1987. He secured financial backing from the Walsin Lihwa corporation, and founded Winbond (whose Chinese characters, Hua Bang, can be interpreted to mean 'a self-governing community of professionals'). Winbond grew rapidly under Yang's guidance to become the island's largest producer of branded ICs. The company has paired off with the world's leading multinationals like Hewlett-Packard and Toshiba to secure advanced technologies and act as second-source producer. In this way, Winbond entered DRAM production in the mid-1990s, through a technology transfer and second-source production agreement with Toshiba. It has continued to expand its wafer-fabrication facilities, opening a fourth plant in 1998 in Hsinchu, and by the end of the 1990s plans to open several more facilities in Taiwan's second science-based industry park at Tainan.

The scale and breadth of the semiconductor industry in Taiwan is based on these strong foundations laid by visionary pioneers. Like the cat in the fairy story, Taiwan looked the leaders of the world semiconductor industry in the eye as an equal. Its wide range of firms producing at the world's technological frontier reflects the depth of training provided to the original cadre of engineers in ERSO's pilot plant in the late 1970s. The former leaders Sun, Pan and Li would be pleased with all this, but probably not surprised. After all, this is what they planned for.

The Nurturing and Flowering of a Semiconductor Industry in Taiwan

Taiwan's creation of a semiconductor industry can be described within the framework of the four-stage process we are calling 'developmental resource leverage'.[3] There was a preparatory stage before any firms or activities were established, as the electronics industry as end-user was building its strength, and as a technology-intensive industrial direction for Taiwan was being established as a policy goal. There was a 'seeding' phase, as the initial technology transfer for semiconductor fabrication

Table 4.1　Stages in the evolution of the Taiwanese semiconductor industry

Stage I Pre-1976 Preparation	Stage II 1976–79 Seeding	Stage III 1980–88 Technology Absorption and Propagation	Stage IV 1989–98 Sustainability
Labour-intensive semiconductor back-end operations (assembly) and testing Dominated by foreign multinationals Establishment of ITRI and ERSO	Licensing of IC fabrication technology, and its adoption by public sector R&D institute Phase I of Electronics Industry Development Program	Technology absorption and enterprise diffusion Establishment of secure infrastructure in the form of the Hsinchu Science-based Industry Park ERSO acquires skills covering all phases of semiconductor manufacturing, moving from LSI to VSLI Spin-off of private companies and entry of private sector	Entry of firms to cover all phases of semiconductor manufacturing and full product range, including DRAMs From VLSI to ULSI technology Submicron stage of public-sector led R&D Cooperative R&D system of innovation established

was effected, and allowed to take root. This was followed by a third diffusion or propagation phase, as more and more companies entered the industry, and the institutional structures in Taiwan ensured rapid transmission of technological capability throughout the sector. The fourth and final phase brings us into the 1990s, as the industry has expanded and developed the institutional, technical and financial sources of sustainability through the range of firms involved, the breadth of products and processes employed, the depth of expertise developed and the internationalisation of its activities. The four phases we use in this exposition are given in Table 4.1.[4]

Stage I: Pre-1976 – Preparation

The 1960s saw the 'miracle' of Taiwan's industrialisation take off, with rapid build-up of manufacturing industries and export-led growth. Unlike Japan and Korea, where large firms had led the export effort, in Taiwan it was mainly small and medium-sized firms, often involved in direct contract manufacturing relations with US and European manufacturers, or retail chains such as J. C. Penney in the US.

The 1960s also saw US electronics and semiconductor firms looking to invest in low-cost manufacturing operations in East Asia, to transfer the production of discrete components, then assembly of chips, and finally test and assembly operations. Taiwan was not slow in encouraging such investment, establishing the world's first 'Export Processing Zone' for this purpose in 1965.[5] This opened the way to considerable investment by US, Japanese and European firms, particularly in the back end of the semiconductor cycle, encompassing testing, packaging and assembling. The first of these was a semiconductor assembly line established by the Microelectronics Division of the US firm, General Instruments. It marks the start of Taiwan's involvement in the world semiconductor industry. These activities tended to be rather isolated from the rest of the economy, and were encouraged for their export earnings rather than for any potential in terms of industrial development.

This period also saw the nascent indigenous Taiwanese electronics and IT industry becoming organised within the Taiwan Electrical Appliances Manufacturers Association (TEAMA), which represented the interests of the industry with government and ensured that multinationals did not monopolise the government's attention.

The 1960s and 1970s saw a period of intense debate in Taiwan about the country's future, and its ability to sustain a model of high-tech development without depending on multinationals or on large existing firms as in Korea or Japan.[6] The issue for the country was to identify and build the institutions which could successfully 'seed' new high-technology industries such as semiconductors.

A decisive phase in Taiwan's industrial development was opened in 1973 with the establishment of the Industrial Technology Research Institute (ITRI) to promote technological leverage, and the Development Fund to promote financial or capital leverage. ITRI was modelled in many ways on Korea's successful establishment of the Korean Institute of Science and Technology (with UN assistance), which in turn had been modelled closely on Japan's Agency for Science and Technology. Thus the patterns of East Asian high-technology industrialisation are diffused and disseminated.

Stage II: 1976–79 – Seeding

Electronics and semiconductors were recognised by the founders of ITRI and the country's science and technology elite as necessary 'drivers' of Taiwan's high-technology development. Firms such as Tatung and Sampo emerged as early exponents of successful mass production in electronic goods. Until the early 1970s they were dependent for technology leverage on their own efforts, through the contract manufacturing arrangements they were able to secure. ITRI had been established in 1973 with public funds under the direct sponsorship of the Minister of Economic Affairs, Y. S. Sun, to support the growing electronics industry and to develop a components industry, particularly semiconductors. It formulated plans for the production of integrated circuits as its very first project. To focus activities on this topic the Electronics Research Centre (later renamed ERSO: Electronics Research Service Organization) was established in 1974. This marks the beginning of a conscious and planned strategy for seeding the development of an indigenous IC-producing semiconductor industry.

It was clear that if Taiwan were to enter the semiconductor industry, it would have to do so through some form of technology acquisition from one of the then dominant firms, such as Philips, RCA, National Semiconductor or Texas Instruments. A strategy of technology licensing and transfer – a comprehensive 'technology transfer agreement' – would have seemed the most attractive. After all, Taiwan had few established large firms in electronics, and they were unable or unwilling at this stage to run the risks associated with major technological upgrading – as were their counterparts in Korea at this time. Thus the public sector was chosen as the means for Taiwan's acquisition of a new industry, rather than relying on multinationals to transfer technology within their own operations, or on the further development of indigenous giant firms, as in Korea. This was a political choice, taken at the highest levels of the Taiwan government and the Kuomintang.

The strategy was finessed with the assistance of an informal Technical Advisory Committee consisting of Chinese engineers working for leading US electronics firms, which prepared a report to the Taiwan Cabinet on how a semiconductor industry could be seeded. The report made the following recommendations: that Taiwan should entertain the possibility of developing an advanced semiconductor industry as the core of its electronics sector; technology transfer should be implemented initially by inviting US companies to bid for a contract (Japanese firms were considered too closed and unlikely to respond to such an approach); CMOS was to be the technology of choice – a far-sighted decision given its subsequent significance as dominant semiconductor manufacturing technology; technical training for engineers was essential, preferably to be carried out in the US with government funds to be found to support the engineers during their training; and a promotion centre of the semiconductor industry should be established within a state agency.

This was an intelligent strategy that had a long-term focus. At this stage it was not concerned with any specific products (for instance, DRAMs versus logic circuits) but with the build-up of a core level of expertise that would nourish an indigenous industry. Its focus was institutional support for the development of technological capability and its rapid diffusion. Its recommendations were followed through meticulously.

Technology Transfer

The government charged ERSO with the task of 'seeding' a semi-conductor industry, through technology transfer, in line with the recommendations of the Pan report.[7] This was to be effected through a comprehensive international technology transfer agreement. ERSO, the public-sector agency, was looking for a partner firm that would be prepared to divulge the secrets of semiconductors. Candidates in Europe, Japan and the US were approached, but none showed interest. Finally, under the influence of the technical advisory group headed by Dr Pan, then working for the US electronics firm RCA, ERSO was successful in signing a technology transfer agreement with RCA. This firm agreed to transfer its obsolete 7-micron IC technology for a royalty charge, and to train a group of up to 40 engineers in the design and fabrication of chips.[8] Over the course of a year the engineers acquired these skills and learned to produce simple chips for watches and calculators. The group of young engineers who were trained in RCA laboratories and IC design studios returned to ITRI/ERSO, and with public funds from the Electronic Industry Development Program were able to put together a pilot IC fabrication plant that was soon turning out commercial-grade chips.

This was 1977, and it marks the point where an IC industry in Taiwan could be said to have started – even though there were no firms directly involved. Over the next few years the yields from the ERSO pilot plant were steadily improved, in a form of 'learning by doing', and the ERSO staff built up and deepened their technical capabilities in the semi-conductor industry. This provided the 'absorptive capacity' needed to launch a successful industry.

Public funding of this first step in building semiconductor competencies was provided under a program called the Electronic Industry Development Program (EIDP). A total of NT$410 million (around $11 million) was expended by the public agencies, principally ERSO, to purchase equipment, in payments to RCA, and in the employment and training of engineers. This was small beer compared to the huge investments being made by Japanese and US firms at the time, but it was a significant expenditure for a small latecomer like Taiwan, with what must have seemed at the time a very low chance of achieving a payback.

By the close of the 1970s, semiconductor technology had been leveraged by ITRI from RCA, and absorbed and assimilated by a young group of engineers who were anxious to see Taiwan make an impression in the world of high technology. By now public debate, spurred on by the science and technology forum staged by Dr Li in 1978, was favouring a stronger push towards knowledge and skill-intensive industrial development, backed by intensive efforts to upgrade the quality and quantity of technical university training of engineers. The stage was set for dissemination – but as yet no Taiwanese companies were prepared to invest in this high-risk industry. The high-technology industrialisation effort threatened to abort, in the absence of further decisive interventions.

Stage III: 1980–88 – Technology Absorption and Propagation

Propagation called for the creation of new infrastructure, enhancement of the technological capabilities located within ERSO and a determined push to create a private sector for semiconductor activities. In 1978 a Science and Technology congress managed to generate all-important political support for the push to lift Taiwan's technological competence, and in particular to continue with the (relatively) expensive promotion of an IC industry, whose prospects of a financial return were still remote. The congress also managed to start up a Science and Technology development program and have its major recommendations adopted by Cabinet.

One outcome of the forum was the formation of a Science and Technology Advisory Group (STAG), chaired by Dr K. T. Li, reporting directly to Premier Sun. This group, consisting largely of foreign experts who would meet for several days at a time to debate potential technology options and strategies, came to play an influential role in the development of Taiwan's high-technology industries generally, and its semiconductor industry in particular. STAG was in turn divided into two Technical Review Boards, covering the semiconductor industry and the electronics industry generally.[9]

By far the most significant of the forum's recommendations was for the creation of high-technology infrastructure in the form of a Science-based Industry Park. It is the creation of this Park in 1980 that we take as the milestone signalling the opening of a new phase of 'propagation' of high-technology capabilities in Taiwan. The task of creating this institution was entrusted to the National Science Council, which after much searching in crowded Taiwan eventually appropriated land near Hsinchu from the Taiwan military as the site of the Park. Taiwan has had many industry parks before and since, but this one was very special, designed to create the 'industrial ecology' in which high-technology industries could flourish.[10]

Private-sector Encouragement

Despite the strenuous urging of the Ministry of Economic Affairs, leading electronics firms in Taiwan such as Mitac, Sampo and Tatung elected not to enter the semiconductor field at this stage, viewing it as still too risky. (At the same time, Korean electronics firms were likewise resisting the urging of government; Samsung and Hyundai delayed making major commitments until 1982–83.) Thus the government elected to become a 'collective entrepreneur', in Gerschenkronian fashion, and undertook the launching of the first private-sector firm itself.

This was to be the first in a series of successful 'spin-off' ventures designed to establish a private-sector semiconductor capability in Taiwan. A 100 per cent publicly owned venture was quickly ruled out, due to the already large size of the Taiwanese public sector.[11] A proposal was submitted to the Ministry of Economic Affairs (MoEA) from ERSO for the formation of a public–private joint venture in 1978.[12] The Ministry eventually accepted the proposal, and mobilised capital input from the private sector. The venture was launched as United Microelectronics Corporation (UMC) with capital of NT$500 million (around $14 million), raised from a consortium put together under the 'guidance' of the MoEA.[13] ERSO provided all its initial resources, including technical staff.

UMC quickly raised further capital to build an independent fabrication facility, on a site in the newly established Hsinchu Park. From this facility, UMC turned out a variety of profitable chips for such consumer applications as digital watches, calculators, musical equipment and television. It was able to commence pilot runs in April 1982, and by November 1982 it had reached commercial break-even point.[14] Taiwan's semiconductor fabrication industry was now launched.[15]

Public-sector Capabilities Enhancement

Phase I of the EIDP had been charged with acquiring the basics of semiconductor technology, and in this it had been highly successful. A new phase of the program, Stage II, which lasted from 1979 to 1983, provided the framework within which these basics could be extended to such associated operations as IC mask making, computer-aided IC design and high-density process technology. This was the time when the US–Japanese 'DRAM wars' were intensifying. Taiwan wisely chose to steer clear of this controversial product, and instead devoted its resources to designing and fabricating the host of semiconductor devices – logic chips, input-output devices, customised circuits – that were being demanded by the electronics industry as the possibilities of large-scale integration became clear. This was a product strategy quite similar to that pursued by Japan in the late 1960s and 1970s before the focus on DRAMs, in that it was geared towards consumer demand and entailed relatively simple technology.

The early 1980s saw ERSO expanding the breadth of its semiconductor technical capabilities and its range of IC products in areas such as IC design, IC applications, testing, and mastering the various phases of process technology. New advanced process equipment was acquired (such as computer-aided IC design systems) and engineers trained in their operation. ITRI adopted a liberal attitude to skilled staff leaving to start their own companies; this was after all one of the goals with which the organisation had been founded. Thus the early 1980s also saw the founding of several IC design studios, such as Syntek, by former ITRI staff; these firms found a natural home on the Hsinchu Park. More technology was licensed by ERSO from abroad to expand its capabilities – such as in advanced mask fabrication technology, licensed from the Californian firm International Materials Research (IMR). All this was accomplished within the ambit of Phase II of the Electronic Industry Development Project, with public funding of NT$796 million (around $22 million).[16] Thus leverage and diffusion promotion were being exercised through acquisition of equipment, the movement and transfer of staff, and licensing of technologies from abroad. However, healthy though the Taiwan industry was at this stage, it was still confined to a single IC fabrication company, UMC, in terms of contract testing and IC assembly, and operating at a relatively low (LSI) technical level. The majority of activity was in contract or multinational IC test and assembly activities, and some IC design work. There was as yet no advanced VLSI semiconductor activity.

Technological upgrading was the essential price of entry into the exclusive club of the semiconductor industry. By its own efforts, ERSO managed to improve its fabrication technology from 7-micron geometry to 5 micron in 1980, and 4.5 micron by 1981. At this time the world leaders in Japan and the US were starting production of 64K DRAMs using VLSI geometry of 2-micron line-width. Taiwan was still well behind the world leaders. Could the gap be closed at the current rate of progress?

The Push for VLSI Capability

The foreign advisers grouped in STAG expressed a forceful view that the gap was not being closed, and indeed was widening. While great progress had been made in Phases I and II of the EIDP, and a new company,

UMC, had been launched, nevertheless a visitor to ERSO in 1981 or 1982 would not have regarded the 4.5-micron pilot fab line as being in the same league as the operations already underway in the US, Europe and Japan. The STAG advisers argued strongly that Taiwan should set its sights higher to achieve VLSI capability of 1-micron standard or better, which would bring it on a par with the world's best.[17] This view was opposed equally as vigorously by many in ERSO, who argued that Taiwan should proceed patiently in its acquisition of an expanding spectrum of technologies and processes and not risk a major commercial setback by pressing ahead too fast. The STAG view was also opposed forcefully by economic officials in the Ministry of Finance and the Council for Economic Planning and Development (CEPD), who were more concerned with Taiwan's macroeconomic stability than with the promotion of any particular technology. The early 1980s saw this debate pursued with some vigour in government circles.[18]

At this point, senior figures in the government intervened to 'raise the bar' of technical expectations in Taiwan. Strong support was expressed, by the President and Premier Sun, for Taiwan's achieving VLSI capability, and efforts were set in train to secure the financial resources needed to reach such an ambitious goal. Their efforts put ITRI/ERSO on 'red alert' while work continued on the LSI pilot fabrication line. Eventually the new goal was agreed and released publicly in 1983 in the form of a new Phase III of the EIDP. It was backed by a huge increase in public funds, of the order of $72.5 million (NT$2.9 billion), nearly *four* times the level of expenditure on Phase II.

The goal was explicit: Taiwan was to achieve 1-micron VLSI capability by 1988 or earlier, an extraordinarily ambitious goal given the level of development of Taiwan industry at the time and the still marginal involvement of the private sector.[19]

Phase III of EIDP: VLSI Project, 1984–88

The VLSI project was entrusted by the government once again to ERSO, which embarked on plans for the assault on 1-micron technological capability. While UMC had argued that it was the appropriate vehicle, the view prevailed that it was premature to entrust such an important mission to a still small private firm. The aim of the VLSI project was to build a working VLSI plant at ERSO using VLSI technology and provide a Common Design Centre for chip design firms to develop application products. This time, ERSO did not turn to a large established multinational like RCA for technology import, but instead signed joint development agreements with Silicon Valley start-up firms such as Mosel and Vitelic to develop VLSI chips.[20]

ERSO was also active in seeding VLSI capabilities in the technical universities, providing projects to professors and their students. By April 1985 a geometry of 1.25 micron had been reached for CMOS memory ICs; by June 1986, the technology for a 1M CMOS memory chip became available. However there were no manufacturing facilities in Taiwan to produce these chips. While Taiwan's design capabilities were leaping ahead, its fabrication facilities lagged behind.[21] The immediate consequence was that designs had to be licensed to third parties for fabrication.[22]

There were comparable developments in the private sector, some successful and some decidedly unsuccessful. As a private firm UMC was also seeking to upgrade its product and process technologies, with the goal of achieving VLSI standard. UMC had acquired its own R&D staff of 75 engineers. US expertise was tapped through purchase of an equity stake in a small Silicon Valley company, Unicorn Microelectronics Corp. UMC thus provided itself with a 'listening post' in the heart of Silicon Valley. Through these leveraging and internal upgrading efforts, UMC achieved 1.25-micron VLSI capability in mid-1986, with the 16K and 64K static RAM memory chips. But process technology and fabrication capability were still lacking.[23]

The most dramatic failure in Taiwan at this time was that of Quasel, which attempted to create a major DRAM fabrication venture at Hsinchu in 1984 and 1985.[24] Large sums of money were raised by Quasel, but it was unable to bring DRAMs into the market profitably, and collapsed in 1986. Its failure shows that there were limits to the capabilities of the Taiwanese at this time. Likewise Mosel and Vitelic tried, but failed, to launch DRAM manufacturing ventures in Taiwan.[25] Further leverage was needed to bring the industry to a point where world-class firms could be launched.

Another failure involved the DRAM product designs Vitelic developed for ERSO. When Vitelic sold its design (developed on Taiwan public-sector funds) to the Korean firm Hyundai, it caused some disquiet among government ranks in Taiwan. This incident no doubt played some part in strengthening the hand of those arguing for a stronger push into full-scale commercial VLSI development. It was these mixed experiences of failure and success that brought discussions on VLSI manufacturing capability in Taiwan to a head.

VLSI Fabrication: TSMC The outcome of the VLSI project was a set of designs and state-of-the-art technology in a specially built laboratory housed within ERSO, with a view to spinning it off as a going concern. But the large scale of the funds involved proved to be an obstacle. In 1984, when a proposal was first mooted by ERSO and the MoEA for such a spin-off, no action was taken. But after the embarrassment of Vitelic's and Mosel's designer chips being licensed abroad for want of an adequate Taiwanese manufacturing capacity (UMC not proving to be a willing partner), talks to establish a new VLSI manufacturing facility progressed.

In 1985 Dr Morris Chang was recruited as the new President of ITRI. He had wide experience of the global semiconductor industry and within weeks of his appointment, was invited by the government to propose a new spin-off venture from ERSO that would take Taiwan into the VLSI era. Instead of proposing a conventional semiconductor company with its own product portfolio, Chang advocated for a pure-play 'silicon foundry' operating VLSI process technology to manufacture chips for small Taiwanese firms and international clients.[26] This was a radical and innovative proposal, which promised to create not only a company with commercial success, but one that could extend fabrication facilities to the island's IC design houses. It was accepted by government leaders on ITRI's recommendation. The source of capital for such a large project – it was costed at $220 million – remained the stumbling block.

Premier Yu stipulated that this spin-off was not to be financed entirely by the government; indeed it was to have majority private-sector support. This was a way of forcing the pace of private-sector involvement in the semiconductor industry. But it proved very difficult to attract funds of the required order. So Premier Yu gave ITRI the go-ahead to find a multi-national backer whose involvement would give the project greater credibility. This too was a radical step, and out of line with prevailing Taiwan thinking on direct foreign investment at the time. Chang got to work, canvassing support among his international business contacts and erstwhile colleagues – but 1985 was not a good year for seeking such investments, given the recession in the industry and the tough time many US companies were having because of the Japanese onslaught in the DRAM sector. Initial interest was expressed by four companies: Texas Instruments (Dr Chang's old firm), Intel, Matsushita and Philips. In the end, only Philips was a serious candidate for the new venture.[27] Negotiations with the multinational proceeded, and soon a deal was done, providing Philips with substantial equity in the new venture, and calling on it to transfer VLSI technology.[28] After some more arm-twisting by the government, a group of Taiwanese firms were persuaded to make up the balance of the investment. In June 1986 it was announced that TSMC would be established, with Philips as its leading equity holder.[29] The concept of involving a major multinational was a bold one, and not altogether supported by ERSO. The aim, however, was to lift the Taiwanese semiconductor industry up to a new level of world-best practice. In this, the initiative has been quite remarkably successful. TSMC's launch in 1986 signals the serious arrival of Taiwan as a semiconductor producer, coincident with the settlement of US–Japanese hostilities in the form of the Semiconductor Trade Agreement, and the early successes of Korean firms in DRAMs.

How TSMC Acquired its Initial Technological Capabilities It was envisaged that TSMC would build its own 6-inch wafer foundry and in the intervening period, take over (rent) the VLSI fab from ERSO.[30] Philips agreed to transfer technology to the new company, as well as its own portfolio of cross-licensing agreements. These proved to be a most valuable asset for the fledgling company since they made it virtually immune from the kind of intellectual property disputes that plagued Korean and some Taiwan firms. Under the equity agreement, Philips supplied 2-micron and 1.5-micron technology for producing VLSI devices at no charge; it would collect fees for the more advanced technologies envisaged as being supplied in the future. These initial technology inputs, which accounted for 80 per cent of TSMC's initial competence, were in the form of Philips fabrication sequences, to be followed precisely.[31] A further 15 per cent of TSMC's know-how was transferred across from ERSO, and perhaps 5 per cent was acquired with the hiring of technical staff. The initial operations for customers forced a rapid move towards more advanced 1.2-micron process technology, with 50 per cent of the know-how coming from such customers as Philips and VLSI Technology (which demanded 1.2-micron processing for their chips, and transferred their specifications to assist TSMC to upgrade) and 50 per cent representing TSMC's own internal learning. By the time TSMC was able to make the move to 0.8-micron process technology, it was no longer dependent on transfer from Philips, and had moved on to a new leverage trajectory of relying on specification transfers from customers.

The immediate effect of TSMC's launch and its success was to take Taiwan to a new level of technical sophistication, and to spark the formation of dozens of small IC design houses in the Hsinchu region. Its demonstration also attracted serious Taiwan capital to invest in the semiconductor industry. Thus the object of the exercise – to launch UMC and then TSMC as 'demonstration' vehicles – was achieved, as skilled engineers voted with their feet, and capitalists with their finance, to enter the new industry. First the textiles giant Hualon invested in a semiconductor operation, Hualon Microelectronics Corporation (HMC), which has been a moderate success, and then the Walsin Lihwa conglomerate provided backing for a new start-up, Winbond, in 1987. This firm, barely into its second decade, has become the star of the Taiwan semiconductor industry, growing rapidly and acquiring expertise in

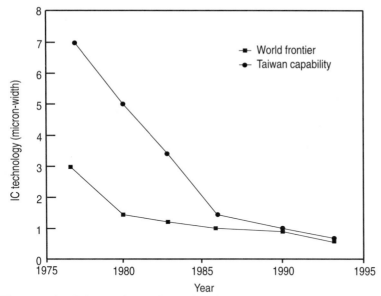

Figure 4.1   Taiwan closes the technology gap in semiconductors.
Source: ERSO.

designing, producing and marketing ICs in every segment of the market.

Meanwhile ERSO continued to expand its capabilities, and to transfer these across to the private sector as they became commercially viable. A third venture, the Taiwan Mask Corporation (TMC), embodying ERSO's chip mask-making capabilities, was launched in late 1989. This continued the leverage and diffusion drive which was now midway through its second decade since the establishment of ITRI in 1973 and ERSO in 1974.

By the close of the 1980s, one could say that the 'propagation' phase of a Taiwan semiconductor industry had been well set in train. A series of ventures had been established in IC wafer fabrication so that revenue from wafer fabrication was fast gaining on those earned from IC test and assembly, and IC design. (They would actually overtake them in 1992.) These firms exhibited technical capabilities across the board with the singular exception of DRAMs, which were still held to be too risky and capital-hungry for Taiwan's (relatively) small semiconductor firms, compared to the integrated corporate giants in Japan and Korea which had specialised in DRAMs and achieved stunning success in this field. The progress Taiwan made in closing the 'technology gap' with the advanced semiconductor firms is shown in Figure 4.1. Public policy now shifted towards eliminating this gap definitively and deepening the industry's 'roots' of sustainability.

Behind this achievement lay the efforts of the extraordinary companies that were starting to populate the Taiwan semiconductor industry. Winbond and Macronix represent cases where there was sufficient capability in the industry to launch specialist IC producers without explicit technology transfer agreements. TMC was a case of further leverage from ITRI/ERSO. Meanwhile UMC and TSMC made dramatic progress in developing and expanding their own capabilities through various leverage devices as well as their own internal R&D.

Winbond – Taiwan's Premier Specialist Semiconductor Producer The name Winbond is highly significant: its Chinese characters are '*hwa*' (Chinese kingdom) and '*bang*' (city state), which in combination can be taken to imply a self-governing community of professionals. The 'in' was added in English to denote 'intelligence' (as in the name of the US firm, Intel). The sense conveyed is that the company will grow through the collective application of intelligence.

Founded in 1987 as an 'unofficial' spin-off from ERSO, it is now emerging as one of Taiwan's most innovative semiconductor companies, producing a wide range of chips and operating several advanced fabrication facilities. Yet the company is still only very young. Since beginning operations in 1989, it expanded rapidly in terms of revenue, scale of production and scope of activities.[32] At the end of 1995 Winbond entered an agreement with Toshiba to become a DRAM producer. By the end of the 1990s it had emerged as Taiwan's number one 'own brand' semiconductor company.

Winbond is a particularly interesting semiconductor company because, perhaps more than any other company in Taiwan, it captures the spirit of high-technology capitalism being 'managed' to generate wealth. Winbond is the product of pure entrepreneurial spirit.[33] In 1987, the ERSO pilot plant (demonstration plant) had been functioning for ten years, and was looking for a new direction. UMC had been established, and TSMC was shortly to take over the operations of the VLSI project. At this point, Dr Yang elected to leave and in effect 'privatised' the ERSO lab through his own initiative. He found an investor, Walsin Lihwa Corporation, which had been one of the original investors in UMC, and which was keen to get more deeply involved in semiconductors.[34] Dr Yang then formed Winbond as an independent company, and with the capital contributed by his investors, hired most of the ERSO staff working on the now-defunct demonstration lab. Thus things renew themselves in Taiwan.

Winbond never intended to be a fabless IC company. From the outset, it determined to operate at a scale that would support the operation of a state-of-the-art fabrication facility. With the initial capital, facilities and equipment were bought. This fab, built in 1988, was the prime asset of the fledgling company. But demand soon outstripped its capacity, and a second was commissioned in 1991, and went on-line in 1992. It incorporated the most advanced submicron technology, taking Winbond to a prime position in the Taiwan industry. The funds to build Fab II were not raised externally, but had to be generated internally and through capital drawings on the existing investors. This is characteristic of Taiwan's cautious approach to expansion – a factor in its survival through financial storms that have afflicted other East Asian players.[35] In fact, the building of Fab II plunged Winbond into negative cash-flow for a time.

As a start-up only four years old, Winbond was one of the first firms in Taiwan to enter the submicron era and chose to specialise in strategically important semiconductor market segments. The company began as a memory and PC-chip maker, and moved on to ASICs, imaging chips and embedded processors, each requiring more sophisticated technological capabilities.[36]

What is quite remarkable is that by the early 1990s no less than 80 per cent of Winbond's sales were through its own brand name. Thus Winbond leapt past the OEM stage of manufacturing directly to 'Own Brand Manufacture' (OBM). These own-brand efforts were backed by a worldwide sales and distribution system with major sales offices in Hong Kong and Silicon Valley, California. The balance of its sales came not from OEM but mainly from foundry services, which accounted for around 20 per cent of revenue in the mid-1990s.

Ever growth-oriented, Winbond announced in 1994 a ten-year $3.8 billion expansion plan that encompassed a 200-mm wafer fab, an R&D centre, and a test and assembly plant. All this happened, and more. As Dr Yang modestly puts it, 'We weren't smart, just lucky'.

Macronix – A Taiwanese 'Smart' IC Producer Founded in 1989 by two of Taiwan's most experienced semiconductor engineer-technologists, Macronix International Co Ltd (MXIC) emerged as one of the most technically sophisticated of Taiwan's new crop of semiconductor companies. It is Taiwan's leading manufacturer of ROM memory devices, and also produces a variety of ICs for use in communications and computer products. The company was on track to earn sales revenues of $1 billion by 2000.[37]

MXIC was founded in Taiwan with venture capital. From the start, it pursued a business strategy of new product development rather than technology importing or foundry/OEM work. Sufficient funds were raised to establish a VLSI fab in Hsinchu Science-based Industry Park, equipped with some of the most advanced processing technology in the world.[38] Funds were also spent on an extremely high-calibre technical staff, including around 40 Chinese–Americans with lengthy experience in the US semiconductor industry.

The initial product strategy was one of developing a range of technically demanding memory products to enhance in-house expertise and maintain cashflow during the company's early years.[39] Then, in a major departure for Taiwan, MXIC forged a link with the Japanese steelmaker and silicon wafer producer, NKK, to jointly develop the technology needed for flash memory products.[40] This was the first of several major international strategic alliances entered into by MXIC, leading the way for the Taiwan semiconductor industry, with the private sector setting the pace for leveraged development, rather than ERSO/ITRI.

Meanwhile the Logic Product group at MXIC targeted a range of niche products needed by next-generation PCs and communication products.[41] From the start MXIC built up a global marketing presence, with sales and distribution channels in all the leading IC-using areas of the world. Its business was to be focused increasingly on Japan, North America and Europe as well as Asia.[42] Cash-flow in the early years was enhanced by securing OEM contracts with some of the leading companies in the US, Japan and Korea for such products as Mask ROM and EPROMs. The list of customers for these OEM accounts with MXIC reads like a *Who's Who* of the international IC industry.[43]

One of the most significant steps in the company's evolution has been its development of a 32-bit RISC microprocessor, produced in conjunction with the US firm MIPS (now part of Silicon Graphics). Likewise, Macronix entered into a partnership with the US multinational VLSI in 1998 to co-develop embedded flash memory chips. In the same year it took another big step forward into DRAM production, through a technology alliance with the Japanese firm, Matsushita Electric Industrial, which licensed its 16M and 64M DRAM technology to the Taiwanese chipmaker. In the early stages of the partnership, Macronix was to build DRAMs for Matsushita on a foundry basis, but it was expected that Macronix would soon use the expertise gained to produce specialised DRAMs – such as embedded memory products – under its own logo. From the perspective of Macronix, securing DRAM fabrication technologies from Matsushita was not a step towards competing in the commodity DRAM market, but a way of building technological expertise which could be used by the company in its strategy of becoming an embedded memory and a 'systems-on-a-chip' supplier.

MXIC is a fascinating example of a high-technology company founded with high levels of technical capabilities but still using judicious resource leverage via partnerships with leading US, European and Japanese firms. It developed a profile as an innovative product producer, while taking in

OEM work to supplement its income and take up slack capacity. It has financed much of its expansion from internal funds as well as external sources.[44] In early 1994, MXIC was approved for listing on the Taipei Stock Exchange as a 'Category C' high-technology company – the first company listed in this category. This listing allowed MXIC to raise future capital requirements through share offerings, and to attract bright engineers by offering them share options in the company.[45] It is demonstrating as much financial sophistication as technological in its rapid expansion to the front ranks of Taiwan's semiconductor industry.

UMC – Shifting Strategies Fuelling Rapid Growth Launched in 1980, UMC is the 'grandfather' of the Taiwan semiconductor industry. It was the first spin-off from ERSO's pilot fabrication operations and came to grow at an impressive rate, expanding its product line from simple consumer goods ICs in the early 1980s to encompass logic and memory chips. UMC led the Taiwan semiconductor industry into the submicron era, with a facility which was able to produce a 1M SRAM chip in 1989. In the 1990s UMC diversified further into microprocessor production, initially with ventures to 'clone' the popular Intel x86 series. (UMC sought to build its microprocessor capabilities through the classic Taiwanese approach of forging a strategic alliance with a small, Silicon Valley firm, Meridian. The alliance was not a success.) Despite taking precautions not to sell its Intel clones in the US market, UMC attracted the legal attention of Intel, which sued the Taiwanese chipmaker for breach of intellectual property rights (just as it sued US cloners such as AMD). In the end UMC was forced to beat a retreat on its Intel-cloning microprocessor strategy. This no doubt hastened a strategic rethink.

In the mid-1990s the company began a dramatic reorientation towards becoming a 'pure' silicon foundry, divesting itself of existing product-based businesses, and entering long-term supply arrangements (involving equity partnerships) with several US fabless IC firms. These arrangements involved the formation of several new ventures, such as United Semiconductor Corporation (USC) – a joint venture to establish a silicon foundry between UMC and the US firms, Alliance Semiconductor Corporation and S3 Inc.[46] UMC followed up these partnerships with plans for huge new investments in foundry fabrication capacity, announcing an investment plan of NT$500 billion (around $18 billion) in 1997 to build six new advanced wafer-fabrication plants over the next ten years. These plans were inevitably scaled back by the Asian financial crisis, but the impetus for expansion remained very much alive at UMC.

By the late 1990s the UMC Group had emerged as the number two silicon foundry in the world behind TSMC, and competing fiercely with its Taiwan rival. Both companies are very successful internationally – in apparent compliance with Porter's notion of international competitiveness being founded in intense national rivalry.[47]

How TSMC Has Forced the Pace of Technological Upgrading TSMC was founded as a public–private joint venture to force the pace of Taiwan's semiconductor development. In little more than a decade, it emerged as Taiwan's largest and most profitable semiconductor venture, and also the largest (and reputedly the most profitable) 'silicon foundry' in the world. Its establishment as a joint venture with Philips called for the leverage of 2-micron VLSI wafer-fabrication process technology, then the most advanced in Taiwan; Philips in turn was a major customer for the VLSI chips produced in the foundry. Since its establishment TSMC has continued to regularly upgrade its technological capabilities through similar means, offering leading US and Japanese IC firms a 'partnership' arrangement through which they received favoured customer access to the foundry, in return for transfer of more advanced process technology.[48] In this way, TSMC can offer an astonishingly broad range of process technology capabilities, consistent with its business strategy of being the foundry of first choice for the world's leading IC companies.

TSMC introduced to Taiwan a new processing technology termed SMIF (Standard Mechanical Inter-Face) in which wafers are isolated in mini or micro-environments by containment in pods. This had two major advantages: it enables high yields to be obtained since the 'contaminant-free' environment is contained within the pods; and it gives great flexibility, enabling multiple processes to run concurrently, which is exactly what a silicon foundry needs.[49]

TSMC acted as a foundry for the Taiwanese IC design houses, thus enabling them to accept product commissions from around the world and deliver chips manufactured to the highest standards. This triggered the formation of dozens of such 'fabless' IC houses, which took up residence in the Hsinchu Park. TSMC introduced to the Taiwanese design houses the concept of 'design geometry', in which the foundry specifies a certain resolution and a series of 'design rules' associated with it. This is an extremely efficient method of design, marrying product and process technology that is employed only by the most advanced semiconductor firms.[50]

TSMC has also led the Taiwan industry in investment in offshore production facilities, starting with its $1.3 billion US venture, Wafer Tech. This is a business established by TSMC jointly with US IC firms Altera, Analog Devices and Integrated Silicon Solution. Wafer Tech built its first foundry in Camas, Washington, coming into full production in advance of schedule, in 1998. The financing of the deal was as innovative as its production: the customer firms financed part of the construction costs in return for tradeable options on the output of the foundry. Thus if their needs decline, they can sell their output options to other fabless IC firms.

More significantly TSMC became the first Taiwan firm to list on the New York Stock Exchange in October 1997. On the opening day of trading, some 120 million shares were released through American Depositary Receipts by Philips, still one of TSMC's major shareholders. The listing, and the prospects it created for raising large capital investment funds, was greeted in Taiwan as a major achievement, and as another milestone in the island becoming known as a high-technology 'Silicon Valley of the East'.[51]

Stage IV: 1989–98 – Sustainability

In this phase firms like Winbond, Macronix, UMC and TSMC became the mainstay of the Taiwan semiconductor industry, and rapidly deepened their roots of sustainability. But Taiwan policy-makers had their sights set on a much larger and more diversified industry. This meant tackling the memory chips – and especially DRAMs – issue, and the broadening of industry activities to cover more links in the value-adding chain. It also meant finding ways to offer further encouragement for private-sector initiatives, and to foster developments through judicious public-sector interventions. Renewed efforts were mounted in the 1990s to consolidate the industry through broadening private-sector capabilities and activities (including DRAM initiatives); ITRI-sponsored technological capabilities expansion (the submicron project), the forging of strategic linkages and strategic technology alliances; establishment of supporting industries; Hsinchu infrastructure improvements and expansions; expansion beyond Taiwan; and further refinement of government support and coordination programs.

Private-sector Capabilities Expansion

The major indicator of the growing sustainability of the Taiwan semiconductor industry has been the flourishing of private-sector developments in the 1990s. New firms such as Winbond, Macronix and Mosel-Vitelic have not had to go through an 'apprenticeship' in simple IC product development, since they were launched from the higher level of collective learning achieved by the Taiwan industry as a whole. In the 1990s new firms entered the industry through private-sector technology leverage arrangements. The computer and IT firms Acer and Umax became involved in DRAM manufacture in this way, through joint ventures with Texas Instruments and Mitsubishi respectively.

The TI–Acer joint venture, which was first mooted in 1989 and came to fruition in 1992 with financial assistance from the CDC, was actually Taiwan's first DRAM fabricating operation, and as such a controversial initiative. But it broke the long-running debate in Taiwan as to whether DRAM fabrication was feasible or desirable; Acer's Stan Shih showed that it was both.

The scanner firm Umax became involved later in the 1990s; its DRAM business, Powerchip Semiconductor, was producing chips by the end of 1996. Likewise Taiwan's largest industrial group, Formosa Plastics, became involved through Nan Ya Technology, securing DRAM technology from the Japanese firm Oki.

The established firms Winbond, MXIC and MV also moved into DRAM fabrication through technology-enhancing leverage deals. Winbond's strategy involved a comprehensive technology sourcing arrangement with Toshiba, under which it became a second-source supplier for 4M and 16M DRAMs.[52] MXIC entered advanced DRAM production, such as embedded DRAM chips, through a technical tie-up with Matsushita. Mosel-Vitelic leveraged 64M DRAM technology from the European firm Siemens in its joint venture ProMos.

By contrast, TSMC entered DRAM production in 1996 through the 'traditional' Taiwanese route, via public-sector leverage. TSMC became the principal shareholder in Vanguard International Semiconductor Corporation, the consortium that took over the pilot plant of the ERSO Submicron project, with TSMC as the largest investor. TSMC kept itself at arm's length from the management of VISC in order to protect its reputation as a pure foundry.

Thus the scale and scope of the semiconductor industry in Taiwan expanded, based on its secure foundation in the technological capabilities acquired within ITRI/ERSO and diffused to a small number of firms. What is remarkable is how rapidly the process of technology leverage moved from the public sector to the private sector, with firms like Acer, Umax, Nan Ya, Winbond and MXIC becoming involved in DRAM production by entering private technology transfer agreements with Japanese, European and US firms.

Submicron Capabilities

Meanwhile, ITRI/ERSO was not standing still. In the late 1980s, ERSO was gearing up for a 'final' push to bring Taiwan into the submicron era, even though the significance of this public-sector effort was diminished somewhat by the simultaneous announcement of entry into submicron fabrication by TI-Acer and UMC. Nevertheless the submicron project proved to be an important means for boosting the technological capability of the Taiwan industry and for transferring its capability across to the private sector. The project was formally launched in 1990 as Stage IV of Taiwan's EIDP, with public funding of NT$5.5 billion (around $220 million) over five years, making it Taiwan's largest public sector-led development program in the IT and electronics sectors. It rapidly produced advanced products, and established the country's first submicron fabrication facility – a large, industrial-strength pilot plant, located away from ITRI in the Hsinchu Science-based Industry Park.

The project benefited Taiwan industry through the transfer of personnel, and when the operation was auctioned off and acquired by TSMC and a group of investors in 1994. This led to the launch of a fourth ERSO spin-off venture, Vanguard International Semiconductor Corporation (VISC). By 1995, VISC was already moving into profit, and had carved out a place for itself as a leading manufacturer of DRAMs (although it did suffer major losses during the global DRAM downturn in 1997–98).

Strategic Alliances and Private-sector Technology Leverage

While ERSO was the vehicle for technology transfer and adaptation in the 1970s and 1980s, in the final phase of development of the semiconductor industry the private sector has itself become involved in a series of technology import measures. The activities of UMC, Winbond, MXIC, HMC and TSMC may be taken as exemplary. Some of the technology alliances in Taiwan in the 1990s are displayed in Figure 4.2.

Winbond followed a judicious strategy of acquiring technology and enhancing its capabilities by linking up with major players such as NCR, Hewlett-Packard and Toshiba. For example Winbond acquired flash memory technology from Silicon Storage Technology, and the two companies went on to jointly develop advanced memory chips such as low-voltage EPROM devices.[53] Winbond licensed Hewlett-Packard's PA-RISC microprocessor technology, and in 1994 offered sample copies of the chips designed exclusively for printers, graphics terminals and other 'embedded controller' applications.[54]

Winbond also took small equity stakes in fast-growing Silicon Valley firms. For example, Winbond has an equity stake in C-Cube Microsystems (San Jose, California), and acts as a second source for C-Cube's image-compression ICs used in multimedia applications. It acquired a 70 per cent equity stake in the US design house Symphony Lab to boost its capacity in chip-set production and purchased a stake, since grown to 100 per cent ownership, in Winbic, which became its US design centre and gateway to the US.

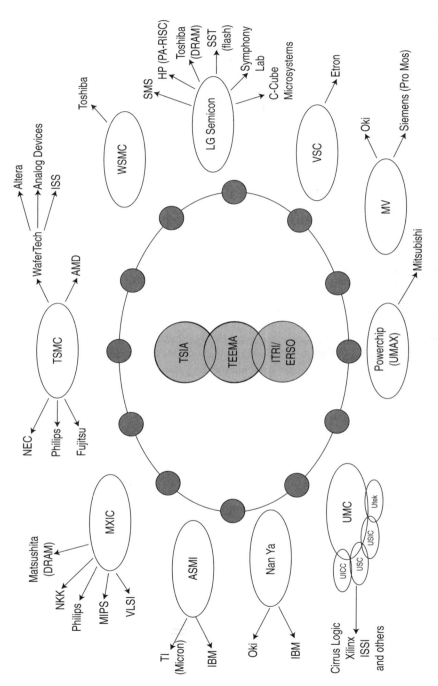

Figure 4.2 Taiwan's strategic alliances.

Winbond has also been active in local Taiwan organised R&D alliances. The firm joined a local consortium promoting the PowerPC, developing chip sets, SRAMs and other ICs to complement the PowerPC microprocessor. Winbond continued this tradition of forging strategic alliances, announcing an agreement with Standard Microsystems Corporation (SMSC) of Happauge, New York, in 1998, providing Winbond with an important new marketing channel into the US. These collaborations appear to be carefully chosen to give Winbond access to the best available intelligence concerning new product developments and shifts in such intangibles as 'architecture' as well as maximising marketing opportunities. It is significant that all the collaborations are with US companies, which Winbond sees as technical leaders in the multimedia and microprocessor area.

MXIC has fostered strategic partnerships from the outset. With the Japanese steel maker NKK, it jointly developed Mask ROM and EPROM products, transferring technology along the way to the Japanese company. (And claiming to be the only Taiwanese company to have done so!) It transferred technology from MIPS Computer Systems for the 32-bit RISC microprocessor. MXIC has increasingly moved into joint development arrangements rather than licensed technology transfer. For example, in 1997 it entered into an arrangement to co-develop embedded flash memory ICs with the Dutch multinational Philips; it extended this kind of collaboration in 1998 when it signed a joint development agreement with VLSI to produce embedded flash memory system-on-a-chip ICs targeted at cellular phones and handheld computing.

An indication of MXIC's growing international sophistication was its cross-licensing agreement with IBM, covering all patents, in early 1996. Such an agreement allows both parties to design chips without fear of infringing each other's patents. Since IBM holds more than 32 000 computer-related patents worldwide, such an agreement puts a newcomer firm like MXIC at a great advantage; for IBM, the agreement provides it with an ally in Taiwan.

TSMC has expanded its foundry capabilities into a greater range of products through a clever combination of seeking new customers and having appropriate production technology transferred from them. These involve leading US firms such as AMD and Japanese firms such as NEC and Fujitsu.[55] TSMC is also a member of some significant international research consortia, such as the Competitive Semiconductor Manufacturing project and the VSI Alliance. This gives it insight into emerging developments in the semiconductor industry as well as into the best practice of the industry leaders.[56]

After experimenting in the mid-1990s with alliances such as the ill-fated link-up with Meridian to produce Intel microprocessor clones,

UMC swung towards a very different approach, forging close alliances with a number of US 'fabless' IC producers, and spinning off new ventures dedicated to serving these customers. By 1998 UMC had evolved into the UMC Group, consisting of five core firms, three of which were joint ventures with US customers.

These initiatives reveal that technology leverage is very much in vogue in Taiwan, but now under the management of the private sector. The technology alliances of the 1990s indicate not catching-up mode by Taiwan, but participation by its firms in the world's leading-edge innovation networks. This is an important indicator of maturity on the part of the Taiwan semiconductor industry.

Innovation Alliances: ITRI-sponsored Collaborative Ventures

The 1990s saw the rise of a new breed of innovation alliances in Taiwan that maintain the innovation momentum. They consist of product development consortia brought together under the auspices of ITRI laboratories such as the CCL. This represents a singular evolution of the supportive infrastructure for technological upgrading in Taiwan beyond the direct public-sector based facilitation of the EIDP in its various phases. It is worth highlighting a recent example to show how Taiwanese firms are able to leverage themselves abreast of larger players through collaboration.

PowerPC Consortium

Under the aegis of ITRI, a group of Taiwanese firms has been developing application products for the PowerPC microprocessor that had been jointly produced by IBM and Motorola for Apple in its PCs. Formed in November 1993, the consortium aimed to establish the PowerPC microprocessor as the new industry standard, and the 'New PC' as a world leader that exploited the full power of the new processor. Members of the consortium included major Taiwanese computer manufacturers, and UMC as chip-set supplier.[57] The initiative in forming the consortium, and in ensuring that it covered all facets of development from chips supply to final assembly was taken by the Computer and Communications Laboratory of ITRI (spun off from ERSO in 1992) and the industry association, Taiwan Electronic Appliances Manufacturers Association (TEAMA).[58] A working model of the New PC based on the PowerPC version 601 was constructed and demonstrated at the Taiwan Computex fair in June 1994. This prototype was then adapted by the consortium members who produced their own commercial versions of the product. Although the market for PowerPC-based computers has not proven to be very large, the consortium proved its worth in introducing Taiwan IT firms to the inner workings of an advanced PC operating

ITRI Laboratory	Alliance	Firms involved
CCL	HDTV	UMC
	NewPC/PowerPC	Umax, Winbond, UMC
	SPARC workstation	
	Notebook PC	UMC
	High-speed digital loop	MXIC
ERSO	LCD Consortium	Nan Ya
	Interactive TV	Winbond, UMC
	Ethernet switch	Winbond

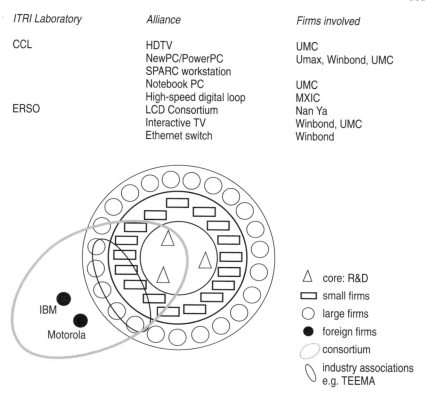

△   core: R&D
▭   small firms
○   large firms
●   foreign firms
⌒   consortium
◡   industry associations
     e.g. TEEMA

IBM
Motorola

Figure 4.3   Technology innovation alliances organised by ITRI: 1990.

system and the chip design that goes with it.

The dozens of technology alliances organised through the laboratories of ITRI provide a powerful institutional mechanism through which small and medium-sized Taiwanese firms can keep abreast of world technological developments, and compete effectively with firms many times their size in East Asia and the West. Alliances which have been influential in the 1990s and are of direct relevance to the semiconductor industry are summarised in Figure 4.3.

Ancillary Industries and Infrastructure

The early focus of the Taiwan semiconductor industry was on the creation of firms capable of producing a variety of chips, together with support in the form of foundry services and mask making. In the 1990s, attention shifted to expanding the breadth of the industry with ancillary services.

At the front end of the industry there is silicon wafer production. In

1994 an important initiative was announced, involving China Steel and the world's leading silicon wafer producer, MEMC, in forming Taisil Electronic Materials Corp (TEM).[59] A new silicon wafer plant was built on the Hsinchu Science-based Industry Park in 1995, and production of silicon wafers began in early 1996. Taiwan public-finance sources facilitated this development.[60]

This initial commitment sparked two further initiatives, announced in 1995. One involved the leading Japanese firm, Shin-Etsu Handotai (SEH).[61] The Taiwan plant's operations will be limited to cutting and polishing the wafers which are produced in Shin-Etsu's Japanese and Malaysian plants. Taiwanese semiconductor firms TSMC and UMC were to hold small equity stakes in this venture, giving them priority for receiving its output. The other initiative brought the Japanese firm Komatsu Electronic Metals into a joint venture with the Formosa Plastics group, through its Nan Ya Technology semiconductor enterprise. Capital for this venture, to be named the Taiwan Komatsu Electronic Materials (TKEM) company, was reported to be $250 million. This joint venture was an important part of Nan Ya's plans to become a significant player in the semiconductor industry in Taiwan.

By the late 1990s, then, Taiwan boasted three internationally competitive wafer production ventures; in each of which there is substantial or majority Taiwanese involvement. This is a significant development for the sustainability of the Taiwanese IC industry and a potentially lucrative export industry in its own right.

Other initiatives involve the expansion of local capacities by lead-frame and chemicals suppliers and by IC testing companies. Again the Hsinchu Science-based Industry Park acts as the focal point for the development of new companies in this sector.[62] This is still only small beer compared to what has been achieved in Japan and, to some extent, Korea, but it is a beginning. And the trend was towards further development of this sector as the market for IC supplies and materials expands in Taiwan, driven by the growth in output of ICs themselves. In any case, the Taiwanese argue that there is sufficient competition between Japanese, American and European suppliers of materials and equipment to guarantee supplies at reasonable prices and delivery to Taiwanese producers. Earlier fears of a monopoly over supply that might potentially strangle a new industry at birth, appear to be groundless.

Expansion beyond Taiwan

By the late 1990s plans were being developed and acted on to take the Taiwanese semiconductor industry out into the wider world and into direct competition with US, European and Japanese companies in major markets. TSMC announced plans in late 1995 to establish its first overseas foundry in the US with the US semiconductor firm Altera Corp and other long-standing customers. This venture, named WaferTech, is being built by the combined efforts of TSMC, Altera, Analog Devices and Integrated Silicon Solution.[63]

Taiwan's largest chip testing and assembly operation, Advanced Semiconductor Engineering Inc (ASE) also embarked on major overseas expansion strategies by establishing important operating subsidiaries in Penang, Malaysia, and in the US. ASE's operating base is Kaohsiung in southern Taiwan, but the company sees itself as evolving into a global player, able to bid for a growing share of the seemingly endlessly expanding market for chip assembly and testing.

Other developments, while not involving Taiwanese production beyond the island, bring Taiwanese firms into direct partnership with US and other advanced firms. The most important initiatives here are the series of wafer foundry agreements entered into by UMC with US semiconductor firms. The first of these, announced in 1995, was UMC in joint venture with US firms Alliance Semiconductor Corp and S3 Inc to form United Semiconductor Corp (USC). It was backed with a syndicated loan of nearly NT$8 billion.[64] These agreements take UMC to a new position as one of the world's leading silicon foundry companies, and the Taiwanese industry out into the world as a major player able and willing to invest in joint agreements.

Developmental Resource Leverage

By the late 1990s, a major semiconductor industry had been established in Taiwan, expanding internationally and into all parts of the IC product spectrum. About half of the Taiwan output is branded product, while half is contract work (OEM or foundry) in the wafer-fabrication end of the spectrum and in IC packaging and assembly. Both have proven to be very profitable for Taiwanese firms, and allowed for technology capability enhancement.

The Taiwanese approach to the upgrading of technological capabilities within industry has been pursued using innovative institutional frameworks over the course of the three decades, 1965 to 1995. These frameworks have co-evolved with the industries they have fostered. The major sources for leverage have been training and engineering development; multinational investments and joint ventures; institutional support in the form of ITRI/ERSO; infrastructure such as the Hsinchu Science-based Industry Park; the EIDP – phases I, II, III and IV (ULSI project); technology diffusion via new firm formation; innovation alliances; and government coordination.

Training and Engineering Development

A constant concern of Taiwan's technological competence acquisition has been the building of an adequate skills base. Educational investments were a priority throughout the 1950s and 1960s, with an emphasis on bringing technical cadres into being, and sending students abroad for postgraduate study. The Science and Technology Forum that convened in 1978 likewise made skills a matter of major concern. In 1983, the Commission on Research, Development and Evaluation, formed by Cabinet as a result of the recommendations of the Forum, issued a policy document 'Scheme to Strengthen the Cultivation and Recruitment of High Technology Experts', approved by Cabinet. This document spelt out the prospective needs for high-technology talent, comparing them with the current sources of supply, and discussed options for bridging the gap.[65] The study estimated the cost of the program and identified sources of finance.

The task of building up a large intellectual base in a very short time was to be achieved in two phases. The first focused on bringing back to Taiwan those who had studied abroad and were pursuing successful technical careers, particularly in the US. Many of these had studied at the best American universities, and had taken up positions of great responsibility in management and engineering in US corporations. Measures were taken to attract them back to Taiwan. New institutes were established in which they could take leading positions, for example, within the framework of ITRI. Facilities were created on the Hsinchu Science-based Industry Park which would help them form companies of their own. In selected areas of high technology, start-up capital was provided by the government.[66]

The short-term measures were backed by the longer-term strategy of rapid expansion of Taiwan's technical educational superstructure. In 1952, there were four universities and four junior colleges, with total enrolment of 10 037 students. Of these, 2590 studied engineering. By 1989, this infrastructure had expanded to the point where Taiwan had 42 universities and 75 polytechnics or colleges.[67] This was a massive expansion in a very short period of time. The programs that were started in 1978 have been remarkably successful, turning Taiwan into an 'Intelligent Island', and creating the basis for high-technology 'absorptive capacity'.

Multinational Investments and Joint Ventures

In the preparatory and seeding phases, Taiwan relied on multinationals for its technology leverage activities. Thus the early semiconductor (discrete and IC) test and assembly industry was created in the 1960s and

Table 4.2 Multinational linkages: Taiwan semiconductor industry

Year	Multinational corporation	Initiative	Technology
1976	RCA	ERSO pilot plant	IC fabrication (LSI)
1986	Philips	TSMC	VLSI IC fabrication
1989–91	TI	TI-Acer	DRAMs
1994	Oki	Mosel-Vitelic	DRAM fabrication
1994	MEMC	TEM	Silicon wafers
1994	HP	Winbond	RISC processor
1994	MIPS (Sun)	MXIC	RISC processor
1994	IBM, Motorola	NewPC consortium	PowerPC processor
1995	SEH	SEHT	Silicon wafers
1995	Kanematsu	TKEM (NanYa)	Silicon wafers
1995	Oki	NanYa	DRAMs
1995	Mitsubishi	Powerchip	DRAMs
1995	Toshiba	Winbond	4M DRAMs

1970s through initial multinational FDI, which sparked some complementary domestic investment at a fairly low technical level. Stepwise upgradings in technological capabilities were secured through leverage from multinationals, including the initial 7-micron IC CMOS fabrication technology from RCA acquired by ERSO in 1976; the step up to VLSI fabrication in 1986 by TSMC, acquired partially from Philips; and the advances to DRAM fabrication in the 1990s, acquired initially from Texas Instruments through the 1991 TI-Acer joint venture and then from Japanese firms such as Oki (Mosel-Vitelic; Nan Ya), Mitsubishi (Powerchip) and Toshiba (Winbond). The multinational linkages are summarised in Table 4.2.

Even with this impressive record of multinational leverage, the Taiwan authorities have ensured that the semiconductor industry is almost entirely domestically owned, and that foreign-equity participation (as in TSMC by Philips, and in UMC by US partners in the 1990s) is kept to levels below a controlling interest.

Institutional Support: ITRI/ERSO

The Industrial Technology Research Institute (ITRI) is the powerhouse behind Taiwan's entry into semiconductors, and generally, is a source of information and other advanced technologies. It is the most visible and dynamic institution in Taiwan's national system of innovation, charged with working closely with Taiwan's private sector. It conducts precompetitive research on projects sponsored by the Ministry of Economic Affairs, with a view to transferring the outcomes to the private-sector nonexclusively. It also conducts short and medium-term research that is sponsored by private firms, and is engaged with industry associations in the formation of various R&D collaborative consortia, designed to bring Taiwanese firms abreast of world technological best practice.

The business of ITRI is not research so much as *technology transfer* or what we would call 'technology leverage'. It is arguably the most capable institution of its kind in the world in scanning the global technological horizon for developments of interest to Taiwanese industry, and executing the steps required to import the technology – either under licence or through joint development – and then absorbing and adapting the technology for Taiwanese firms to use, transferring across the products, equipment and know-how so that further commercial development can be managed.[68] This is not so much a 'national system of innovation' as a 'national system of economic learning' of prodigious effect.

Programs undertaken by ITRI were designed both to facilitate the creation of new industries, as in the case of semiconductors (but also fine chemicals, pharmaceuticals, optoelectronics, aerospace), and to upgrade existing industries. In the latter case, a good example is ITRI's efforts to upgrade the technologies used in bicycle fabrication (such as carbon fibre).[69] In the 1990s, ITRI sought to promote a series of technological collaborative alliances that made Taiwanese firms participants in current technological developments in partnership with ITRI specialists. The submicron consortium formed in 1991 was one such project, which brought the consortium members (mainly TSMC and UMC) into contact with the world's best DRAM process technology suppliers.

The semiconductor industry has certainly been ITRI's greatest industry creation success story. Through ERSO, ITRI was centrally involved in the promotion of the private-sector development of the semiconductor industry, which it achieved via its initial pilot wafer-fabrication facility and subsequent spin-off ventures: UMC (1979), TSMC (1986), TMC (1988) and VISC (1994). ITRI has been actively promoting other technologies and industries which in many cases build on the prior success with semiconductors, such as in flat panel displays.

Electronic Industry Development Program

Central to the process of guiding Taiwan's development of a semiconductor industry were a series of public-sector R&D projects, each of which was designed (and implemented) to effect strategic leverage and bring the private sector up to a new level of capability. The successive projects, which are Taiwan's equivalent of the famed Japanese VLSI project of the late 1970s, coordinated by MITI, are shown in Table 4.3.

In developmental terms, the effect of these successive projects was to overcome the entry barriers that would otherwise have inhibited small

Table 4.3   Taiwan: public R&D coordination projects

	EIDP-I	EIDP-II	VLSI Project	ULSI Project
Timeframe	1976–79	1979–83	1983–88	1990–94
Expenditure (NT$m)	489	796	2921	5500
Objectives	IC design and manufacturing technology acquisition Establish pilot operation	Improve pilot CMOS facility Acquire mask technology Promote IC applications in industry	Establish VLSI process technology Acquire CAD for VLSI ICs Promote VLSI IC applications	Acquire ULSI (sub-micron) process technology Establish ULSI pilot plant Promote ULSI IC applications
Major features	Pilot plant established Technology acquisition and transfer	Pilot plant improved LSI chips Mask shop	VLSI chips VLSI pilot plant	ULSI chips ULSI pilot plant
Technology capability	7.0-micron CMOS	3.5-micron CMOS	1.0-micron CMOS	0.5 micron CMOS
Spin-offs	none	UMC Syntek Holtek	TSMC TMC Winbond	VISC

Source: Adapted from Liu (1993): Table 2, p. 303.

private firms from entering a demanding high-technology industry like semiconductors. This is an extraordinarily effective use of public-sector institutions by Taiwan, which complements the predominance of small and medium-sized firms in its economy.

Infrastructure Provision: Hsinchu Science-based Industry Park

Underpinning all these Taiwanese semiconductor firms is the Hsinchu Science-based Industry Park. All the semiconductor companies have their fabrication and design facilities here, clustered around the foundry facilities of TSMC and the research and design facilities of ITRI/ERSO and the leading national technical universities of Chiaotung and Tsinghua.

To many observers, such as the US Semiconductor Industry Association (SIA), Hsinchu has taken the best features of Silicon Valley and adapted them to the Taiwanese situation.[70] The National Science Council established the Park in December 1980 to attract investment in high-technology industries of the future. Ease of access, clean environment, good housing and educational facilities and land made available by the government, plus generous investment and taxation allowances,

were the inducements. The park continues to offer a supportive environment for all the firms located there.

Hsinchu Park offers firms an attractive working environment and
living conditions (much better than the crowded conditions of cities like
Taipei and Kaohsiung) as well as proximity to technical expertise.[71]
Because it is government-owned, it also offers firms which settle there a
range of special benefits such as low-interest government loans (5.25 per
cent), R&D matching funds, tax benefits, special exemptions from tariffs,
commodity and business taxes, government purchase of technology
abroad for transfer to participating companies, government equity
investment of up to 49 per cent of enterprise capitalisation and access to
government laboratories and test facilities located in the Park.[72]

By the mid-1990s Hsinchu was full: the park's existing 360 hectares had
been entirely used up. A third stage extended its reach by another 200
hectares, but this too was fully booked even before any soil was turned.
A subsidiary Hsinchu Park at nearby Houlung, in Miaoli county, with an
area of 370 hectares, was promoted. The tight land situation has been
taking its toll – HSIP had to knock back a request from Philips to locate
a major LCD plant at the park.

It was these conditions that led the NSC to create a second park at
Tainan in southern Taiwan, on a 660-hectare property formerly owned
by the Taiwan Sugar Corporation. Construction started at the beginning
of 1996, and was completed over 1996 and 1997. The new park accom-
modates firms in four major industrial sectors: microelectronics and ICs,
precision machinery, biotechnology and agriculture. The latter two are
based on the abundant agricultural resources of southern Taiwan, to
which value can be added by high-technology firms. Investment in the
infrastructure of the second park is likely to be of the order of NT$80
billion ($2.9 billion), channelled from the Hsinchu Park's own operating
fund, and from loans raised using existing assets. Ever cautious, the
Taiwan authorities have thus created a second science park without
drawing on government appropriations. This is also a case where
regional development policy is reinforcing industry development policy
– a goal that many countries have found difficult to achieve. Taiwan's
science parks have attracted much comment in the West, even from
critics of East Asian development strategies.[73]

Technology Diffusion via New Firm Formation

While the 'genealogy' of firms located in California's Silicon Valley has
become famous (Fairchild begat Intel, which begat . . .) the same process
has been working its magic in Taiwan. The first firms in the semiconductor industry were seeded by ITRI/ERSO. The ERSO-managed

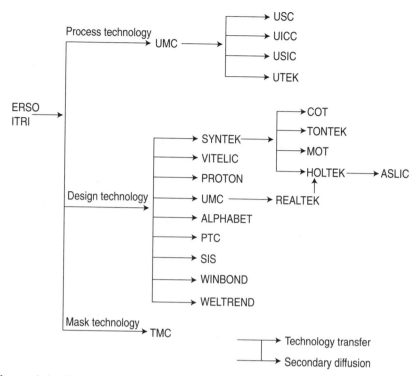

Figure 4.4   Genealogy of Taiwanese semiconductor firms.

spin-offs included UMC, TSMC and TMC, and the MoEA-managed sale of the submicron project facilities to form VISC. Indirectly there was great encouragement for small IC design firms to be set up in Hsinchu by the creation of the silicon foundry service provided by TSMC. A 'genealogy' of Taiwanese firms tracing their origins to ITRI is given in Figure 4.4.

The stated intention of UMC to focus its activities on foundry work and to spin off its existing product-oriented businesses as new ventures brings the story of the Taiwan semiconductor industry genealogy full-circle. UMC, a product of the ERSO spin-off, thus becomes the source for a new 'generation' of Taiwan semiconductor firms, renewing the vitality and sustainability of the industry as a whole.

Public Coordination in the 1990s

With the establishment of the semiconductor industry in Taiwan, the role of public support and coordination inevitably changes. With the close of the submicron project, ERSO no longer played a major role in providing leading-edge pilot plants – something that the established companies can provide for themselves. Neither is financial assistance needed for the launch of new companies and ventures. All the new DRAM initiatives, for example, have been privately funded.

Nevertheless the public sector continues to play an important role. Its most significant function is in the provision of good infrastructure. The Hsinchu Science-based Industry Park is an example and the second park in Tainan will play a similar role in the twenty-first century.

To support the further development of the semiconductor industry some issues have to be addressed. The Industrial Development Bureau has highlighted goals such as shortening the gap between domestic technological levels and those of the most advanced companies; establishing an ability to develop critical production equipment (that is, the equivalent of the Korean 'local production' strategy); coordinating future investment to avoid situations of 'excessive competition'; supporting upstream activities such as systems design and downstream activities such as packaging to improve the coverage of the span of operations involved in semiconductor manufacturing; and encouraging cooperation between semiconductor firms through collaborative R&D.

Some of the supporting measures taken in pursuit of this strategic focus in the semiconductor sector include the identification of future strategic technologies and industries, which were then supported through the 'Science-Technology R&D Projects' and the 'Critical components and products' programs of the MoEA; basic research on fundamental technologies conducted through a new 'Submicron CMOS process technology development project' in the newly formed National Laboratory for Nanotechnology established by the NSC; and assisting in the financing of R&D to produce new leading-edge products (such as 64M DRAMs, digital signal processors) under the IDB's program of assistance in 'New Leading Products'. This pattern of public and private-sector collaboration in Taiwan is set to continue until well into the twenty-first century, guiding and coordinating activities to ensure that Taiwan's semiconductor industry remains at the cutting edge of technological developments.

The aim of this chapter has been to demonstrate that the semiconductor industry in Taiwan did not simply 'evolve' through the operation of market forces or through decisions of multinational corporations to include Taiwan in their global production networks. Rather, the industry was created as a deliberate series of acts of public policy by the Taiwanese authorities. In the 1970s, these steps started with the building of technological capabilities, leveraging the skills and knowledge required from all available sources, but concentrating them first in the public-sector laboratories of ITRI. When the time was judged ripe to involve firms, it was again the public authorities who seeded the development with the creation of UMC as an act of public entre-preneurship, in pure Gerschenkronian fashion.

Likewise the industry was propagated through the creation of public resources in the form of the Hsinchu Park, the Common Design Centre located on the park (to spark the formation of small IC design firms) and the provision of a public IC foundry in the form of TSMC. The industry's technological capabilities were deepened through such programs as the submicron project, while they were broadened through the managed extension of the scope of activities, for example, in silicon wafer fabri-cation. All the while the Taiwan authorities were encouraging the private sector to take initiatives and assume more responsibility for technological and market expansion.

This the industry was doing by the 1990s, as firms initiated technology leverage agreements for themselves – notably in the case of DRAMs – and internationalised their operations. The public authorities meanwhile turned their attention to the sparking of new follow-up industries, such as LCDs and other flat panel displays which, after repeated efforts, were flourishing in Taiwan by the end of the 1990s. All of this adds up to a powerful system of continuous technological leverage and diffusion, managed by institutions crafted for the purpose. It can most fittingly be described as a national system of economic learning.

Notes

1   One of us (JM) had the honour of meeting Dr Li at the STAG offices in Taipei, in 1997. He was then in his nineties, and spoke lucidly for over two hours on Taiwan's development policies. For some apposite remarks on Li's career, from one who was his equal in Singapore, see the text of the Fourth K.T. Li Lecture delivered at Harvard by Dr Goh Keng Swee in 1993 (Low 1995). See Li 1988 for a personal account of the evolution of policy behind Taiwan's successes.

2   Dr Chang granted one of us (JM) a lengthy interview in his office in March 1996.

3   On the development of Taiwan's semiconductor industry, and government's role in its foundation, see the following: Schive (1989), Chiang (1990), San and Kuo (1993), Liu (1993), Hsu (1994), Chang, Shih and Hsu (1994), Meaney (1994), Lin, Shih and Yang (1994), Wang (1994), Sung (1997) and Lee and Pecht (1997). On the national institutional system that has underpinned the semiconductor effort, see Hou and San (1993).

4   This periodisation is in line with ITRI/ERSO 1994; Hong (1992) and Liu (1993). It differs from that of Meaney (1994) because of the different theoretical frameworks being used.

5   On Taiwan's development strategies, see for example Chu (1995), Schive
    (1990), and Wade (1990). On the origins of the EPZ, see the account by the
    man who invented it, in Li (1988).

6   It was government leaders like the Minister for Economic Affairs, Sun, and
    the Finance Minister, Li, allied with leading technologists such as Shu, who
    won the debate in favour of non-dependent development through 'leverage
    and learning'.

7   After a short interregnum, a Taiwanese electronics engineer, Dr Hu Ding-
    Hua, was appointed to be head of ERSO. He was recruited by Professor S. S.
    Shu, who was at the time President of the National Science Council and
    Chair of ITRI. Hu was the manager of the initial technology transfer
    exercise involving ERSO and RCA, and has since gone on to play an
    important role as President of the firm Macronix, and in further efforts to
    launch a flat panel display industry in Taiwan.

8   This arrangement made sense for RCA. A once-great US technology
    corporation, it had already withdrawn from the computer business, and was
    starting to withdraw from the chips business. Its 7-micron technology was
    completely obsolete, at a time when the world's best firms were approaching
    1.5 micron or even finer resolutions, and the chance to earn some royalties
    from its sale would have been hard to resist.

9   The idea for forming STAG is attributed to Pat Haggerty, former CEO of
    Texas Instruments; he died before the group was formed. The group was
    chaired by Fred Seitz, who was to become President of Rockefeller Uni-
    versity; it also included Bob Evans of IBM, who in 1995 assumed an
    important role in Taiwan as President of the new Vanguard International
    Semiconductor Corporation. Dr Li was convenor of the group and
    remained as an honorary adviser in the mid-1990s.

10 Hsinchu remained the only industrial park under the administrative control
    of the NSC up until the creation of a second park in the mid-1990s. An
    administrative body was established to oversee the park's development and
    management, under the Statute for the Establishment and Administration
    of a Science-based Industry Park, September 1979.

11 Contrary to popular conception, the Kuomintang in Taiwan resorted to
    state-owned firms for most of the critical economic activities in Taiwan, such
    as power generation, upstream chemicals production, steel production and
    so on. These created the stream of products and processes within which the
    private sector could operate profitably.

12 The proposal was formulated by Dr Shih, one of the 'RCA 37', and Dr Hu,
    head of ERSO. Shih went on to become head of ITRI, while Hu became co-
    founder and chairman of Macronix.

13 UMC's major shareholders were ITRI, the Bank of Communications (later
    called the Chiao Tung Bank), Sampo Electronics, Pacific Wire and Cable,
    and Teco Electric and Machinery Co.

14 By June 1983, UMC's sales were exceeding NT$100 million per month, and
    the company was finding sales for its simple chips with electronics
    producers in Taiwan, Hong Kong, Korea and the US.

15 UMC's success must clearly have been a factor in convincing the Korean
    chaebol to lift their efforts in semiconductors, given the intense rivalry
    between the two former Japanese colonies.

16 Of this, ITRI alone spent NT$670 million on such activities as improving its
    process technology capabilities from chip densities of 7 micron to 4.5
    micron.

17 This view was put strongly by Bob Evans, then the adviser on micro-electronics and IT (personal interview in 1995).

18 The Taiwan debate mirrors a parallel development in Korea that broke out in 1982–83, as Samsung *et al.* stepped up their capital expenditures, provoking opposition from the MoF and EPB but strong support from the MTI and MoST.

19 All funds were raised entirely within Taiwan; there was no foreign money involved. By this time the Korean *chaebol* were announcing their intentions to become major players in VLSI semiconductor device production. Thus Korea's and Taiwan's commitment to the VLSI semiconductor industry was contemporaneous – and in clear competition with each other – but through radically different vehicles for leverage of technology and finance.

20 Mosel and Vitelic were semiconductor start-up firms founded by Chinese–Americans; they subsequently played a major role in the Taiwan semiconductor industry, and in the 1990s merged to become a full-fledged DRAM producer, Mosel-Vitelic.

21 None of the five IC design houses in 1985 possessed VLSI fabrication facilities; UMC possessed LSI facilities which were adequate for linear IC production, but not for state-of-the art 64K and 256K DRAMs.

22 Mosel sold its design for the 16K SRAM chip to Fujitsu, and its next-generation 64K SRAM to the Korean latestarter, Hyundai. Vitelic licensed its designs to such firms as Sony and NMBS in Japan and Hyundai in Korea.

23 At the same time in Korea, Samsung, Hyundai and Goldstar were producing similar products, based on their capacity to establish similar 'listening posts' in Silicon Valley and to acquire designs.

24 Quasel was founded by a Chinese–American entrepreneur, Liu, who had worked at Xerox. The DRAM venture in Taiwan was headed by Dr Ronald Chwang, who was hired from Intel for this purpose. Acer was an investor in the Quasel venture, and when it failed, Stan Shih of Acer offered Chwang a position with his company. Chwang was a strong technological influence on Acer, and certainly one of the factors in the company's success.

25 The firms did not collapse, and became major forces in Taiwan's IC industry in the 1990s after their merger.

26 At this time, there were no 'pure' foundries in existence; there were simply firms that offered foundry services to third-party clients when they had excess capacity.

27 Philips already had considerable involvement in Taiwan. It had established an IC Design Centre in Taiwan, along with a transistor plant and a TV tube factory on the Kaohsiung EPZ; the tube factory was in fact the world's largest, employing some 3500 staff.

28 The attraction for Philips, presumably, was that this would allow it to secure an important footing in the emerging Taiwan market; it was also attracted by the concept of a foundry that would not be competing directly with Philips' own semiconductor products in Taiwan. In the event, TSMC proved to be extremely profitable, to the great benefit of Philips. The model was repeated in China, where Philips was co-developer of a similar wafer foundry in Shanghai called Advanced Semiconductor Manufacturing Co (ASMC).

29 TSMC was founded with total investment of $207 million, of which $145 million was capital, subscribed by: Philips (27.5 per cent, with an option to increase this to 51 per cent after three years); the China Development Fund (48.3 per cent); and other private investors (24.2 per cent) including

Formosa Plastics (5 per cent) and Sino-American Petroleum (4 per cent). Philips had been given the option of purchasing up to 51 per cent of the ownership during the fourth and tenth year after the establishment of TSMC. In 1992, Philips increased its stake to 40 per cent, agreeing to make this the limit of its holding. In 1995 it was announced that part of Philips' equity would be floated on the New York Stock Exchange, taking its stake down to 26 per cent, and freeing up considerable capital for new investments by the multinational. Its involvement in the Taiwan semiconductor industry proved to be very profitable.

30   TSMC leased the ERSO pilot plant facilities, which had been built on the Hsinchu Park in anticipation of such an arrangement, for a ten-year period. This was an imaginative public–private sector linkage, with the public sector underwriting the risks of entry by the 'private' firm – in this case, a firm created through public sponsorship.

31   Personal interview with Tseng Pin-Nan at TSMC, March 1997.

32   Sales grew from $48 million in 1990, $96 million in 1991, $123 million in 1992, $215 million in 1993, to $326 million in 1994 and an astonishing $669 million in 1995. In 1996 it suffered its first-ever reverse, due to the worldwide cutbacks in the semiconductor industry, and revenue fell to $433 million. Growth resumed in 1997, despite further difficulties such as a major fire at one of its Hsinchu-based fabs.

33   Dr Yang Ding Yuan has a PhD in engineering from Princeton; his classmates there included Dr Shih Chintay, the first director of the IC Demonstration Lab at ERSO in 1977, and now the President of ITRI, and Dr C. C. Chang, former Director of ERSO and now Executive Vice-President of Winbond. Dr Yang joined ERSO in 1976, and has been associated with the IC industry in Taiwan ever since. He led the group of engineers to RCA in 1977, and worked with Dr Shih on the first demonstration lab at ERSO. He led the IC Design Lab at ERSO (which was not actually as successful as the manufacturing lab) and in 1985–86 was sent by ERSO to complete a Master of Management Science at Stanford Business School. From 1978 to 1986, Dr Yang was head of the Computer Technology Development Operation of ERSO, which laid the groundwork for Taiwan's phenomenal success in personal computers. After his return from Stanford, he became the head of the Office of Planning and Marketing at ITRI, and president of ITIC, the ITRI fully owned venture capital fund. During his last year at ITRI, he was head of the Industrial Economic Research Centre, where he conducted an internal review of success and failure factors of ITRI projects.

34   Walsin Lihwa Corporation was a very significant investor in the Taiwanese semiconductor industry. It invested originally in UMC in 1980; in Mosel, then a Silicon Valley start-up, in the early 1980s; then in Winbond in 1987; and finally in 1994 the group emerged as the second most significant investor in the new DRAM manufacturing business spun off from ERSO, Vanguard Semiconductor Corp. It has also spun off related investments such as Walsin Advanced Electronics. In the mid-1990s, Winbond was the most profitable of the group's activities.

35   It also reflects the reluctance of the founding investors to dilute their shareholdings with further equity issues.

36   In general, Winbond targeted the multimedia market. It developed multimedia ICs such as speech synthesisers, speech controllers and video compressors. In conjunction with C-Cube, a Silicon Valley firm, it pioneered

the development of chips which can 'squeeze' sound and visual data for packaging in a CD-ROM.

37   The President and promoter of Macronix was Miin Wu, who had sixteen years' experience working at the highest levels in US semiconductor companies such as Intel and VLSI Technology before the launch of MXIC. The chairman was Dr Hu Ding-Hua. In the mid-1970s, Hu, then working for RCA, was responsible for taking a group of Taiwanese engineers to RCA for semiconductor training and technology transfer.

38   This fabrication facility, with a Class 1 clean-room for the submicron chip fabrication areas, achieved 0.8-micron geometry in 1992 and 0.6-micron capability in 1993.

39   Initial product offerings were Mask ROM (4M to 16M), graduating to the more technically demanding EPROM (256K to 1M) within a year of the company's establishment. Flash memory products, which are recognised as providing ideal memory ICs for the next generation of PCs, were targeted as the next major product offering. A 4M Flash EPROM was released in October 1992.

40   NKK was one of the most recent of the Japanese steelmakers to enter the semiconductor fabrication field.

41   The product groups selected were digital signal processors, micro-controllers and analog ICs (for interfacing electronics products with the real world). In each case, the emphasis was to be on 'total system' solutions to be contained in the chip, with low power requirements and maximum portability. Early examples of this strategy include 386 and 486 chipsets, graphics controllers, digital answering machine chip and a 64-bit accelerator chip for graphical user interface. These were innovative, state-of-the-art ICs.

42   Sales in 1994 were distributed as follows: Japan 36 per cent, Taiwan 35 per cent, the US 17 per cent, and 12 per cent elsewhere.

43   They included Nintendo, Sharp, HP, IBM, Motorola and Philips.

44   The company was able to break even in its first two years, then slipped back into a loss of $23 million in its third year (during the ramp-up of the VLSI fab), before establishing a profit of $18 million in 1993 (15 per cent net profit) and a $42 million profit in 1994 (18 per cent net).

45   MXIC continued to use advanced financial methods to raise the capital needed for its expansion plans. A meeting of shareholders in January 1996 approved a plan to issue $200 million in American depositary receipts.

46   The two US firms each took 20 per cent of the equity, while UMC took 50 per cent, and a variety of other investors the remaining 10 per cent. The joint venture was launched in January 1996 at a signing ceremony where a syndicate of fourteen Taiwanese banks pledged a loan of NT$7.7 billion (around $285 million) to start construction of a foundry fab.

47   See Porter's 1990 study of the competitive advantage of nations.

48   Firms which have partnered TSMC in this way include Advanced Micro Devices (AMD), and the Japanese firms NEC and Fujitsu. In 1994, AMD and TSMC signed an agreement, under which AMD was able to double its output of Am486 microprocessors through TSMC's foundry, in return for transferring 0.5-micron processor technology. In the same year, TSMC signed a foundry partnership agreement with NEC, providing the Japanese firm with guaranteed foundry capacity for gate arrays and other ASICs in return for the transfer of NEC's 0.8-micron CMOS gate array process

technology. TSMC entered a similar deal with Fujitsu. This was a powerful leverage technique for the acquisition of enhanced technological capabilities.

49 On the concepts behind SMIF fabrication procedures, see Shu and Tu (1992).

50 This approach makes for great economy in design since it allows circuits to be designed in a general way, introducing the current geometry as a parameter only at the end. Its origins go back to the conceptual innovations in design introduced in the US by the computer prophet Carver Mead. It has since been adopted by the leading chip producers in the US. On the conceptual innovations introduced by Carver Mead, see the illuminating account by Gilder (1989) and Mead and Conway (1980).

51 This means of raising finance protected Taiwanese firms like TSMC from the pitfalls of highly debt-leveraged development; this was certainly one of the factors involved in Taiwan's coming through the 1997–98 Asian financial crisis in better shape than its neighbours.

52 Presumably the interest of a Japanese partner would be to secure access to the Taiwan DRAM market, engage a competent Taiwanese firm such as Winbond as a 'second source', and receive some cash royalties for a superseded 4M and 16M DRAM technology. Winbond's interests would be access to a sector of the semiconductor business that had been unavailable.

53 SST provided the non-volatile memory products, and Winbond made them manufacturable. A 1M flash memory product was released shortly thereafter from this collaboration.

54 Embedded controllers (chips that perform a dedicated function with control built in, rather than applied from an external source) promise to be a leading product area in the early years of the twenty-first century.

55 TSMC and AMD reached a foundry agreement in 1994, under which AMD doubled its production capacity for its Am486 microprocessors by the end of 1995. Under the agreement, AMD transferred 0.5-micron technology to TSMC. In the same year, TSMC signed an agreement with NEC of Japan, giving it foundry capacity for gate arrays and other ASICs, with transfer of NEC's 0.8-micron CMOS technology. Then TSMC signed a further agreement with Fujitsu of Japan to produce microcontrollers and ASICs. Fujitsu agreed to transfer the necessary CMOS process technology.

56 The Competitive Semiconductor Manufacturing Project was a research program coordinated by the University of California at Berkeley that brought together fifteen leading semiconductor fabrication companies (ten from the US; four from Japan, and one from Taiwan – TSMC) in a phased series of surveys of manufacturing methods in the industry on the development of coordinated metrics of manufacturing performance (e.g. die yields). The program was directed by Professor Robert Leachman of the Engineering Systems Research Center at UC Berkeley. The VSI Alliance was an international collaborative effort to develop open standards for the production of 'systems on a chip' through 'virtual socket interface' (VSI) standards. The inaugural members of the VSI alliance, who were concerned to hasten worldwide adoption of system-chips through agreed interface protocols, were 38 companies, most of which are leading US firms and Japanese firms such as Sony, Toshiba, Fujitsu, Hitachi, as well as the Taiwanese firm TSMC.

57 The computer firms included Tatung, Mitac, DTK, FIC and Umax; Taiwan Auto-Design as systems solutions provider; and UMC as chip-set supplier.

The full complement of 32 companies were allocated to four working groups (for the platform, the add-on card, components and software), each of which developed 'core' technology that consortium members were then free to elaborate to their own specification.

58   Further details on this and other Taiwanese technology development collaborative alliances are given in Weiss and Mathews (1994). For a discussion of the PowerPC consortium, see Mathews and Poon (1995).

59   MEMC is the world's leading supplier of silicon wafers, with plants in the US, Europe, Japan, Malaysia and Korea. The Korean operation was also a joint venture, involving Samsung and the Korean steel company, POSCO.

60   The China Development Corporation and the Chiao Tung Bank were involved in financing the deal, which was capitalised to a level of NT$2 billion, with a further NT$3 billion ($150 million) financed by a consortium of banks.

61   This calls for a Taiwan-based wafer firm, with capital of $182 million (NT$5 billion) in which the Japanese hold 70 per cent of the equity, and Taiwanese partners take the remainder.

62   By the late 1990s the fledgling Taiwanese semiconductors supply and ancillaries industry encompassed firms such as the following. Chemicals: Merck-Kanto; design tools: Cadence, Mentor, Compass, E-Team; mask making: TMC, Innova; Testing: Vate, Siliconware, ASE Test, FIC; lead frame: Getmore, Hi-Tech, SDI, Sitron; and equipment: Advantest, Applied Materials.

63   The foundry cost in the region of $1.2 billion, and TSMC financed a large proportion of this sum by offering customer firms a share in the venture in return for guaranteed output. Moreover, these shares would be issued as tradeable options. This is a novel but seemingly effective way of raising finance.

64   By the end of the 1990s the UMC Group consisted of UMC plus four joint ventures with largely US 'fabless' semiconductor firms such as Alliance Semiconductor, Xilinx, Lattice and Trident. The joint ventures included United Semiconductor Corp. (USC); United Integrated Circuits Corp. (UICC); United Silicon Inc. (USIC); and UTEK Semiconductor Corp., formed by the merger of Holtek with UMC. Internationalisation of the group was extended in 1998 through incorporation of Nippon Foundry Inc. (NFI) in Japan, when UMC took over the former Nippon Steel Semiconductor Corporation. In mid-1999 UMC changed tack again, and announced the consolidation of all these group members (with the exception of NFI) back into UMC. This was part of a new phase of consolidation in the Taiwan industry.

65   See the Harvard K. T. Li Memorial Lecture 1993, in Goh (1995).

66   In total, 19 000 scientists and engineers returned from abroad between 1950 and 1988, with their families being accommodated in superior housing and their children going to bilingual schools.

67   In these, there were 37 247 students enrolled in engineering courses, and 135 788 in technician courses. In addition, there were 33 530 students enrolled in the natural sciences and engineering in US universities in 1990–91, over three-quarters of whom were at postgraduate level.

68   The statistics of this process are impressive. In 1995 ITRI obtained 381 patents, and transferred technology to 418 Taiwan companies that it engaged in 1430 joint development projects. All the indicators point to further growth.

69 The systematic transfer of carbon fibre technology to the bicycle industry and its upgrading (with some government assistance) led to a revival of Taiwan's bicycle exports (and export earnings) in the 1990s, after they were headed downwards in the 1980s (Lin, Shih and Yang 1994: 13–14). Taiwan's bicycle industry is now one of the most advanced and successful in the world.

70 See Howell, Bartlett and Davis (1992).

71 HSIP continues to provide high-quality employment for a growing number of well-educated staff. By 1995, there were 42 257 people employed by the 180 firms located on the park. Of these, over 60 per cent held junior or technical college qualifications, while more than 30 per cent held university degrees.

72 See Statute for the Establishment and Administration of a Science-based Industrial Park, September 1989.

73 Ferguson and Morris (1994), two harsh critics of the East Asian approach to the computer and semiconductor industry, nevertheless view Taiwan favourably as the next 'Silicon Valley'. In the context of a discussion of high technology strategies by 'Silicon Valley'-type entrepreneurial firms, which they promote as the saviours of American high-technology industries, they state:

> The Silicon Valley model firm is obviously not one for the fainthearted, nor is it suited for every industry. To date, however, America is the only country that has mastered it. We expect Taiwan to be the second; its population has a strong entrepreneurial tradition and close relations with the California business and educational system. (1994: 179)

Interesting as this comment is, it misses the point that what Taiwan has created is a 'Silicon Valley' in Hsinchu Science-based Industry Park, organised and administered by a *public-sector agency*.

CHAPTER 5

Jack and the Beanstalk:
How Singapore and Malaysia are Doing it

In the mid-1980s, when the US and Japan were struggling for world supremacy in semiconductors, and Korea and Taiwan were making their first moves into the industry, the South East Asian countries Singapore and Malaysia were following a quite different trajectory. Lacking anything like the technological sophistication of their North East Asian neighbours, these countries sought to leverage themselves up the technology ladder by attracting investments from multinational corporations (MNCs) – and indeed had some success in this endeavour, particularly in semiconductor packaging and assembly, and electronics.

But the strategy these countries had been pursuing appeared to unravel in the mid-1980s. Impressive as their industrial output was, it was produced by multinationals rather than by domestic firms – and the activities were decidedly at the low-technology end of the spectrum. Then amidst a worldwide electronics industry recession, the multinationals cut back investments in both Singapore and Malaysia, underlining the vulnerability of the countries. With high wages being advocated by the government in each country as part of a social justice campaign focused on the multinationals, local enterprises found themselves squeezed.

It was out of this crisis that new policies and programs were developed which have resulted in a sustained period of growth and industrial upgrading in Singapore and Malaysia, and a breakthrough by both into the most sophisticated 'front end' of the semiconductor industry, namely wafer fabrication. The activities are carried out at three dedicated wafer-fabrication industrial parks in Singapore, and at the Kulim high-technology park development in Kedah, northern Malaysia. Even more significantly, numerous local firms have emerged as suppliers of materials, equipment and services to these multinationals, and – in the case of Singapore – an indigenous firm, Chartered Semiconductor, is holding its own internationally as a wafer fabricator.

Like Jack in the fairy story, *Jack and the Beanstalk*, Singapore and, to some extent, Malaysia have been able to grow enormous industries from very small beginnings. They have learned to face down the giant (the multinationals) and made good use of the fruits taken. In the fairy story, Jack acquires assets such as the hen that lays the golden eggs – in much the same way, these countries have been able to leverage skills and technology from the multinationals, while offering them a stable and safe environment in which to conduct their operations. This has been a good deal for both sides.

The roots of the transformation go back to the 1960s and 1970s, as Singapore, and Malaysia, a few years behind, began the turn to multinational investment and continuous upgrading that is now their high-technology signature.

In 1965, Singapore's future looked bleak. The fledgling Malaysian federation, which included the former British colonies of Singapore and Malaya and two of the Borneo states, Sarawak and Sabah, had just sundered. The new People's Action Party (PAP) government, led by the brilliant young lawyer, Lee Kwan Yew, which had fought so hard for independence and union with Malaya, and had come through such an ordeal in its struggle with the communist opposition, faced a highly uncertain future as a tiny city-state ringed by hostile neighbours. It was in these desperate circumstances that Lee and his able colleagues, led by Goh Keng Swee at the economic helm, devised a new 'industrialisation-by-leverage' strategy. At the time, Singapore had no industry to speak of, and its free-port operations faced decline because of its political isolation. It had few entrepreneurs but plenty of militant unions, a legacy of the declining years of Britain's colonial administration.

The PAP leaders took stock of the situation, and concluded that their future depended on their ability to attract foreign investment to build up manufacturing industries. This was also the gist of a strategy devised by a UN Economic Adviser whom Goh called in upon taking office in 1961. There were multinationals like US electronics firms keen to invest in production facilities in Singapore, which had the advantage of an English-speaking workforce. But before Singapore could compete with Hong Kong, Taiwan or Korea in attracting MNCs, the PAP government had to put its own house in order. The anti-capitalist rhetoric which had brought it to power had to be tempered, and it had to find a way to bring the militant unions to heel without suppressing them, which it did through a new compulsory arbitration system, modelled on the Australian system. It had to provide infrastructure in Singapore's marshy swamps. It needed to create an economic development agency, as recommended to Goh by the UN Advisory team. Such an agency was duly created in 1961, in the form of the Economic Development Board (EDB), headed by Singapore's most able public servant, Hon Sui Sen.

The EDB embarked on a frenetic program of building industrial parkland, and cooperating with other statutory authorities to provide worker housing. It scoured the world for potential investors and created an efficient bureau for packaging investment deals and acting as a 'one-stop shop' for multinational clients. All this was driven by the indefatigable Goh, a product, like Lee, of the British university system. The EDB was Goh's initiative, as was the decision to level the Jurong swamps to make an industrial parkland. (If the strategy failed, he joked, the empty wasteland would be called 'Goh's folly'.) It was his initiative to orient the strategy towards exports, in defiance of the prevailing orthodoxy that favoured import substitution as a development strategy, and foreign investment as a way of building exports, in defiance of the orthodoxy that favoured domestic industries' promotion.

Against the odds, this strategy paid off. The first multinationals to show an interest were US and European electronics firms, then scouring East Asia for places to situate their labour-intensive chip assembly and packaging plants. In 1968, two of these firms, Texas Instruments and National Semiconductor, committed to building semiconductor assembly plants in Singapore. It was a development of slight significance for the companies concerned (after all, they had plenty of alternative sites) but it had enormous ramifications for Singapore. The new plants were duly established and the workers trained. The plants performed well, with productivity levels rapidly increasing. More MNCs followed in their wake and within five years, Singapore became a thriving hub of manufacturing based on foreign investment. Unemployment was eliminated. Export earnings underpinned the government's ambitious programs for housing, health and education. 'Goh's folly' looked as though it would pay off.

Goh himself went on to serve in other capacities in the Singapore government, as Minister of Education to upgrade the technical levels of the island's workforce, as Deputy Chair of the Government of Singapore Investment Corporation, Deputy Chair of the Monetary Authority of Singapore (its equivalent of a central bank) and as Minister of Defence, where he emerged as architect of Singapore's military self-sufficiency. Goh took the initiative in establishing a number of state-owned enterprises charged with the responsibility of providing the military hardware needed by the armed forces in the name of national independence. But these enterprises were also required to operate as businesses, and were expected to expand and find markets for their products beyond Singapore's immediate military requirements. Out of this pragmatic but principled approach has emerged a strong public enterprise sector that has been the driving force behind Singapore's indigenous technology development. One of these enterprises, Singapore Technologies Group (STG), launched Chartered Semiconductor Manufacturing in 1988. Within ten years it grew to become Singapore's largest indigenous wafer-fabrication operation, and the third largest silicon foundry in the world.[1]

Singapore's successes sparked emulation in Malaysia. In the island state of Penang, for example, moves were underway to imitate Singapore's approach as a way of solving Malaysia's racial and ethnic conflicts. Riots had broken out in 1969, leading to a change of government in Penang, and accession of a new premier, Dr Lim Chong Eu. He emerged as political and economic architect of Penang's remarkable industrialisation over the course of the next twenty years. The first act of the new Lim government was to create a Singapore-style development agency, the Penang Development Corporation (PDC). This body has been at the centre of Penang's development ever since. Lim then negotiated with the world's leading multinationals to come to Penang – a move that Intel made. It has been a good corporate citizen of Penang ever since, making its Penang plant technically the most sophisticated in South East Asia. By 1990, when Lim handed over the reins of state government to his successor, another tertiary-trained economist, Dr Koh Tsu-Koon, Penang was a thriving centre for advanced electronic, IT and semiconductor activities – a quite remarkable transformation in the space of a generation.

By the late 1990s entrepreneurs were taking the lead in transforming Malaysia's economy in the direction of knowledge-intensive industries based on the technological capabilities transferred from multinational corporations. One of the most remarkable is surely Ku Hong Hai, founder of the enormously successful IC contract packaging and testing firm, Unisem. A wholly Malaysian-owned operation based in Ipoh, it does business with the world's leading semiconductor multinationals.

Ku's own story parallels the evolution of the Malaysian semiconductor industry. He started without any family wealth or business background. He completed his undergraduate studies in engineering at Taiwan's prestigious NTU, and then went on to complete postgraduate studies at the University of Wales in Cardiff. This gave him insight into both the Chinese-speaking and English-speaking worlds of international business. On his return to Malaysia he joined Motorola, and worked in various capacities in its semiconductor business for the next twelve years.

In 1985 the Malaysian industrial conglomerate Hong Leong made a move into semiconductors, buying the dilapidated operations of Carter Semiconductor in Ipoh, the capital of the north-west state of Perak.

Table 5.1 Stages in the evolution of the Singapore and Malaysian semiconductor industries

Singapore

Stage I Pre-1976 Preparation	Stage II 1976–85 Seeding/ Implantation	Stage III 1986–present Diffusion	Stage IV 1991–present Roots of sustainability
Preparation by Economic Development Board Attraction of MNCs Assembly and test operations established by foreign companies Expansion of technical education	Upgrading of MNC activities and expansion of their scope Internal and external leverage via MNCs Beginnings of indigenous industry established as contract service providers to MNCs	Further upgrading and expansion of MNC activities Beginnings of MNC-based wafer fabrication Beginnings of local wafer fabrication Expansion of local service industries	Stock of both MNC and indigenous firms engaged in all phases of IC and wafer fabrication Framework of R&D support to upgrade activities Establishment of institutional R&D support, such as IME Development of Woodlands wafer fab 'park'

Malaysia

Stage I Pre-1980 Preparation	Stage II 1981–present Seeding/ Implantation	Stage III 1991–present Diffusion	
Preparation by state agencies such as Penang Development Corporation Attraction of MNCs Assembly and test operations established by foreign companies Expansion of technical education	Upgrading of MNC activities and expansion of their scope Internal and external leverage via MNCs Beginnings of indigenous industry established as contract service providers to MNCs and as contract test and assembly firms	Further upgrading and expansion of MNC activities Beginnings of MNC-based wafer fabrication Expansion of local service firms Establishment of institutional R&D support, such as through pilot plant at MIMOS Establishment of infrastructure such as Kulim High-Tech Park	

Hong Leong renovated the firm and called it Carsem; they brought in new equipment, a new workforce, and appointed Ku as the new manager. For the next six years Ku built Carsem into an internationally competitive IC package and assembly operation, drawing on his Motorola contacts and knowledge.

The privately financed Hong Leong group was reluctant to treat Ku as anything more than an employee, so in 1991 he made the move to establish his own firm in partnership with a former colleague, with the plan to establish an IC contract package and testing house using the most advanced technology available. A financing consortium was eventually formed from local investors, and a new company, Unisem was launched. Ku built his new plant on the outskirts of Ipoh (not far from the Carsem plant), where it stood in splendid isolation, nestling between hills that provided excellent '*feng shui*'. Carsem immediately attracted major semiconductor clients, including a long-term contract from Korea's Samsung.

Together, Carsem and Unisem have become the largest employers in Ipoh, once the tin-mining centre of Malaysia. Unisem continued to grow, even during the world semiconductor downturn of 1997–98, and 'came of age' in July 1998 with its initial public offering on the Kuala Lumpur Stock Exchange. It is engineer–entrepreneurs like Ku and far-sighted political leaders like Goh and Lim who stand behind the transformation of Singapore and Malaysia into hubs of knowledge-intensive industrial activity.

In this chapter we look first at Singapore, analysing the developments using our developmental resource leverage (DRL) framework – with the qualifier that the final stage of 'sustainability' cannot be said to have matured as yet – and the industrial ecology that has developed, and then, briefly, at the case of Malaysia. The stages involved, and their time periods, are shown in Table 5.1.

Singapore

Stage I: Pre-1976 – Preparation

The foundations of Singapore's present success in the modern manufacturing sector go back to the mid-1960s.[2] By 1960, just a year after its election and before formal independence, the Singapore government under Goh Keng Swee invited a UN study team to examine and evaluate the city-state's economic prospects. This study, now known as the First Economic Plan for Singapore, prepared under the guidance of Dutch economist Dr Albert Winsemius, recommended the establishment of an Economic Development Board (EDB) to accelerate (or rather, initiate) industrialisation.[3] Such a body was duly founded in August 1961, with an initial capital budget of S$100 million.[4] The collapse of federation with Malaysia in 1965, lent even more urgency to the economic groundwork being prepared. It was not domestic firms that Singapore was seeking to attract, but investments from multinationals, which were seen as the only feasible source of rapid employment growth. The preparatory steps put in place were rigorous and comprehensive: they covered such matters as provision of infrastructure, development finance, investment incentives for foreign firms, active sourcing of investment, labour and human resources, as well as acquisition of technical skills through university and technical training.

Infrastructure

The EDB was charged with the primary responsibility of attracting foreign manufacturing investment. Once the first industrial estates had been established, the Jurong Town Corporation was spun off from the EDB to take charge of these lands and their management.[5] The Corporation, along with the Singapore Housing Board, provided extensive worker housing for the employees in these new industrial estates. In 1963 the Public Utilities Board was created to ensure the reliable and cost-effective supply of utilities – power, water and gas – to the industrial estates. All of this represented effective infrastructure to underpin multinational manufacturing activities.

Development Finance

The Development Bank of Singapore was also established in 1968, a spin-off from the EDB, and equipped with funds. Half the equity was owned by the government, and half by a consortium of commercial banks. This financial institution was to be a key vehicle for assisting with the establishment of new ventures in Singapore, particularly those which met the government's goal of raising the technological level of the island's economy.

Investment Incentives

Tax breaks and other incentives for investing companies were formulated.[6] The government was able to maintain tight control over the incentives to ensure that they were working as anticipated, and not as an encouragement for rentier activities. In effect, taxation revenues were being foregone in favour of employment and technology transfer, in the expectation that tax would be recouped subsequently from those placed in employment and from the MNCs themselves once they were established.

Active Sourcing of Investment

The EDB was refocused in 1968 as primary agent for attracting foreign investment. In this capacity the EDB opened new offices, starting with one in New York, and sent missions abroad to argue the case for Singapore as a desirable investment location. It followed up with offices in the world's financial capitals. Nothing was left to chance in Singapore's drive to industrialise.

Labour and Human Resources

The issue of union militancy was met head on – but not with the kind of repression meted out in Korea. The PAP government leaders tirelessly put the case that unions and their members stood to gain more from economic growth and prosperity than from strikes and rioting in the streets. The militants were isolated, while gung-ho employers were curbed with the introduction of industrial arbitration. Fairness was emphasised as the goal of this system. It was complemented by training initiatives, which demonstrated that worker skills and therefore prospects could be improved in ways other than through union militancy. Eventually, in 1968, with the support of the NTUC, the *Employment Act* was passed, establishing an industrial relations system conducive to rapid industrial development.

University and Technical Training

Singapore spared no effort upgrading its technical training activities. A Technical Education department was created in the Ministry of Education in 1968 to drastically enhance training levels. The EDB made technical training and 'manpower development' (now called 'human resource development') one of its principal priorities, forming a Manpower and Training Unit for the purpose.[7] Another spin-off from the EDB's training efforts was the Singapore Institute of Management, founded in 1964. Enrolments in technical and educational training programs expanded dramatically.[8]

Professional Immigration

Perhaps even more significantly, Singapore recognised that the real bottleneck to its rapid development would be skilled engineers and managers, not skilled workers. In order to make up the immediate shortfall, it liberalised its immigration and work permit systems for foreign professionals being employed by foreign firms. This proved to be an astute move, solving one of the hidden problems that bedevil MNC operations.

The results of these preparations were readily apparent: between 1966 and 1973, Singapore's real GDP grew by 13 per cent per annum – a record even for East Asia. At the beginning, in 1959, industry accounted for 13 per cent of a small GNP; by 1975 it accounted for 35 per cent of a much larger GNP. The spectacular growth in the industrial sector not only solved Singapore's unemployment problem, but actually created labour shortages. By the early 1970s it was necessary to import guest workers from Malaysia.[9]

Singapore found quick success in attracting multinational semiconductor operations because of its careful preparatory steps. The semiconductor industry in Singapore started with chip assembly plants established by US-based multinationals such as Texas Instruments and National Semiconductor. They were soon followed by other US firms such as Hewlett-Packard, and by Europeans such as SGS (which became SGS-Thomson and, in 1998, ST Microelectronics). The Japanese came in the 1970s, with firms like NEC establishing their own chip packaging and assembly plants. After the initial employment stimulus from these investments had been absorbed, Singapore began to insist that future operations have a substantial skill component; otherwise they should go elsewhere, for example to Malaysia. Singapore also insisted on companies raising technological levels within existing operations. Some MNCs such as Hewlett-Packard and SGS-Thomson saw this as being in their own interests, and were happy to comply.

Hewlett-Packard, for example, was one of the first of the electronics and semiconductor multinationals to locate its operations in Singapore. In 1970 the US company outsourced the labour-intensive assembly of its core memory chips to a small operation there. The venture began in a rented factory in Redhill with 62 employees, mostly young women. The experiment took hold as the reliability and quality of the Singaporean operation proved itself. A sales office was added in 1975, and by 1977, HP Singapore moved into its own factory; by then it employed a staff of 1500. Indigenisation of the local operation was further underlined in 1984, when a Singaporean, Koh Boon Hwee, was appointed Managing Director of HP Singapore.

The European electronics and semiconductor firm SGS-Thomson is another typical story of a multinational settling in Singapore because of the favourable local conditions. SGS founded an electronics assembly plant in Singapore as early as 1969, taking advantage of incentives offered by the government and the low-cost labour available. It was the first European multinational to do so. The first operations were the assembly of transistors, involving rows of women sealing chips with drops of epoxy resin. The decision to locate this labour-intensive activity in

Singapore was made purely on the basis of labour costs. At the time, SGS had five factories in Europe – in Germany, Sweden, UK, France and Italy. Competition with US firms had been in terms of technology – but with Fairchild setting up assembly operations in Hong Kong, the basis of competition changed, and moved towards costs as the decisive factor. Costs of assembling in Hong Kong and Singapore were about one-twelfth those in Europe or the US. This was Singapore's competitive advantage – indeed its only advantage – but it would have to be turned into an actual advantage through active intervention.

The choice for SGS between Hong Kong and Singapore was made, in fact, through an intervention by the EDB. An approach was made to SGS in the US to visit Singapore in January 1969; the general manager of SGS met with the EDB at the site and made a commitment on the spot.[10] The Singapore company was incorporated in April 1969, and operations were underway by May 1969 – EDB efficiency at work. Soon SGS moved to its own site at Toa Payoh and within four years, it had opened new production lines, engaging in a full range of semiconductor assembly as well as testing activities. By 1973–74 a shortage of labour was making itself felt, so SGS moved its low-end operations to Malaysia, and started the same chain of upgrading there, a few years behind the process in Singapore. Today SGS-Thomson is a major player in the Malaysian and Singapore semiconductor industries.

Stage II: 1975–85 – Seeding/Implantation

As the early approach of attracting investment indiscriminately to mop up unemployment and kickstart a process of industrialisation began to achieve its goals, so attention turned to a more 'strategic' approach to take the city-state beyond labour-intensive activities. The framework for the seeding of semiconductor capabilities was established by the EDB through a number of initiatives. In 1975 it embarked on a targeted promotion strategy, and published Singapore's first list of priority industries that would henceforth receive favoured treatment – including electronics and semiconductors, but not heavy industries like chemicals or shipbuilding. Singapore was picking up on a strategy pioneered by Japan and was being used to great effect by Korea and Taiwan at the time. The list of priority industries indicated where government support would be focused, with a view to securing the maximum leverage of technologies and skills.

By the end of the 1970s, economic restructuring out of labour-intensive industries in Singapore was proceeding in earnest.[11] A new Ministry of Trade and Industry (MTI) was formed to take charge of the process and devise relief programs for the industries being run down while the EDB maintained its targeted programs to promote the industries of the future, particularly electronics and semiconductors. In 1980 the Second Economic Plan was launched by the MTI, reflecting Singapore's new emphasis on technology-intensive industries, and the achievement of higher levels of productivity and quality. In response to this, in 1981 the EDB published a revised list of priority industries, emphasising those which promised higher levels of investment in R&D. Again electronics and semiconductors were top of the list. The multinationals that had settled in Singapore, and the new ones arriving in the 1970s, were the source for the implantation of skills and technologies in the economy.

Hewlett-Packard, for example, adopted an enlightened policy towards internal skills transfer. The company took the position that it would benefit from an upgrading of engineering skills, which were broadened from an initial concern with process engineering to encompass design skills. An IC design centre was opened in the 1980s; this was HP's first in Asia and a first for Singapore. The design centre successfully developed new ICs for use in HP's worldwide product range of calculators, keyboards and displays. HP has since upgraded its Singapore operation to include IC wafer fabrication, involving production of specialised gallium–arsenide wafers for optoelectronic devices. Further expansion of responsibilities followed. In 1988 HP established its Asia-Pacific Distribution Centre in Singapore, and the following year set up a Network Software Development Centre to produce networking software for telecommunications developments in the Asia-Pacific region. This is a case of progressive expansion of functional capabilities that serves to deepen the 'absorptive capacity' of the economy as a whole.

The European MNC, SGS, followed a similar trajectory. Up to the end of the 1970s, SGS and other MNCs were producing in Singapore and Malaysia as a low-cost platform for sales to the world, rather than to Asia. But in 1980 the emphasis shifted to Asia. Pursuing a strategy of locating marketing expertise around the world, SGS now gradually built up the Singapore operation as a base for Asia-Pacific, gradually adding new capabilities in the domains of R&D, design, advanced assembly and test (A&T) services, customer support and service, and eventually in wafer fabrication. A design centre was established in 1982, and in 1984 the decision to locate a wafer-fabrication facility at the new industrial site of Ang Mo Kio was made – a big leap forward for Singapore. SGS's decision was closely linked to overcoming the labour rigidities found elsewhere, particularly in Europe. In Singapore, automated lines could run for 24 hours, on two 12-hour shifts, a practice introduced with union support. Investments in automation were therefore attractive in Singapore, not just because of rising labour costs but on account of the fast payback of the investments made. The establishment of this plant also had the effect of stimulating new supply activities and training a new cadre of technicians in wafer fabrication.

Singapore's Efforts to Encourage Seeding

The transfer of technologies and skills was not a one-way street – Singapore had to set the tone and direction of leverage. In this seeding phase, Singaporean agencies insisted that MNCs provide adequate skills transfer, mostly through on-the-job training and sending technicians back to firms' headquarters for training. A policy of high wages was implemented in the early 1980s, partly to induce firms to invest in greater levels of training and to force out firms that wished to pursue simple low-cost assembly operations without skill or technology transfer. This was backed by the initiative of the Skills Development Fund, which initially imposed a levy of 4 per cent of payroll on firms; the funds accumulated were used to upgrade skills, particularly in the small and medium-sized contract firms which had sprung up throughout Singapore to supply parts and services to the multinational operations.

These requirements were underpinned by massive public investments in industrial training, financed out of the Skills Development Fund. Besides the efforts of the Ministry of Education, and of the EDB's Manpower Services Division, major initiatives were taken to establish focused industrial training institutes in partnership with leading MNCs. Three such institutes were established by the EDB with Philips, Tata and Brown-Boveri. Because of the close association with the MNCs, these institutes could provide short training courses in subjects such as precision engineering and electronics assembly using the latest industrial equipment. The Skills Development Fund, backed by its payroll levy, ensured that these new institutes would actually be used for advanced training purposes, a very effective way of ensuring that firms would see a coincidence of interest between their own needs for skilled operators and the upgrading of Singapore's general technological level. Thus, even in the most basic provision of industrial skills training, Singapore was able to leverage the required resources from the MNCs.

Stage III: 1986–present – Diffusion

The 1985–86 recession was a turning point for Singapore. It revealed weaknesses in the previous high-wage policy, which had the desired effect of forcing technological and business upgrading, as well as improving worker welfare, made life very difficult for the smaller firms struggling to survive. The recession underlined Singapore's extreme dependence on multinationals, and catalysed a new approach that would be oriented more strongly to the encouragement of local enterprises.

The new strategy was outlined by the Ministry of Trade and Industry in its 1986 document *The Singapore Economy: New Directions* (MTI 1986). It was marked by an intense effort to propagate knowledge-intensive activity, with the EDB again spearheading the new effort, using a range of vehicles and avenues, including direct leveraging from multinationals (local industry upgrading); investment in front-end wafer-fabrication semiconductor activities by multinationals; further MNC investment in a broader functional range of semiconductor activities; and propagation from Singapore's state-owned enterprise sector.[12]

Direct Leveraging: Local Industry Upgrading

Rather than offer general incentives to small firms, the Singapore approach to local industry upgrading was to use the multinationals, encouraging them to enter into closer supply relations with local firms. The government sought to facilitate such developments through a Local Industry Upgrading Program (LIUP), which provided benefits to small firms in selected local industries. Multinationals were encouraged to enter into long-term supply contracts with a select group of such firms, upgrading their quality and reliability, and technological levels, in the process. Small firms supplying maintenance services, components and equipment to the semiconductor MNCs particularly benefited by this new approach.[13] The effects were sometimes dramatic, as in the cases of Advanced Systems Automation (ASA) and Manufacturing Integration Technology (MIT).

How ASA Leveraged Skills

ASA was started as a small engineering operation in 1978 by Singaporean engineer Jimmy Chew, who had worked for Fairchild, and three other colleagues previously at National Semiconductor, to supply tooling spare parts to the MNCs. The basis of the business was that the MNCs would prefer to source simple tooling parts locally rather than have to wait for a shipment from the US or Europe whenever something minor went wrong. The founders started small, with little capital, and with an initial contract from NEC, a Japanese semiconductor producer. Later they acquired contracts from US multinationals as well, and expanded the range of their services. Skilled machinists were acquired through the EDB's training centres.

By 1982 M&M had trebled in size, but was facing intense competition, not only from bigger suppliers in Japan and the US, but also from lower-cost new entrants in Malaysia. This was a turning point for the company.

Instead of simply continuing in its current strategy with tighter cost controls (a recipe for slow decline) it took the bold step of upgrading its skills and capabilities to become a producer of complete semiconductor encapsulation moulds.[14]

Chew's colleague, C. H. Kwok, was given responsibility for developing new equipment through the new venture, named ASA, deriving technology initially from a US engineering firm, with financial assistance from the EDB. Its special niche was an ability to supply Chinese firms with mouldings as Chinese semiconductor operations started to build up in Shanghai and Wuxi. Indeed, the company was able to weather the 1985 recession in the semiconductor industry (to which it might otherwise have succumbed) because of its continuing contracts to supply Chinese producers. A further joint venture was taken with the UK firm Alan Grinders to establish a connector tooling firm, Precise Connector Tooling (PCT).

ASA has become a world player in IC lead-frame equipment supply. After a shaky start – a first joint venture with a German firm resulted in the development of a mould that was too complex and had to be abandoned – the founder and his engineers developed a new automoulding concept, embodied in the form of the ASA 808, which attracted seed funding from the EDB.

By the 1990s, ASA had perfected these leveraging techniques, and was embarking on major initiatives in the latest packaging technologies, involving ball grid array and 'wafer bumping'. A further venture, Advanced Packaging (Advanpack), formed in the late 1990s, took the leverage approach to the point of purchasing a small firm in the US, FITC, because of its expertise in the new packaging technology of wafer bumping. Advanpack was able to use this as platform for developing a range of improved packaging options. In this way, ASA and its offshoots became a highly successful cluster of advanced technology firms, were listed on the Singapore Stock Exchange and internationalised their operations.[15]

Another such success story is Manufacturing Integrated Technology (MIT), a supplier of semiconductor testing equipment. This company was founded by another engineer, Tony Kwong, in 1989, and in little more than a decade had grown to become one of the most significant of Singapore 'Enterprise 50' firms, expanding its operations into Europe, North America and Asia. It has done so by following its multinational customers, providing equipment and service wherever their operations are located.[16]

Many of the multinationals themselves saw it as being in their direct interests to have local vendors/suppliers whose quality and delivery could be relied upon, and therefore participated in the LIUP. One of these was SGS-Thomson, which has been instrumental in helping a number of small local firms to upgrade their operations. On several occasions SGS-Thomson has taken a group of Singapore suppliers to Europe, and introduced them to suppliers there. In some cases this would lead to joint ventures between the two, with each enhancing their own capabilities, thereby making life a little easier for SGS-Thomson globally – they would then have one superior supplier instead of two. SGS-Thomson was also helping local Singapore suppliers to expand their operations into the East Asian region, particularly into China, again with a view to supplying their regional operations. Through this, the local suppliers were encouraged to become mini-MNCs themselves.

Investment in Wafer Fabrication by MNCs

The wider diffusion of semiconductor capabilities through the Singapore economy was driven, as in previous phases, by MNC initiatives. A breakthrough to 'front end' wafer fabrication was eagerly sought by Singapore. The first multinational to establish a front-end wafer-fabrication facility in Singapore was SGS-Thomson in 1985 (then the Italian half of the operation, SGS).[17] At the time it was a bold move by SGS, but it was a decision that has proven to be far-sighted. Another of the multinationals to invest in advanced front-end semiconductor fabrication activities was Hewlett-Packard, which established the company's first overseas wafer-fabrication facility in Singapore in 1987.

A third major MNC-led venture of the late 1980s took Singapore into the realm of memory chips fabrication. This was an initiative of Texas Instruments and Hewlett-Packard, together with the Japanese firm Canon, and Singapore's EDB, in a venture called TECH Semiconductor. Tech Semiconductor was the first DRAM producer to be located in Singapore. It is a venture in which Texas Instruments supplies the technology and receives the bulk of the product; the minority shareholders also receive a guaranteed share of the output.[18] TECH Semiconductor was launched in April 1991. By September 1993 – in record time – it had opened a DRAM-fabricating facility in Woodlands, on the northern edge of Singapore. It was soon shipping 4M DRAMs, and moved on to 16M DRAMs in 1996.[19]

Broadening of MNC Activities

All these direct leveraging initiatives did not distract Singapore and the EDB from the basic strategy of attracting multinationals and pressuring them to broaden their range of activities, which remained the bedrock of Singapore's development strategy. The later they came, the more stringent the requirements imposed on the multinationals by the

Singapore government. The Singapore authorities were acquiring more maturity and confidence in dealing with MNCs as it became clear that Singapore had something important to offer.

Take the case of Linear Technology as typical of the later arrivals. The company is the world's leading supplier of high-performance linear analog ICs, which are needed in huge numbers to provide links between real-world operations and the digital operations of computers. The company was founded in 1981 and first came to Singapore in 1989, when it opened a small testing and finishing operation in leased premises in Kallang. Since then, Linear Technology has expanded these operations to become a significant provider of test and finish operations for the company's global activities. It has added two further functions of IC design, and warehousing and distribution to Asia-Pacific, and in 1994 it upgraded its Singapore operation to make it Linear's regional head-quarters for Asia-Pacific. These activities complement the IC assembly plant built at the same time in Penang, Malaysia.

Many of the new arrivals in Singapore rapidly expanded their IC-related activities. In the case of the German electronics giant, Siemens, it established a microelectronics design centre in 1992, with the assistance and encouragement of a development grant from the National Science and Technology Board. By 1995 the centre employed a staff of 65 research engineers, engaged in development of such products as microcontrollers for automotive applications and digital signal pro-cessors for desktop video-conferencing systems.[20] Siemens also invested in advanced IC packaging technologies, making its Singapore plant one of its four global centres of excellence. Siemens is by no means the only multinational to have broadened the scope and depth of its tech-nological activities in Singapore in the semiconductor sector. Others such as Apple, Sony, Sharp and Hitachi have also made notable invest-ments in IC design facilities there.

For earlier arrivals such as SGS-Thomson and Hewlett-Packard, the process of broadening the scope of their Singapore operations con-tinued unabated. There was a common interest between the firms and the Singapore authorities – the firms were looking for greater efficiencies and responsibility to be exercised by their Asia-Pacific operations, while the government agencies were looking for higher levels of func-tional responsibilities to be transferred, in the interests of knowledge leverage.

SGS-Thomson, for example, continually expanded its activities after the building of the IC fabrication plant in 1985. The plant's techno-logical capabilities were broadened to encompass MOS ICs in 1988, and several R&D projects have since been located at the Singapore operation. By the mid-1990s the firm had designated Singapore as the leading centre for three such worldwide projects.[21] In the 1990s SGS-Thomson established its regional headquarters in Singapore, in recognition of the growing significance of Asia-Pacific in the company's world operations.

By the mid-1990s Hewlett-Packard was ranked as the most advanced manufacturing and engineering centre in the city-state. It had a staff of 8000, with activities spanning such HP products as palmtop computers, integrated circuits, optoelectronic components, inkjet printers, keyboards and computer peripherals and network software. Indeed, by the mid-1990s, the Singapore operation held global responsibility for two of HP's product lines, namely mobile printers and hand-held products (such as personal data assistants), meaning that it carries responsibility for all stages of these products from R&D through to manufacturing, marketing and customer support. HP has been one of the multinationals which has given most justification to the soundness of the Singapore version of the developmental resource leverage strategy. In pursuing its own interests in South East Asia, it has also accommodated the needs of Singapore for the transfer of skills, technology and resources.

Investments by Singapore's State-owned Sector

Central to the Singaporean strategy for the implantation of high-technology capabilities has been its use of the large firms which have grown within the state-owned sector. This sector, established in the 1960s as a far-sighted Singaporean initiative, has proven to be the seedbed for many of Singapore's present high-technology indigenous firms, such as Keppel Corporation and Singapore Technologies Group (STG).

STG, which can be taken as typical of these firms, was founded early on in Singapore's evolution as a defence equipment producer, but one that was forced from the beginning to operate along sound commercial lines. Under Goh Keng Swee's leadership, firms such as STG were encouraged to diversify, to take on commercial contracts where these would not interfere with their basic equipment manufacturing and supply functions, and to act as technology leveragers in their own right. Thus Singapore rapidly acquired skills and technologies in the fields of ship repair and maintenance, shipbuilding, weapons manufacture, aircraft maintenance – all within a carefully controlled and nurtured commercial environment.

Diversification into semiconductors was a natural and sensible step for STG to undertake. It was delayed until the late 1980s, when STG was focused clearly on its future need for semiconductor-based products and systems, and then was effected via a major technology transfer agreement to create Chartered Semiconductor. Singapore Technologies represented the first critical test of Singapore's version of the resource leverage strategy in semiconductors: would it be capable of sustaining Singaporean ventures in the most advanced stages of semiconductor activity? Singapore Technologies' wafer-fabrication venture, Chartered Semiconductor Manufacturing (CSM) is also one of Singapore's few conscious cases of direct technology transfer, undertaken in collaboration with the US fabless firm, Sierra Semiconductor. It is for these two reasons a particularly interesting case.

How Chartered Semiconductor Became South East Asia's Premier Silicon Foundry In the 1980s, the Singapore Technology Group (STG) was keen to get into the semiconductor industry, partly due to its market potential, and partly to support its own growing operations in electronics.[22] Singapore Technologies scoured the world for joint venture partners, and in 1987 secured agreements with US semiconductor firms National Semiconductor (NS) and Sierra Semiconductor. While NS came into the venture as an investor, Sierra agreed to transfer its 3-micron process technology and offered training for over 100 technical staff recruited in Singapore during 1988. The gain from Sierra's viewpoint would be to establish a secure manufacturing base for its products in East Asia. CSM was duly formed in November 1987 as a division of STG, and began commercial operations as Singapore's first indigenous wafer-fabrication facility in June 1989. The investment for STG was substantial, running to around S$200 million. Sierra transferred its manufacturing, product and test technologies to the joint venture.[23]

CSM started with Sierra and NS as its sole customers, and with VLSI technology transferred from Sierra, produced mixed-signal ICs to 3-micron design. However its initial experiences were rocky. In 1988 NS dropped out, due to over-capacity in its own operations, leaving Sierra as sole customer. Despite great efforts it proved to be difficult to attract further customers under the existing ownership arrangements. By 1990, CSM faced a crisis that could have brought it down. It was clear that Sierra could not take all the facility's output, and so the strategy of the enterprise was rethought. A shift towards a foundry operation was decided upon, and a new CEO, recruited from TSMC in Taiwan, was appointed to implement it. This was an astute move on CSM's part, which bore fruit. The foundry strategy was implemented from May 1991, effectively constituting a fresh start for CSM. In the same year, Singapore Technologies bought out Sierra's holding, on amicable terms, and sought to broaden the company's customer base in the new foundry business venture. It split Chartered into two operations, Chartered Semiconductor Manufacturing (to operate the fabrication facility) and TriTech Microelectronics (to offer design services), building on the expertise transferred across from Sierra.

CSM made strenuous moves to upgrade its own technological capabilities. A technology development group was created in-house to improve on the technology transferred across from Sierra. By 1990 it achieved 1.5-micron process technology, improving to 1.2-micron in 1991 and 0.8-micron in 1992, and 0.6-micron in 1993. In 1994 a further technology transfer agreement with Toshiba enabled CSM to leap forward to 0.5-micron technology; in return Toshiba secured the facilities of CSM as a 'second source' for its products. This technical partnership with Toshiba blossomed, so that in 1997 Toshiba was providing Chartered with its embedded DRAM technology, again for purposes of using CSM as its foundry 'second source'. Thus CSM leveraged itself abreast of the world technology frontier.

CSM grew rapidly in the 1990s after recovering from the crisis involving Sierra. It opened a second wafer fab in 1995, in Woodlands, and by year end was constructing a third. Meanwhile the first fab, built in 1989 in the Singapore Science Park, operated at full capacity for years, producing chips on 6-inch wafers for 50 industrial customers around the world.[24] The second fab was built in Woodlands (next to the TECH DRAM fabrication facility) and started shipping 8-inch wafers in mid-1995, barely a year after construction began. The operation was breaking even by the end of 1995, but not enough to keep up with demand.[25] By the end of the year construction had started on a third fab, which opened for business in 1997.

These fabs were financed through innovative equity deals with customer firms. For example, Fab 2 attracted equity investments of $60 million from four US firms anxious to have a guaranteed share of the facility's capacity.[26] The EDB also facilitated CSM's expansion by investing S$100 million in Fab 2; this was in fact one of the first investments made by the EDB from its new Cluster Development Fund, established to facilitate the development in Singapore of an electronics/semiconductor cluster of industries.

CSM took this concept further with its fourth and fifth fabs, also built on the Woodlands site, which were launched as joint ventures with major customers, Hewlett-Packard and Lucent. The joint venture foundry with HP is called *Chartered Silicon Partners*, with HP a major equity partner alongside Singapore's EDB. The fab went into production early in 1999. The joint venture with Lucent, named *Silicon Manufacturing Partners*, had to delay its plans for fab construction (due to the 1997–98 financial crisis) but was expected to be up and running by 2000.

CSM continued to invest heavily in technological upgrading through its own development efforts and by technology leverage such as licensing (from IBM and AT&T, for instance) and more comprehensive technology transfer, as with Toshiba. In November 1994 CSM announced that it had signed a five-year technology collaboration agreement with Toshiba, under which the Japanese company agreed to transfer its advanced process technology in return for a guaranteed share of CSM's capacity (as a second source) and an equity participation.[27] These alliances – with Hewlett-Packard, Toshiba and other leading firms such as VLSI Technology – all provide the evidence that Chartered has 'come of age' in the semiconductor industry, and is now accepted as a peer by the world's elite IT and semiconductor firms.

The Singapore Technologies group has further diversified its semi-conductor operations, launching a test and assembly contract operation to complement its wafer foundry operations. This business, known as Singapore Technology Assembly Test Services (STATS) was launched in the mid-1990s, and quickly established itself as a strong competitor with existing South East Asian operations. It attracted the support of such Japanese giants as Seiko Epson, which transferred specialist technology to STATS in return for a guaranteed share of the company's activities. Thus the same process of technology leverage that starts a new venture is employed over and over as the venture is extended.

By the late 1990s, Singapore Technologies' activities encompassed IC design (through TriTech), wafer fabrication (through CSM) and test and assembly (through STATS) – all on a contract basis, without producing products of its own. The Singapore Technologies group is a perfect example of a technology leverage player, lifting itself into new phases of the industry through joint ventures, technology transfer agreements and by expanding its customer base.

Stage IV: 1991–present – Roots of Sustainability

It is only in the 1990s that the Singapore government has taken steps to prepare the city-state for 'advanced country' status, and to accelerate the shift towards knowledge-intensive industries. This has involved, for the first time, sustained investment in Singapore's own R&D facilities, set up in the public sector according to the Taiwan model. The framework for the new strategy, which would take Singapore around the 'next lap' of its development trajectory, was issued by the Ministry of Trade and Industry in 1991.[28] *The Next Lap* called for more adventurous industrial-isation policies to take Singapore to a qualitatively higher-level of tech-nological and commercial sophistication.

One approach was to consider how Singapore's various industries could be conceived as 'clusters', and to formulate government policy in the future by identifying the gaps that needed to be filled if the clusters were to operate effectively. From Porter's notion of industry clusters, the EDB started to formulate plans to encourage certain industrial 'clusters' in Singapore rather than single industries.[29] For example, an 'electronics cluster' was identified as a key component of the future Singaporean economy, based on the fact that electronics contributed 46 per cent of the manufacturing sector's output in 1993, and rose to more than 50 per cent in 1995.

The 1990s also saw Singapore restructure its institutional framework to encourage the uptake of technology and the generation of new technological knowledge by local firms. The principal initiatives were the formation of the National Science and Technology Board (NSTB), taking over functions previously exercised by other bodies, and the establishment of the new Nanyang Technological University. Under the NSTB a number of new R&D institutes were established. This was an important step – the first series of investments by Singapore itself in collective public-sector development of technological capabilities – nearly twenty years after the comparable step had been taken in Taiwan. For the semiconductor industry, the most important of these initiatives is that of the creation of a new Institute of Microelectronics.

Institute of Microelectronics

The Institute of Microelectronics (IME) was formed in 1991 as a research institute under the auspices of the National University of Singapore and the NSTB.[30] Its mission, as spelt out in its founding charter, is to engage in relevant R&D in strategic microelectronics fields; support and partner with the electronics industry in Singapore; and develop skilled R&D personnel.

Projects undertaken within the IME are industry-driven and have a high level of industrial participation from local companies as well as multinationals. Some of the projects are commissioned directly by firms operating in Singapore; some are initiatives taken by IME in conjunction with groups of firms (on a Taiwan innovation model).

In 1995, for example, a group of companies joined with the IME to form a twelve-firm consortium to improve packaging technologies such as ball grid array. The project focused on core technological characteristics such as enhanced electrical performance and miniaturisation technologies that will be available to all participants.[31] A broader consortium was formed subsequently by the IME to encompass a range of electronic packaging research and development initiatives. The Electronic Packaging Research Consortium (ERPC) enrolled eleven member companies in its first year.[32] One of the members of the consortium was Siemens – a company that restructured its semiconductor operations around four global centres of excellence, of which Singapore is one, with responsibility for advanced IC-packaging technologies. In this way, the IME acts as 'technology broker' in bringing together companies with advanced skills to ensure that these are diffused and extended.

Signs that Singapore's semiconductor industry is putting down roots of sustainability come from various quarters. These include the variety and expanding scale of wafer fabrication, the proliferation of R&D centres, and the international alliances being made by Singaporean firms. Singapore is also actively seeking to strengthen itself in certain areas, including the location of ancillary industries (for example, silicon wafer supply) in Singapore, and the expansion abroad of Singaporean firms.

The latest and most important phase of the propagation and sustainability phases is the formulation by the EDB of three wafer-fabrication parks at Woodlands, Pasir Ris and Tampines. Thus by the late 1990s Singapore was presenting a very confident face to the world. The manufacturing and business services, of which the semiconductor sector was an important part, accounted for a full 40 per cent of the economy, and strong commitments had been made to maintain Singapore's manufacturing excellence. The Ministry of Finance had approved funds of S$3 billion under the Economic Development Assistance Scheme to the EDB over the five years from 1995 to 2000, to support initiatives and programs taken under the programs developed in the early 1990s.[33] The initiatives covered four main issues.

First, innovation support to promote and maintain the development of new ideas and projects through the provision of major new resources to the NSTB. This is designed to promote innovation activities in Singaporean companies and by entrepreneurs.[34]

Second, overseas expansion via regional promotion to replicate Singapore's high-technology activities and strategies abroad in a series of 'technology parks' being jointly developed in India, China, Vietnam and Indonesia. The EDB, for example, co-invested with Hitachi Semiconductor, which already operates an advanced plant in Singapore, to attract the Japanese firm to the China–Singapore Suzhou Industrial Park. It is anticipated that Singapore's high-technology activities will take place in several continents by the twenty-first century.[35]

Third, by promoting process capabilities enhancement through the public sector as stimulus for similar developments in private firms. These programs are focused on Singapore's critical high-technology industries. In 1996 the NSTB launched its Semiconductor Process Capability Development (SPCD) program, a S$200 million scheme to upgrade companies' capabilities in wafer fabrication, lithography and display process technology. The first contract under the scheme was awarded to Chartered, to develop 0.25-micron wafer capabilities at its Woodlands fabrication facility in conjunction with the Institute of Microelectronics and tertiary institutions.[36]

Finally, the labour and skills needs of high-technology industries had to be deepened. In 1995 the EDB and NSTB initiated several specialist skills development programs specifically in the area of IC wafer-fabrication skills, to ensure that new wafer-fab projects being sought for Singapore would be able to draw on reliable skilled labour.[37]

By the late 1990s Singapore was finally taking the necessary steps to support a genuine innovative capability and to promote the self-sustaining efforts of its own companies. It was looking to establish high-technology foundations that complemented but were at the same time independent of the activities of its multinational clusters.

That a promotion framework is needed at all is a sign that Singapore considers its high-technology activities to be very vulnerable – as indeed they are. It competes vigorously for new investment by multinationals, but is now actively encouraging the efforts of its local firms. The practical engagement of these programs is striking. They are complemented by an array of reforms to administrative infrastructure and relentless IT upgrading which, when combined with Singapore's clean and efficient administrative procedures, make for a formidably competitive manufacturing centre. But no-one is more aware of the vulnerabilities of Singapore than its own elite. It was able to pass through the 1997–98 Asian financial crisis virtually unscathed, but nevertheless anticipated major downturns in 1998 simply because of its regional ties. These are the realities of Singapore's existence. Like Jack of the fairy story, Singapore has faced down the giant (the multinationals) but claimed from this giant no more than is its due – and has made good use of the fruits leveraged.[38] This is the heart of the Singapore model.

Malaysia

The high-technology experience in Malaysia has been complicated by the country's greater population – in 1995, nearly 20 million compared with Singapore's nearly 3 million – and its federal political structure, which has not made for an easy national focus. The country also had three quite distinct ethnic groups – the Malays, Indians and Chinese – each with quite different patterns of income and wealth distribution. In very broad terms, the Indians had been imported in the late-nineteenth and early-twentieth centuries to work on the plantations – they were the 'industrial proletariat' of Malaysia. The Chinese had been allowed to migrate to provide service functions and form the 'small business' class of Malaysia. The Malays had by and large been ignored by the British, and allowed to stay in their villages in a state of economic backwardness, entering the economy only as providers of fresh food. With political independence from the British in 1957, Malaysia had to wrestle as much with issues of equity between the ethnic groups as with questions of growth and development.

The 'new economic policy', introduced in 1972 in response to the continued racial and communal riots, was a plan to raise the economic participation of the Malays (*bumiputera*) – growth took a secondary position. It was not until Dr Mahathir Mohamad's federal government took office in 1981 that technology-accelerated growth policies came into vogue. Dr Mahathir's government spent the first five years of its life pursuing capital-intensive strategies modelled on Korea's and Japan's Heavy and Chemical Industrialisation push of the 1970s. With some important exceptions such as the Proton car these strategies were not wholly successful, and to its credit the government swung behind a new export-led strategy driven by foreign investment by multinationals in 1986. Malaysia benefited with over a decade of uninterrupted growth, brought to an end only in 1997 by the Asian financial crisis.[39]

While federal development strategies have been important in Malaysia, the most significant initiatives in the semiconductor industry have come from the state level. As noted previously, Penang stands out for its capacity to pursue technology-intensive industrialisation strategies in advance of the rest of the country. From 1970, Penang had become Malaysia's 'Silicon Island', housing semiconductor and electronics assembly operations of the world's leading US, European and Japanese MNCs. More recently, it has hosted newer North East Asian investments from Taiwan, such as a major Acer PC components plant. We look briefly at how technology leverage strategies have worked in Penang, before examining other parts of the Malaysian federation.

The Story of Penang

Penang is a tropical island that has transformed itself from tourist paradise to a bustling industrial centre of electronic and associated manufacturing within the space of a generation. Under the leadership of Dr Lim Chong Eu, who was state premier in 1970, Penang embarked on a rapid industrialisation program, modelled on the success of Singapore. The first act of the new state government was to create a Singapore-style development agency, the Penang Development Corporation (PDC), charged with the tasks of industrialisation. This body has been at the centre of Penang's development ever since. It threw itself into the tasks of industrial development and planning, new township development and industrial estate establishment. Its initial focus in the early 1970s was on the creation of export-oriented labour-intensive industries, to take advantage of the abundance of labour reserves in the state. This phase was concentrated on attracting MNCs, like Singapore a few years earlier. With the first factories established, from 1975 the PDC ventured into township development, housing and industrial estate formation. In the 1980s, there was further consolidation of these activities, until the 1985–86 recession, which caused lay-offs and some permanent cutbacks. In 1987 growth resumed in Penang – and it was the same year that marks Penang's take-off as a dynamic new centre of excellence in manufacturing, particularly electronics and semiconductors. The changes of these years can be told through the story of two multinationals – Motorola and Intel – and some of the small companies which have been spawned to service them.

Motorola in Penang

Motorola's roots in Penang go back to the beginnings of the island's industrialisation drive. The story starts in 1970, when its Paging Product group in the US came up with a new device that was dramatically smaller and lighter than anything then available, based on the revolutionary miniaturisation concept of hybrid circuitry. It was manufactured at the Motorola facility in Plantation, Florida, but at cost levels that made it unattractive commercially.

Motorola looked for an offshore manufacturing site for the hybrid circuit, which called for labour-intensive assembly. A small management team was formed to investigate potential sites in Asia, in Japan, Hong Kong, Thailand, Singapore and Malaysia. (They might have saved themselves the trouble of investigating Japan!) They settled on Penang, and how they did so tells a lot about the capacity to 'manage' the process of technological and business diffusion.

Two Motorola managers were in the Kuala Lumpur Merlin Hotel when they bumped into a senior manager with the PDC. He immediately invited them to Penang, arranging a visit that night. Next morning they were met at the Penang airport and shown the Bayan Lepas industrial zone. They booked a site for Motorola on the spot.

A hybrid circuits assembly plant was established in 1973, and hybrid modules were assembled by hand, by women workers in the factory. The results were so promising that within a year, Motorola transferred assembly of the entire pager to this facility. A new computer-controlled testing machine was installed, as well as automated welding and assembly equipment, and Malaysian engineers were trained to operate and maintain it. The yields obtained through this mechanisation improved dramatically, which led to further enlargement of functional responsibilities, including the manufacture of two-way radios, and the establishment of a development centre for pagers in 1976.

This was an astonishing rate of engineering evolution and development in a facility still surrounded by rice paddies and palm trees.[40] Penang was now responsible for designing, assembling and shipping to customers one of the most popular portable radios in Motorola's history. Mechanisation of the 'front-end' operations, namely assembly of the hybrid circuits themselves, was introduced only in 1980, with a 'Pick and Place' machine imported from Florida. Within two years, two Malaysian engineers had adapted and extended it and built their own Auto Test Handler. This was technology leverage and 'improvement engineering' in action.[41]

By 1975 the first wave of foreign investment had settled in Penang. There were more than 30 factories operating in the FTZ, employing some 22 700 workers. All were MNCs, and almost all were involved in electronics and semiconductor packaging and assembly. Some of the tasks that had been necessary in Singapore, such as the curbing of a militant trade union movement, were unnecessary in Penang. It was an island that went literally from rice paddies to chip factories, with young women as the major source of industrial employment. Unions would come eventually, but they were not a factor in the early stages of development. MNCs who were looking for stable and efficient work conditions found it – and stayed.

How Intel Came to Penang

Penang was Intel's first offshore assembly plant, established in 1972 just three years after the company was first formed in California. It started as a small operation of 100 employees (again, mostly young women) assembling into packages a small 1K memory chip, Intel's 1103 DRAM. Just one building on a 5-acre site housed the packaging operations. Barely three years later, a disastrous fire destroyed a good part of the plant, and severely tested Intel's patience and commitment. However, the efforts of the locals, backed by confidence from the corporate parent, enabled the Penang operation to get back on its feet, and by 1978 it had added Intel's first offshore test plant to its operations. It advanced from the testing of DRAMs and EPROMs to the testing of the more complex microcontrollers and microprocessors, and was the first plant in Penang to link IC testing with assembly. Since then, the expansion of responsibilities and capabilities at the Penang Intel operation has been impressive.

In 1985 an important advance occurred with the transfer of technical responsibilities, giving engineers in Penang responsibility for new features such as failure analysis, yield improvement and test software.[42] In support of this transfer, a large investment was made in training, with Penang engineers sent to attend in-house courses in California – the first major integration between the Penang operations and those of the parent company. At the same time, productivity of the Penang operation improved dramatically, with the introduction of round-the-clock work. These improvements provided the platform for yet further developments.

The late 1980s saw another round of expansion of the functional responsibilities of the Penang plant. One of the first functions bequeathed to the plant was customer support. This enabled customer firms in the Asia-Pacific region to have their problems dealt with by engineers in Penang, without having to refer everything to the parent corporation. In 'Intel-speak' this was referred to as the establishment in Penang of an Asia-Pacific Correlation Centre. Intel was not transferring these responsibilities for 'free', and had to be coaxed and induced to do so, and it had to see tangible benefits. The strategy on the part of the Penang Intel senior (Malaysian) management was clever: they offered Intel the chance to offload responsibility for dealing with customers in relation to products that were becoming obsolete. As new products were developed, which absorbed most of Intel's time and energy, there was a tendency to let the customer support for existing and soon-to-be-obsolete products slip. Penang saw this as its 'window of opportunity'.

Intel was only too pleased to be able to transfer responsibility for supporting these soon-to-be-obsolete products to its subsidiary. From Penang's perspective, however, it represented a quantum leap in its functional responsibilities and a further reason why Intel had to transfer the engineering skill – product and process technology – involved in dealing with customers who used these products. The point of this story is that functional responsibilities are expanded through conscious leverage initiatives; they do not just 'happen'.

By 1988 the Penang engineers were becoming involved in the early development of new Intel products, given the responsibilities they would be exercising for the testing and assembly of these products. Increasingly, the introduction of new products revolved around the issues of production, with efficiencies in process technology taking precedence over the pure questions of product technology. This shift favoured the transfer of further skills and technology to Penang. This period also saw the start of a determined quality drive within Intel worldwide (named the QIP program) and it called for further massive training efforts and greater responsibilities to be carried by engineers and production staff throughout the organisation.

Training was stepped up with the formation of a special training facility in the Penang plant in 1990 called the Intel University. This is now the centre for induction and further development programs offered to all employees at the plant. 1992 saw an important further step, with the founding of the Intel Penang Design Centre. This has involved Intel transferring design responsibilities for a range of products (starting with 8-bit and 16-bit microcontrollers) to its South East Asian operation – transferring the skills and responsibilities for designing these products from its US base to its Penang plant. This Design Centre has been a great success. It started with 30 members doing simple design enhancements for 8-bit and 16-bit microcontrollers (that is, microprocessors embedded in certain applications, such as in VCRs or photocopying machines). Within three years, this team had grown to 150 staff, who were engaged in 8-bit and 16-bit architecture designs for new products, as well as some design work at the new generation 32-bit level. Over 70 new products were introduced in this time, including new chips featuring Intel's next-generation architecture.

Behind these successes again lies a story of heavy investment in training. Some of the product engineers spent between two and three years in on-the-job training in the US and other Intel sites, learning the in-house techniques of design, use of computer-aided tools and participating in active design projects. These engineers would then pass on their knowledge through their leadership of design teams in Penang, as well as through advanced courses offered at the Intel University.

The culmination of this process was the establishment of an integrated 'business centre' at Penang to take responsibility for Intel's 8-bit microcontroller business worldwide. Thus Intel Penang in 1993–94 assumed responsibility for the design, production, testing, assembly, marketing and customer support for Intel's 8-bit worldwide microcontroller business, dealing with customers around the world. Again the strategy on the part of Penang was to offer to take responsibility for products which were being phased out by newer 16-bit and 32-bit architectures. But 8-bit microcontrollers are workhorses that have been around for a long time, and will continue to be an important source of business. Intel Penang's design involvement in 16-bit and 32-bit microcontrollers shows that it does not expect to have its total business responsibilities limited to 8-bit products for very long.

By the mid-1990s, the process of internal technology transfer within Intel had proceeded to an irreversible point, with Intel Penang an integral and irreplaceable part of the Intel global business. But Intel's commitment to Malaysia is not confined to Penang. In 1995 it announced its intention to develop a second plant in Malaysia to produce motherboards for PCs and boards for communication systems. This plant was to be located on the Kulim High-technology Park in Kedah state, adjacent to Penang. The plant was built and started operating in 1996.

Intel's experience thus captures the essence of the Penang story, and takes it across the water to neighbouring Kedah, where the Malaysian story was being taken up in the 1990s.

External Leveraging from Multinational Corporations

Like Singapore before it, Penang pursued a vigorous strategy of leveraging skills, knowledge and technology from the multinationals operating on the island to seed the skills needed for development of indigenous industry clusters. The Penang counterpart of the Singapore 'Local Industry Upgrading Program' was the Vendor Partnership Program (VPP), initiated with Intel in the 1980s and spreading to other multinationals. At the beginning of the 1980s, there were a number of small tooling workshops in Penang, with names like Atlan Industries, Loh Kim Teow and Eng Hardware. They had low staff numbers (usually fewer than ten), cramped quarters and low-technology tooling. There were too many small firms competing with each other to allow them to compete on anything other than least cost terms. As the MNCs upgraded their automation and production operations, they found that they needed local supplies of tooling, fixtures and fittings rather than depending on overseas supplies. Intel, in particular, recognised that some drastic action was needed to bring local tooling vendors up to the MNCs' quality standards.

Intel's VPP worked as follows. Intel engineers selected a few local suppliers and worked with them as 'partners'.[43] This eliminated the cut-throat competition, and enabled a selected group of vendors to develop up to Intel's standards. The first step for Intel was to identify and select vendors who had potential for future growth – these were the ones who became Intel's partners. Next, Intel offered premium prices to these vendors to ensure their profitability and to enable them to invest in improved technologies and upgrade skills. Thirdly, vendors were provided with a dependable volume of business, which allowed them to make longer-term calculations. Intel's expectation was that the profits generated by these actions would be reinvested to upgrade the vendors' capacities, technologies and capabilities – an expectation that was not dashed, as in the case of a local company LKT/SEM. The company was consolidated in 1995 and listed on the KL Stock Exchange as LKT Industrial Berhad. It is an exemplar of the multinational leverage strategy bearing fruit.

How LKT Has Expanded through Leverage

LKT group is a sophisticated supplier of automation equipment to the semiconductor assembling industry. It was materially helped by the multinational, AMD, as well as by the Intel VPP. LKT traces its beginnings to the 1950s when a Chinese-Malaysian engineer, Loh Kim Teow, opened his own metal-working shop. The products turned out initially included household fencing, window grilles and metal doors. In the 1960s Loh ploughed back profits to upgrade technology, specifically investing in heavy machinery to service the engine maintenance and rebuilding sector. This machinery was then leveraged to take the firm into servicing the construction industry, with piling equipment and mobile cement mixers. An idea of the conditions involved can be gleaned from the description of these activities given by Loh's son in 1995:

> My father, the late Loh Kim Teow, designed the mobile crane, cement lifter and mixer, when hardly any companies were in the same industry at that time in this region (Penang). There was hardly any equipment available to produce the gear system for the crane's gear drive. Gears had to be salvaged from unused lorries and mixed and matched.[44]

In 1978 LKTE was incorporated to further expand as a provider of tooling and precision instruments for the semiconductor industry. The company was taken on by Intel as a partner in its VPP. In the 1980s, under the leadership of Loh's son, Vincent Loh Khee Lian, LKTE created its own division for the development of automation equipment targeted at the semiconductor industry. This business was incorporated as Semiconductor Equipment Manufacturers (SEM) in 1988. Today, SEM is one of a few companies in Malaysia involved in both the design and manufacture of automation equipment. The machines produced, such as Eutectic Die Attach machines or Auto Lead Straighteners, are used by semiconductor assembly and packaging firms, mainly MNCs.

SEM is the product of Vincent Loh's determination. SEM's technological development was encouraged by Intel, which awarded the company the 'vendor of the year' prize over three consecutive years, from 1991 to 1993. SEM's first venture came in the automating of the die-attach process, one of the most difficult in the packaging of a chip. (It involves attaching the sawn die to its package, prior to the leads being connected.) In the early 1980s, the MNC AMD allowed Vincent Loh to experiment with different approaches to the automation of this process. The best solution was embodied in a machine that was sold to AMD, and then on-sold to AMD's affiliate in the Philippines. The same kind of machine was then sold to the Penang MNC IDT, and then to IDT's parent company in the US. AMD ordered 30 of the machines, and SEM was in business! Thus are ventures created and grown in Penang.

The story of LKT/SEM provides evidence of external leveraging from multinationals – in this case, AMD and Intel – by indigenous local firms, which in turn grow to become mini-multinationals as they service clients around the region.

Penang's Leveraging Efforts in the 1990s

In the 1990s, Penang faced problems of success such as overcrowding in its industrial parks, severe skills shortages and infrastructure problems, particularly in its antiquated airport and unreliable power supply (which comes via cable from the mainland). It also faced competition from other emerging Malaysian states as well as federal initiatives. The Penang state government, under the leadership of Dr Koh Tsu-Koon, new Chief Minister from October 1990, embarked on an ambitious plan to seek to remedy these deficiencies.

Its blueprint, issued in 1991, was a strategic plan drafted by a team of local consultants from the Institute of Strategic and International Studies (ISIS) and the Penang Development Corporation. The plan focused on measures which were within the powers of the Penang government, such as broadening and deepening the technology base of the Penang economy, and upgrading the skills of the workforce. But the plan was swimming against the natural barriers posed by the island's size and the critical shortages of land and skilled labour, and against the political barriers of Malaysia's federal structure and the unwillingness of Kuala Lumpur to see Penang get too far out of line with the rest of the country.

There have been some high-technology start-ups by Penang-based firms in the semiconductor sector, but they are very few, and not on anything like the scale of Singapore with its DRAM and other wafer-fabrication initiatives. These are likely to be found elsewhere in Malaysia, such as in central Perak state or northern Kedah state.

Nevertheless there have been some Penang-based semiconductor start-ups, of which Globetronics is one. It is of interest as an example of a Malaysian high-technology firm founded through investment by an established company which had made its fortune in palm oil plantations. It is also of interest as the first joint venture in Penang between a Malaysian firm and a Japanese firm, Sumitomo Metal Ceramics Inc (SMCi), a wholly owned subsidiary of the giant Sumitomo Metal Industries.

Globetronics: From Palm Oil to Chip Packaging

Globetronics is a Malaysian-financed firm in Penang which has entered the semiconductor industry as a major contract provider of IC packaging. Leverage was effected in this case from a major multinational, which provided the training needed for the entrepreneur starting the business, as well as early business contracts.[45]

Globetronics was formed in 1990 by Michael Ng, a Chinese–Malaysian entrepreneur, with capital from his family trust, General Produce Agency (GPA), and a partner who has since left the business. The family trust had built up a business over the past 40 years in rubber and palm oil plantations. Globetronics represents its first investment in a high-technology venture.[46]

Globetronics represents an exemplary case of Malaysian high-technology development, in that it has been nurtured all along by a major multinational operating in Penang.[47] This MNC provided equipment to Globetronics at its inception, and gave the company its first orders. The arrangement allowed the MNC to subcontract its lower-end packaging to Globetronics, while it concentrated on the higher value-adding products such as microprocessors for its own internal packaging operations. The Globetronics initiative was taken in response to the acute need felt by the MNCs for capable local contract houses which would enable the multinationals to even out their production flows without having to expand and contract their own operations. Senior management of Globetronics has been drawn from former employees of local MNCs. This further underlines the significance of the MNC in the company's foundation and development.

Globetronics took off in its present form in 1991. It employed an initial staff of 250 in 1991, and grew rapidly to employ over 1000 by the mid-1990s. Revenue expansion was just as impressive.[48] Instead of competing across the board with existing suppliers of packaging contracting services in Korea (Anam), Taiwan (ASE) and Thailand (Alphatec) and in Malaysia itself (Carsem and Unisem), Globetronics pursued a niche strategy within the packaging business, concentrating on high-end ceramics packaging and 'burn-in' testing. The company has been most discriminating in its choice of customers. Initially it provided services for two firms only, namely a major MNC in Penang and Shinca, a local producer of electronics products. In 1992–93 a third firm, Hewlett-Packard, was added. Globetronics continued to grow through the 1990s. Further capital was acquired in 1993 to allow for expansion from the Malaysian Technology Development Corporation, which took up a 30 per cent stake in the company.

In 1994, Globetronics undertook a major strategic shift and aligned itself with the Japanese giant Sumitomo to produce state-of-the-art ceramic chip packages. A joint venture was created between Globetronics and SMCi – termed Sumitomo Globetronics Technology – 51 per cent owned by Sumitomo and 49 per cent by Globetronics. This is the first joint venture for the Sumitomo affiliate outside Japan, and a first for the Malaysian fledgling semiconductor materials supply industry. A new plant was constructed next to Globetronics' building in the Bayan Lepas industrial zone for the manufacture of the ceramic dual-in-line packages, with technology transferred from Sumitomo.[49] Thus Globetronics has lifted itself to its present position through leverage from Penang-based multinationals from the Japanese giant Sumitomo, and from the

Malaysian federal financial structures, all the while drawing its staff from the well-trained pool of managers and engineers available in Penang.

Perak – An Emerging Centre for Chip Packaging

Not all of Malaysia's states can boast of Penang's experiences. But one that has made headway in semiconductors is the central state of Perak, which had been the centre of tin-mining in the colonial era. It is now one of the most heavily industrialised areas in the Malaysian federation, with no fewer than 35 industrial estates, most of them created under the auspices of the Perak State Development Corporation (PSDC). Seagate Technology Inc of California, the world's largest producer of hard disk drives, and already well-established in South East Asia, chose Ipoh for its fourth plant in Malaysia. The factory opened for production in 1995.

Not all the enterprises in Perak are multinationals – some are Malaysian investments in the semiconductor industry, and one was a small semiconductor contract assembly firm, Carter Semiconductor, set up in 1972 in Perak. Like its counterparts at the time in Korea and Taiwan, it offered MNCs cheap assembly services using rows of highly dexterous but poorly paid young women. There was little, if any, technological investment in Carter Semiconductor.

In the mid-1980s, however, one of the Malaysian industrial groups created by the country's pro-development policies, the Hong Leong group, bought the firm as a going concern and proceeded to build an advanced facility equipped with state-of-the-art chip assembly technology. The venture was renamed Carsem, and sparked a chip assembly mini-industry in Perak that now employs over 7000 Malaysians. Carsem in turn spawned an independent chip assembly and packaging house, Unisem. Both are examples of the enterprise gains to be won by assiduous entrepreneurs through leverage from multinationals.

Unisem: A Malaysian Entrepreneurial Initiative

Unisem is a wholly Malaysian-owned semiconductor test and assembly contract house serving the overseas semiconductor fabrication industry. It was founded in Ipoh in 1991 by a Malaysian entrepreneur, Ku Hong Hai and Colin MacDonald, as outlined previously. Operations commenced at Unisem's Ipoh headquarters in March 1992. Ku and MacDonald developed their plan for a contract IC test and assembly house that would start its operations with the very best and latest production technology. Venture capital funds were raised from several sources in Malaysia and South East Asia. It was not easy to raise capital, but their efforts came at a time when Malaysian business was becoming aware of the rich possibilities available in semiconductors. They managed to raise an initial working capital of $7.5 million. A plant was built in record time, in six months. Ground was broken for the construction of a state-of-the-art plant in September 1991, located in the newly created Pulai Jaya industrial area in Simpang Pulai, Ipoh (Perak). The plant incorporated the latest in automated test and assembly equipment.[50]

Unisem's production system was built in an over-arching U-shape to incorporate the most advanced features of IC assembly, packaging and testing. It was the first semiconductor plant to be designed and built by a local Malaysian engineering firm; in the past, semiconductor plants were normally built by Japanese contractors.[51] An initial management team was assembled, again recruited largely from Ku's professional acquaintances. (The joke at Unisem is that they call themselves Motor Car, since they all came from Motorola or Carsem.) This management team has virtually stayed intact from day one – one of the secret assets of the company and an important factor in its success.

Orders were secured for the assembly and packaging of ICs from three multinationals in the US, Japan and Europe. For each of these customers, Unisem had to undergo rigorous quality certification tests and procedures, which they passed. Indeed they passed the first test in April 1991, less than a month after the occupation of the company's plant. The fledgling company gained an initial precious asset – a reputation for outstanding quality and reliability from inception. In 1993, barely six months into full production, Unisem secured an extremely important $35 million (RM100 million) three-year order from Samsung. Officials from Samsung awarded the contract competitively, after visiting seven subcontracting test and assembly firms in four East Asian countries during 1992. The Samsung order was for assembly and final testing of ICs, including shipment to final customers. This is rarely entrusted to contract firms, underlining Samsung's high regard for the Unisem facilities.

Unisem announced an expansion costing RM10–20 million in order to undertake the Samsung business. It has not seen fit to establish any marketing office outside Ipoh, operating exclusively by word of mouth and reputation. By 1995 it had acquired over two dozen multinational semiconductor firms as customers, some with business even larger than Samsung.[52] They are all connected to Unisem through dedicated computer links, including EDI that enable US customers, for example, to interact with Unisem's database during US business hours.

Unisem set a standard for the rest of the Malaysian industry in its insistence on entering the business at the highest and most demanding level of technology, seeking and attracting customers through the quality and reliability of its operations, rather than simply depending on low costs. Whether it expands further into front-end contracting such as a wafer fab, like its counterpart Anam in Korea, remains to be seen.

Wafer Fabrication in Malaysia

The late 1990s saw announcements of several IC fabrication initiatives slated for Malaysia, as well as of supporting operations such as silicon wafer production. These initiatives, if they are acted on, will bring the long-sought prize of front-end wafer fabrication to Malaysia, and help to maintain its parity with Singapore as a semiconductor operations base. The initiatives reflect the judgement by semiconductor multinationals that the skills of the Malaysian workforce, and the quality of the supply companies, have now reached sufficient level to support this most advanced of activities. Critical to these developments have been the creation of advanced infrastructure and R&D support in the form of the Kulim High-technology Park in Kedah, and the Malaysian Institute of Microelectronic Systems (MIMOS), which was establishing its first IC fabrication pilot plant in the late 1990s.

MIMOS

To assist in the development of the country's semiconductor industry, the Malaysian federal government in 1985 established MIMOS, a research and development agency that had construction of a research fab as one of its earliest aims. Agreements with foreign vendors were signed in July 1995 for the building of a pilot IC wafer-fabrication facility at MIMOS, the first of its kind in Malaysia. Yet it was to take ten years of delays before this goal would be realised – one of the features of Malaysia's high-technology industrialisation that speaks to institutional deficiencies.

The Economic Planning Unit of the federal government allocated funds to the wafer-fab project in the Fifth Malaysian Plan (1986–90) but nothing was done at this stage. The project has since moved through various consultancies, seemingly without getting any closer to fruition.[53] It was apparently only in 1992 that MIMOS made serious approaches to equipment suppliers on its own behalf – seven years after the organisation's foundation. With financial support from UNIDO (again) MIMOS sent representatives abroad to hunt for fabrication technology. A decision to purchase was made in 1994, and contracts exchanged in July 1995. Construction work started on the fab in May 1995, with equipment to be installed and chips coming off the line in 1996.[54]

Despite its difficulties, by the late 1990s MIMOS was gearing up to play the role of public-sector channel for capability enhancement of the

Malaysian semiconductor industry – as ITRI played for Taiwan in the 1970s and 1980s, and KIET for Korea. Whether MIMOS can actually deliver in the same way as these bodies were able to remains to be seen.

Sarawak

In the jungles of Borneo, further high-technology development zones are being created to satisfy the apparently inexhaustible demand for advanced sites in South East Asia by MNCs. Kuching, the capital of Sarawak state, is now one of the most active and sought after of these, through its Sama Jaya FIZ. This is already home to two US high-technology manufacturers, Zycon and Komag, and to two Japanese electronics firms. Komag has built a huge plant for its computer hard disks, which call for advanced clean-room technology. It expects to have several more plants co-located at Sama Jaya in the next few years, as well as plants of its principal supplier firms. At the end of 1995 Zycon committed itself to open a \$29 million plant for multilayered printed circuit boards.[55] Zycon chose the Sarawak site because the state government took the trouble to ensure adequate supplies of basics such as power and water, and the high skills level (including ability to speak English) of the local population. The existing Komag plant in Penang was to be an important training centre for these people. Thus one investment creates the possibilities for further investments, in a familiar upward process of technological enhancement.

In late 1995 the Sarawak state minister for industrial development, Datuk Abang Johari Abang Openg, stunned the semiconductor world and the rest of Malaysia with his announcement that a US consortium calling itself Interconnect had plans to build an IC wafer-fabrication plant in Sarawak. The minister was an energetic campaigner for Sarawak as the site of the next phase of Malaysia's high-technology industrial development. Its future, however, is uncertain; construction was put on hold in 1997.

Kulim High-technology Park

In the late 1990s, the federal government of Malaysia and state government of Kedah combined to form the Kulim Hi-Tech Industrial Park (KHTP), which promises to be a major focus for Malaysia's semiconductor and IT development. The KHTP is designed to act as a natural extension of Penang's further development, providing the land and labour that is in such short supply on the island. The KHTP is a long-term venture that will not be completed in any real sense until 2003 at the earliest. But already by the late 1990s there were substantial commitments made by leading semiconductor firms such as Intel, VLSI Technology, Atmel and specialist suppliers such as Sitt Tatt Industrial Gases and MEMC Electronic Materials.[56] The deal with VLSI Technology, a joint venture named Wafer Technology Malaysia (WTM), reveals how far the Malaysians have been able to exert leverage in semiconductor wafer fabrication.[57]

The Kulim development could well become the site for Malaysia's continued growth and expansion in front-end wafer manufacturing in the semiconductor industry. The Malaysian government formed a high-level Cabinet Taskforce to attract wafer-fabrication plants to the country, and was offering companies special incentive packages to locate their wafer fabs in Malaysia, and specifically at Kulim. But competition from other sites, particularly Singapore, has been intense.

The experiences of Singapore, Penang and other Malaysian centres such as Kedah or Petaling Jaya are constantly recycled as Malaysia moves towards the vision of being a fully developed country by 2020. Our account of developments, including local success stories like Globe-tronics and Unisem, does not seek to overstate the achievements. Globe-tronics is the only local Malaysian high-technology semiconductor firm to have emerged in Penang – after nearly thirty years of developmental leverage. This cannot be described as a high rate of propagation. At the federal level, MIMOS was founded in the late 1980s but it was only in the late 1990s that it was building a pilot IC wafer-fabrication plant. While the achievements are to be admired, the difficulties encountered once again point to the underlying institutional capacity of the country as being the critical factor in its ability to leverage advanced technologies and create indigenous high-technology industries.

Notes

1   Goh was not just an economic visionary and leader, but a prolific author as well. His collected works (Goh [1995a; 1995b; 1996]) provide fascinating insight into the strategies adopted in Singapore.

2   General sources on Singapore's industrialisation strategies include Rodan (1989) and Huff (1994); and on electronics and technology, Hobday (1994a; 1995a) and Wong (1995a, 1997).

3   The report – 'A proposed industrialisation program for the state of Singapore', United Nations Survey Mission – was delivered to the Singapore government in June 1961.

4   On the history of the Economic Development Board, see L. Low *et al.* (1993) and Schein (1996). For the speeches and writings of its first Chairman, Hon Sui Sen, see Low and Lim (1997).

5   By 1975, the Corporation's industrial estates covered nearly 3900 hectares,

on which 613 factories were sited. They employed 68 000 workers. See Goh (1977/1995b: 103).

6   These incentives were formalised in the 1967 *Economic Expansion Incentives (Relief from Income Tax) Act*. This reduced the corporate tax rate from 40 per cent to 4 per cent on export-generated profits, for up to fifteen years, in approved manufacturing occupations.

7   This was the main thrust of the recommendations made by Dr Winsemius in his second visit to Singapore in 1970: output of engineers, accountants and other professionals would have to be drastically upgraded to keep up with potential demand. At the same time, Singapore relaxed its restrictions on immigration and work permits, particularly for foreign professionals.

8   Between 1959, when the PAP government was elected, and 1975, total student enrolment in Singapore increased from 306 000 to 522 000. The increase was largest in the fields of secondary and tertiary education. Enrolment in secondary schools increased from 49 000 to 176 000. Enrolment in tertiary institutions – the two universities and polytechnics – increased from 5000 to 18 000. There was a strong practical and technical bias towards these tertiary enrolments, in keeping with the needs of an expanding and developing economy.

9   By 1975 the number of Malaysian guest workers had grown to close on 100 000.

10   On condition that the EDB official become the founding managing director of the local venture! The condition was accepted by the ever-pragmatic EDB.

11   The same experience of restructuring had occurred in Japan two decades before and was still underway in Korea and Taiwan.

12   By 1985 the EDB had become a victim of its own success, and it too was revitalised in 1986 with the new charter, to be implemented under a new chairman, Philip Yeo.

13   By the mid-1990s there were 32 MNCs enrolled as sponsors of the LIUP. Two of these were actually Singapore multinationals, namely Singapore Telecommunications and the Port Authority of Singapore.

14   For further details, see Low *et al.* (1993: 471–76).

15   Interview by JM with Kwok in Singapore, October 1998.

16   Interview by JM with Kwong in Singapore, October 1998.

17   This was a bipolar technology facility producing chips on 5-inch wafers for a variety of consumer electronics products applications.

18   This is a similar arrangement to ones that Texas Instruments has established elsewhere in East Asia, such as through the joint venture with Acer in Taiwan: TI-Acer. Of the total S$330 million investment, the EDB of Singapore put up 26 per cent, TI 26 per cent (much of it in kind), with Canon and Hewlett-Packard minority shareholders with 24 per cent each. Their interest as equity holders is to secure a supply of DRAMs for their own IT-related products through the 1990s.

19   The Singapore plant was voted one of the two top chip plants in the world in 1994 by the journal *Semiconductor International*, the industry's major publication. The magazine commended TECH Semiconductor for its manufacturing excellence, fast ramp-up, centralised computer monitoring, safety and environmental protection measures, emphasis on training and skills development and stringent quality assurance program.

20   One of its major projects has been the production of a Chinese teletext IC, which would decode teletext information in Latin-based languages as well as in Chinese characters – the first in the world.

21 They covered a design project for digital signal processing (DSP) chips, streamlining the wafer-fabrication process, and new packaging operations.

22 This and the following paragraphs are based on three visits by JM to CSM, in late 1994, in August 1996 and in October 1998, to speak to CSM's then President, Tan Bock Seng; as well as a visit in 1994 to CSM's sister IC design firm, TriTech, and to STATS in October 1998 where Tan had become CEO.

23 Sierra transferred its highly distinctive 'triple technology', through which it provides analog, digital and EEPROM technologies in an integrated fashion on chips. Sierra had only a small fab at its San Jose headquarters, and was looking to the Singapore joint venture to boost its fabrication capacities. Thus there was a match between STG's requirements for technology and Sierra's requirements for fabrication facilities.

24 By 1995 more than 80 per cent of its output was using submicron technology, and yields approached an impressive 94 per cent.

25 Technologically, CSM displayed strong measures of organisational learning in its approach to Fab 2. All the equipment suppliers, for example, were required as part of their contracts to provide support through their technicians stationed in Singapore; the aim of this stipulation was to ensure that tacit knowledge as well as codified technical knowledge would be passed on to CSM's engineers, and technological capability would thus be consolidated in the company. This is technological organisational learning.

26 The four founding members were Actel, Brooktree, Rockwell and LSI Logic. Other companies, such as Alliance, Analog Devices and Standard Microsystems Corporation, also came in as equity partners.

27 Toshiba transferred 0.5 micron, multi-layer metal CMOS wafer manufacturing process technology, along with technologies for reliability testing, failure analysis and process improvement methodologies.

28 This was the 1990s Strategic Economic Plan, prepared by an economic planning committee convened in 1989. See Ministry of Trade and Industry, *The Next Lap* (Singapore: MTI, 1991).

29 See Porter (1990). This has all along been the implicit approach of Japan, Korea and Taiwan. It makes sense to develop such an approach in an economy dominated by DFI, as in Singapore. Note, however, that Porter made a very negative judgement about Singapore's prospects in his 1990 study. We take up this issue later.

30 The IME is headed by Dr Bill Chen, who came to Singapore in 1991, after pursuing a career with the Bell Labs in the US. His appointment is in itself a kind of leverage on the part of Singapore, enabling the IME to draw on Dr Chen's worldwide networks.

31 Ball grid array (BGA) was then a new packaging technology for large lead-count ICs, which cuts through the multiplicity of external connections by making the connections internal to the chip. It is being pursued by such US multinationals as Compaq, Motorola and IBM.

32 The 11 firms were: AMD Singapore, AT&T Microelectronics, Delco Electronics Singapore, HP Singapore, Johnson Matthey Electronics, National Semiconductor Singapore, SGS-Thomson Microelectronics, Siemens Components and Silicon Systems Singapore (these all being multinationals) and the local Singaporean firms Advanced Systems Automation and Plaskon Electronic Materials.

33 The five programs were:
- the Manufacturing 2000 program, which aims to keep manufacturing contributing at least 25 per cent of GDP, and at least 20 per cent of

employment by 2000 (in 1995 manufacturing accounted for 25.3 per cent of GDP and the employment share of manufacturing was 24 per cent)
- the International Business Hub 2000 program, which aims to encourage firms to make Singapore the site for their regional headquarters
- the Promising Local Enterprises (PLE) program, which aims to foster the development of indigenous local firms, at least 100 of which are expected to grow to the point where they produce S$100 million in turnover within 10 years
- the Regionalisation 2000 program, which aims to establish high-technology industrial parks in Riaus (Indonesia); Suzhou and Wuxi (China), Bangalore (India) and Vietnam
- the Co-Investment program, which establishes a fund from which the EDB can make equity investments in strategic projects
  By the end of 1995 over S$200 million had been committed under the Cluster Development Fund in eight projects involving both MNCs and 'promising local enterprises'.

34   A S$500 million Innovation Development Scheme (IDS) was launched at the end of 1995. Under the scheme, companies can seek reimbursement of 50 per cent of the costs involved in undertaking innovation activities in products, processes, applications or services.

35   On Singapore's global expansion, see Yeung (1998).

36   The decision to locate the 0.25-micron 'pilot plant' at Chartered, rather than within IME, can be interpreted as a sign that IME was not yet considered strong enough to play the role in Singapore that ERSO played in Taiwan. This point is explored further in Chapter 6.

37   The NSTB launched a S$30 million Semiconductor Manpower Development Initiative in 1996 to encourage young Singaporeans to pursue postgraduate technical studies in semiconductor engineering at the National University of Singapore and the Nanyang Technological University.

38   In the fairy story, Jack acquires assets such as the hen that lays golden eggs – a good analogy for the skills leveraged by Singapore from multinationals. Jack does not kill the giant deliberately, but only chops down the beanstalk – with the giant in hot pursuit – as a last measure of self-defence. Singapore too maintains this right of self-defence, and will refuse to renew the investment permit of any multinational that refuses to invest in skills enhancement and technological upgrading.

39   On Malaysia's industrialisation strategies, see Ali (1992); Jomo (1993); Rasiah (1994; 1996); Jomo *et al.* (1998) and on electronics and semiconductors specifically, see O'Connor (1993) and Kim (1996).

40   Chan (1994: 5–15).

41   Peck and Tamura (1976), in their description of technology transfer and adaptation in Japan, refer to the phenomenon of 'improvement engineering', by which is meant upgrading the performance characteristics of imported machinery and equipment (1976: 542–43).

42   This transfer was codenamed TY-TX within Intel.

43   Lim (1991: 174).

44   Malaysian *Business Times*, 6 December 1995, p. 3. The case is based on a visit to LKT by JM in October 1995.

45   The identity of this MNC is kept confidential at the specific request of Globetronics.

46   The chairman of Globetronics was Ng Kweng-Hai, an elder of the Ng family business. This is how Chinese family capital renews itself – by backing a new venture by an energetic younger member of the family.

47   Michael Ng himself worked for close to twenty years for Intel, and conceived his new business as a contract supplier of IC assembly and packaging. Personal interview, December 1995.

48   The services offered by Globetronics included IC assembly (glass-sealed ceramic, co-fired laminated ceramic as well as some plastic packaging) and IC burn-in services – that is, Globetronics took wafers from client IC firms and packaged them into usable ICs. It then goes on to stress test some of these chips in various environmental settings, including 'burn in'. Thus the end-customer receives a chip that has actually proved itself as reliable for an extended period.

49   The joint venture initially supplied the Japanese firm's existing customers in the SE Asian region, but it was expected to develop new customers of its own. Ceramics packaging was the dominant trend in the region. In 1995 a second joint venture with Sumitomo was formed, to concentrate on Pin Grid Array (PGA) ceramics packages production. PGAs are high-end packages used for high value-adding ICs such as Intel's Pentium. The new joint venture was called SGT Industries.

50   The plant took investments of RM40 million. Around RM20 million was invested in equipment, RM14 million in building, and RM6 million in working capital to cover wages and other expenses. Construction was completed in February 1992. Production began six months later, in July.

51   The firm was Hiti Engineering, who were turn-key contractors for Motorola.

52   Twenty of these were US-based (including IBM), three were from Japan (including Sony), two from Europe (SGS-Thomson and Philips) and one from Korea (Samsung).

53   A first effort was struck with a consultant from Japan's National Telephone and Telegraph. He recommended establishing a research fabrication facility, at a cost of RM20 million. Next MIMOS engaged a German consultant, with funds secured from the UN Industrial Development Organisation (UNIDO), in 1989. He also recommended the establishment of a research fabrication facility; MIMOS used the report to seek investments from private firms, but none showed any interest. Then with further funds from UNIDO, a further consultant was engaged in 1991, this time from the Netherlands. He again recommended construction of a pilot fab at an estimated cost of RM31.3 million ($12 million). A proposal along these lines was approved as part of Malaysia's Sixth Plan (1991–95) – but apparently never implemented. Yet another consultant (from the US) was engaged to conduct a study on the technology, equipment and skills needed by such a facility. By comparison with other developments, such as the creation of the pilot LSI fabrication facility at ITRI in Taiwan in 1977, progress at MIMOS appears to have been slow.

54   The first phase of the fab incorporated CMOS technology down to 1-micron line-width. The next phase was to incorporate CMOS and BiCMOS fabrication lines operating at 0.5 micron geometry.

55   *Asian Wall Street Journal,* 14 February 1996, pp. 1, 4.

56   Other ventures such as those proposed by Hualon (Taiwan) and Hitachi and LG Semicon, which made earlier commitments, were subsequently dissolved.

57   WTM planned to operate a new wafer-fabrication plant on the Kulim park,

with process technology supplied entirely by VLSI Technology; the US firm
would in addition pass over its existing wafer fab in San Jose, in the heart
of Silicon Valley, for operation by WTM. The joint venture was funded
entirely by Malaysian industrial development banks, BIM and KNB – until
the Asian financial crisis intervened and put the project on hold.

PART III

The Technology Leverage Strategy

CHAPTER 6

East Asian Semiconductor Industries: National Strategies and Sustainability

Our exposition so far has provided a detailed account of the creation of the semiconductor industry in four East Asian countries. We have analysed the organisational and institutional strategies employed, and sought to account for the achievements outlined in Chapter 1. We now shift gear to examine the strategies employed in comparative perspective, probing them for strengths and weaknesses.

In this chapter, we confine our attention to the semiconductor industry, looking at the character of the industry created in each of the different countries, and extrapolating from this to analyse, at least to a first approximation, what may be the core strengths and the potential pitfalls of the leverage and learning approach to creating new industries. The advantage of our approach is that we are focusing on a single industry, over the course of its entire trajectory. Thus, many of the concerns and issues expressed in more general terms by other scholars can be tackled with greater precision in the case of this specific industry, and be subjected to more searching scrutiny. We examine the institutional pathways followed by the industry creation process characteristic of each country, look at their commonalities and differences, and attempt to account for them. The implications of such an analysis are brought out in our study of the sustainability of the industries created.

In Chapter 7 we probe the leverage strategies more generally, examining their strengths and limits to their applicability, and the potential pitfalls involved in using them. We test the proposition that the strategies have a coherence and a replicability that sees them constantly reproduced, not just in East Asia but in the advanced countries, as industries seek to catch up with each other.

Finally in Chapter 8 we pull all the threads together, sketching out the 'national systems of economic learning' that have been created in East Asia for the purposes of industry seeding and development, and seek to draw some general lessons. We find that the leverage strategy emerges virtually intact as a 'model' for high-technology catch-up. Certainly we find it hard to envisage an alternative that can promise as much to firms and countries in catch-up mode, especially within the setting of high-technology industry.

East Asian Pathways to Semiconductor Industry Creation

To begin, a summary of our argument and the evidence presented concerning the creation of semiconductor industries in East Asia. Japan was the first such industry, and we argue that it had achieved essential sustainability, according to all reasonable criteria, by 1979, at the conclusion of the VLSI program.[1] Japan was then ready to launch its DRAM assault of the 1980s.

Korea and Taiwan were well on the way to achieving sustainability by the end of the 1990s (putting down the roots of sustainability from the end of the 1980s), but achieved these results in very different ways. Korea was a world leader in the demanding segment of DRAMs, but achieved little progress beyond this. Taiwan, by contrast, was only becoming a force in DRAMs in the second half of the 1990s, having achieved a greater prior diversity of capabilities that sustained the industry well during the financial crisis of 1997–98.

Singapore had been putting down the roots of sustainability since the beginning of the 1990s, but by any reasonable criteria still had some way to go, while Malaysia still appeared to be in the propagation phase of our DRL framework. These considerations are illustrated in Table 6.1.

We now seek to substantiate these summary conclusions, comparing the evidence for each country in terms of the strategies adopted, their institutional underpinnings, and their effectiveness in creating well-balanced and sustainable semiconductor industries.

Japan

Japan was the first. This was the breakthrough case that made everything else possible. Japan was the first non-Western country to successfully industrialise – the original 'East Asian miracle' with its two decades of high-speed growth in the 1960s and 1970s. But Japan was also the first non-Western country to upgrade its industrial structure in line with a shift to knowledge-intensive industries, which is our central concern.[2] Through a process of trial and error, and remarkable foresight, Japan created an industrial 'system' that was capable of breaking through the

Table 6.1 Developmental resource leverage in the semiconductor industry in East Asia

Year	Japan	Korea	Taiwan	Singapore	Malaysia
1970		DRL I	DRL I	—	—
1974		DRL II		DRL I	—
1975	DRL IV				DRL I
1976			DRL II	DRL II	—
1979	complete				
1980			DRL III	DRL II	DRL II
1982		DRL III			
1983					
1985				DRL III	
1989		DRL IV	DRL IV		
1990					
1991				DRL IV	DRL III
1997	⇩	⇩	⇩	⇩	⇩

Western monopoly on scientific and technological innovation – not through trying to match Western firms initially in terms of R&D-led product development, but through accelerated diffusion of new techniques, combined with unprecedented attention to manufacturing quality and efficiency.

It makes no sense to try to analyse the Japanese system of knowledge-intensive industrial upgrading as it was formulated in the 1960s and 1970s from the perspective of Western innovation strategies. It evolved to achieve something quite different from rapid product development, which was the goal of innovation as understood in the US and Europe. Japan's goal was rapid 'catch-up', to be achieved at any cost and in any way possible through a combination of public and private resources working together in some form of strategic collaboration. The fact that it was successful had remarkable implications not just for Japan, but for other countries in East Asia. Japan's success meant that countries such as Korea and Taiwan could hope to succeed in knowledge-intensive industrial upgrading as well.

While its strategies and methods were successful, they were costly politically, and did not necessarily represent the only 'pathway' to knowledge-intensive industrial upgrading. The later East Asian arrivals would be competing not just against US and European firms, but against Japanese firms as well. It was largely because of the latter two implications that Korea and Taiwan could not hope to succeed by following a 'carbon copy' of Japan's approach. The political costs of the closed-market approach characteristic of Japan would simply be unsustainable (that is, they would not be allowed to upgrade industrially under the same conditions extended to Japan) while pursuit of an identical strategy to Japan's would not hold up against Japanese competitors. Moreover, both nations started with very small domestic markets for semiconductors – their electronics and IT industries purchasing most of their components from the advanced countries – and so had to deal with export markets from the outset, unlike the Japanese situation, where companies could hone their skills first on domestic customers.

The Japanese 'model' of knowledge-intensive industrial upgrading by a non-Western country, *because it was the first*, had to be seen as some kind of benchmark. The main elements of the Japanese system of technology leverage and diffusion management – what we have called developmental resource leverage – which resulted in the creation of an industrial ecology cultivated for the nurturing of the semiconductor industry, were built step by step, as follows.

Strategic Industry and Technology Identification

Japan recognised early on the significance of the semiconductor technology, when the first transistors were being produced and discussed in the 1950s. These were seen as a potential industry in their own right, and as significant components for new electronic products. It seemed a natural step in Japan's case, since after the devastation of war it lacked sophisticated companies operating at the technological frontier to foster technological competence accumulation in these newly identified sectors within public-sector laboratories (initially the Electrotechnical Laboratory (ETL) of MITI and the Electrical Communication Laboratories (ECL) of the NTT). These public facilities were the site of Japan's early competence acquisition in transistor technology, and later in early IC developments.[3]

Industrial Grouping Creation

Rather than leave the transmission of technological competences from the public to the private sector to 'market forces', the Japanese government agencies organised a rather more sophisticated and effective catch-up system for industrial upgrading, involving a group of firms and close coordination between them and leading government agencies. Through administrative coordination and other devices, a group of highly competent firms were assembled to act as primary carriers of the new technological competencies. These competencies were to be used to quickly develop products which could be commercialised, initially for the domestic market and later for exports. Japan's industrial organisation, consisting of a series of interlocking inter-organisational *keiretsu*, was of enormous assistance in assembling a competent group of firms – in effect, one firm from each of the half-dozen *keiretsu*. This is how an initial group of six firms – NEC, Fujitsu, Hitachi and Oki, from the telecommunications side, and Toshiba, Hitachi and Mitsubishi from the electrical equipment side (with Hitachi spanning the two) – was assembled. Firms with interests in electronic consumer goods such as Matsushita, Sanyo, Sony and Sharp were eventually also fitted in.

Institutions of Technological Collaboration

While encouraging a healthy degree of competition between the firms involved in the new sector, the Japanese government agencies were able to build an institutional foundation for collaboration as well, exploiting both competition and collaboration as tools of industrial upgrading. The self-organisation of the private sector, through the formation of such institutions as the Electronic Industries Association of Japan (EIAJ) in 1948 and the Japan Electronic Industry Development Association (JEIDA) in 1958, provided the key to successful public–private sector coordination, with MITI supplying strategic leadership on the public side, and the 'Group of Six' providing the commercial implementation on the private side, of the strategies devised collectively.

This organisation of industry, entirely a product of Japanese genius, owed nothing to Western notions of liberal competitive markets and proved to be remarkably resilient and adaptable, providing the flexible framework within which Japanese firms acquired and upgraded their technological competencies, in one wrenching process of change after another.

Catch-up Technological Goals

Technological and industrial goals were selected for their strategic significance in terms of potential business and of providing a platform for future expansion. This, again, is the essence of the catch-up strategy, consisting of both 'crisis' and 'opportunity' components. The *crisis* is created by the widening of the technological gap – such as IBM introducing a new computer system based on ICs rather than on vacuum tubes. The *opportunity* is created by having a definite target to aim for. These targets were selected through a judicious process of technological sounding and multiple iterations in MITI-sponsored industry councils. Once the targets were selected then the machinery of state promotion, incentive and discipline could be mobilised to accelerate the private sector's achievement of the goals.

The most striking feature of the industrial 'system' that resulted was that it helped to set limits to the competitive development of the industry. 'Excess competition' (*kato kyoso*) that could kill any nascent industry was contained through selected entry, while fierce competition was encouraged between the selected companies, domestically and in export markets. But this competition was tempered by collaboration on selected technological upgrading targets. Industry management on this scale had never been attempted before either in the East or West.

Industry Creation Measures

The early model of MITI-coordinated industry creation and industrial upgrading involved a number of steps, as elaborated by Johnson (1982). There was the formulation of a basic policy or 'vision' statement that sketched out the expected lines of development; this document would serve as a benchmark for future evaluations, and a means of securing consensus across the industry on a set of goals (even if they appeared to be wildly unrealistic, such as Japan's aiming to create super-fast ICs in advance of the leading US firms in the 1970s). Administrative means were then brought into play to support the vision: foreign currency allocations were made and funding lined up by the Development Bank for the purchase of technology; licences for the import of technology would be issued by MITI; special depreciation allowances and other tax incentives could be triggered by declaring the industry 'strategic', and so on. MITI would then coordinate a hand-picked group of firms (normally spanning all the *keiretsu*) to act as drivers of the new industry and as vehicles for technology acquisition, and they would be provided with incentives, tax allowances and exemptions from import duties to encourage their rapid entry into the designated industry. Coordination in this instance meant coordination of investment, regulation of competition, and usually some kind of collaboration with public sector laboratories such as ECL and ETL to hasten the acquisition (diffusion) of technological competencies.

This was the 'MITI model' of the 1960s and early 1970s, which served Japan extremely well for its early phases of labour-intensive and capital-intensive industrial upgrading that generated high-speed growth. But it proved *insufficient* for the demands of knowledge-intensive industrial upgrading. Based on strategies formulated by MITI officials such as Amaya in the mid-1970s, further administrative methods had to be invented to ensure that Japanese firms could keep up, let alone take a leadership position, in sectors such as semiconductors and computers. MITI came up with the novel 'Engineering Research Association' (ERA), which proved to be an enduring institutional innovation adapted from an earlier European innovation.

The ERA brought firms together into collaborative R&D efforts on designated projects without sacrificing their competitive postures in other areas and at other times. In the typical ERA, all the member firms conducted development work in their own laboratories; collaboration was in the pooling of results and the partition of development work into a number of parallel projects which could be undertaken by different firms, thereby accelerating the rate at which all firms involved could absorb new techniques.[4]

As sophisticated as this system was, it was inadequate because of the extraordinary demands made by the goal of catching up in semiconductors. Thus the VLSI project of 1976 to 1979 introduced the further institutional innovation of a 'Common Developmental Laboratory' to which all the member firms assigned some of their best engineers. This institutional innovation had mixed success, and has not been widely repeated in Japan. Nevertheless, it certainly assisted and accelerated the diffusion of best practice in firms producing ICs at VLSI technological level, particularly DRAMs. By 1979 Japan had indeed caught up with the best US firms such as Intel, TI and IBM, and was ready to compete head-to-head with them in international and US markets.

Strategic Selection of Semiconductor Products

The Japanese institutional form for technological catch-up was complemented by strategic selection of certain products (normally, those most amenable to standardisation and commodification – hence, DRAMs in semiconductors) and by painstaking attention to the 'industrial ecology' of the new sector, particularly the support and supply industries providing specialist materials and equipment. Firms judged capable of acting in such support roles were introduced into the more recent collaborative projects so that they would have the benefit of working at the frontier with the firms developing the next-generation product technologies. 'User-driven' innovation, which has attracted so much attention in management literature, was no stranger to the Japanese.

All these ingredients came together in the VLSI project of 1976–79, which was concerned with generating the product and process technologies needed to fabricate next-generation DRAMs, and the firms that were able to produce these technologies. This turned out to be a largely collaborative project for the accelerated development of a materials and equipment supply industry in Japan that would provide full support as leading firms such as NEC, Hitachi and Toshiba drastically racked up their investments in DRAM production at the end of the 1970s and early 1980s.

This same institutional model has been used repeatedly in Japan, subject to institutional refinement, when a clear catch-up target has been identified. A classic instance outside the semiconductor sector was Japan's uptake of the new technology of basic oxygen steel-making in the 1960s, in advance of any other steel industry in the world – even though the technology was not developed in Japan.[5] In semiconductors Japan refined the model as it acquired the characteristics of a leader rather than a follower. Once Japanese firms had achieved parity with the world's best, then a catch-up model could no longer deliver the goods: there would no longer be clear targets for emulation (since from a position of leadership, it is much more difficult to predict the direction of future technological change), and firms would be much more reluctant to collaborate on projects with competitors. It is therefore not surprising that there were no more MITI-coordinated collaborative projects in the 1980s to match the VLSI project in semiconductors. (Of course there were such projects in other technological areas, such as advanced computing.) This should not be interpreted as a 'defeat' of MITI but as the expected evolution of the Japanese industrial system in semiconductors as it moved to a position of global technological parity with US industry.[6] What was created in the first place was a formidable system of technology diffusion management which provided the other countries of East Asia with their template and model – and competitive benchmark.

Korea

The dominant industrial strategy in Korea had always been emulation of Japan, and the catch-up efforts were directed not just at the advanced Western industries, but at the Japanese industries which had already caught up with or even surpassed their Western competitors. Thus Korea's strategy has largely been directed towards creating technological capabilities in sectors where Japan has shown that leveraged catch-up is feasible. This was clearly the case in sectors such as petrochemicals, steel-making, ship-building and automobiles. The semiconductor sector is surely the pre-eminent case of this strategy at work.

The preparatory stage in Korea's case saw the establishment of the vehicles of leverage, which, following the model of Japan, were seen to be industrial conglomerates (*chaebol*). The industrial take-off decade of the 1960s saw a series of export-oriented industrial conglomerates established, with state-rationed credit to provide finance, and careful leveraging of technology for industrial muscle. In most cases, such as Samsung or LG, the company had existed in pre-Korean war times, but only as a very small player, frequently as a trader rather than a manufacturer. It was under the dictatorship of Park Chung-Hee that the

Korean industrial system took shape, modelled on Japan's *keiretsu* or pre-war *zaibatsu* (or, more specifically, on Japan's war-time economic creation in Manchuria, where Park had served as a young officer in the Japanese occupation forces).[7] It was the successes achieved by these conglomerates in relatively low-technology mass production industries that created the vehicles for high-technology industrial upgrading. More than in any other country of East Asia, Korea's high-technology industrialisation has been a product of these firms working independently on their own projects of export-oriented industrial upgrading, fuelled by financial resources provided under tight conditions of surveillance and discipline exercised by state agencies. Indeed, the 'core competencies' of these firms lay not so much in manufacturing techniques – which they were able to absorb from commercial suppliers – as in the systematic and rapid creation of *new businesses*, through which they achieved unprecedented diversification, and in the 'combinative capabilities' they brought to bear on the task of integrating machinery and capital equipment and product designs from a variety of sources.

By the time the *chaebol* were ready to take the plunge into VLSI semiconductors in the early 1980s, the system of corporate oversight provided by government, and the performance benchmarks in terms of export levels, had been settled. This was the overall framework that was used for Korea's push into semiconductors – one that was formulated and driven at the highest levels of the government (the Presidential Blue House) and by the founder–entrepreneurs of the major *chaebol*. These were to become highly effective vehicles for the leveraging of the technologies required.

While Korea strove to recreate the elements of the Japanese model, it fell short on two significant counts. When the Japanese began their 'final' push to technologically upgrade to VLSI capabilities in 1976, the firms involved were already operating at very sophisticated levels, and were indeed leaders in their fields of electric machinery, computers and telecommunications equipment supply. By contrast, when the Korean *chaebol* began their push less than ten years later, they were much less technically sophisticated, and were forced to purchase virtually all the product and process technology needed for the new sector on the open market – making the strategically correct judgement that it would be available, for a price. Further, the coordinating capability of the Japanese public agencies, led by MITI but also encompassing the JEIDA, the EIAJ, and the public–private consortia, far exceeded the capacity of the Korean public agencies to mount a similarly coordinated program, both because of the limited technical and collaborative capabilities of the state agencies themselves, and because of the intense rivalry of the *chaebol*.

This rivalry had been fostered in the earlier industrialisation phase by the Korean state agencies as a weapon to protect against cosiness and rent seeking, and it has weighed heavily on the country's industrial upgrading efforts ever since.

In striking contrast with Taiwan, the Korean strategy called for little dependence on small and medium-sized enterprises (which by the late 1990s were still conspicuously lacking in the Korean political economy) or on public-sector research institutes. This is not to say that great efforts were not made within public institutes to acquire technological capabilities in semiconductor technologies, notably by KIET in the 1970s, where a pilot LSI wafer-fabrication facility had been built with technology transfer from the US firm, VLSI Technology, by 1979. But these efforts had little direct continuity with the major push by the *chaebol* into VLSI production in the 1980s; their links were indirect, such as in passing on skilled staff and contacts in Silicon Valley.

Once the initial investments in VLSI capabilities by Samsung, LG and Hyundai had taken place (with Daewoo following behind), the stage was set for the characteristic Korean pattern of catch-up and innovation systems operating in parallel within the separate *chaebol*. It is reasonable to say that Korea had not one, but three, national innovation or upgrading systems – as represented by Samsung, Hyundai and LG. These firms did everything on their own – there was little effective coordination. (There were joint development efforts, such as the consortia established for the 1M and 4M DRAMs, but they provided the *chaebol* with only marginal benefits.) With continuing access to regulated and rationed finances, as well as with open credit lines across their different operating arms, these *chaebol* were able to purchase the required product and process technologies, and, with determined internal efforts of organisational learning, were able to bring themselves abreast of world technological capabilities. They quickly established global marketing operations and internationalised their R&D efforts, particularly through the purchase of equity stakes in start-up Silicon Valley firms. In the 1990s, they internationalised their production efforts as well, establishing wafer-fabrication plants in Europe, the US and in South East Asia – their semiconductor operations acted both as spur, and as platform, for the globalisation of these giant firms.

It was investment strategy that undoubtedly drove Korean success. Aggressive investment had been the hallmark of the Korean approach to achieving competitiveness: Korean firms actively invested during the 1985 cyclical downturn, when Japanese investment fell away, picking up business in 1986 and 1987. This was their first taste of victory. But the same thing happened in 1991–92 when Japanese investment fell off and Korean investment picked up, resulting in Samsung seizing number one spot in 1993, and the Korean industry dominating the world market for 16M DRAMs by 1994. By the 1997–98 financial crisis, it was Korean investment that was forced to slacken, while that of the Taiwanese industry continued unabated, particularly in DRAMs, leading to a shift in competitive advantage between the two countries.

With the financial crisis of 1997–98, the Korean strategy, with its high debt levels and over-reliance on a single product, namely DRAMs, proved to be extremely vulnerable to any external downturn. Such a downturn occurred with the collapse of memory chip prices in 1995–96 – a collapse that led to a severe contraction in cash-flow for the Korean majors, and to substantial difficulties in meeting repayment schedules. Ambitious overseas expansion plans had to be scrapped – for example, LG Semicon's proposed chip plant in Wales – while new entrants to the industry, such as the Dongbu DRAM venture (with technology supplied by IBM) and the proposed TI-Anam joint venture to produce DRAMs, had to be put on hold. By 1998 the Korean semiconductor industry was looking a lot less buoyant than in 1995, but it was surviving, and had amassed a sufficiently strong technological base that promised to pull it through the crisis intact.[8] This, after all, is the toughest test of sustainability that an industry can be subjected to. The same test was being applied to Taiwan.

Taiwan

If Korea has been a classic instance of large firms cooperating with state agencies to muscle their way into high-technology industry – in a Japanese brand of a Gerschenkronian strategy – the Taiwanese case presents some striking contrasts. For reasons that go deep into its political origins, the developmental process in Taiwan has been carried largely by public-sector agencies working closely with small and medium-sized enterprises.[9] While large industrial conglomerates have indeed emerged in Taiwan, they are not on the same scale as in Korea, nor have they been created as institutions by state-credit rationing. The years of the Taiwan 'miracle' of the 1960s and 1970s saw the island generate literally thousands of hard-working small and medium-sized firms engaged in labour-intensive industrial contracting work, linked direct to industrial customers in the US, Europe and Japan. These firms generated wealth, but not knowledge. They were not to be the bearers of a new stage of high-technology industrial upgrading.

Instead, the Taiwan development and planning agencies concocted an ingenious alternative model of high-technology upgrading. As in the Japanese and Korean cases, the early technological capabilities were acquired and consolidated by public-sector R&D institutes created for this very purpose. Thus ERSO, the electronics laboratory within ITRI that was established only in 1973, was by 1976 already embarking on a major program to build a semiconductor LSI fabrication pilot facility through technology transfer from RCA – at the very same time as Korea's KIET was doing the same through technology transfer from VLSI Technology, and Japan's MITI was coordinating its final push in the VLSI project. But in Taiwan, there were no companies ready and willing to receive the technology adopted and adapted by ITRI. (Electronics firms such as Tatung and Sampo were already large and sophisticated, but they were not prepared to take the plunge into semiconductors.) So Taiwan's solution was to create a private sector in the technological image of the public sector. This was an extraordinarily innovative – and effective – strategy for knowledge-intensive industry creation.

The process began with the Hsinchu Science-based Industry Park in 1980, and the spinning off of UMC from ERSO in the same year. More firms followed, mostly in the design phase of IC fabrication, until a decisive boost was given with TSMC's creation in 1986 through a joint venture with Philips. TSMC's conception as a 'silicon foundry' underpinned much IC activity on the Hsinchu Park and led the sector's technological development (for example, through TSMC setting new 'design rules' for the IC design houses) and paved the way for the first substantial investments from the private sector. Interestingly, these investments came from firms in sunset sectors such as cables and textiles (Walsin Lihwa backing Winbond, and Hualon backing HMC) looking to regenerate their cash flow through high-technology activity.

Why did Taiwan use public-sector enterprises in a high-technology field such as semiconductors against the trend of all advanced countries and the conventional wisdom that sees the private sector as the *only* form of enterprise able to cope with a fast-changing technology-intensive field such as semiconductors? This question goes to the heart of the Taiwanese model of developmental resource leverage. One reason certainly has to do with the absence of large, integrated electronics complex firms in Taiwan, compared with the existence of firms such as NEC, Toshiba or Hitachi in Japan, and Samsung, Goldstar, Daewoo and Hyundai in Korea, which provided a ready vehicle for those countries' forays into the high-technology semiconductor field. Public-sector agencies which could enter joint ventures with foreign partners (such as ERSO with Philips to form TSMC; or CCL with Motorola and IBM for the PowerPC consortium) represented a viable alternative for Taiwan, where small and medium-sized firms were the norm. Another reason lies in the 'demonstration effect' that such public enterprises as UMC and TSMC have had in inducing private-sector firms to make the substantial investments needed to enter the semiconductor industry.[10] The publicly financed firms would take the initial risks of entry into the new sector, but not 'crowd out' other players as private capital followed their lead.

All the major firms which have emerged as key players in the Taiwanese semiconductor industry reflect the influence of leverage and organisational learning, but in different and interesting ways. All were products of leverage in the first place. UMC was the purest expression of this process, deriving all its initial assets from Taiwan's public-sector institutions. TSMC was established with a more elaborated form of leverage, taking over technical capabilities from ITRI's VLSI project, as well as technical know-how and intellectual property from its joint venture partner, Philips. Later, the DRAM spin-off from ITRI, VISC, performed the same role, taking over the assets of the submicron project in the early 1990s. Winbond marked a shift to the private sector in the elaboration of this process, deriving its founder and initial human assets from ERSO/ITRI, but drawing its financial backing from an industrial conglomerate, the Walsin Lihwa group. It was able to develop its own range of initial products through its market research and R&D, supplemented by a range of strategic alliances. Nan Ya Technology, Acer Semiconductor Manufacturing (formerly TI-Acer) and Powerchip all represent later versions of this strategy, in that they were initiated by existing Taiwanese businesses, and leveraged their technology from US or Japanese sources. Macronix and Mosel-Vitelic followed the most R&D intensive routes, but each leveraged required product and process technologies as they entered new product segments. All have continued to use leverage through partnerships with leading firms as a means of broadening their product base and to enter new markets.

The seeding of a private-sector semiconductor industry in Taiwan in the 1980s has been followed by a flowering of talent and capabilities that few could have foreseen. The Taiwan semiconductor industry is technologically advanced, and produces a broad range of IC and discrete products, as well as hybrids and chip-sets which feed directly into its thriving electronics and computer businesses. The semiconductor strategy in Taiwan has been of a piece with its strategy of industrialising through components and OEM manufacturing rather than necessarily concentrating on branded end products – although this is now changing as the electronics and computer industries mature, and are joined by communications and software industries in an 'information technology complex' that is expected to remain Taiwan's top export performer in 2000 and beyond. The most striking feature of the Taiwan case is its capacity to engage in repeated rounds of technological upgrading, always following a similar institutional form of the public-sector agencies such as ITRI and its laboratories working closely with networks or consortia of small and medium-sized firms. This has become a characteristic feature of the Taiwan 'national system of economic learning' and one that demonstrates high learning capacity as its institutional foundations are improved from one technological upgrading experience to another.

Singapore and Malaysia

The institutions of resource leverage in the cases of Singapore and Malaysia are quite different from those encountered in Japan, Korea and Taiwan. Leverage from internal and external MNCs is a distinctive and (it would seem) effective approach to high-technology industrialisation. In this case Singapore and Malaysia are particularly important because they appear to be the first of what will very likely come to be seen as the most widespread and viable strategy for high-technology industrial upgrading in the twenty-first century. While there was only one Japan, and while the institutions of Korea and Taiwan are unlikely to be replicated in full by any other country, the experience of Singapore (and Malaysia) could in principle be replicated – and does appear to be replicated, in early stages, in countries like China. What, then, were the strategies and the institutional underpinnings of their approach?

In both countries, there was a clearly demarcated initial phase in which investment – any kind of investment – was sought, simply to kickstart a process of modernisation and industrialisation. This began in Singapore after 1965; in Penang in 1970; and in other states of Malaysia through the 1970s and 1980s. Singapore provides the clearest example of what 'preparation' calls for in this context. It demands an institutional agency geared towards rapid and decisive dealing with MNCs (in Singapore, the EDB; in Penang, the PDC), and equipped with powers and capabilities that enable it to prepare industrial estates, provide worker housing and welfare amenities, and other social infrastructure such as world-class hotels and a country club, as in Penang. It calls for state provision of basic training and skills formation activities, particularly in the technical skills being targeted by the MNC investors. It calls for industrial relations and human resource management arrangements that favour disciplined work and productivity improvements, while placing obligations on employers to provide training and opportunities for career advancement. It calls for a liberal financial regime in which MNCs can make investment decisions for themselves, laced with tax and other incentives, and in which there are no obstacles put in the way of profit repatriation. Under these circumstances, Singapore and Malaysia have shown that MNCs will work assiduously, provide stable employment and upgrade the technological level of their activities, enriching themselves and the countries in which they operate.[11]

The processes of 'seeding' and 'diffusion' also take quite distinctive institutional form when the engine driving them is MNC-based activity. Both Singapore and Penang reveal the efficacy of leveraging strategies based on *internal* skills and technology transfer within the MNCs, and on *external leveraging* through the creation of various kinds of maintenance and equipment supply firms to service them. In effect, this leverage strategy is based on encouraging the formation of *backward linkages* from the MNC to local firms.[12] In such a process a leading agency like the EDB or PDC is critical, to take the initiative in terms of favouring certain kinds of investment (skills and knowledge-based) and, after the initial phase, rejecting investment based on simple, labour-intensive activities. More restrictive conditions were set on MNC investment, requiring firms to make undertakings regarding the expansion of activities, the inclusion of some R&D and product development, and upgrading to include marketing and product support. These restrictions can only be imposed once a country has established itself as a desirable site for MNC investment. Singapore has shown that the upgrading burdens on MNCs can be increased, not by 'breaking' previous agreements, but by imposing more onerous conditions on new firms as they locate in the region, and by making agreements for set periods of time and periodically renewing them.

The Malaysian institutional framework is less successful. Particularly in the field of technical training, progress has been slow.[13] The Ministry of International Trade and Industry has not been able to demonstrate anything like the 'institutional capacity' of comparable agencies in North East Asia, or indeed of Singapore's EDB, in harnessing advanced technologies from abroad, or in assessing the proposed technological upgradings of firms operating in Malaysia. This problem is compounded in the seeding of dynamic new technology-based small and medium-sized enterprises. A strategy of external leverage via the formation of small and medium-sized service enterprises is a product of facilitation by the public agencies, and the provision of an economic framework that favours the formation of such small firms (a point that Singapore grasped only after the 1985–86 recession). These SMEs can rapidly become high-technology multinational operations in their own right, as shown by numerous examples in Singapore, Penang and elsewhere (such as ASA, MIT, LKT/SEM and Globetronics). Their formation is encouraged and facilitated by the formation of network linkages with the MNCs in ways which are quite foreign to the original model of industrialisation through FDI by MNCs, in isolated foreign investment zones. Such zones, which were popular in Taiwan and Korea in the 1960s, were in effect 'export enclaves' and were rapidly overtaken by the development of an indigenous industry; they have not in general seeded the next phase of technology-intensive development. In Singapore and Malaysia, the zones served by contrast as foci for the formation of tight business networks (supplier networks, vendor partnerships) that have expanded rapidly through the region. But public policy was slow to register and act on this development.

The goal, as in Korea and Taiwan, was the creation of a viable *local* high-technology industry. This can be expected to arise from local firms investing in advanced technology activities (for example, the Malaysian Hong Leong group investing in Carsem, or the General Produce Agency trust investing in Globetronics in Penang). Singapore also showed how a parallel diffusion track can arise from the state-owned sector, which provided a separate source of technology leverage and a base for diversification, in the first instance, through the formation of Chartered Semiconductor and its sister firms, TriTech and STATS, under the umbrella of the Singapore Technologies Group. Neither Singapore nor Malaysia has revealed a propensity to 'seed' semiconductor activities through the formation of a firm with the intention of its taking over public assets and skills, as in the Taiwanese UMC, TSMC and VISC models. However it remained an option that might be taken in Malaysia, as MIMOS was building up its pilot wafer-fabrication activities in the late 1990s.

The putting down of roots of sustainability calls for institutional support of the kind offered in Singapore by IME and in Malaysia by MIMOS. Such bodies play a role as 'collective' providers of R&D support for fledgling firms to enable them to keep abreast of fast-moving technological changes, and perhaps to bring them into technology collaboration alliances that would otherwise lie beyond their ken or resources. Compared with the progress made on this front in Taiwan, activities in this sphere could still only be described as 'early stage' in Singapore, and preparatory in Malaysia. But our argument is that this relative lack of progress reflects the difficulties involved in breaking into a high-technology sector like semiconductors, and reflects the relative under-development of indigenous firms in these economies, rather than structural or intrinsic weaknesses in the leverage strategy itself. Moreover, the leverage strategy itself needs to accommodate developments in the technologies with the creation of new technological trajectories (such as LCDs) and new options, necessitating further choices for follower firms. The shortcomings should not be allowed to dim the perception of the achievements registered which, by the end of the 1990s, were the envy of all other countries in the region.

The Common Factor: Technology Leverage

These diverse national pathways, with their institutional frameworks, hold a common core, namely a process of *technology leverage*. Catching up as a process is all about securing access to knowledge and technologies held by advanced firms in advanced countries in order to create viable firms and viable industries. The latecomer's disadvantage is to be cut off from these sources of knowledge and the markets that sustain them. But the latecomer has the advantage, as formulated by Gerschenkron, of being able to attach itself to a given technological trajectory and import the very latest in technology in order to enter a new industry at the highest levels of efficiency. The latecomer has to have something to offer – and there is usually something tangible that can be offered, such as a (relatively short) period of low wage costs, or controlled access to its domestic market (say, for telecommunications services), or industrial subcontracting at high levels of quality and lean profit margins. The latecomer also has to have access to potential vendors or partners – which limits the scope of applicability of the process.

The semiconductor sector has seen all these elements in play. The Japanese high-technology model, which was elaborated in a process of trial and error during the 1970s, used the capacity of a highly capable state agency, MITI, to control access to foreign technologies, trading off access to these technologies for Japanese firms against controlled access by foreigners to the domestic market. What was created was a kind of 'funnel' or 'vacuum cleaner' that channelled leading-edge technologies to Japan, either through a public-sector R&D institute such as ETL or ECL, or to a Japanese firm via licensing (as in the case of NEC licensing Fairchild's planar technology for producing ICs). In either case the goal was to allow other Japanese firms access to the technology as soon as they had built up the requisite absorptive capacity to receive it and build on it. As technological capabilities were built up domestically, the emphasis of catch-up strategies shifted from external leverage to internal leverage via various 'forced march' collaborative programs, in which the institutional innovation of the Technology Research Association (or Engineering Research Association) was critical. The success of this Japanese model depended on a very high degree of coordination or orchestration of a range of public and private sector agencies by the lead or 'pilot agency' – in this case, MITI. This was the catch-up model, which as we have seen had accomplished its task in semiconductors more or less by the end of the 1970s; the model would subsequently have to evolve to account for the fact that Japan now shared world technological leadership in this sector (except in the case of microprocessors).

While the strengths of this Japanese catch-up model are well recognised, so too are its defects. The MITI-coordinated concentration on DRAMs as technology and product trajectory of choice appears to have had an inertia effect that slowed Japanese semiconductor firms from branching out into related semiconductor fields. While Japanese difficulties in the 1990s had much to do with the country's prolonged recession, it is also arguable that Japan was unable or unwilling to extend its DRAM dominance of the 1980s into an 'architectural dominance' of other IT-related technologies, in particular that of microprocessors, leaving the field to Intel and its US competitors like IBM, Motorola and DEC (all of whom have struggled for dominance in the microprocessor field).[14]

Korea's leverage strategy most closely resembled that of Japan, in its organisational basis in large firms and in its strategic focus on standard-ised, commodity chips like DRAMs. It was a more concentrated or exaggerated version of the Japanese approach, in its being carried by a few very large firms, with less reliance on public-sector institutes and with less institutional capacity for coordination and mobilisation of resources by state agencies. Technology leverage in Korea, more than in any of the countries of East Asia, has been concentrated within the *chaebol* themselves. Government research institutes played a role, particularly in the very early years, but a minor one compared to Taiwan (with its ITRI-sponsored R&D consortia) and Japan (where the VLSI program, for example, was effectively administered and operated by public research agencies and laboratories). Some coordination capabilities were exhib-ited. In the 1980s, when the export performance of the Korean com-panies in the DRAM sector, led by Samsung, started to generate trade friction with the US, the companies were able to make most effective use of their trade association, the EIAK, and in the 1990s the KSIA. But the KSIA played a minimal role in the technological learning and leverage of the industry, which has been in the hands of the companies. In turn, this company-focused strategy called for tight control over and co-ordination of finance for investment, which was ensured in the 1980s during the breakthrough to VLSI semiconductor technology by continuing state rationing of credit, but was dismantled in the 1990s, with severe results for the Korean economy as a whole.[15]

The *channels* through which technology leverage has been exercised in Korea have also changed as technological capabilities were acquired. Table 6.2 shows how the major channels – foreign direct investment (the building of plants by foreign multinationals), technology licensing, the use of technology consultants and purchase of capital equipment – have varied in significance between 1965 and 1990. The data covers all Korean industries, not just semiconductors.

Table 6.2 shows how FDI was a significant source of technological leveraging in the early 1970s, laying the preparatory and seeding foun-dations of the electronics and semiconductor industries. But it declined thereafter as policy emphasised different sources, and sought to keep multinationals at bay (following the Japanese example). Technology

Table 6.2   Korea: Channels of technology leverage in all industries, 1965–91

	1962–66	1967–71	1972–76	1977–81	1982–86	1987–91
			($million)			
FDI	47	219	879	721	1768	5636
Licensing	1	16	97	451	1185	4359
Technology consultants	0	17	18	55	332	1348
Capital goods	316	2541	8841	27 978	44 705	52 155
Total	364	2793	9835	29 205	47 990	63 498

Source: Based on Hong 1994: Table 7.

licensing instead built up as an important source in the late 1970s and increasingly in the 1980s, along with the use of technology consultants. The impact of the semiconductor industry would have been substantial, as we have seen that licensing of both product and process technologies was a critical avenue for rapid adoption of semiconductor technologies by the *chaebol* in the 1980s.

Table 6.2 also reveals how *capital goods purchase* has dominated the channels of technology leverage in Korea from the 1960s. Capital equipment purchased on the open market from suppliers or under contract is a principal source of the knowledge embodied in the equipment. Suppliers can also be prevailed upon to provide technical training and support for the operation of the equipment, particularly in the early years when knowledge transfer – both tacit and codified – is crucial. Although figures for the different sectors are not available, we know from our study of the significance of the semiconductor industry in Korea's high-technology development that purchases of capital equipment for this industry would have been important, particularly in the 1980s when capital goods purchases overall were growing quickly. They reached their peak growth rate in 1982–86, precisely when the Korean majors were establishing their new IC fabrication facilities.

This extreme reliance on capital goods purchase as the dominant channel of technology leverage was characteristically Korean. In Japan there was much greater emphasis on the build-up of indigenous suppliers of equipment based on early leverage; in Taiwan emphasis was on licensing and indigenous development; and in Singapore and Malaysia the transfers were effected largely through the internal operations of multinationals. It was the predominance of large companies in Korea that enabled them to focus their leveraging activities on the purchases of equipment. This strategy was underpinned by their finely honed capabilities in *sourcing of technologies* (through technology monitoring and intelligence gathering) and in *combining equipment from different sources* into an integrated and coherent production system. Such activities complemented the international expansion of the semiconductor equipment industry, and thus were moving in time with dominant trends. These were characteristic and distinctive core competencies of the Korean *chaebol* that explain the rapidity of their technological learning. They saw – and still see themselves – as *hakseup chojik*, learning organisations, and it is these *combinative* capabilities that underpin their learning achievements and establish the platform for further development. The one, potentially large, weakness in this approach was the financing strategy based so heavily on debt; once this was divorced from regulatory coordination and control in the mid-1990s, it led rapidly to wider difficulties for the Korean economy.

In Taiwan, technology leverage was the strategic concern of an institution created expressly for this purpose, namely ITRI and its various specialist laboratories such as ERSO and CCL. These institutions of technology leverage were complemented by the institutions of finance leverage such as the China Development Corporation and a very active stock market on which entrepreneurial high-technology firms could expect to raise considerable sums of capital within only a few years of founding. This combination of technology and financial leverage has served Taiwan's high-technology industry well, in particular the semiconductor industry. During the East Asian financial crisis of 1997–98, it proved to be a robust and resilient foundation on which to build a new industry.

In Singapore and Malaysia, technology leverage was effected through a controlled diffusion of skills, knowledge and techniques from multinationals to local firms and to local public institutions. An evolutionary sequence of firms leveraging their skills and knowledge from MNCs can be posited, corresponding to our four-stage DRL strategy.[16] The firm starts as a supplier of parts and components to the MNCs (as done by firms in Penang in the 1970s). The company then upgrades its manufacturing processes to meet specification standards of the MNCs (for instance, under various multinational vendor partnership programs). The third step is to seek export markets instead of simply catering to the domestic, while venturing into high-technology products (as practised by several Penang-based firms in the 1990s). A variant on this involves seeking stock exchange listing, providing further funds for expansion and continuous growth.[17] The final step is to put down roots of sustainability such as training institutions to ensure that the company and its industry has an adequate supply of skilled workers. In Penang, this sequence provides an 'evolutionary' description of the development of the latecomer industry and its expansion of capabilities through leverage

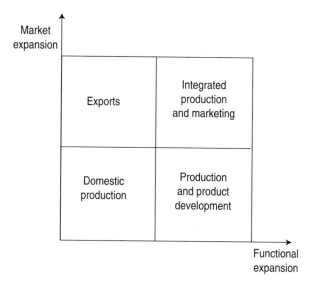

Figure 6.1   Map of technology diffusion: leverage from MNCs.

from multinationals. Figure 6.1 maps out the diffusion of capabilities leveraged from multinationals. It corresponds to the more general case of mapping of degrees of leverage discussed in Chapter 2.

The Semiconductor Industries Created

Leverage strategies have been applied in East Asia to create high-technology industries over the past 25 years. What can we say about the character of the industries created? How sustainable are they? Are they well-balanced industries with deep technological roots or shallow creations that can be expected to wither and die as technological trends shift and new capabilities are called for? To what extent have leverage strategies left their mark on the industries created, for good or ill?

Sustainability of the Industries Created

Table 6.3 summarises our account of the creation of semiconductor industries in East Asia. It conveys the configurations of the national industries created: Korea, a bit top-heavy and still without solid foundations; Taiwan, well-balanced with great diversity of firms and product strategies; Singapore and Malaysia, thriving industries based on multinational investments, but as yet little evidence of indigenous activity.

Table 6.3   Sustainability of East Asian semiconductor industries

Criteria	Japan	Korea	Taiwan	Singapore
Range of firms	***	*	**	*
Range of products	***	**	**	*
Spread of activities	***	*	**	*
Domestic market supply	***	*	*	*
Domestic ownership	***	***	**	*
Profitability	**	**	**	**
Investment efficiency	**	***	**	**
Minimisation of leverage costs	***	*	**	**
Marketing/pricing	***	**	**	*
Innovation capabilities	***	*	**	*

Note: ***   High level of sustainability
    **   Moderate level of sustainability
     *   Weak level of sustainability

Korea

Despite its huge success in semiconductors, particularly memory chips, by the end of the 1990s Korea was in many respects still in aggressive and expansionist mode, rather than in sustainability mode. Its continuing high levels of investment, for example, in our view constituted an indication not of strength but of immaturity. But Korea was undoubtedly moving up the technological ladder. By the late 1990s the major firms were moving into higher value-added segments of the DRAM market, such as synchronous DRAMs, flash memories and embedded DRAMs (stimulated by the Taiwanese challenge in lower value-added commodity chips). The Koreans were forced to replicate the survival strategy adopted earlier by the Japanese in the face of their own earlier challenge, and in the process, enhanced the sustainability of their own industry. Certainly Korean firms were actively leveraging the technological capabilities needed for more diverse production, but they did not seem to be accomplishing this diversification as fast as was warranted. As its DRL phase for semiconductors approached completion, so new cycles were being established, such as in LCDs and CDMA cellular telephony. These views put us at odds with those industry observers who claim that market share indicators reveal that Korea had 'arrived' as a semiconductor power much earlier. It also puts us at odds with those scholars who claim that the Korean innovation model is fundamentally flawed.[18]

    The great strength of the Korean industry lies in the powerful achievements of the three major *chaebol*, and their channelling profits into diversification and innovation activities. The weaknesses lie in the continued concentration and narrow range of products produced. By the end of the 1990s the Korean semiconductor industry still clearly suffered from imbalances, in its dependence on three huge firms (or rather, on two, if the mooted merger between LG Semicon and Hyundai Electronics was to proceed). While each of these firms is a very large and sophisticated player, over-dependence on so few companies renders the Korean industry vulnerable (for example, to political upheaval). Furthermore the growth of the *chaebol* stifled the development of smaller, innovative firms.

In terms of spread of activities, the Korean *chaebol* effectively span all stages of the IC fabrication process. Although it was still largely dependent on Japanese and US suppliers, which were being used as sources of leverage for this new expansion phase of the industry, Korea made a start in attempting to establish ancillary equipment and materials supply industry, particularly in the region around Chonan. Dependence is less of an issue than earlier commentators might have expected, given the continuing rivalry of the US and Japanese equipment and materials industries, and their eagerness to supply East Asian customers, such as through opening local supply offices and production facilities.[19]

The domestic Korean market for ICs is open to foreign supply – a factor that Korea has been able to exploit in trade negotiations with the US. Korean firms supplied less than 20 per cent of their domestic market in 1991, rising to just over 30 per cent in 1995, with the trend continuing upward. This constituted a healthy balance between domestic supply and imports, and stands in stark contrast with the situation in Japan. In terms of ownership, the Korean semiconductor industry has been very firmly in the hands of Korean capital; this was all along an object of public policy, and it has proven to be remarkably effective, at least until the financial crisis of 1997. Subsequent to the IMF intervention in Korea, foreign ownership of parts of the semiconductor industry was likely to increase, with firms selling off assets (such as Hyundai disposing of Symbios in the US in 1998).

By the end of the 1990s the cost structure of the Korean firms remained a source of weakness, reflecting the huge costs of leverage of their crash-through approach to the semiconductor industry. Table 6.4 shows the breakdown of costs of a Korean semiconductor firm, as of the mid-1990s (compared with the cost proportions of a typical Japanese firm); it can be taken as typical of the Korean industry as a whole at that time.

Table 6.4 provides a revealing comparison of the relative sources of competitive advantage between Korean and Japanese semiconductor firms. Some factors are quite similar. Costs of materials, for example, accounted for around 10 per cent. Investment costs (depreciation) were of comparable proportions (with absolute Japanese investment levels still exceeding those of Korea). But our interest lies in the revealing

Table 6.4   Costs of a Korean semiconductor firm, compared with a
Japanese firm

Cost item	Korea	Japan
	per cent	
Materials	9.9	10.4
Labour	4.4	8.2
Depreciation	21.5	22.0
Overheads	6.1	10.4
Royalties	14.7	2.6
Sales/management	16.0	23.1
Interest	12.7	5.8
R&D	14.7	17.5
Total	100.0	100.0

Note: Costs normalised to an index of 100 for Korean and Japanese firms.
Source: Industry figures.

contrasts. Korean overheads and costs of sales were proportionately
smaller than for Japanese firms, indicating that the Koreans were leaner
enterprises. Labour accounted for less than 5 per cent of costs for the
Koreans, and only 8.2 per cent for the Japanese. The real costs for the
Koreans lie in interest payments on loans and royalties on licensed
technologies; these are the costs of resource leverage for the Koreans,
who carried proportionately much higher charges for these items than
their Japanese competitors. The combined effect of these 'leveraging
costs' was 27.4 per cent – dwarfing the labour component of 4.4 per
cent.[20] While much of this would carry through to 2000 and beyond, it
was a once-off leverage cost (albeit a very large one) that is unlikely to
be repeated as the firms gain their own technological capabilities and
run down their licensing obligations.

In terms of marketing and pricing, the Koreans were able to follow a
Japanese model closely, pricing their memory chips according to a strict
'product cycle' pattern and thus putting maximum pressure on their
competitors, mainly the Japanese. The Korean *chaebol* are strong in
developing a marketing presence and brand awareness. Their pricing
policies were investigated by the US Department of Commerce and the
chaebols were eventually cleared of dumping charges.[21]

While the Korean model had formidable strengths, its weaknesses were
no less apparent in the late 1990s. The overwhelming focus on DRAMs
made the firms top heavy in their technological development. Decentral-
isation of the industry away from the three central *chaebol* also achieved
modest success, with Anam set to become a major producer of ICs through
its joint venture with Texas Instruments, and new players such as Dongbu
electing to join the IC industry.[22] The big weakness in the Korean

political economy remained the absence of small, high-technology start-ups. These firms abound in the US Silicon Valley and its Taiwanese counterpart. But there are very few incentives in Korea for young entre-preneurs to start such firms, and those that do get off the ground are rapidly absorbed or squeezed by the existing *chaebol.*

Thus the greatest problems appear to lie in the innovation capabilities of the Korean industrial system. The Korean *chaebol* themselves have been massively upgrading their R&D capabilities, but on its own this does not address the issue of sustaining the formation and survival of innovative small firms. This remained at the end of the 1990s the single biggest issue to be addressed in Korea. The 1997 financial crisis may indeed have triggered the beginnings of a solution, as both policy-makers and the *chaebol* oriented their purchasing and joint-development strategies towards smaller firms.[23]

Taiwan

The scale of the Taiwan IC industry remained, up to the end of the 1990s, inferior to Korea's. But the *scope* of the Taiwanese industry, in terms of the range of firms and products produced, was superior. Consistent with the broad range of firms involved in the Taiwan semiconductor industry, and the range of products fabricated and designed, the outstanding feature of the Taiwan industry is its diversity. The range of firms is impressive: many of the small Taiwanese producers have grown to become large companies in their own right, such as TSMC, UMC and Winbond, while others were growing rapidly such as MXIC and Mosel-Vitelic. Meanwhile there is a plentiful supply of small and medium-sized firms, while industry policy and infrastructure such as the Hsinchu and Tainan Science-based Industry Parks, ensure that the environment favours such small high-technology firms.

The weakness of the Taiwanese industry in the 1980s was its absence of serious DRAM production. By the mid-1990s, this had already been remedied as firms and industrial groups entered DRAM production in a big way, largely through technology transfer from the Japanese.[24] By the late 1990s they were already considered a major factor in the market-place by Korean firms, which were considering how they could move up the DRAM value-adding chain, such as by moving to more specialised flash memories or synchronous DRAMs. Taiwanese firms like Winbond, MV and MXIC were looking to follow them into these more advanced segments of the DRAM market.

It is entirely possible that Taiwan could become a larger producer of DRAMs in the twenty-first century than Korea, or even Japan, based on the massive and sustained investment made by Taiwanese firms in the late 1990s, even during the financial crisis of 1997–98. Despite cutbacks to their ambitious investment targets, firms like TSMC and UMC were still investing close to 100 per cent of their revenue in the late 1990s, well above the comparable proportion for Korean and Japanese firms.

Taiwanese firms were unable to take the plunge into DRAM production in the 1980s because of the massive investment costs and their inadequate absorptive capacity at that time. Early failures like Quasel, Mosel and Vitelic (then trying separately to build DRAMs) provide an index of this incapacity. By the 1990s the absorptive capacity was greatly enhanced, with the provision of a skilled workforce and ancillary services. Technology transfer arrangements with the Japanese became feasible, as Japanese firms such as Toshiba, Mitsubishi and Fujitsu looked to outsource and second source many of their memory products. The Taiwanese firms were able to rapidly internalise the DRAM production skills thus acquired, based on their already substantial absorptive capacity. Thus by the end of the 1990s, Taiwanese expertise in DRAM and advanced memory chips generally represented a significant new component in its sustainability arsenal.

The greatest strength of the Taiwanese industry lies in its capacity for self-generation of new firms and the continual upgrading of technological expertise of existing firms. The clustering of Taiwan's semiconductor firms on the Hsinchu Park gives them economies of scale that are not available to firms scattered around large continents, as in the US and Europe.[25] It is in securing economies of scale through clustering that the small and medium-sized firms of Taiwan have proven to be a match for the larger players in other countries. This is where the breadth of the industry is crucial – all aspects of the process of production of chips need to be available on-site from design to mask-making to manufacture, and testing and packaging. It is to ERSO/ITRI's credit that such coverage exists through spin-off firms such as TSMC with its wafer foundry and TMC with its mask-making services – and the arrival in the mid-1990s of silicon wafer producing firms such as MEMC and SEH. The Taiwanese industry has secured all the advantages of large-scale firms through clustering while keeping the advantages of nimbleness and responsiveness of smaller firms. They do not carry the bureaucratic overheads that slow down larger firms. This appears to be the key to its entrepreneurial flair.[26] Investment efficiency and financial accessibility has also been high. The Taiwanese firms are not too small to secure capital investments on a very large scale – these have been financed from a variety of sources, all of which are sustainable.[27]

Marketing has been a particular strength of the Taiwanese. The Hsinchu-based semiconductor firms have shown themselves to be the masters of customer relations, developing very high levels of customer interaction in their IC-design activities. This reflects the fact that many Taiwanese engineers and entrepreneurs have a background in North America – they speak English well and understand the workings of the US market. Their Japanese language skills and knowledge of Japan are also generally good. This is consistent with the continuation of a relatively high level of contract manufacturing in the Taiwan semi-conductor industry (contract wafer fabrication, as in foundry activities, and contract test and assembly of chips) which co-exists with a strong presence of branded product in the marketplace (Winbond, UMC, MXIC, Mosel-Vitelic).

In terms of human resources, the Taiwan semiconductor industry has made great efforts to attract high-calibre staff, and allows them to share in its prosperity through stock issues and bonuses. Professionals working for the IC industry in Taiwan do comparatively well.[28] It is ironic that it was precisely this aspect of the Taiwan industry that US firms chose to target in a concerted 'anti-dumping' petition brought by Micron *et al.* in 1998, charging the Taiwanese with understating their costs because of their system of stock bonuses.

The most fundamental strength of the Taiwanese industry lies in its innovative capabilities. Taiwan has devised ways of bringing its small and medium-sized firms abreast of world trends in technological innovation without sacrificing their independence or their flexibility. This is not innovation in the conventional sense of massive R&D expenditure by large firms, but it is effective and it boasts organisational innovations of the highest calibre. The Taiwanese system of 'innovation alliances' is a unique institutional creation which assists in developing expertise in new products and processors, such as the PowerPC.[29] It is a powerful system for replenishing the supply of small high-technology firms which keep the incumbents on their toes.

Singapore and Malaysia

Singapore has made significant strides towards the establishment of a world-class semiconductor industry, but in terms of many of the criteria of sustainability, its industry is still in the early stages of development. There is a wide range of semiconductor activities undertaken, much of it high value-adding such as IC design and new chip development, but for the most part this is conducted by MNCs and therefore cannot be counted as evidence of the Singaporean semiconductor industry's sustainability.[30] What counts in terms of sustainability is the quality and skills of the workforce (something to which the MNCs have made major contributions), the number of Singapore-capitalised firms entering the industry (still small but growing), and the linkages established between these firms and the international semiconductor industry. The STG initiative in semiconductors, encompassing Chartered Semiconductor for manufacturing, TriTech for IC design and STATS for test and assembly, ranks as one of the most successful silicon-integrated services firms in the world. New additions to the Singaporean fabrication operations, such as the Hitachi/Nippon Steel wafer fab and the TSMC/Philips joint venture, also augur well for the Singapore industry. Moves to establish the Institute of Microelectronics and its bid to organise Singapore-based product development consortia based on the Taiwan model (for example, the Ball Grid Array consortium) is yet another indicator of incipient sustainability.

The key to judging the viability of an industry is by evaluating its indigenous capabilities. So a special potential weakness raises its head in regard to the strategy of leveraging from multinationals, as practised so extensively by Singapore and Malaysia. One of the most stringent judgements made about Singaporean industry in general comes from Michael Porter, who declared in 1990 that Singapore was pursuing a 'dead-end' route. According to him its efforts have been 'too little, too late'.[31] To what extent may it be considered valid when applied to the semiconductor industry? On one measure, namely output of indigenous product, it must be considered valid – the output of the semiconductor cluster consisted in the late 1990s entirely of chips manufactured by or on behalf of international firms; there was as yet no branded production by any Singaporean firm.[32] But against this must be set the solid output of contract or OEM semiconductor products by Chartered and other contract firms which, while not branded, are nevertheless an indigenous product, and an important business in its own right.

On balance, it seems reasonable to reject Porter's assessment. The grounds for doing so rest with the dynamic features of Singapore's industry, and the demonstrable efforts made to diversify and extend it. These include at least the following five features.

Scope and Depth of Semiconductor Cluster Activities

Enormous efforts have been expended to ensure that all steps in the 'value chain' linking the various stages in semiconductor fabrication have been covered. By the late 1990s, all had been done, including even the case of silicon wafer production (covered by the construction of a plant by the German-based MNC, Wacker-Siltronics, in 1998). Thus, Singapore is not just a 'foreign production site' but is becoming an integrated semiconductor industrial cluster through deliberate public policy.

Quality of Semiconductor Services

Singapore is not to be confused with some 'low cost' subcontractor for MNCs. It is attracting the cream of US and Japanese semiconductor firms, not just to locate their own activities on the island, but to purchase high-quality wafer-fabrication services. Thus, the silicon foundry established by Chartered Semiconductor now attracts as customers – not just leading US semiconductor houses such as Actel and Brooktree (both of which have taken equity positions in Chartered's new foundry), but, in the mid-1990s, major Japanese firms as well. The significance of the links with Toshiba (by CSM) and Seiko Epson (with STATS), involving both guaranteed production capacity and a reverse flow of technology, underpinned by an equity stake, are profound. This was replicated in the later joint ventures between Chartered and HP and Lucent. It means that Chartered and STATS have been subjected to the ultimate test in quality by their Japanese and US customer firms, and have been found capable.

Supportive Infrastructure

The services provided in the wafer-fabrication parks, including reliable power, clean water and environmental controls, as well as good training services and human resource support, add up to a favourable environment for conducting high-technology business. This environment is the result of highly focused policy implementation rather than the outcome of the operation of 'market forces', and adds to the emergence of a genuine industrial cluster in Singapore.

Links with Other Industrial Clusters

The viability of the semiconductor sector depends on firms having access to advanced chemical and precision engineering firms (for fixtures and jigs on the assembly and testing equipment). Great efforts have been expended to ensure that such industries are brought into existence and nurtured — involving both foreign firms and indigenous Singaporean firms such as ASA and MIT.

Spawning of Local Firms

The charge that Singapore is dependent entirely on multinationals is rebutted by the spate of indigenous firms that have been founded in the IT, electronics and semiconductor services sectors, and in particular the high-technology ventures spawned from the state-owned enterprise sector such as Chartered Semiconductor. Their combined output might not yet come close to matching that of the multinationals, but the foundations have been laid, and the value added by this domestic sector continues to expand.

These strengths are attributable in no small way to the continuing efforts of agencies such as the EDB and NSTB to shape and foster the industry's development, particularly its ancillary and support clusters such as precision machining and materials supply. Given such considerations, it seems reasonable to rebut Porter's charges, at least in the case of the semiconductor industry.

Singapore's strategy in leveraging its semiconductor industry from MNCs has been amply rewarded in creating an internationally competitive industry. While the industry is not yet, by any yardstick, in a state of sustainability and independence, it is nevertheless on a clear trajectory towards achieving such a state.

Porter's strictures may apply with greater force to Malaysia. Here the efforts to attract wafer-fabrication plants, and to diffuse industry capability across to indigenous firms, have not met with the same success as in Singapore. By the late 1990s the KL region and Penang still had no front-end wafer-fabrication facilities, compared with the eleven plants built or commissioned in Singapore. Malaysia's best hope for a breakthrough in wafer fabrication remains the Kulim High-technology Park. In terms of diffusion, indigenous Malaysian firms linked backwards or forwards to MNCs such as Globetronics, Unisem, Carsem and AIC remain rare. The direction towards upgrading is undoubtedly there, but its execution has been slow – although much more advanced than in neighbouring countries like Thailand or the Philippines.

Malaysia's slowness to extend its semiconductor industry is undoubtedly due to the inferiority of its institutional support compared with that available in Singapore. The government agency MIDA has not been able to match the technical and financial virtuosity of Singapore's EDB, while MIMOS as a technology diffusing and promoting institute appears to have played a role that is barely comparable to Singapore's IME, let alone Taiwan's ITRI/ERSO. The real factor in the ongoing viability of the Singapore semiconductor industry would appear to be the continued presence and active intervention of the EDB in scouring the world for potential partners for local firms, creating 'wafer-fabrication parks' in Woodlands, Pasir Ris and in Tampines, securing the best services for the firms that locate there, and putting together attractive packages for newcomer firms. In these and many other ways, the EDB continues to play a critical role as the 'field high command' of the Singapore advanced technology economy.

For some critics, this might be taken as evidence that the Singapore industry is 'dependent' on a government agency, and hence, unsustainable. We see the matter differently. The continuing involvement of the

EDB is evidence of a sustained high level of institutional capacity in directing, coordinating (and disciplining) the evolution of the Singaporean high-technology industrial upgrading process. Institutional capacity – measured in terms of the government agencies' ability to marshal intelligence, formulate feasible programs directed towards realistic goals and intervene sensibly to usher private-sector players towards the fulfilment of those goals – is probably as high in Singapore as it is in Japan.[33]

The Institutional Framework: Changing Patterns of Government Industry Collaboration and Coordination

Governments and government agencies have been central to the process of creating and nurturing a semiconductor industry in East Asia.[34] But how are the relations between government agencies and the industry to be characterised? As opposed to the perception of 'cronyism' that inflects government–business relations in East Asia, the reality of the relationship observed in the creation of the semiconductor industry is one of 'governed interdependence'.[35] By this phrase is meant a productive and complementary relationship, in which each side provides a necessary complement to the other: government agencies need the private sector for implementation of policies, while the private sector needs public agencies for coordination of catch-up activities, particularly in financial allocation and risk-sharing and technological upgrading. The point is that the relations between the public and private sectors are not fixed, but evolve along with the industry that is being created. It is a case of co-evolution of the firms and public agencies (linked bilaterally and in clusters), each of which adapts to changes in the others, thus stimulating a mutually dependent process of change and development.

Taiwan's semiconductor industry provides a test case of this co-evolution. Government strategies for the creation of the industry have been open and explicit, with the government agencies such as ITRI and the Industrial Development Bureau (IDB) being equally insistent that firms must learn to survive and prosper in a world of fierce competition. It is striking that government assistance to the industry – the nurturing of enterprises while in a fledgling state – never moved beyond this to encompass trade protection or rescue of enterprises which hit operational difficulties. Indeed the history of the creation of the industry in Taiwan is littered with bankruptcies – such as that of Quasel in the mid-1980s – where government refused to intervene to rescue the company in distress. In Taiwan it is understood that this would completely defeat the goal of public policy, which is to ensure that firms become independent of nurturing assistance as soon as practicable, and are able to hold their own in

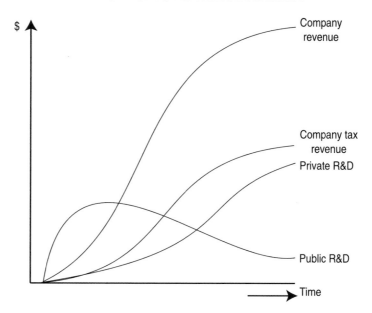

Figure 6.2   Taiwan's model of recoupment of public investments.

international competition. But the forms of nurturing and public coordination evolve as the industry becomes established.

Consider the process in the case of the semiconductor industry. The early years saw ERSO and its pilot plant play a leading role in acquiring technological capability and then in propagating that capability as quickly as possible to the private sector, through spin-off ventures and staff leaving to take up employment in semiconductor firms. With the close of the submicron project in the early 1990s, ERSO no longer played a major role in providing leading-edge pilot plants; this is something that the major companies could provide for themselves. Neither was financial assistance needed in the launch of new companies and ventures. Most of the new DRAM initiatives, for example, have been privately funded or, in some cases, assisted by public investment vehicles that came to act like venture capital funds.

Recovery of Public Investments

Part of Taiwan's institutional capacity lay in its highly innovative approach to evaluating the worth of public investments in industry creation, and to taking a long-term view of the returns that flow from this. It is of interest to note how Taiwan computes the return on the

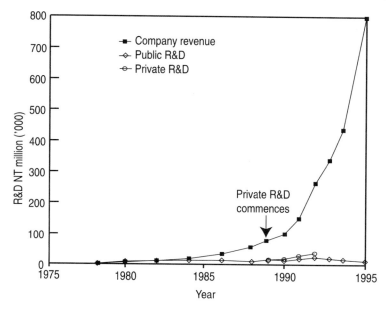

Figure 6.3 Return on public R&D expenditure in Taiwan's semiconductor industry.
Source: ERSO.

public investments made in firms such as UMC. They are not seen as having to be immediately 'cost-effective' in paying for themselves. Rather the government looks to the long term for a return in taxes paid by companies that are successfully launched. The idea of this 'Taiwan model' of recovery of public investment is depicted in Figure 6.2.

The model rests on the twin propositions that private R&D expenditure will eventually exceed public R&D expenditure, and that company tax revenues will eventually exceed public funds paid out as R&D support. These are realistic propositions, and account for the public support granted to ITRI's programs of R&D leadership to date. The actual revenue and expenditure figures for the semiconductor industry are shown in Figure 6.3.

From 1977 to 1995, a cumulative total of NT$12.7 billion was spent in R&D funds by government through ERSO/ITRI to develop and sustain the semiconductor industry, while the cumulative revenues of the companies which received technology transfer assistance has amounted over the same period to NT$225 billion. This is a near twenty-fold return to the country as a whole. Figure 6.3 shows the annual funding of projects sponsored by government and carried out at ERSO, together with the annual revenues earned by companies which had been the beneficiaries of technology transfer activities. Note that the companies received *no* direct financial assistance from government – they were expected to stand on their own financial feet, and any assistance was in the form of technology transfer. This is a characteristic feature of the Taiwanese model of developmental resource leverage.

As the industry matures, the initiative for technological upgrading gradually passes to the private sector. This is revealed most clearly in the series of second-sourcing arrangements struck in the mid-1990s between firms such as Umax, Nan Ya and Winbond with Japanese firms for the transfer of DRAM production technology. The same process was repeated in the late 1990s with the transfer of LCD technology from Japan. Meanwhile public-sector research institutes such as ITRI were by the late 1990s turning their attention to more fundamental technological issues (such as ERSO's prosecution of the 'deep submicron' project) and to seeding new technological capabilities – and thus initiating new DRL cycles – as in the case of LCDs.[36] Their technological role was being reassessed, as in their ability to provide complementary resources for established firms (trialling new process technology combinations, for example) rather than in seeking to continue to provide leadership for an increasingly sophisticated private sector.

By the late 1990s, the Taiwan government agencies were assessing the future of the semiconductor sector in terms of its ability to generate innovations and work with public-sector facilities to further intensify and upgrade its technological capabilities, such as through the Center for Semiconductor Research, which was established in 1998 as a collaborative effort to bring Taiwanese firms abreast of 'deep submicron' technological capabilities. The capacity of the industry itself to generate new firms, and for public-sector agencies and universities likewise to stimulate the formation of new firms, was identified as a major policy issue.[37] Thus the pattern of public and private-sector collaboration in Taiwan, as in East Asia more generally, continues to evolve, with public agencies guiding and coordinating activities to ensure that the semiconductor industry remains at the cutting edge of technological developments.

Hong Kong provides a critical test of our leverage framework, and the role of government–business coordination (or 'governed interdependence') in effecting catch-up in technologically advanced industries. As described in Chapter 1, Hong Kong started at the same technical level as Taiwan in electronics in the 1960s, but fell behind in the most advanced sectors such as semiconductors and sophisticated IT equipment. The difference between the two countries was the presence of co-evolving technological guidance and diffusion management in Taiwan, and its absence in Hong Kong. The role of state agencies in guiding the process of technological upgrading, setting new standards and driving firms to reach them, is not a luxury but a necessity. Once catch-up has been achieved, the situation changes drastically, and the role of state agencies changes accordingly. But the historical record so far in catch-up strategies in knowledge-intensive industries like semiconductors indicates that the role of activist state agencies is a critical factor in accelerating the organisational learning that firms have to accomplish. This is the fundamental lesson that East Asian high-technology development has to teach.

Notes

1   In the absence of easily defined sustainability criteria (linked to a general absence in the economic literature of consideration of the viability of whole industries generally) we consider the following ten factors as relevant to sustainability: range of firms, range of products, spread of activities, domestic market supply, domestic ownership, profitability, investment efficiency, minimisation of leverage costs, marketing/pricing and innovation capabilities.

2   On Japan's development of a semiconductor industry, and the strategies it used to penetrate the world semiconductor industry, see Flamm (1996), particularly Chapter 2. The rise of the semiconductor industry in Japan, treated as a case of knowledge-intensive development, is the subject of Okimoto (1989) while the technology leverage strategies used by the Japanese in many industries are analysed in Odagiri and Goto (1996). For the semiconductor industry's role in underpinning broader industry developments in Japan, see Fransman (1995).

3   This was not through any kind of 'social democratic' commitment to the public sector over the private sector, but because in Gerschenkronian terms it was simplest to acquire the basics of a completely new technology in a public sector setting, with a view to passing the expertise across to the private sector as soon as practicable.

4   On Japan's ERAs, see Sigurdson (1986), revised and republished in 1998.

5   On Japan's leverage of basic oxygen technology for steel-making, and the remarkably rapid diffusion of the technology through Japan's steel industry, see Lynn (1982).

6   See for example, Callon (1995). Callon demonstrates that MITI collaborative projects declined in effectiveness through the 1980s and were hardly attempted in the 1990s. This is consistent with a view of Japan's industrial policies moving from a 'catch-up' mode to a 'leadership' mode. However Callon seems to draw the wrong conclusions from his analysis if he points to MITI's difficulties as support for the view that R&D collaboration is passé. On the contrary, R&D collaboration has been pursued with great effectiveness in the US through such consortia as SEMATECH and the EUV alliance. In Japan, some collaborative consortia were formed in the mid-1990s, partly in response to the effectiveness of US initiatives. This time, the consortia such as SELETE and J300I were formed at the instigation of the industry rather than of MITI.

7   Scholarly recognition of the significance of Manchuria in Japan's own postwar development strategies, and particularly in Korea's, is still slow in coming. A brief discussion is provided by Johnson (1982: 130–32). The Japanese occupation army developed a comprehensive plan for Manchuria's development in 1937, in which the lead role was given to the Nissan corporation. It was envisaged that Nissan would spin off a number of 'satellite firms', one for each new industry.

8   While some commentary has linked the global strategic aspirations of the Korean semiconductor firms to the collapse of the Korean economy at the end of 1997, this is in our view drawing a rather long bow. The Korean economic collapse had multiple causes, which to detail here would take us too far afield. While some Korean *chaebol* had excessive debt–equity ratios, the top five, including all three semiconductor majors, had relatively responsible levels (given their strategy of raising funds externally to buy their way into the industry). It was middle-ranking *chaebol* looking to rise up the ladder that took excessive risks and triggered financial collapse. We have discussed these issues in Mathews (1998a; 1998c) and Cho (1998).

9   Scholarly debate as to the origins of the Taiwan model of industrialisation has been heated. A prominent line of argument is that the KMT, when retreating to Taiwan after its loss to the Communists on the mainland, was forced to encourage local industrial enterprise as a means of securing political legitimacy. But the KMT did not trust local Taiwanese entrepreneurs enough to allow some of them to grow to be leaders of huge conglomerates, as in the Korean case. Indeed, most of the 'heavy and chemical' industrialisation phase of the 1970s was entrusted to state corporations, who supplied the materials and energy for the thousands of small firms that proliferated. One exception to this rule was the native Taiwanese entrepreneur Wang, who founded Formosa Plastics and has since grown to become head of the island's largest industrial conglomerate, and is now a leader of Taiwan's push into high technology through Nan Ya Technology.

10 See Wade (1990) for a discussion of earlier uses by Taiwan of public-sector enterprises to open up new industrial sectors. As Wade puts it:

> The public enterprise sector is also used (in Taiwan) . . . as a substitute for attempts to induce private firms to enter new fields with high entry barriers. The main import-substituting projects of the 1970s – petroleum and petrochemicals, steel and other basic metals, shipbuilding and nuclear power – were carried out by public enterprises; and major expansion projects in heavy machinery, heavy electrical machinery, trucks and *integrated circuit production* have been undertaken by public enterprises. (1990: 179)

Our study substantiates this claim for the case of the semiconductor sector.

11 This was the point made by Quinn (1969) whose analysis received its strongest endorsement from Singapore.

12 The World Bank report by Battat, Frank and Shen (1996) offers strong support for the approach taken by Singapore and Malaysia in this regard, as does Meyanathan (1994).

13 In 1986, only 12 per cent of Malaysia's 40 804 students were enrolled in engineering programs; by 1992 the number of students had grown to 54 177, but the proportion in engineering remained at 12 per cent. This

failure to keep pace with the demand for technical graduates is seen in Malaysia itself as a major blockage to further high-technology development.

14   This is the position argued by such US commentators as Ferguson and Morris (1993) and Itami (1995). While acknowledging the strength of these arguments, we set out our own position, with its different emphases, in the next chapter.

15   For discussion of this aspect of the Korean strategies, see Weiss (1998) and Mathews (1998a).

16   Such a sequence was proposed by the Chief Minister of Penang, Dr Koh Tsu-Koon. In 1995 he outlined his five-point model at the launch of the prospectus for Atlan, a local engineering and services supply company in Penang.

17   Listing on local stock exchanges also carries the penalty of loss of complete control, which some entrepreneurs are reluctant to accept.

18   See, for example, Ernst (1994; 1997). We agree with many of the strictures Ernst proposes, but depart from his conclusion that the weaknesses of the Korean industry are essential characteristics beyond remedy. The point is discussed further in the next chapter.

19   Earlier fears of a Japanese monopoly of such supplies, which drove efforts to create national ancillary industries, have proven to be groundless.

20   In 1993, royalties of $125 million were paid by Korean producers to US firms. Given that revenue of the Big Three that year was just over $4 billion, this means that royalties costs had fallen to 6 per cent of revenues by the early 1990s. The source for the $125 million is KSIA, and so this can be taken as reliable.

21   This investigation of Korean pricing and cost levels was undertaken by the US Department of Commerce as part of the investigation of dumping allegations brought against Korean semiconductor firms in the early 1990s. The KSIA intervened most effectively to represent the Korean firms' case, producing cost accounting data to show that pricing strategies were sustainable.

22   These efforts were frustrated by the 1997–98 financial crisis. The Anam joint venture with TI was thrown off course by the withdrawal of TI from DRAM production in 1998, while Dongbu's efforts, based on a comprehensive technology transfer agreement with IBM, were put on hold in early 1998 until financial conditions improved.

23   The strictures of scholars such as Ernst (1994; 1997) on this point highlighted real difficulties which were being addressed by the end of the decade.

24   It is conceivable that one of the factors motivating the Japanese firms involved in these memory chip technology transfer agreements – besides commercial calculations about royalties and 'second sourcing' of product – may be a desire to curb the Korean DRAM assault.

25   Treating this cluster as a single value-adding entity (looking only at design and manufacture, and leaving packaging to one side) Hsinchu Semiconductor Inc had an output in 1995 of $5.6 billion, and investment of just over $2 billion. This was comparable to the semiconductor output of IBM, or to the combined activities in Korea of LG and Hyundai.

26   The US technology consultants Ferguson and Morris agree with us on this point. They describe Taiwan (favourably) as the world's 'first (non-American) Silicon Valley'. They state: 'The Taiwanese have developed in an entirely different direction [i.e. away from Japanese/Korean large,

integrated firms] and are well on their way toward creating the first non-American Silicon Valley. The Chinese entrepreneurial tradition, the predilection for small firms, ample government-funded venture capital, and close family and business ties with the California university and business system are all coming together to create possibly a major new center of computer innovation'. (1994: 222)

27   Firstly finance has been generated internally, through high cash flow rates (as in the early production expansions of Winbond or MXIC). Secondly, outside industries have acted as a source of capital (as in the case of the textiles, plastics and metal products industries investing in HMC, Nan Ya, and Winbond, Mosel-Vitelic and VISC). Thirdly, investment capital has been raised on the Taipei Stock Exchange, through initial public offerings, pioneered by UMC and since emulated by TSMC, Winbond, MXIC, Umax (Powerchip) and others. These sources have been supplemented, particularly in strategic instances such as the TI-Acer joint venture for DRAMs, through the mobilisation of public funds, such as the China Development Corporation. Most recently capital has been raised through listing on foreign stock exchanges (such as the New York Stock Exchange in the case of TSMC) to raise equity. The formation of international multi-bank syndicates to raise debt capital has been practised in Taiwan on a more modest scale than in Korea, with the result that the country's semiconductor industry weathered the 1997/98 Asian financial crisis better than others.

28   Leading firms such as UMC and TSMC use bonus stock issues as a principal means of attracting and retaining staff.

29   On the technology alliances, see Weiss and Mathews (1994) and Mathews and Poon (1995).

30   It is welcome nevertheless to Singapore, which continues to press the MNCs hard to leverage skills and knowledge from their global operations.

31   Porter discusses the Singapore case tangentially in his 1990 study, *The Competitive Advantage of Nations*. In the context of a discussion about the relative merits of Korea and Singapore, he notes: 'Singapore is still a foreign production site, not a real home base. Singapore's approach to economic development, built mostly on foreign multinationals, has produced rapid progress and is lower risk than Korea's. Until Singapore becomes a home base, however, its upside potential will be capped.' (1990: 566)

Later, in the context of economic development strategies and multinationals, Porter notes: 'Foreign multinationals should be only *one component* of a developing nation's economic strategy, and an evolving component. At some stage in the development process, the focus should shift to indigenous companies. In Singapore . . . my view is that the shift has been *too little and too late*. (Singapore has not) truly committed to the slow process of developing a broader base of indigenous firms.' (1990: 679; our italics).

32   There were some exceptions by the end of the 1990s. TriTech for example produces chips under its own brand name, and has them fabricated in foundries, including in its sister firm, CSM.

33   The two cases are not strictly comparable, given their respective populations of 3 million versus 120 million or thereabouts.

34   Dahlman (1993) identifies eight instruments of government influence in shaping the development of the electronics industry in various countries:

direct participation; trade protection; public R&D; fiscal/financial incentives; government procurement; direct foreign investment control; industrial organisation; and special human resource strategies.

35 The concept of 'governed interdependence' in the context of an extended analysis of state capacity in East Asia was introduced by Weiss (1995) and elaborated in Weiss (1998).

36 As discussed above, ERSO mounted a determined effort to seed LCD capabilities through an R&D consortium in the early 1990s, but was frustrated by semiconductor incumbents (notably UMC). It continued to support the dissemination of LCD capabilities up until the point where Taiwanese firms felt able to enter into direct technology transfer arrangements with Japanese firms. Thus the forms of technological collaboration within East Asia continue to evolve.

37 This is all the more important given that by the end of the 1990s there was a marked trend towards consolidation of the Taiwan industry. In June 1999 there were two such announcements: the reconsolidation of UMC into a single corporation, and the purchase by TSMC of a 30 per cent stake in Acer's ASMI, to form TSMC-Acer (effectively to be managed by TSMC). Further consolidation is to be expected.

CHAPTER 7

Limits to Technology Leverage Strategies

This chapter probes the strengths and weaknesses of the model of high-technology industry creation through leverage, and the underlying conditions that account for the industry's success or failure. We have shown in previous chapters that Korea, Taiwan, Singapore and, to some extent, Malaysia have mastered leverage strategies for the creation of high-technology industries, in particular semiconductors, while similar strategies appear to be working well in other countries of the region, notably China.

But how effective have these strategies really been? They may have created viable and well-balanced semiconductor industries that are capable of sustaining themselves, but have they worked in other sectors and cases? Is there a coherence in their repeated applications? Are there counter-examples? How widespread is their applicability? Is their success, such as it is, contingent on certain industry characteristics? Is a leverage strategy more likely to work in one kind of industry than another? We aim, then, to look at the leverage strategies to find out *how* and *why* they work. We also seek to establish the extent to which they are spreading and why.

There are three cases to consider: further leverage in the same core countries of East Asia as they continue to upgrade their knowledge-intensive industries; leverage by other countries in East Asia such as China; and leverage by advanced firms in the technologically advanced countries. We shall look for evidence of coherent application of leverage strategies in all three cases in order to establish their significance. To what extent are 'diffusion management' strategies themselves diffusing? Such questions cannot be avoided in any systematic presentation of the creation of new industries through the management of technological diffusion.

Limits to Applicability

We acknowledge at the outset that there are limits to the success of leverage strategies. Both Taiwan and Korea, for example, have attempted to create other high-technology industries through similar leverage strategies, in sectors such as biotechnology and aerospace, with little success to date. While Korea has managed to leverage the ingredients of an automotive industry, Taiwan has been less successful in this sector. The Taiwanese have established several motor vehicle companies, and linked them through technology leverage to Japanese automotive producers, but they have remained tied to these Japanese firms, producing under their brand for over two decades, with little prospect of breaking free to design and produce cars of their own – the expected outcome of the leverage strategy. So, with certain qualifications, one might say that the leverage strategy has not served the Taiwanese particularly well in automotive products.[1] Likewise in aerospace, attempts by the Taiwanese to launch aircraft projects through technology transfer from European and US producers have yet to meet with substantial success.

There are many reasons for these shortcomings. While there were failings on the Taiwanese side in terms of technological or marketing deficiencies, there were also powerful factors working against their success in the nature of the industry. Whereas the semiconductor industry and electronics and IT generally are characterised by many competitors, short product life-cycles and rapid company turnover, none of these conditions applies in either the automotive or aerospace sectors. These, on the contrary, are characterised by few players, large investments in long product development cycles and very low company turnover. All are factors militating against the prospects of securing technology through leverage other than on the terms dictated by the incumbents for what they perceive to be their own interests (for example, some technology transfer associated with OEM contracting), or in aerospace, associated with defence and security issues.

In South East Asian countries such as Indonesia, attempts to enter high-technology sectors such as aerospace without the accumulated technological capabilities and 'absorptive capacity' that Taiwan can demonstrate have been even more controversial and problematic. The Indonesian case demonstrates quite vividly the limits and obstacles to catch-up by latecomers in technologically complex fields like aircraft manufacture.[2] Technology leverage is not destined to succeed without the requisite preparation and investment in absorptive capacity.

Even in the IT and electronics sector, the Taiwanese have had patchy success. While Taiwan firms ride high in the production of PCs and PC components such as motherboards, mouse pointers, monitors and scanners, they have made little headway in ultra-sophisticated products such as hard disk drives and, until the late 1990s, in CD-ROMs and flat panel displays. They have virtually zero penetration in such areas as video cassette recorders and players. What is required in these kinds of products is not just digital electronics and video technology, but capabilities in precision engineering for the micromotors and bearings on which these products depend. In the absence of a strong infrastructure of precision engineering firms, which themselves may have been leveraged from supply contracts to incumbent players and multinationals, it has been very difficult for Taiwan to leverage and implement the technologies associated with these precision drive-based products. This contrasts dramatically with Singapore, which has been able to develop a strong infrastructure of small-firm precision engineering whose business is initiated by servicing the multinationals. The point being made here is that there are clear limits to the likely success of a technology leverage strategy in the absence of the requisite technological foundations ('absorptive capacity') and public technological learning infrastructure and associated industrial clusters.

Against these less successful cases are many instances of repeated successful application of technology leverage techniques in industrial and technological upgrading of established industries. This points to something more than mere casual application of disjointed techniques, to something systematic. Let us first review the evidence relating to the systematic application of technology leverage in the East Asian countries.

Repeated Application: The Coherence of Leverage Strategies

The process of 'developmental resource leverage' as applied through various iterations has a coherence and systemicity that strongly points to deliberate and carefully honed public skills in industry creation. The coherence strongly argues against random adaptations or just plain 'luck' in accounting for East Asian success in knowledge-intensive industries. If the approach to industry creation and industry upgrading works once, why not try it again – and again, and again? We use some examples from Taiwan and Korea to reinforce this point.

Taiwan DRAMs

Taiwanese firms mastered DRAM technology only in the 1990s. Earlier efforts to enter the industry by firms such as Quasel, Mosel and Vitelic all failed. (Quasel disappeared as a company; Mosel and Vitelic merged in the 1990s and have since become strong DRAM producers.) The supporting infrastructure and skills – the absorptive capacity of the Taiwan semiconductor industry – were not at that time able to support the demands of advanced DRAM fabrication. But the absorptive capacity was enhanced by the activities of semiconductor firms in various non-memory devices, which rapidly deepened their experience through the various stages of developmental resource leverage in the 1980s, while judicious targeting by the Taiwan public agencies (such as the Industrial Development Bureau and ITRI) ensured that as many of the steps as possible in the semiconductor value-chain were being covered (such as IC design, mask production and supply of specialist materials and equipment). The decisive contribution to raising the industry's absorptive capacity to produce DRAMs was made by ERSO with its submicron project, in which a major pilot fabrication plant was built and subsequently passed across to the private sector (thus accounting for the launch of the new firm, Vanguard International Semiconductor Corporation). In the 1990s, one Taiwan firm after another announced the intention of becoming a DRAM producer based on technology transfer agreements with US or Japanese firms.[3] By the late 1990s, these Taiwanese firms were established as serious and highly competitive DRAM producers, putting great pressure on their Korean, Japanese and US counterparts. (By the late 1990s the Europeans had just about given up on DRAMs.) Thus the initiative for moving to the next stage of semiconductor capabilities was taken by both the private and public sectors, with the initiative for technology leverage gradually moving to the private sector as the industry matured.

Taiwan Communications Chips

Likewise in the communications chips sector, Taiwanese firms used various forms of technology leverage to become players in the 1990s. Here the technological challenge is to meet international standards for data transmission protocols. In the 1980s, before the industry's absorptive capacity had reached the appropriate level, some small firms tried to enter this industry as 'knock off' practitioners, taking US or Japanese products and copying them to sell for a lower price. Strict enforcement of property rights put a stop to this. A new wave of Taiwanese ventures emerged in the 1990s, driven by technology leverage taking place through both the public and private sectors.

In the private sector, firms like Silicon Integrated Systems entered the fast Ethernet data-switching IC business by licensing technology from one of the leading US firms, National Semiconductor. In the public sector, ITRI's ERSO and CCL have developed Ethernet switches and the ICs to drive them, and then formed R&D alliances with small firms to pass across the technology for rapid commercialisation. Firms such as DLink and Accton have prospered through this process.

Korean CDMA Cellular Telephony

In the 1990s Korean firms extended their technology leverage strategies to enter totally new technology-intensive sectors such as cellular telephony. Again the strategy was to bet on a new technological standard and then to 'leapfrog' ahead of established players. Korean government agencies and firms committed to a new and untried technological standard, Code Division Multiple Access (CDMA) as early as 1993, when it was first being developed by its US inventor firm, Qualcomm. The technology was licensed (a boost for Qualcomm at the time) and developed partly competitively and partly collaboratively by Samsung, LG and newcomer SK Telecom.

Because of their strategy of being a 'fast follower' Korean firms were able to win substantial export orders in Brazil and in China, against the competition of US giants including Motorola and Lucent Technologies. The Korean domestic market was used as test bed for the new cellular system. SK Telecom launched its Korean cellular telephone service in 1996, and it had grown to be the world's largest such network by year's end.

LCDs in Taiwan

Finally consider the case of Taiwanese development of an LCD industry in the late 1990s. Taiwan grew in the second half of the 1990s to become the world's second largest supplier of notebook PCs (based partly on highly innovative developmental consortia in the 1980s) after Japan. But it was unable to penetrate the key component segment of flat panel displays, which were dominated by Japanese firms including Sharp, Fujitsu, Toshiba and Matsushita. This meant that much of the value-added in notebook PCs was lost to Japan and represented a drain on Taiwan's balance of trade. Efforts by ITRI/ERSO to launch a Liquid Crystal Display (LCD) industry in Taiwan in the early 1990s were frustrated, partly due to lack of sufficient absorptive capacity, and partly due to resistance from semiconductor incumbents.[4] But in the second half of the 1990s one Taiwan firm after another committed to LCD production, as it became clear that Thin-Film Transistor (TFT) LCDs were becoming the technological standard for notebook PCs, and as Japanese firms sought to outsource and 'second source' much of their LCD work to Taiwanese firms.[5] By the late 1990s, through these several efforts, Taiwan was moving to establish itself as the world's third largest supplier of TFT LCDs, after Japan and Korea, all of whom were considerably ahead of US and European firms in terms of mass production.

The point to emphasise here is that there is a coherence to these continuing leverage processes, which evolve as competencies are accumulated. The earlier competencies in basic semiconductor fabrication and marketing – themselves leveraged mainly through the public sector – serve as a platform for later, more specialised and sophisticated devices leveraged through the public and private sectors. Private firms come to take more and more of the initiative in such leveraging, while the public-sector laboratories serve as the repository of technical capabilities that can be upgraded and diffused across to the private sector through R&D alliances.

Industry Characteristics Favouring Leverage

Given these experiences, what are the characteristics of successful application of leverage techniques in the semiconductor sector both in terms of the industry and the strategies followed by the firms and public agencies in the countries concerned? Several industry characteristics immediately present themselves as relevant: rapid turnover of products and high levels of competition, predictability of technological trajectories in semiconductors, availability of product and process technologies, availability of leverage trade-offs, and underlying reliance by firms on their own organisational learning.

Rapid Product Turnover and High Levels of Competition

The key to successful leverage strategy lies in new opportunities being generated by the fundamental dynamics of technological change – with new product and process technologies being created and putting pressure on incumbents to keep transforming their own organisational routines. In the case of the semiconductor sector such restless technological change is readily apparent, as in the case of DRAMs product turnover, with each product generation lasting for no more than two or three years at most. Other semiconductor products, such as ICs for multimedia, likewise demonstrate rapid product turnover. The industry is also highly competitive, with start-ups being generated constantly to keep up the competitive pressure on incumbents – unlike the case of steel, automobiles or aerospace, where incumbents have much longer to adjust and fewer competitors. On these grounds, the semiconductor industry presents latecomers with numerous opportunities, which have been taken advantage of by East Asian firms.[6]

Predictable Technological Trajectories in Semiconductors

Technological change takes place in the 'clumping' or 'path-dependent' fashion of technological trajectories, which can be read by the latecomer as well as by any incumbent firm.[7] Japanese firms were able to read the DRAM technological trajectory, and the CMOS sub-trajectory within it, with great insight, and build an industry around this product specialisation in the first instance. The Koreans were able to follow the Japanese example, at lower costs and with yields and quality measures that eventually matched those of Japanese firms. For the Taiwanese firms in the 1980s, the huge investments in DRAM production systems ruled out this option, and instead they pursued other technological trajectories in ASICs and logic chips, which had smaller markets but which were just as predictable in terms of their likely technological evolution. In the 1990s they were able to move into DRAM production based on the continued extension of this technological trajectory. Taiwanese and Korean firms leveraged LCD technologies from the Japanese once it was clear that these had stabilised around a TF LCD trajectory. And so the examples can be multiplied.

Availability of Product and Process Technologies

Access to technology is the key to catch-up, followed by its adoption and internalisation by firms through processes of learning. But if the product and process technologies are held as proprietary by the incumbent firms to form one of their inimitable sources of competitive advantage, then the scope for catch-up through leverage is minimal.

In the semiconductor sector, early pioneers such as Fairchild, Intel and Texas Instruments held proprietory product and process technologies that they guarded carefully. But as the industry matured, firms which specialised in certain aspects of these technologies – for example, non-fabricating designers of logic chips and semiconductor fabrication equipment – were formed. Such firms are the 'technology vendors' looking for buyers, and not just in the industry's originating country.

The key strategic decision involved in creating new high-technology industries is to know when the critical product and process technologies become available, either through licensing (for example, from technology-rich but cash-poor Silicon Valley start-up firms), the use of engineering consultants, acquisition of capital equipment or a combination of all three. The resources targeted for leveraging are those which are most transferable, transparent and least susceptible to 'time compression economies'.[8]

Successful leveraging is a matter of *strategic choice* for the latecomer firm, and for the latecomer nations' public research institutes. The strategic issues involve making a judgement as to the direction of the technological trajectory, the availability of product and process technology, and the strategies of incumbents in favour of OEM outsourcing contracts, second sourcing or licensing. Our insistence on this element of strategic choice distinguishes our analysis from that of scholars who emphasise the decisions of incumbents, for example, in creating international production networks. We see such networks as providing a strategic opportunity which latecomers can take advantage of – but do not see them as the primary driving influences behind the technological upgrading of East Asia.

Availability of Leverage Trade-offs

This brings us to the heart of the matter. Leveraging involves a strategic exchange. One party gives the other technology in return for which it receives something that it needs or wants. How has this worked? This 'something' might be cash: an upfront fee or fees paid for equipment and the training that goes with it, or royalties paid as a product is produced. It might be a productive partnership: one party develops the products, and outsources their production or testing to the other. This can be a very profitable arrangement for both, as is attested by many fabless IC companies in Silicon Valley that have used the contract fabrication and test services of East Asian firms to great strategic effect. The East Asian foundries and test houses have done very well out of this arrangement, and look like doing so for some time to come. The 'something' might also be market access – as in the case of telecommunications, where government agencies have been instrumental in trading access to the domestic market in return for technology transfer by multinationals.

In all these instances, the East Asians have found a strategically apt way of fashioning a response to a strategic initiative on the part of incumbents. There is a strategic initiative on the part of the incumbents to outsource production and build an international production network. But it is *complemented* by a strategic initiative on the part of the East Asians to use this opportunity for purposes of technology leverage. Complementarity is the strategic key, as we see it, to understanding the success of East Asian technology leverage approaches to industry creation.

Strategic Factors Necessary for Leverage to Work

The object of leverage is to *accelerate* the enhancement of technological capabilities by the firm, to *improve* its learning. How firms and institutions approach this issue is a matter of strategic calculation. If companies have good cash reserves – built up, for example, by years of mass production of low-cost products – then they can leverage more rapidly and in greater 'chunks' than would otherwise be the case. These are the 'footprints' of the Korean *chaebol*, whose actions in acquiring and internalising the technology of semiconductors at the most advanced VLSI level in the 1980s represent a remarkable case whose scale and scope and speed are unlikely to be repeated. If companies have *agility*, they can find out the potential partnership arrangements and quickly take advantage of them, offering services that integrate them into wider, global chains of value-adding activities. This was the forte of the Taiwanese – with the assistance of the technology intelligence gathering activities of ITRI and its specialist laboratories such as ERSO.

If companies have good *production capabilities*, that is, the 'combinative capabilities' to put together items of equipment from different sources, then these can be enhanced and extended, for example, by OEM contracts and leveraging devices that place such companies in partnership arrangements. Companies can exploit the advantages of being local, particularly as providers of maintenance services and replacement equipment for multinationals operating in their domestic market. The point is that none of these leveraging strategies comes gratis, and all require a leveraging strategy on the part of the companies initiating the contacts, that is, on the part of the latecomer firm. These are all firm-level or organisational capabilities.

Of equal significance are the institutional capabilities that shape or frame the firms' efforts. These include issues such as the capability to foresee the need for technically trained staff and provide for the requisite training programs; the availability of adequate R&D capabilities, such as might be provided through public-sector research institutes; and the capability to secure access to adequate financial support for the development of long-term, high-technology industries. None of these factors can be expected to be produced through the operation of market mechanisms on their own, or through the benevolent actions of international firms or international agencies. These are institutional capabilities that have to be created by the latecomer countries themselves. The strategic factors identified are summarised in Table 7.1.

The resource leverage strategy of the latecomer firm is a very different beast from the kind of strategies developed and implemented by incumbent firms in advanced countries. It is the latter that dominate discussion in the management literature and in the business schools. 'Strategy' from this dominant perspective refers to the identification of competitive advantages and their defence, such as through focusing on company resources which are not easily imitable by others and using these to build

Table 7.1   Strategic capabilities involved in successful technology leverage

Organisational capabilities	
Adequate cash reserves and cash management	For securing rapid access to technological opportunities
Organisational agility	For discovery of potential technology sources and internalising the technologies leveraged
Production capabilities	The 'combinative capabilities' needed to secure and integrate technologies from a variety of sources
Localisation	The ability to capture local advantages and build on them, e.g. in supplying services to multinationals
Institutional capabilities	
Supply of skilled personnel	Through targeted government-funded training programs
Core R&D services	For uptake of new technologies and their dissemination to firms
Financing of high-technology initiatives	Through foreign direct investment or by arranging for access to international finance

sustainable competitive advantages.[9] The latecomer's strategy, by contrast, is concerned with identifying the resources that might be leveraged in order to bring the latecomer into contact with advanced firms, exploiting its meagre initial advantages such as low costs or locality.

The latecomer firm's strategy is not about defending assets and resources, but *creating* them through leverage, and then *enhancing* them through further leverage and internal organisational learning. It is the demonstrated capacity of latecomer firms to engage in such learning to enhance their technological capabilities that forms the core of our argument as to the efficacy of leverage as a viable strategy.

Underlying Reliance by Firms on Their Organisational Learning

The processes of technology leverage call for firms and institutions to make their own efforts to identify, acquire and internalise technologies and technological capabilities. If such efforts cannot be demonstrated, then the case for 'developmental resource leverage' as the means through which high-technology industries have been created in East Asia is very much weaker.

Is there evidence of organisational learning in the East Asian semiconductor industry, for example, of improved yields within each product generation, and at handover from pilot production to mass production with successive generations of chips? It is possible to demonstrate such efforts in single-loop and double-loop organisational

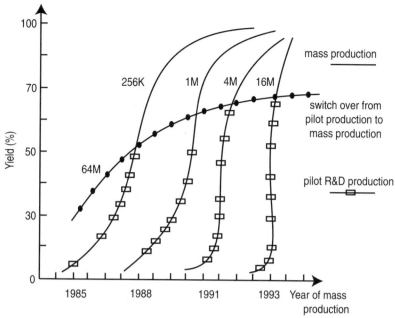

Figure 7.1   Organisational learning: yield improvements in DRAM fabrication.
Source: Mathews and Cho (1999).

learning in the DRAM sector, which argues against extrinsic or transient factors being the most important explanations for East Asian success.

Consider Figure 7.1, which shows the experience of a typical Korean semiconductor company improving its yields of DRAM chips, generation by generation. This case can be taken as representative of the Korean industry as a whole up to the mid-1990s.

The data shows that the Korean firm was able to engage in considerable 'learning by doing', by improving efficiencies – as measured by 'yield' of good chips per wafer – in each generation of the DRAM product cycle. This is called 'single-loop' learning by organisational theorists.[10] But there is something much more significant going on here. In each new product generation, there is a period of operation of the fabrication process on pilot or R&D fabrication lines, where the aim is to improve yields up to something approximating commercial efficiency, before handing the process over to the production department for mass production. Figure 7.1 shows how this Korean semiconductor firm improved the yield at the point of handover from pilot operation to mass production with each product generation. From one product generation to the next, the firm was learning 'how to learn' to improve yields faster and with greater reliability. Organisational theorists call this 'double-loop learning', which concerns the organisational capability of improving operations over time so that the results of earlier experiences are embodied in later organisational routines. What we have here is rich data collected from an actual firm that shows directly how efficiency improvement has been a central and prime factor in the firm's ability to enter and sustain its presence in a high-technology sector like semiconductors. The evidence can be taken as typical for the Korean industry as a whole – and by extension, for firms from other countries such as Taiwan.

Thus it can be argued that East Asian success in semiconductors is due not to a fortunate combination of external factors, or to calculations by foreign firms that leave East Asian firms as prisoners of others' calculations, but rather is attributable directly to their own efforts and achievements in mastering and improving the technologies of the semiconductor industry – as measured directly by single and double-loop learning rates in the DRAM sector. Such an argument leads one to search for East Asian success in terms of the various 'knowledge-enhancing' processes that companies engage in, such as technology licensing and contract manufacturing – which collectively we have called 'resource leveraging' and in the developmental context of East Asia, 'developmental resource leveraging'. Consistent with a Gerschenkronian perspective, firms have not had to develop these competence-enhancing processes on their own but have been able to draw on a series of innovative institutional frameworks to encourage a higher form of supra-organisational or economic learning.

Limits to Technology Leverage

From the semiconductor case, we can posit several strategic conditions that must be satisfied for leveraging techniques to work. They represent limits to the applicability of leverage from one perspective, but from another, might be interpreted as weaknesses or traps awaiting the latecomer firm. For example, the availability of technological trajectories is seen as a fundamental necessary condition for leverage to work, but once embarked on a trajectory, does a latecomer firm run the risk of becoming 'trapped' in this technology while more advanced firms perhaps change the underlying technological trends and thereby undermine the competitiveness of the latecomer? This might be called the trap of 'path dependence'.

Another such instance concerns the strategy of fast followership, which is an effective strategy for leverage on the one hand, but from another might be seen as a recipe for permanent dependence. Let us discuss these two issues as representative of a broad class of such concerns (some of which are more realistic than others).[11]

Technological Trajectories – Opportunities or Traps?

One commonly expressed critique of the leverage strategies employed in semiconductors goes like this: perhaps it works well in commodity-like, standardised products like DRAMs, but will it work beyond this kind of product? Expressed more generally, this concern can be characterised as one of 'path dependency', that is, a latecomer company can 'lock on' to a particular technological trajectory by leveraging product and process technology, but will remain 'locked in' to this trajectory – be path dependent – and will not develop the capabilities to move on or keep up with the shifting technological frontier.[12] Commentators like Ferguson and Morris make a clever and appealing argument. It renders the Japanese and Korean success in 'commodity' items like DRAMs appear easy and dangerously circumscribed. This argument is buttressed by Ferguson and Morris's case that competition outside these commodity sectors will be driven by standard architecture considerations; the American firms (particularly start-ups, but also established firms like HP and Intel) are better at this technological development than their Japanese and East Asian competitors.

Is this plausible when applied to the Japanese, Korean and other East Asian firms' semiconductor competences? Certainly it does *not* apply to the Taiwanese, who developed their semiconductor industry on a well-balanced growth path across a wide spectrum of semiconductor products, and maintained a diversity of product and process technological capabilities towards the end of the 1990s. But it does have some force in the case of the Koreans, who bet heavily on DRAMs and, as we have seen, remained heavily dependent on DRAMs even by the late 1990s. Does this imply that the Koreans will never escape from a purported 'DRAM trap'?

There is a kernel of truth to this critique. It is clear that the Japanese, and subsequently the Koreans, made a strategic decision to focus on the most standardised of semiconductor chips because this was where they saw the best prospects for mass production and mass marketing. But whether this locked them into a particular trajectory or not appears to be an exaggerated concern. Take the case of Japan. Its Japanese semiconductor industry is technologically highly competent in all aspects of semiconductor operations, including microprocessors. (If NEC does not rule the world in microprocessors like Intel, it is because of strategic marketing errors, as well as insuperable barriers to entry in the PC world erected by Intel – which have been as effective against other US firms like AMD, Motorola and IBM, as against Japanese firms like NEC.) In the late 1990s, Japanese firms were leading the world in some of the most advanced areas of semiconductor technology, such as liquid crystal displays and 'system on a chip' technology (which is likely to supersede stand-alone microprocessors early in the twenty-first century). Neverthe-less Japanese firms stayed with commodity DRAMs for longer than warranted by the value-added they represented, and perhaps allowed themselves to be outmanoeuvred by US firms like Intel on microproces-sors. So Ferguson and Morris might have a point – but only in the sense of strategic decisions, rather than capabilities.

With Korea, it is certainly true that firms like Samsung were having difficulty breaking out of the DRAM trajectory. Difficulties, yes – but insuperable problems, no. The Koreans were using their well-honed leveraging techniques to break out of DRAMs and acquire expertise in other IC areas such as logic chips and microprocessors, as discussed in Chapter 3. But again it is strategic choices that count. Samsung's efforts to acquire microprocessor capabilities through leverage from DEC's Alpha processor may have been a strategic miscalculation (given DEC's decline and takeover by Compaq in 1997).

To summarise, 'lock-in' does not seem to be a serious objection to a technology leverage strategy, provided the company (or country) practis-ing leverage is prepared to make the efforts involved to continually upgrade its technological capabilities. This is axiomatic for sophisticated latecomers. Our argument does not depend on our being able to show that latecomers practising leverage have rapidly reached positions of world dominance. Demonstrably they have not. All our argument requires us to show is that they have arrived and are retaining their com-petitive positions in the face of determined counterattacks (for example, from European firms), and that they are enhancing their technological and organisational capabilities. This is all we have to show to defend the leverage strategy against the charge that it locks firms (and countries) into losing trajectories.

That latecomers succeed at all is a small miracle. Success in high-technology industries is inherently implausible and unlikely. It was a daring gamble for Korea to try to enter the memory chips industry in the mid-1980s. The working assumption must be that the gamble would not pay off. Therefore we seek to account for how some countries have succeeded against the odds rather than starting with some preconceived limits to the success of a leverage strategy in principle.

Fast Followership – Effective Leverage Strategy or Recipe for Permanent Dependence?

Does a strategy of leverage and learning condemn a country or firm to permanent followership? This is a more serious objection, since it is couched in terms of strategy, not capabilities, and implies that there is something intrinsically defective in the latecomer's leverage strategy. We answer this question in two parts. First, how limiting is a strategy of followership in general? There appears to be an uncritical acceptance in much of the management literature of the supposed benefits that firms derive from the pursuit of 'leadership' strategies. A little reflection indicates, however, that only one or two firms can actually succeed. What happens to the others? A less biased survey of the evidence that traces case studies of industrial innovation from initial invention to ultimate market saturation leads to the conclusion that most of the benefits in a new industry are actually secured by follower firms. This has been demonstrated in one new industry or product market after another, such as ballpoint pens, CAT scanners, telephone answering machines, magnetic resonance imaging, and so the list goes on.[13]

From this perspective, the 'followership' strategies of East Asian firms might make a lot of sense – provided they have access to adequate financial and other resources. But a 'copycat' strategy taken to extremes can rebound against the practitioner. This is essentially the gist of our argument against Hong Kong's strategies, where fast followership and low-cost manufacturing have been pursued at the expense of technological sophistication (at least until the late 1990s).

Second, the evidence already indicates that if East Asian semi-conductor firms wish to strike out for product or technology leadership, they can do so. There is, for example, a modified 'followership' in which Taiwanese firms align themselves with a technology, but then introduce improvements or innovations of their own. A case in point is new products based on the PowerPC microprocessor. Here, the Taiwanese IT firms do not invent the new microprocessor – it is in fact co-developed by IBM and Motorola – but they lead the world in developing new IT products based on the new microprocessor, even to the point of developing new PowerPC-based products in advance of the originators, IBM and Motorola themselves. And there is the case of straight, world-first innovation, for instance Winbond's multimedia chips, which achieve digital signal compression rates that are the envy of the world.

Perhaps the best way to respond to the issue of perpetual 'followership' is to redefine what is conventionally meant by 'innovation'. Japanese scholars such as Nonaka and Takeuchi have already made substantial headway in showing how Japanese firms are extraordinarily creative in the way they formulate and pursue their product development strategies, whether these are seen as being 'innovators' or 'followers'.[14] We have also shown how Korean firms have demonstrated enormous ingenuity in improving their process technology in the semiconductor industry, raising yields of good chips per wafer to sustainable levels.

Is this 'innovation'? Such a discussion leads us full circle, back to the points made at the start of the book, that the novelty of high-technology industrial upgrading in East Asia lies in its focusing less on the generation of 'new knowledge' as on the more efficient diffusion and dissemination of existing knowledge. The overwhelming emphasis of Western literature on innovation, oriented towards the generation of 'new knowledge' through basic R&D, at the expense of all other forms of diffusion and dissemination of knowledge, has blinded many scholars to the wider processes of diffusion. Yet these are actually the source of *national wealth* rather than of *individual wealth*. The formulation and implementation of a strategy for innovation understood in this broader sense, and its sustainability, have been given an institutional foundation in East Asia that is a major social and economic innovation in itself, and a source of collective prosperity.

Thus we reject the notion that technology leverage has *intrinsic defects* which constrain its applicability. We see its limits set by existing technological and competitive dynamics that set the context within which leverage can be practised. But we do not see its limits lying in strategic defects that condemn practitioners to irremediable insufficiencies and inadequacies. Where these exist (and demonstrably they do) then we seek an explanation either in terms of the strategic choices made or the fact that companies and countries need time to establish the full range of absorptive capacities and combinative capabilities needed to sustain advanced technologies. They cannot accomplish these overnight.

These considerations bring us naturally to the next issue. If technology leverage is intrinsically plausible, how might it be replicated and diffused to firms in other countries?

The Replicability and Spread of Leverage Strategies

The plausibility of the account we offer is strongly supported by the fact that it is clearly replicated by the countries of East Asia, both in the originating countries as they upgrade to more and more sophisticated technologies and by others such as Malaysia and Thailand and, above all, China. The clinching argument for the growing significance of leverage is provided by the demonstration of its increasing use by advanced firms in the advanced countries as they seek to catch up with each other and with their East Asian competitors. There are three cases to consider: the repeated applications of technology leverage by Korea, Taiwan, Singapore and Malaysia; the diffusion of leverage strategies to other countries in East Asia through adoption of various institutional vehicles; and the adoption of technology leverage strategies in advanced countries.

Repeated Applications of Leverage

We have already discussed this case by pointing to the coherence of repeated applications of the leverage strategy by Korea, Taiwan and Singapore as they seek to upgrade and extend the semiconductor industry. The point to be made in this context is that such repeated applications do not condemn the country to endless technological dependence, rather they represent a means of maintaining and enhancing an 'absorptive capacity' ready to identify and acquire technological capabilities as they present themselves as of strategic significance. The application of repeated leveraging techniques in Taiwan's evolving 'collaborative alliances' between ITRI and the consortia of small and medium-sized firms represents a significant form of 'economic learning' on the part of these core East Asian countries.

Diffusion of Leverage Strategies to Other East Asian Countries

Much of our narrative in this book has been concerned with the spread of semiconductor firms throughout East Asia, where the striking feature of their acquisition of technological capabilities is that they use various forms of leverage on the model of the core East Asian leveraging pioneers. As elaborated in Chapter 2, we may identify three forms of such leverage, based on the chosen vehicles. They are Model A, that is, leverage using large, established firms; Model B, leverage using public research agencies and networks of smaller firms; and Model C, leverage from multinational enterprises. All three models are actively used throughout East Asia, singly and in combination.

Model A

With its emphasis on the role of large firms, Model A is a powerful approach to leveraged high-technology development. Large firms are generally sophisticated exponents of leverage, both technological and financial, and can bring these skills to bear on the acquisition of advanced skills and technological capabilities, as did the Korean *chaebol*. But many Korean companies tried, and only few succeeded. The successful *chaebol* made many strategic decisions that turned out to be wrong; they had to exercise quick corrective action to stay in the game (as with Hyundai's early espousal of SRAMs rather than DRAMs, and LG's aborted approach with ASICs). Model A encourages large firms to make large investment decisions and take large risks, emphasising the essential vulnerability of these high-risk strategies.

Singapore has also been an exponent of Model A, using its state-owned sector as the source of large companies which could be the vehicles of high-technology leverage. This is the case of STG, with its entry into IC wafer fabrication via Chartered Semiconductor. Due to the contingencies of the initial leverage arrangements (STG entering into an exclusive production arrangement with Sierra Semiconductor), the Singapore experiment was nearly aborted within a few years of its launch; but quick corrective action, and a new strategy based on the wafer foundry business, saw Chartered pick itself up and move onto a rapid growth trajectory.

The major potential weakness of Model A is its neglect of the role of small and medium-sized firms. This has not been an issue in Singapore, but has been in Korea where credit policies in the 1980s choked off investment finance from the small-firm sector and stunted its development.

Model B

This approach emphasises the role that small and medium-sized firms can play, in the absence or unwillingness of large firms, provided the public sector acts as a collective agent for the early stages of the leveraged development process. This is what Taiwan has proven to be so adept at doing. Moreover, Taiwan's approach evolved with the semiconductor industry, so that in the 1990s the major institutional mechanism for propagation of new technological capabilities has not been ITRI working on its own and spinning off companies, but ITRI working in close collaboration with groups of small or medium-sized firms in 'innovation alliances'.

Model B emphasises the need for a balanced industry structure and the gradual accumulation of technological capabilities – at the risk of being too 'gradual' and falling behind the more aggressive players. This was the situation faced by Taiwan in the early 1980s before its decision to go all out for VLSI capability; and in the 1990s before the decisions of firms to enter DRAM production activities.

Singapore showed signs of becoming an exponent of Model B in the 1990s, with the establishment of the Institute of Microelectronics as a collective source of technological capability enhancement, and the adoption of collaborative alliances as a means of upgrading and diffusing technological capabilities. However this was still at a relatively early stage of development by the late 1990s.

Model C

The option of choice for any country that lacks both large sophisticated firms and small technologically agile firms is Model C with its focus on leverage from multinationals. This is a description that must fit virtually all the underdeveloped countries of the world. In the face of so many predictions to the contrary by theorists of 'under-development' and by socialist governments East and West, the experiences of Singapore and Malaysia prove conclusively that multinationals can be used to good effect as vehicles of leveraged skills and technology. But for an industry to become 'sustainable' (in our sense) there must be some commitment on the part of local capital to invest in the high-technology sector, and some mechanism for allowing domestic companies to enter the market without excessively favouring the interests of the multinationals. This is a fine line that Singapore and, to a lesser extent, Malaysia have so far managed to walk, at least in the semiconductor sector. It involves balancing multiple pressures between early and late arrivals among the MNCs, and between the foreign and indigenous firm sector. To effect such balances calls for high levels of political capacity.

We appear to have exhausted all the possibilities in our framing of DRL models, so that we do not expect to see the next round of 'late-comers' inventing entirely new leverage models. What we expect to see is a range of *combinations* of these models, depending on the circumstances in which each country finds itself.

Model A is an approach that commends itself to any country that possesses an abundance of large, sophisticated firms, created in earlier phases of industrialisation. China comes to mind, with its large stock of state-owned enterprises. The most nimble of these enterprises were gearing up in the 1990s for major technology leveraging exercises through joint ventures and technology licensing to accelerate their entry into semiconductor production. The lesson of Korea and Japan is that if such enterprises are to succeed in advanced activities such as semiconductors, they need to be equipped with a diversification and leverage strategy, and not a 'sticking to the knitting' strategy that was popularised by the 'corporate excellence' literature of the 1980s.[15]

The second model is the generation of new and sophisticated firms through seeding from public sector agencies acting as 'collective entrepreneur'. The viability of such a model was in doubt until Taiwan's experience revealed it to be eminently practical. Indeed it is the model of choice in that what it generates is a well-balanced industrial structure and broad-based innovation capability, sustained as it is by the constant *replenishment* of sophisticated firms through the new-firm creation systems of such institutional arrangements as technology consortia and alliances. Thus this model is available to any country that has a stock of small and medium-sized enterprises and an institutional framework that is capable of inducing these SMEs into collaborative processes demanding increasing levels of knowledge intensity. This description must apply to many countries, particularly those that have relied extensively on SMEs in earlier phases of their industrialisation. Again this situation applies in particular to China, which has a huge supply of SMEs, such as in the emerging private sector based on town and village cooperative enterprises, many of which are high-technology oriented and have strong links to the country's vast array of scientific research institutes.[16]

Model C depends on direct foreign investment from MNCs to create an initial base of operations in the country, importing skills and technologies to do so. While Japan actively opposed such an approach, keeping MNCs like Fairchild, Texas Instruments and IBM at bay (and at great political risk to itself) during the 1960s, we have seen that Singapore and Malaysia have pursued this strategy with great success.[17] The lesson of these countries is that they must be able to impose their own leverage demands on the MNCs for internal skills and technology transfer, and for external leverage via direct components and services supply, while meeting the needs of the MNCs for stable and disciplined operation, freedom to import the equipment and components desired, and to repatriate profits without interference. This is a political trade-off that calls for a high level of state capacity on the part of the countries negotiating such arrangements.

Model C is clearly the strategy of choice for any country that lacks sophisticated firms of its own, or that wishes to accelerate its access to advanced technologies by tapping into the current activities of MNCs. This description must apply to half the countries in the world. In particular, it applies to China, Indonesia and to some extent India, which are looking in their different ways to bring their huge countries through early-stage industrialisation (the transition from rural agriculture-based economies to urban industrial-based systems) and late-stage high-technology industrialisation simultaneously.[18] They can expect to succeed in such an accelerated industrialisation strategy only by co-operating with MNCs (particularly those from the second-tier NIEs Korea and Taiwan) rather than by keeping them at bay.

China: Simultaneous Application of All Three Models

By the late 1990s, after two decades of open-door policy towards FDI, China was displaying capacities in technology upgrading that use not just one of the institutional models we identify in East Asia, but all of them, simultaneously. Thus, China was basing much of its upgrading on the capacities of large, established firms to reach out and forge technology alliances with other large firms in Japan, Europe and the US, to tap their internally generated semiconductor capabilities. This was the pattern pursued by Japan and subsequently by Korea. China was also using its multitude of small and medium-sized enterprises, many of them newly renovated collective village-based enterprises that can form partnerships with public-sector R&D institutes, to act as channels for the diffusion of technological capabilities from these institutes into the wider Chinese economy. This was the pattern pursued by Taiwan.

Thirdly, China was pursuing an open-door policy in relation to FDI, inviting the world's multinational enterprises to establish operations in China, subject to their agreeing to involve themselves in local skills upgrading and supply contracts with local firms.[19] This is the Singapore model, or the wider South East Asian model in general. Thus China shows determination to use all three of the institutional models we have identified – and it is large enough to do so. Success or failure in the creation of a semiconductor industry in China will provide a critical test of the aptness of the technology leverage strategy now being pursued in such determined fashion by a multitude of Chinese enterprises. As noted in Chapter 1, China appeared to have made significant headway towards the creation of a viable industry by the end of the 1990s.

From the mid-twenty-first century, when China is likely to have advanced much further along the road of industrialisation and urbanisation, and assumed its place among the world's economic superpowers, the technology leverage strategy that underpinned its success might be scorned or forgotten, as the European powers have largely forgotten how they acquired their technological capabilities in the eighteenth and nineteenth centuries, and the US has largely forgotten its dependence on technology transfer in the nineteenth century. But there is an important reason why this is unlikely to be the case. By then, *technology leverage promises to be the norm for advanced firms in advanced countries as well.*

Uptake of Resource Leverage Strategies in Advanced Countries

The final strand of our argument concerns the uptake of leverage strategies by advanced firms in the advanced countries. The processes of technology leverage that we have identified as being critical to the recent successes of East Asia are being widely emulated. In the US, Sematech is certainly the most successful instance of an R&D consortium being formed to counter growing Japanese influence in the semiconductor equipment and materials supply sector. Sematech has been credited with having renewed US strengths in this sector, with firms such as Advanced Materials moving to global leadership in the 1990s. The pace of alliance and consortium formation in the US has not slackened. Under Sematech's sponsorship, an international 300 mm wafer initiative (I300I) was put together in the mid-1990s, in which Taiwanese and Korean firms were invited participants for the first time; the Japanese went their own way with the J300 consortium.[20] In 1998, Sematech institutionalised this case of cooperation to encompass an International Sematech, involving Korean, Taiwanese and European firms with the existing US participants.

By the late 1990s, consortium formation was becoming routine in the US. In 1997 three leading semiconductor firms – Intel, AMD and Motorola – joined with three leading national R&D laboratories – Sandia, Lawrence Livermore and Lawrence Berkeley – to form an advanced lithography consortium: the Extreme UltraViolet Limited Liability Company (EUV LLC).[21] This is a pattern of development that is strongly at odds with earlier patterns that emphasised go-it-alone strategies of individual firms.

The flat panel display (FPD) industry provides a highly instructive case of 'catch-up' alliance formation in the US. While US firms developed advanced laboratory versions of FPDs, including the most popular versions such as active matrix liquid crystal displays, they did not move on to establish mass-production industries for these high-technology products, allowing Japan to take a decisive lead in the late 1980s that continued into the 1990s. This lead was challenged by Korea in the early 1990s, and then by Taiwan in the late 1990s both using leverage techniques – but not yet by US firms themselves, while European firms such as Philips remained small players in the global industry.[22] Since FPDs will play an ever more significant role in industrial, consumer and military applications in the twenty-first century, this absence of a domestic industry in the US has excited an intense national debate. In 1994, the US Department of Defense, worried that the future security of the country could be compromised by extreme technological dependence on other countries (read Japan) for the displays to be used in advanced weapons systems, orchestrated a determined effort to bring US firms up to the technological level of their East Asian competitors. The methods used? Joint R&D consortia, strong government procurement incentives, public-sector funded pilot production operations, powerful development incentives with an emphasis on mass-production capabilities, and technology alliances with advanced players. That is, methods that resemble very closely the technology leverage strategies of the East Asians. The result has been the formation of a publicly funded consortium, the US Display Consortium, and a flurry of activity in R&D and pilot production, although not yet on the scale envisaged by the DoD or by the report it commissioned in 1994.[23]

There is considerable irony in the fact that the Americans were resorting to 'Japanese-style' R&D consortia and technology leverage strategies to catch up in this most strategic of industries, since the Japanese themselves developed the FPD industry in the 1980s with little or no government or collective involvement at all; the Japanese moved on to 'US-style' industry strategies while the Americans sought to catch up with 'Japanese-style' programs in this high-technology industry.[24] The point here is not to promote or belittle any particular efforts but to demonstrate that by the late 1990s, all three major world centres of industrial innovation, in the US, Japan and Europe, national R&D consortia and international consortia were becoming frequent and unexceptionable. They represented an index of technological strength rather than weakness. That East Asian latecomers were becoming integrated in such consortia was a further index of their having 'arrived' as serious players in knowledge-intensive industries. Are these isolated examples, or are there reasons to believe that technology leverage strategies will become the norm in advanced countries?

Technology leverage presents itself as a strategy of choice in advanced countries in conditions where firms are looking to enter new industries, or are seeking to catch up with the technological leaders, and where technological resources are available (for example, through international joint ventures) and product turnover is sufficiently rapid to put constant pressure on incumbents.

These conditions are strikingly similar to those described by D'Aveni (1994) as 'hypercompetition'. Thus we hazard the proposition that leverage strategies will work whenever hypercompetitive conditions prevail – whether in East Asia, other developing countries or the advanced countries. We close this discussion with the intriguing observation that perhaps leveraging techniques have much broader applicability than is at first evident. Such an observation attests to the wide replicability of leverage strategies even beyond East Asia, provided institutional capacities to underpin the process can be generated. It is these capacities which continue to separate the successful from the unsuccessful practitioners of knowledge and resource leverage.

Notes

1   There are important qualifications. In the mid-1990s, for example, the Taiwanese launched a collaborative R&D exercise to jointly develop a four-stroke automotive engine (after an earlier attempt to develop a two-stroke engine in the 1980s ended in failure). Technology in this instance was leveraged from the UK firm, Lotus, under the auspices of ITRI's Mechanical Engineering Laboratory. Four of Taiwan's auto firms were involved in this project (later falling to three). This collaboration has been successful, and a joint Taiwan Engine Company was launched in 1996, and was producing engines, largely for Taiwanese cars being sold in the China market, by 1997. The second qualification is that the Taiwanese have been successful in leveraging themselves into the automotive components industry rather than

in the production of fully assembled vehicles in head-to-head competition with the Japanese. This is a characteristic strategy of the Taiwanese: to avoid head-to-head competition and secure niches instead as suppliers of key components and industrial OEM contracts.

2   See McKendrick (1992) for an assessment of Indonesia's 'catch-up' efforts in the aircraft industry, where the accumulation of impressive technological capabilities was not matched by managerial competencies.

3   The process started with the TI-Acer joint venture of 1991, and proceeded through several tie-ups with Japanese firms, for example Nan Ya Technology with Oki; Umax with Mitsubishi (Powerchip Semiconductor), Mosel-Vitelic with Oki, and Winbond with Toshiba.

4   Incumbents argued that ITRI's industry promotion efforts resulted in too many competitors being crushed.

5   By the late 1990s the Taiwanese firms involved in mass production of TTF LCDs, based on technology leverage from Japanese firms, included the following:

   • Unipac Optoelectronics: A UMC affiliate that signed with Japan's Matsushita Electronics in October 1998 to manufacture TTF LCDs using Matsushita's technology.
   • Chung Hwa Picture Tubes: Affiliate of the electronics giant Tatung (and itself the largest producer of TV and PC picture tubes in the world) moved to production of TTF LCDs in 1998, based on technology transferred from Mitsubishi.
   • Acer Display Technologies: Affiliate of the global Acer group licensed TTF LCD technology from IBM and entered mass production of screens, both for its own use and for the OEM market, in 1998.
   • Winbond: A semiconductor producer that diversified into flat panel display production initially through technology for producing TTF LCDs transferred from Toshiba.
   • Prime View: A Taiwanese firm that developed its own LCD technology, based initially on some technological assistance from ERSO.

6   These factors can be overdone to the point that they represent a constraint, as in the case of the hard disk drive industry which has seen product innovation become so rapid that a 'fast follower' strategy becomes impractical.

7   Dosi (1982) provides the classic exposition of the concept of technological trajectory.

8   Note how these criteria reverse those usually advanced to explain the sustainability of competitive advantage which have such resources to begin with. This reversal, which calls into question the universality of the criteria of sustained competitive advantage as used in the 'resource-based' theory of competitive advantage, was first raised and discussed in Mathews (1997b).

9   See Porter (1985) and Barney (1997).

10   See the canonical discussion on this issue by Argyris and Schon (1978).

11   The 'path dependent' thesis on the limitations of East Asian strategies is developed by numerous authors, including Ferguson and Morris (1993). The notion of permanent dependence on advanced sources is developed by Ernst (1994), while that of permanent dependence on government guidance is a popular theme in the trade press. The successful diversification and expansion of high-technology clusters in East Asia is sufficient response to such points.

12   US technology commentators Charles Ferguson and Charles Morris, contend that in spite of the undeniable successes of East Asian firms, they suffer from a 'fatal flaw' in that they have chosen relatively easy 'commodity-like' products and then poured their energies into improving process technology for these products, without acquiring an all-round technological and innovative capability. See Ferguson and Morris (1994: 113–14).

13   See Schnaars (1994) for the definitive account.

14   See Nonaka (1994) and Nonaka and Takeuchi (1995) for the most comprehensive discussion of this issue.

15   In our view it is failure to diversify on the part of most well-established large firms in countries such as Canada and Australia, and the failure of government agencies to encourage or force them to do so that accounts for their failure to become serious players in semiconductors. By contrast, it was the almost reckless diversification pursued by Korea's large firms, backed by strong government encouragement and incentives, that lie at the core of Korea's success in semiconductors.

16   See Turpin et al. (1995) for a description of the emergence of advanced technology industries in China, in which such township enterprise and research institution linkages played a vital role, based on a case study of radiation-based high voltage cable technology.

17   See Hill (1990) for a review of the literature on foreign direct investment and economic development in South East Asia, with particular emphasis on the role played by multinationals.

18   The literature on this topic is growing rapidly. For an account that is consistent with our analysis, see Amsden et al. (1996).

19   See Zhao (1995) or Hayter and Han (1998) for representative studies of these processes in China.

20   Actually the two international consortia reached an agreement, the Global Joint Guidance Agreement, in 1997, forming the world's first truly global process technology consortium to ease the transition for a global industry to the next upgrade in process technology (from 200 mm to 300 mm wafers).

21   The EUV LLC announced plans to invest $250 million in private funding over three years, to develop EUV lithography for use by all three consortium members, over and above the funds already invested by the Department of Defense channelled through the three national laboratories. This is the largest investment ever by private industry in a DoD semiconductor research project, an indication of how seriously US firms now take collaborative joint leverage as an organisational option.

22   See Linden, Hart, Lenway and Murtha (1998).

23   The Department of Defense and other agencies such as ARPA commissioned a special study of the US display industry by the Brookings scholar, Kenneth Flamm, to use the 'dual use' strategy enunciated by Defense Secretary William Perry. The report was publicly available on the Internet in the late 1990s: see www.acq.osd.mil/es/fpd. A summary was published in the special issue of *Industry and Innovation* on the 'global dynamics of the flat panel display industry' (June 1998).

24   For further discussion of this theme, see the introduction by Wong and Mathews (1998) to the special issue of *Industry and Innovation* on the global dynamics of the flat panel display industry.

CHAPTER 8

National Systems of Economic Learning: Lessons from East Asia

Our aim in this book has been to document, account and appraise the methods and achievements of the East Asian countries in establishing semiconductor industries. We have compared the variety of knowledge leverage strategies developed in East Asia in some detail: the long, patient process of leverage laced with autarchy pursued by Japan; the accelerated export-driven leverage strategy of the Koreans using large, diversified firms; the patient build-up of private sector capabilities using the leverage of the public sector in Taiwan; and the skilful leveraging of technologies from the multinationals in Singapore and Malaysia. Our aim has been to demonstrate that in creating a high-technology industry such as semiconductors, these East Asian countries have pioneered new strategies and techniques – not of technological innovation, but of *industry creation* itself.

They have developed a new and powerful focus for their efforts, not to generate new knowledge, but to accelerate the *leverage* and *diffusion* of existing knowledge, first from overseas advanced countries into their own institutions, and then from firm to firm within their own countries. We have sought to demonstrate how these East Asian countries have developed unique institutional frameworks adapted for this purpose – which in themselves constitute an important form of economic innovation. We have argued that the East Asian countries have pioneered the development of three institutional models of accelerated diffusion of technological capabilities, which we have designated in neutral terms as Models A, B and C. We have sought to demonstrate the subtleties of the workings of these institutional frameworks which we have dubbed 'national systems of economic learning'.

The spirit of our exposition is Schumpeterian, Gerschenkronian, Chandlerian and Johnsonian. It is Schumpeterian in our insistence that

313

the *feasibility* of the project of latecomer high-technology industrialisation lies in the restless turnover of technologies that characterises industries such as semiconductors, destroying the power of incumbents and creating endless new opportunities for newcomers – provided they can learn to read technological trajectories, and can work within the constraints of technology and product life-cycles. These are demanding requirements, and much of our narrative has been concerned with the drama of the attempts, both successful and unsuccessful, by firms and agencies in the East Asian countries to learn and master these subtleties.

Our account is Gerschenkronian in that we have sought to highlight the means through which the East Asian countries were able to turn the disadvantages of being latecomers into advantages by leveraging the very latest technologies and building technological infrastructure unencumbered by earlier industrial phases. They were Gerschenkronian in the sense that firms in latecomer countries have not been left to tackle the high-technology industrial upgrading tasks on their own. They establish and enter leveraging channels, and conduct their technological learning activities in an institutional setting adapted to facilitate, accelerate and discipline their efforts. This is where public agencies and infrastructure and the disciplined government–business collaboration they make possible – in short, institutional capacity – has made a difference. Just as Gerschenkron hypothesised that latecomer industrialisation in Europe in the nineteenth century was accelerated by state institutions, where the state could play the role of a 'collective entrepreneur', so we sought to demonstrate the same process at work in East Asia in the late twentieth century in the semiconductor industry. Here the setting is not labour or capital-intensive industrial upgrading, but knowledge-intensive industrial transformation that works on the levels of organisational and collective economic learning.

Our account is Chandlerian in the sense that we recognise that countries' catch-up efforts must depend on the role of firms that are frequently created by public agencies specifically to play the role of vehicles of technology leverage and diffusion. It was Chandler who insisted on the role played by large firms in driving the process of catch-up industrialisation in the US in the nineteenth century, laying the groundwork, through their readiness to invest in huge plants that captured unprecedented economies of scale, for their dominance of global industries in the twentieth centuries.[1] We have seen how large firms have played a significant role in the high-technology catch-up efforts of Japan and Korea, while in Taiwan small and medium-sized firms have been able to match the resources of larger competitors through their collaborative efforts and their links with public agencies. In Singapore and Malaysia it was large firms – the multinational corporations – that provided the vehicles for enhancement of technological capabilities.

Our account is Johnsonian in the sense that we have insisted on the importance and specificity of the institutional frameworks within which the different countries created their advanced industries through leverage. It was Johnson's account of MITI that firmly established the institutional factor as decisive in the emergent Japanese political economy, and likewise we have sought to bring out the significance of institutional arrangements in our own account of high-technology industrial upgrading in East Asia. Moreover we have sought to demonstrate in detail how the relations between the public and private sectors in each of the East Asian countries have not assumed a static, once-off cast, but have evolved together, changing as the industry evolves and matures. It is the *co-evolution* of the *public* (laboratories like ECL and ETL in Japan; ITRI in Taiwan; KIET in Korea) and the *private* (the high-technology firms) and the *intermediate* institutions between them (the industry associations, development consortia and innovation alliances) that are of interest in accounting for successful transformations, and for the strengths and weaknesses of the different institutional settings. Some systems of economic learning are clearly better than others in achieving high-technology industrialisation. The East Asian countries, as we have shown, are innovative pioneers of such systems, and have made them work better than others.

In this chapter we widen the focus and apply these perspectives to the process of knowledge-intensive industry creation more generally. It is highly probable that knowledge-intensive industries will in the future be the primary sources of wealth generation – as opposed to the resource, labour and capital-intensive industries that dominated the twentieth century. Thus the methods that have worked so well for the four East Asian countries studied here are likely to have much wider applicability, in East Asia and beyond, in the twenty-first century.

The Schumpeterian Perspective

Chapter 6 examined the industry constraints that impinged on the process of leverage as a successful system, highlighting factors such as rapid product turnover, widespread entry by new firms into the industry (for example, as start-ups), and availability of process technology from merchant vendors. These factors are concentrated in the IT, electronics and semiconductor industries, making them prime candidates for catch-up and leverage strategies. In our view it is the evolution of technology in trajectories, rather than its 'random' development, that provides the fundamental possibility for technology leverage by latecomer firms. A new firm can read the technological trajectory just as well as the old, even if it does not as yet possess all the skills and knowledge needed to implement the technology and become a serious player. There are 'technological options' that a developing firm can read as well as an incumbent. Indeed, the trends might be read better by the developing firm precisely because it lacks the intellectual baggage from the past that might confuse or bias an incumbent's perceptions.

Underpinning successful technology leverage strategies are the features of 'Schumpeterian competition' in high-technology industries, and the observed characteristic pattern of technological evolution in 'lumpy' trajectories.[2] Success depends ultimately on technologies that follow defined trajectories. If an industry is based on technologies that have no identifiable trajectory, then it is, quite simply, not a candidate for catch-up through leverage.

The Gerschenkronian Perspective

Our concern is with catch-up, not technological leadership. There is a vast literature that debates the respective merits of the US industrial system, with its purported emphasis on individualism and innovation, versus the Japanese system, with its purported emphasis on collaboration and imitation. We say 'purported' because we find much more collaboration and state sponsorship in the US system than is normally admitted, and much more fierce competition and sheer, brilliant innovation (witness Sharp's worldwide leadership in LCDs and its record of pathbreaking innovation in this technology over the past 25 years) in the Japanese system than is admitted. But our point is that neither the US nor the Japanese systems of the 1990s are relevant models since they are industrial systems oriented towards maintaining world technological leadership, not catch-up.

The East Asian Gerschenkronian systems of economic learning are certainly innovative, but not in the sense of the fast turnover of new firms and new ideas in a 'Silicon Valley'. The difference is absolutely critical. Catch-up through leverage demands a quite different strategy ('fast followership') and institutional framework for its implementation than that associated with the conventional approach to innovation. It calls for a Gerschenkronian understanding of the ways that latecomer firms can turn their disadvantages into sources of advantage by focusing on resources that are most susceptible to leverage, even if this works only for a limited time and 'window' of opportunity. And it calls for a sophisticated understanding of the institutional foundations of the processes of technology leverage and diffusion management. These frameworks are not driving the generation of new ideas, as in a Silicon Valley, but rapid technological upgrading and adjustment to world conditions.

The Chandlerian Perspective

Latecomer firms are created through entrepreneurship, but the concept of 'entrepreneurship' needs to be given a sufficiently broad interpretation. By entrepreneurship we understand the capability of assembling and recombining existing business elements to create something that did not or would not otherwise exist. In this sense, entrepreneurship has been fundamental to the creation of the semiconductor industry in East Asia and, by extension, to the creation of any new industry by leverage anywhere.

But entrepreneurship takes many different forms. Consider the semiconductor firms in Korea, Taiwan and Singapore. With the Korean *chaebol*, it was entrepreneurship that created the firms in the first place and drove their extraordinary diversification. Samsung demonstrated a quite dramatic history of such diversification from food supply to food manufacturing, to woollen textile manufacturing, to fertiliser production and so on, where the mechanism in each case involved the spinning off of new businesses using the expertise acquired in running the earlier businesses, but adding each time new technological capabilities acquired through leverage.

In Taiwan, firms like UMC were created through the entrepreneurship of public agencies, including ITRI and financing vehicles like the CDC. The entrepreneurship involved was directed towards giving a firm like UMC a strong start, with the assets, skills, a product range and process technology needed to produce them all transferred from the public sector at minimal charges to the new company. Once established in this manner, it was up to the company to fend for itself in the international marketplace, which UMC and other such creations in Taiwan (like TSMC, VIS and TMC) have been able to do most effectively.

In Singapore, the entrepreneurship demonstrated by Singapore Technologies Group in its creation of Chartered Semiconductor Manufacturing and its sister firms is that of the public sector playing a role as 'state capitalist' with the express intent of stimulating a private sector into existence. This is a very different situation from one discussed by economists when they point to public-sector activities 'crowding out' those of the private sector. In each case, the institutional frameworks favoured entrepreneurship rather than constrained it – and in places such as Taiwan, better than in others.

The Johnsonian Perspective

The World Bank's 'East Asian miracle' report attributed East Asian success to good macroeconomic management and to market friendly interventions.[3] While these elements were certainly present in the rise of high-technology sectors, they do not take us very far in understanding high-technology industrialisation such as in semiconductors. Once the central role of learning is acknowledged, the issue of the institutional setting in which it takes place becomes unavoidable. Our analysis of the semiconductor industry has shown how the East Asian national systems of economic learning have embodied the following elements.

Technology Leverage

This has been carried out by public-sector R&D institutes, whose main mission is to scan the world's technological developments and rapidly build a capability in new techniques. The institutes' purpose is to diffuse them to the private sector as quickly as possible. Examples are ITRI in Taiwan, with its specialist laboratories ERSO and CCL; KIET, ETRI and KAIST in Korea; IME in Singapore and MIMOS in Malaysia.

Financial Leverage

Some development banks or investment vehicles have been charged with the mission of identifying worthwhile strategic investments, such as those that further the goals of catching up and organising the financing required. In Taiwan there was the China Development Corporation; in Korea the state-owned or regulated development banks; in Singapore the Singapore Development Bank (spun off from the EDB in the 1960s) and in Malaysia the Bank Industri Malaysia and the Khazana Nasional Berhad (the National Treasury investment arm of the Malaysian government).[4] These operate either through the mobilisation of domestic savings, or through the creation of international bank syndicates and the issuance of debt instruments such as depositary receipts.

Nurturing Environment for the Formation of Knowledge-intensive Firms

All the cases of semiconductor industry formation have involved provision of suitable infrastructure such as the Hsinchu Science-based Industry Park in 1980 and its successor the Tainan Park in the late 1990s; the Singapore science parks in Jurong and the new semiconductor fab parks in Woodlands, Pasir Ris and Tampines, and comparable Malaysian developments such as Kulim; as well as taxation and R&D incentives schemes designed to facilitate the formation of new firms in the semiconductor sector. With Taiwan's ITRI, this has extended in the 1990s to the creation of a multi-storey 'incubator' building on the campus to house the operations of new technology-intensive firms, started mainly by ITRI staff.

Investment-attracting Vehicles

Bodies such as Singapore's Economic Development Board or Penang's Penang Development Corporation – termed, collectively, economic development agencies – have been central to the process of attracting and monitoring investment in high-technology activities by multinationals. The East Asian agencies have been so successful in attracting multinational investment that they have been paid the compliment of emulation in places such as Scotland, Wales and Ireland, where the SDA, WDA and IDA have played major roles in attracting foreign investment to areas formerly stricken with industrial decline.

Industry Self-organisation

Bodies such as the KSIA in Korea, the TEEMA and more recently, TSIA in Taiwan, have emerged to provide a means for communication between government and firms, and to fashion a consensus over new directions for the industry to move in. It is the capacity for such an industry to self-organise for more than merely defensive ends that is an important factor in its ability to be continuously upgraded and thereby sustain its competitiveness.

Industrial Upgrading Incentives and Discipline

None of the public agencies in East Asia has been content to create new firms or seed technologies without also setting in place processes for continual technological upgrading and enhancement. The world technological frontier moves ahead relentlessly, and firms and agencies need to be focused on keeping up with these developments through all the means of open technological communication available.

Skills Upgrading and Technical Training

Technological capabilities rest on an infrastructure of specialist industrial training that is not created by markets, but calls for institutional innovations to ensure that firms can employ skilled staff and engineers as they need them. Singapore, for example, created specialist training centres with selected multinational corporations. In the 1990s the expansion of its wafer-fabrication activities has been underpinned by a specialist technical training program funded through the EDB.

Market Shaping and Creation

In all the cases of semiconductor industry formation in East Asia, markets for the products did not exist initially. They had to be conjured into place to complement the markets in advanced countries that acted as the export drivers for the nascent industries. Thus institutions like the Institute for Information Industry in Taiwan helped to create a public and private-sector market for IT products by driving the associated standards for IT use in government agencies. In Singapore the National Computer Board played a similar role.

Export Promotion

The collective enhancement of export performance through institutions such as KOTRA in Korea and the Trade Development Board in Singapore has been a significant source of institutional support as firms in East Asian countries seek to enter new markets.

Lead Agency (Johnson's 'Pilot Agency')

Since industry adaptation and adjustment depends for its success on coordination, the need for some form of pilot or lead agency to set the overall strategic directions and coordinate the activities of the various agencies and trade/industry associations, is apparent. Prominent examples are the CEPD in Taiwan, the EDB in Singapore and the former EPB in Korea.[5]

We capture the sense of these Johnsonian institutional frameworks that drive economic learning in Figure 8.1. On their own, these agencies and organisational innovations are not so remarkable, and easily replicated (as for example, the economic development agencies that have been emulated in Europe, such as the Welsh Development Agency). What is remarkable is the total system formed by their interaction and mutual support. It is this systemic character of the elements that accounts for the capacity to learn.

Learning is a process of adaptation to changing circumstances based not just on random trial and error, but on stored experience and tested responses. This is the core of the emergent field of organisational learning, as developed in the field of organisational behaviour. It is certainly the core of the new field of knowledge we have identified in the way that new industries are created and upgraded in East Asia and beyond, which

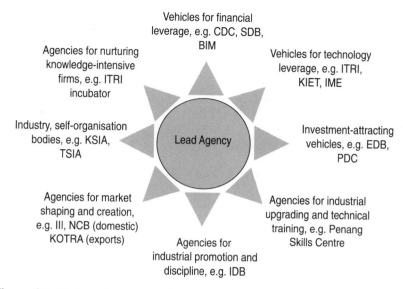

Figure 8.1 National systems of economic learning in East Asia.

we call 'economic learning'. It is the adaptability of the total system that counts, with the facility to improve adaptation over time as experience is gained and stored in appropriate institutional form, generating what we call 'institutional capacity'.

What, then, are the features of a national system of economic learning viewed as a coherent totality? What are the core elements and the synergies between them, abstracted from any specific institutional framework and any specific part of the world?

Features of National Systems of Economic Learning

Successful national systems of economic learning created for purposes of technological catch-up will exhibit *at least* the following six features. How these features are realised in institutional form will depend on a country's starting point and history.

A Core Institutional Capacity for Technological Capability Enhancement

At the centre of the economic learning/technological upgrading through leverage approach is a public-sector core capacity to acquire, absorb and disseminate technologies. It might be a public-sector research laboratory, like Taiwan's ITRI or it might be a series of such laboratories, specialising in certain areas like solar technology and alternative energy sources, environmental control technology and recycling, new materials and chemical processing technologies and so on.

Core capability also includes universities equipped with faculties teaching in core technological areas, as well as laboratories where good graduate students can experience the challenges of working at the technological frontier. All the East Asian countries we have looked at have understood profoundly the significance of creating such institutions – witness the efforts to establish KAIST in Korea, Tsinghua University in Taiwan, Nanyang Technological University in Singapore and recently, Hong Kong University of Science and Technology. The great centres of innovation in the West, such as Silicon Valley in California, and the Route 128 complex in Boston, have great public institutions at their core – Stanford University and its offshoots in Silicon Valley, and MIT in the Boston high-technology complex.[6]

From the perspective of a national system of economic learning, these core public institutions provide the wellsprings of sustainable industrial learning and technological upgrading. They combine disinterested scanning of the world's technological horizon for new and interesting technological developments with a teaching and research capability to acquire, replicate, adopt and adapt these technologies. While private firms can provide many of these features for themselves (in Korea today the leading *chaebol* such as Samsung, Hyundai and LG do so) the firm is involved in a constant struggle over trade-offs, with the potential profits of the *new* having to contend with the current profits of the status quo.

The great advantage of a public-sector institution is that it can take a disinterested approach to the evaluation of new technologies, uncluttered by existing technological commitments. If such institutions combine research with teaching, they also provide a constant stream of graduates equipped with new technological insights and an eagerness to find applications for them, thus creating a bias towards innovation and its diffusion.

Institutional Capacity for Promoting the Formation of Networks of Technology-based Firms

To complement the core public-sector institutions of leverage are the firms that cooperate with them to commercialise the new technological developments, or that engage in their own leverage activities to bring themselves abreast of the world technological frontier. Instead of the conventional view that sees firms as atomistic entities rising and growing through their own intrinsic efforts, the economic learning perspective sees firms as carriers of technological capabilities and their creation and enhancement as prime goals or outcomes of the process of learning. Not just any old firm pursuing any old strategy is sought, but sophisticated firms equipped with 'absorptive capacities' that will function effectively as agents of technology leverage, individually and in collaborative networks, to link upstream and downstream activities to the mutual benefit of both.

The creation and nurturing of new technology-based firms is one of the most striking institutional features of the East Asian systems of economic learning. This capability rests on a number of institutional innovations, including: the formation of science-based industry parks, for example, Hsinchu in Taiwan or R&D parks in Singapore, with their first-class facilities and services, and their proximity to tertiary technical institutions; the encouragement of entrepreneurship among staff of tertiary technical institutes; in some cases, active encouragement through the provision of 'incubator' facilities on campus (as in the creation of such a facility for new firm start-ups at ITRI in the late 1990s); the framing of tax and other incentives to encourage firms to pursue technology-intensive strategies rather than low risk, low cost and low value-adding strategies; and the provision of a range of financial and other resources through development banks and financial agencies, with special remit to encourage the formation of new firms with long-term potential.

Such a system of incentives and structures has the capacity to evolve towards a leading-edge system like California's Silicon Valley as the technological sophistication of its firms grows and their international experience accumulates.

Institutional Capacity for Promoting and Managing Technology Diffusion

Economic catch-up is about technology leverage – the accelerated diffusion of technological capabilities and their enhancement within firms. Thus, given the prior existence of strong public-sector core institutional capacities and the formation of new, sophisticated firms, the essential feature of the learning economy is the institutional capacity to accelerate the diffusion or uptake of new technological capabilities. The first major institutional innovation designed to achieve such an outcome in East Asia was the Japanese innovation (adaptation) of the ERA, which has been used as the vehicle for public–private collaboration and inter-firm diffusion, through the entire high-technology catch-up phase of Japan. Likewise, Korean collaborative programs have sought similar ends, while in Taiwan there have been numerous experiments and institutional improvements in R&D alliances that bring together public-sector agencies such as ITRI, the IDB, networks of firms and trade associations (such as TEEMA), where self-organisation reinforces the institutional capacity for rapid technological learning and diffusion.

Institutional Capacity for Attracting International Investment

In virtually all cases in the twenty-first century, efforts to encourage and promote indigenous capabilities will have to be complemented by efforts to attract foreign direct investment (FDI), in the form of operations of MNCs. It is these MNCs that will act as a direct source of technology leverage. FDI is superior as a direct source of technology leverage to alternatives such as licensing and company purchase, but it carries the risk that the company establishing its operations will seek to limit the degree of skill and knowledge transferred and will potentially obstruct the formation of local enterprises by bringing with it its own sources of supply. Given that these are recognised problems, the issue for any country or sector pursuing such a leverage route is to guard against them. Institutional capacities are needed to monitor such FDI agreements and to ensure that technology transfer is built into any agreements that allow such investment to take place. Competitive underbidding (for example, by states in a federal system) is clearly incompatible with such a requirement and needs to be remedied by an institutional capacity at national level.

Steering of the System

The most significant feature of the institutional capacity to effect technological learning is the capacity for 'steering' the system within strategically identified technological trajectories. The more we examine the processes of high-technology industry creation, the more we are struck by the subtle but important role played by the institutional capacity to decide on strategic directions and then to 'steer' the interactions of the players involved. This cannot be done by a 'strong' state that bullies the private sector into submission or by a 'weak' state that cannot stand up to special pleading and impose fair business conditions on all players. It can only be effected within a context of give-and-take between the public and private agencies in an institutional setting best described as 'governed interdependence'.[7]

We are impressed by the continuing ability of state agencies to fashion the direction of technological upgrading in East Asia. For example, in Taiwan in the late 1990s there were determined efforts to shift private transport options towards electric vehicles, particularly to silent and energy-saving electric motor cycles. Taiwan's Ministry of Economic Affairs promoted this option not just by stimulating the development of certain technical options (such as efficient batteries) but also by 'shaping' markets that would support them, by intervening to create a public infrastructure for battery recharging that would be price competitive with the existing infrastructure serving petrol-engine driven vehicles. This is not just a 'market-friendly' view (in terms used by the World Bank) or even a 'market-enhancing' one (as developed by Aoki *et al.*), but a 'market-shaping' view that seems to be most compatible with the successful instances of technological upgrading and adaptation that we describe as economic learning.

Economic Learning, Technological Upgrading and Institutional Capacities

The national systems of economic learning we have described are concerned with the specific tasks of technological leverage and upgrading to maintain and enhance the competitiveness of knowledge-intensive industries. Over and above the ingredients or elements described is the *operation of the system as a whole*, in an integrated or coherent fashion.

Our interest lies in developing the notion of 'economic learning', that is, the system by which an economy adapts to new circumstances using measures that are more than random, price-guided reactions. Learning involves adapting intelligently to new circumstances by developing a repertoire of routines that are stored in memory and which can be drawn on as circumstances change. Great progress has been made in developing the notion of 'organisational learning', that is, an adaptive response on the part of an organisation to changing circumstances which calls on something more than random explorations of new technological or market spaces. Organisational learning implies the existence and acquisition of 'organisational competencies' as the outcome of learning. The 'learning organisation' is one that can translate the learning of individual members or sections into something that belongs to the organisation as a whole; it is the creation of supra-individual competencies. Quick and nimble organisations are those that can develop and call on such resources. Learning here implies the existence of an organisational memory in the form of behavioural routines such as standard operating procedures and the ability to 'learn' from mistakes.

A clear analogy presents itself at the economic level when we deal with specific industries rather than a single organisation. Thus 'economic learning' is about the capacity of an economy to react intelligently to changing circumstances – by forms of economic adjustment that follow certain 'learned' routines (like firms working together in collaborative networks) and which demonstrate a capacity to improve over time. It implies the ability of an economy to react intelligently to new circumstances, drawing on a 'memory' that encompasses similar prior experiences and the results of earlier efforts to react to change in technologies or markets.

By analogy, the outcome of economic learning must be a set of competencies that we might call 'economic', namely, competencies to do with economic or industrial adjustment – such as by developing new industries and running down old industries, creating circumstances that facilitate the emergence of firms in new sectors or the adaptation of firms in existing sectors, and disseminating technological and market intelligence. These are 'supra-organisational' competencies or institutional capacities that inhere in no single organisation but are shared by many, embodied in institutions spanning the public and private sectors.

Economic learning is above all a capacity to experiment with new organisational forms, adopting those which work and discarding those which do not, and improving these forms through further rounds of controlled variation and selection. What we are describing, then, is a process that is consistent with the notion of the economy as an evolutionary system, dynamically adapting through time, using processes of variation and selection, as described by Nelson and Winter (1982). What we are doing is adding some explicit institutional detail to the process, and a notion of controlled variation and repeatability of organisational forms, inspired by the recent experiences of East Asian countries in successful rounds of industrial upgrading.

Cases of economic learning can be found in Japan, Korea and Taiwan in the semiconductor industry. In Japan, the FONTAC program was an initial economic learning experiment in which the new institutional form of the ERA was tested, and which proved to have some survival value for the firms which became participants. It was varied and refined over time to become an 'economic routine' (by analogy with organisational routines) that Japan was able to invoke each time there was a step change in technological competence to be accomplished by Japanese firms, culminating in the VLSI program. Likewise in Korea early attempts to promote major changes in technological capabilities by the *chaebol* through simple imitation of Japanese organisational forms – as in the 1988–89 ULSI program – were not very successful, but later programs launched by the KSIA have embodied the 'learning' from these earlier experiences and have demonstrably been more effective.

In Taiwan there are numerous cases of economic learning, particularly the changes in organisational form of the R&D alliances, which became more effective in diffusing technological capabilities to participant firms as experience in their operation was accumulated. In the sense that we use the term, some countries 'learn' economically better than others.

The key to successful economic learning is not just the 'elements' of the process, which are described very well in the comparative institutional analysis of 'national systems of innovation' (Nelson 1993). Our concept of NSEL seeks to go further in bringing out the coherence of these elements into an operational system, focusing in particular on how it mimics 'learning' through its dynamic capacity to make mistakes and profit from them. A national system of economic learning stamps an evolutionary economic direction with public purpose and institutional means for dynamic improvement. It calls for the highest levels of institutional capacity in tying together the separate elements into a coherent and dynamic system.

Conclusion

We have sought to show how catch-up development strategies using various institutional forms of technology leverage have worked for the East Asian countries that have successfully created semiconductor industries. We argue that success in these industries was not because of a reliance on external, contingent factors (like low costs, government handouts, or just plain 'luck'), all of which are transient or non-repeatable, but on the concentrated and determined efforts of the countries themselves. These efforts were focused on building institutional structures which could accelerate processes of organisational learning (acquisition of enhanced technical capabilities) within firms. That organisational learning does indeed take place and can be demonstrated, for example, in yields across successive generations of DRAMs as companies shift from pilot production to mass production, lends strong support to our argument.

We have demonstrated a coherence to these leverage strategies by seeking the core technology acquisition and diffusion activities in each case of semiconductor industry creation, and their replication and repetition over time, in a process of expanding technological capability enhancement. This coherence and the evidence of its repeated application in East Asian countries substantiate the use of leverage as a deliberate and effective strategy. We have sought to account for this coherence conceptually in terms of the notions of 'absorptive capacity' and 'combinative capabilities' as the 'core competences' created and sustained by the countries concerned.

We have critically examined the effectiveness of the strategies involved by looking at the characteristics of the semiconductor industries created and their sustainability. Based on this analysis, we have concluded that the industries created are surprisingly robust, and not subject to the various forms of intrinsic and strategic weakness (such as path-dependence) hypothesised in the literature.

We then sought to buttress these findings by looking at the various institutional forms that have been 'invented' so far by countries in East Asia for such processes, which we have dubbed 'Model A' (large firms as carriers of leverage activities), 'Model B' (small and medium-sized firms acting with public-sector research institutes), and 'Model C' (leverage from multinationals), and inquiring into the replicability of the strategies based on these different forms. We sought to show that the strategies are indeed replicable. China provides compelling evidence of all three 'models' being used simultaneously in its efforts to acquire semiconductor capabilities.

The coherence of the leverage strategies involved in creating semiconductor industries rests on an interlocking series of institutional capacities involving public agencies, networks of firms and industry associations. It is these institutional capacities that provide the core competence to initiate and drive through the technological upgrading experiences, which are always wrenching in their effects and destroy firms as well as create new ones. It is the capable steering of such upgrading processes, in providing adequate incentives for undertaking the new while buttressing firms against the worst effects of change, that provide the strategic core of the East Asians' success in creating such demanding new industries as semiconductors.

We then subjected our argument to the test by considering counter-examples and cases of failure to leverage. Hong Kong was a critical counter-example, since it had shared with the other East Asian countries a grounding in electronics and IT, but had not gone on to conquer such knowledge-intensive industries as semiconductors. The absence of institutional capacities for strategic high-technology coordination of the economy was the critical absence in Hong Kong. This argument is reinforced by the fact that efforts were clearly underway in the late 1990s to create such capacities in Hong Kong with a view to building knowledge-intensive industries by leverage in the twenty-first century.

Based on this analysis, we posited that the key institutional innovation is a 'national system of economic learning' that can implement successive waves of 'developmental resource leverage' to create and upgrade knowledge-intensive industries in East Asia. We sought to demonstrate that the capabilities built through creation of the semiconductor industries have acted as a platform for subsequent developments of new industries such as flat panel displays, which take the East Asian countries to positions of world technological leadership.

We have also demonstrated that there is nothing intrinsically East

Asian in the national systems of economic learning created. Our final point is that the institutional elements of economic learning are not confined to East Asia countries, but are, in principle, applicable to any country seeking to catch up in any area of advanced, knowledge-intensive technology. We have shown this by analysing the institutional forms being used by advanced countries, such as the US, in its efforts to catch up in sectors where it has fallen behind East Asia, most notably in flat panel displays.

This conclusion has far-reaching implications. It means that there is an institutional system that various countries can use for technological catch-up, whether they be developing or developed, located in the East or West. This institutional system appears to have advantages over conventional ones based solely on market-mediated diffusion or, more realistically, over systems based on processes of intra-firm innovation. Standing in the way of the application of these processes is the political will to do so and the capacity to enact the institutional structures and processes needed. As knowledge-intensive industries will become ever more central in all advanced economies in the twenty-first century, this process of catch-up will, perforce, become the key to economic prosperity and wealth generation.

The distinction of being the first to create national systems for technological catch-up through leverage in the postwar period belongs to the East Asians.[8] In this context, the semiconductor industry is their greatest achievement. Developmental resource leverage, as we have defined and analysed it, is an East Asian innovation. But it is an innovation available to all who can apprehend its institutional demands. Institutions of management of diffusion through leverage are now spreading throughout the world, to the benefit of the world as a whole.

Innovation in one company, as mastered in the West, enriches one individual or, at best, the members of the company. Management of leverage and diffusion, as mastered in the East, enriches a wider spectrum of industry. This perhaps captures, more than any other economic or social characteristic, the difference between the innovation goals of East and West. As the world enters the twenty-first century, both will play a vital role in enhancing the wealth of nations.

Notes

1   See Chandler (1977; 1990) for his major expositions of the role of large firms in creating the configurations of industrial capitalism and Chandler (1992) for a summary statement of his position. For an overview of the

Chandlerian opus, reviewing the role of big business in industrial wealth, see Chandler, Amatori and Hikino (1997).

2   On Schumpeterian competition, see the exposition in Nelson and Winter (1982).

3   See the World Bank report (1993).

4   For example, both the Industrial Bank of Malaysia and the Khazana Nasional Berhad were funding the wafer fabrication initiative, Wafer Technology (Malaysia), to be established on the Kulim High-technology Park in a joint venture with the US firm, VLSI Technology, announced in 1997.

5   The Korean EPB was restructured and incorporated within the Ministry for Finance and Economics in the mid-1990s, in what is widely seen as a downgrading of its lead agency role.

6   Some qualifications are in order here. Stanford University and MIT are public institutions, but privately endowed. It is not their mode of financing that makes them great public institutions. In Silicon Valley, it is not just Stanford University but also leading Universities of the California State system, such as Berkeley, which have played a role in the seeding of new technologies and firms. On the role of MIT in generating new technologies and new technology-based firms, see the Bank Boston report on *MIT: The Impact of Innovation* (1997). This study examined 4000-plus high-tech companies founded by MIT graduates, employing 1.1 million people and achieving world sales of $232 billion. This is equivalent to the GDP of a nation with the 24th largest economy in the world – all from just one institute of technology.

7   See Weiss (1998) for an exposition of this concept, where the focus is on the continuing role of state agencies in an era of 'globalisation'.

8   Important institutions of technology leverage and diffusion were built in the US and Europe in the nineteenth century to accelerate their industrialisation and catch-up with the UK. These tend to be forgotten in the current discussions of Silicon Valley and EU funding programs. The East Asian institutions have been able to build on this solid institutional foundation. On the contribution of the 'dynamic firm' to the generation of national wealth, encompassing the role of technology, strategy, organisation and regions, see Chandler, Hagström and Sölvell (1998).

Appendix I

Exchange rates: 1975–97[*]

East Asian equivalents to US$

Year	Japan Yen	Korea won	Taiwan NT$	Singapore S$	Malaysia RM
1975	297	484	38.0	2.49	2.59
1976	297	484	38.0	2.46	2.54
1977	269	484	38.0	2.34	2.37
1978	210	484	36.0	2.16	2.21
1979	219	484	36.0	2.16	2.19
1980	227	660	36.0	2.09	2.22
1981	221	700	37.8	2.05	2.24
1982	249	749	39.9	2.11	2.32
1983	238	796	40.3	2.13	2.34
1984	238	827	39.5	2.18	2.43
1985	239	890	39.9	2.11	2.43
1986	169	861	35.5	2.18	2.60
1987	145	792	28.6	2.00	2.49
1988	128	684	28.2	1.95	2.72
1989	138	680	26.2	1.89	2.70
1990	145	716	27.1	1.74	2.70
1991	135	761	25.7	1.63	2.72
1992	127	788	25.4	1.64	2.61
1993	111	808	26.7	1.61	2.70
1994	102	789	26.2	1.46	2.56
1995	94	775	27.3	1.41	2.54
1996	109	844	27.5	1.40	2.52
1997	121	1695	28.7	1.68	3.89

[*] Data for 1998–99 are not included because of wide fluctuations caused by the Asian financial crisis.

Sources: IMF: International Financial Statistics Yearbook, Taiwan Statistical Data Book, Council for Economic Planning and Development.

Appendix II

Chronology

Korea   *Taiwan*

1962		
1962–64		
1963		
1964		

1965	Korean government selects electronics industry as one of 13 priority sectors for exports Komi (US) establishes first Korean transistor assembly operation Normalisation Treaty with Japan: opens up Japanese investment in electronics	
1966	Fairchild, Signetics establish semiconductor assembly operations in Korea Korean Institute for Science and Technology (KIST) established	Philips establishes electronics plant in Taiwan, in new Export Processing Zone National Science Council formed
1967		
1968	Five-year plan for the promotion of the electronics industry (1967–72)	National Long-Term Science Development Plan issued Texas Instruments establishes electronics operation in Taiwan

| 1969 | Promulgation of Law for Electronics Industry Promotion (1969–76)
Toshiba establishes silicon transistor plant in Korea
Goldstar Electronics formed to manufacture transistors (JV with National Semiconductor)
Samsung enters electronics industry, through joint ventures with Sanyo and NEC | Philips starts IC packaging
General Instruments starts diode (discrete) manufacturing
First local electronics company starts transistor and IC packaging |
| 1970 | Electronics Industry Development Plan (1970–78)
Kumi Electronics Industrial Complex established
Masan Free Export Zone (MAFEZ) established | |

Singapore   *Malaysia*

Singapore	Malaysia	
EDB founded (August) with capital budget of S$100 million		1962
EDB builds first industrial park in Singapore out of marshlands of Jurong		1962–64
		1963
Malaysian federation formed from Malaya, Singapore and Kalimantan states		1964
Anti-Chinese agitation in Malaysia; Singapore leaves federation		
Singapore reconstituted as sovereign state; joins UN (September); Singapore swings behind export led strategy; EDB charged with inviting MNCs to Singapore to establish labour-intensive industries		1965
		1966
		1967
Britain announces military withdrawal from Singapore; EDB divested of some tasks: Jurong Town Council formed to develop and administer industrial parks; Development Bank of Singapore formed to channel capital to export-oriented industrial projects		1968
First investments by US multinationals in electronics assembly operations in Singapore: Texas Instruments leads the way	Malaysian People's Movement Party wins State government in Penang; Dr Lim Chong Eu installed as First Minister	1969
	Penang Development Corporation (PDC) incorporated	
	PDC launches Penang Electronics as wholly owned subsidiary, to begin manufacturing in Penang	1970

Korea   Taiwan

1970   Anam starts semiconductor contract
        assembly operation (first indigenous
        company)
1971   KIST develops/transfers semiconductor
        fabrication technology
1972   Samsung takes over Sanyo's share in JV
        and establishes Samsung Electronics

1973   Launch of Korea's 'Heavy and Chemical   ITRI established with charter to bring
        Industrialisation' drive   technology to Taiwan
        Establishment of National Investment   Liberalisation of import controls on
        Fund (NIF)   2367 items (with 465 items
                                       remaining controlled)
1974   First Korean IC wafer fabrication plant   Semiconductor industry strategy
        established – Korea Semiconductor   formulated (TAC)
        Samsung takes over NEC's share in JV   Electronics Industry Research Centre
        and establishes Samsung   established (becomes ERSO in
        Semiconductor   1979) as part of ITRI
1975   KIST identifies semiconductors as top
        research priority
        Samsung buys into KESEC, and forms
        Samsung Electronics Co.
        (SEC) – first *chaebol* to become involved
        in IC wafer fabrication at LSI level
        KEC (Korean Electronics Corp) formed
        through JV with Toshiba, for
        manufacture of discrete
        semiconductors (transistors)
        KIET established on Kumi complex, as
1976   primary R&D centre for   Electronic Industry Development
        semiconductors   Program (EIDP) Phase I launched
        MCI announces six-year plan to   (1976–79)
        indigenise electronic components   ERSO signs technology transfer
        (including silicon wafer fabrication   contract with RCA
        and memory ICs)
        Electronic Industries Association of
        Korea (EIAK) formed by
        amalgamation of industry
        cooperative and export associations

Singapore   *Malaysia*

		1970

Malaysia launches the 'New Economic   1971
Policy' (NEP) backed by Outline
Perspective Plan   1972
PDC launches Malaysia's first Free
Trade Zone at Bayan Lepas;
multinationals such National
Semiconductor, AMD and Intel
locate there
Carter Semiconductor founded as
contract assembly firm in Ipoh
Motorola and other MNCs locate in
Klang Valley (Petaling Jaya)

Singapore achieves full employment   1973

                                                               1974

EDB publishes list of priority industries   1975
to promote, including electronics
and semiconductors but not
including heavy industries like
chemicals or shipbuilding

EDB enters first joint venture in   1976
electronics field: takes a 33.3 per
cent share in International Display
Systems Pte Ltd (total capital of
S$0.5 million) formed to produce
liquid crystal displays for electronic
watches

Korea   *Taiwan*

1976	Daewoo enters electronics business, with formation of Daewoo Electronics, and plans $20 million plant in Kumi (built 1978)	
1977	Korea Telecommunications Corp formed to manufacture electronic switchboards (technology transfer from ITT)	IC demonstration plant established at ITRI; first CMOS ICs manufactured
	Korea Raw Silk establishes Hansaeng Semiconductor – takes over Fairchild assembly plant	
	Electronics Industry Sectoral Plan prepared (Arthur D. Little)	
1978	KIET establishes VLSI pilot plant, through technology transfer from VLSI Technology (US)	Formulation of Science & Technology Development Plan
	Korea Explosives (Hankuk) group seeks to enter semiconductor industry (technology transfer from National Semiconductor)	
	Ssangyong attempts to enter semiconductor industry (joint venture with Philips-Signetics)	
1979	Hansaeng Semiconductor wound up	First domestic-designed commercial IC produced at ERSO
	Goldstar Semiconductor established with acquisition of Taihan Semiconductor (plus other faltering semiconductor projects initiated by Kukje and Seoul Trading)	Electronics Industry Development Program Phase II launched (1979–83)
	Samsung Semiconductor merged with Samsung Electronics	Information Industry Institute (III) established
	Korea Electronics (formerly Korea Toshiba) expands from contract assembly to silicon transistor fabrication (technology licensed from Toshiba)	
	Three Korean firms survive in semiconductor fabrication industry – Samsung, Goldstar and Korea Electronics (KEC); many foreign firms engaged in fabrication and assembly	
1980	Economic stabilisation measures introduced	Hsinchu Science-based Industrial Park established
	Samsung takes 49 per cent stake in Korea Telecommunications Corp, and forms Samsung Semiconductor and Telecommunications Co. (SSTC)	Ten-year plan for development of the electronics industry (1980–89)
		UMC launched

Singapore   *Malaysia*

	1976
	1977
Intel establishes first semiconductor test plant in Penang	1978
Ministry of Trade and Industry formed; economic restructuring of labour-intensive industries begins in earnest	1979
Second Economic Plan, developed by Ministry of Trade and Industry; initiates push for high quality and productivity	1980

Korea   *Taiwan*

1980	KIET develops 4-bit microprocessor IC	
(cont.)	Goldstar Semiconductor produces first ICs from new Kumi plant, with technology transfer from Western Electric (now Lucent)	
1981	Promulgation of Basic Long Term Plan for the Semiconductor Industry (1982–86)	Promulgation of Long-Term Science & Technology Promotion Plan
	KIST develops 4-inch wafer fabrication CMOS technology	
	Long-term plan for promotion of electronics industry: 1982–91 (MTI)	
1982		UMC establishes Fab on Hsinchu and starts manufacturing
		Syntek IC design house established on Hsinchu
		Strategic Industries initiative (145 strategic products), including ICs and other semiconductors, targeted for preferential loans and tax breaks
		ITRI develops range of ICs for commercial application
1983	Increased availability of investment capital for semiconductor, computer and other advanced industries; Samsung, Goldstar announce major investments in VLSI fabrication; set up 'listening posts' in Silicon Valley, CA	Electronics Industry Development Program Phase III launched: VLSI capability
		ITRI and NSC cooperate to establish IC CAD design facilities in universities
	Hyundai enters electronics and semiconductor industry; likewise sets up US subsidiary, Modern Electrosystems, in Sunnyvale, CA	Electrical and electronic products become top export items
	Samsung produces 64K DRAM, under licence from Micron (US)	
	Daewoo enters semiconductor industry	
1984	Electronics Industry Promotion Fund (2 billion *won*, interest rate 1.6 per cent)	
	Imports of 185 designated electronic components restricted (e.g. ban on imports of microcomputers until 1988)	
	Goldstar Semiconductor sets up US subsidiary in Silicon Valley	
	Goldstar enters joint venture with AT&T; takes over ETRI R&D lab	
	Anam creates own R&D lab	

Singapore   *Malaysia*

		1980 (cont.)
EDB publishes a revised list of priority industries, emphasising high R&D	New federal government launch of capital-intensive industrialisation strategy	1981
		1982
		1983
SGS-Thomson invests in wafer fabrication plant in Singapore		1984

Korea   *Taiwan*

	Korea	Taiwan
1985	Samsung ships first VLSI product (64K DRAM); develops 256K DRAM	Dr Morris Chang appointed Chairman of ITRI ERSO establishes Common Design Centre to promote IC design services VLSI project: ERSO and Vitelic develop 64K then 256K DRAM
1986	Omnibus Law for Industrial Development enacted (repealing previous sector-specific laws) US–Japanese Semiconductor Trade Agreement TI sues Samsung and 8 Japanese firms for breach of IC patent Intel sues Hyundai for breach of IC patent Samsung produces 1M DRAM Daewoo Semiconductor acquires US-based Zymos Corp KIET and KETRI merged to form ETRI (coordinates joint development project for 4M DRAM)	Cadence CAD and other design houses established
1987	ETRI consortium produces 4M DRAM prototype Samsung, HEI produce 1M DRAM	TSMC spun off from ERSO: first VLSI fabrication (joint venture with Philips)
1988	Samsung, HEI mass produce 1M DRAM Samsung merges semiconductor operations with electronics to form Samsung Electronics Corp (SEC) Korea Semiconductor Equipment Association (KSEA) established Institute of Semiconductor Research formed by consortium at Seoul National University	Electronics Industry Development Program Phase IV (Submicron project) TSMC foundry begins mass production
1989	Goldstar Electron formed, taking over joint venture with AT&T, and enters technology transfer arrangement with Hitachi Five-Year plan to establish local semiconductor materials and equipment industry in Korea	Taiwan Mask Company spun off from ERSO, and establishes itself on Hsinchu Weltrend sets up in HSIP; specialising in digital/analog ICs MXIC sets up in HSIP TI and Acer form joint venture to produce DRAMs Taiwan now has ten IC manufacturers

Singapore   Malaysia

Singapore	Malaysia	
Singapore experiences first major recession; government devalues Singapore dollar and stimulates domestic consumption with Central Provident Fund	Hong Leong group makes move into IC contract assembly, with purchase of Carter Semiconductor; relaunched as high technology operation Carsem	1985
Third Economic Plan; initiates push for wage flexibility and 'business-friendly' environment; ushers in a decade of growth	Industrial Master Plan launched MIMOS established	1986
		1987
		1988
Chartered Semiconductor Manufacturing established as joint venture between Singapore Technologies and the US firm Sierra Semiconductor: this is first major involvement of Singapore capital in semiconductor wafer fabrication	The Penang Skills Development Centre established (industry-led training)	1989

Korea   *Taiwan*

	Korea	Taiwan
1990	GSE ships 1M DRAM licensed from Hitachi Samsung, Hyundai and Goldstar all ramp up to production of 4M DRAM	Innova, a second mask company, established Etron sets up in HSIP: memory IC design as part of submicron ERSO project IDB Ten-year technology development plan: Semiconductors listed as one of eight key technologies in Taiwan's future ERSO restructured, leading to separate establishment of Computer & Communication Research Laboratories (CCL)
1991	Korean Semiconductor Industry Association (KSIA) formed Samsung, HEI and GSE mass produce 4M DRAM	Acer-TI joint venture begins construction of DRAM fabrication facility
1992	Chonan Industrial Complex designated for development of Korea's equipment supply industry ETRI consortium develops 64M DRAM prototype	
1993	Samsung becomes world's number one DRAM supplier HEI enters joint development agreement with Fujitsu Samsung enters joint development agreements with NEC, Toshiba	Mosel-Vitelic begins DRAM manufacture, with technology imported from Oki

Singapore   Malaysia

	Globetronics founded as high technology contract IC packaging operation	1990
Strategic Economic Plan (Fourth) – targeted towards making Singapore an advanced industrial country by the year 2020; heavy emphasis on developing strategic industrial clusters NSTB formed and laboratories established, including Institute of Microelectronics TECH Semiconductor formed as $300 million joint venture between Texas Instruments, EDB, Canon, and Hewlett Packard EDB makes first investment of S$100 million out of new Cluster Development Fund to assist Chartered to build its second wafer fabrication plant Toshiba and CSM announce technology collaboration agreement, under which Toshiba transfers its 0.5 micron CMOS technology to CSM's silicon foundry	Vision 2020 launched by Malaysian PM Dr Mahathir National Development Plan (NDP) backed by Second Outline Perspective Plan Unisem founded as high technology contract IC assembly house	1991
	Kulim High-technology Park created – looks for wafer-fab operations	1992
		1993

Korea   # *Taiwan*

1994	MoTIE announces 3-year program to promote local production of equipment and materials supply MCI announces vision and development roadmap for high technology industry Samsung develops 256M DRAM prototype	Vanguard International Semiconductor Corp. launched
1995	Samsung and Hyundai given approval by Korean government to build $1 billion-plus wafer fabrication facilities in the US Goldstar interests split into LG Semicon and LG Electronics Samsung announces 5-year $65 billion DRAM supply contract with six US computer firms, including IBM Hyundai purchases NCR, forming Symbios Logic	Nan Ya Technology establishes DRAM operation (technology from Oki) Powerchip established to produce DRAMs (technology from Mitsubishi) VISC begins manufacturing DRAMs Winbond enters agreement with Toshiba over DRAM-manufacturing technology TSMC commences construction of Fabs IV and V TSMC announces plan to establish IC foundry in the US in partnership with US firm Altera and other US firms UMC forms multiple IC foundry consortia, starting with USC (United Semiconductor Corp)
1996		

Singapore   Malaysia

	ASE established in Penang; subsidiary of Taiwan IC contract assembly firm	1994
CSM opens Fab 2 in new Woodlands wafer fab park EDB announces second wafer fab park, at Tampines IME announces formation of Electronic Packaging Research Consortium	MIMOS signs contracts to build research wafer fab Interconnect announces new wafer fab to be built in Sarawak Intel announces new PC motherboard plant to be built on Kulim HT Park	1995
Singapore declared a 'developed nation' by the OECD		1996

Glossary

Bipolar devices   The earliest forms of transistors, which worked like a switch through p and n junctions inserted in silicon wafers by the introduction of contaminants.

Customisation   The technology of semiconductor manufacturing lends itself to varying degrees of customisation, from totally standardised devices such as DRAMs to totally customer-specific ICs (CSICs). The variation in customisation is achieved technically by customising one or more layers of the masks (since complex circuits can have up to twelve mask layers, this gives twelve degrees of customisation); through use of 'cells' in circuits (i.e. blocks of standard architecture) – a 'standard cell IC' is customised on all mask levels using a cell 'library' of preformatted circuit structures, termed 'intellectual property' (IP); through use of metal interconnect between layers of a circuit, between blocks of transistors organised in rows and columns (gates), hence a 'gate array'; through programming by user – a programmable logic device (PLD) – e.g. FPGAs (field programmable gate arrays) and EPACs (electrically programmable analog circuit).

Fabrication stages   The production of ICs entails a number of highly synchronised and delicate steps in which impurities and coatings are introduced into or on silicon wafers to get them to behave as circuits according to a particular design. The design is transferred to a transparent silicon sliver called a 'mask', and its image is deposited (etched) on the silicon wafer through the action of light. This is termed photolithography (from the Greek 'writing on stone'). The analogy with printing, where an inked image on paper is achieved through first producing a plate, is quite close. The major steps involved are as follows.

Silicon wafer preparation: Ingots of pure silicon are produced and sliced to produce 'wafers'. These are polished, and may have materials deposited on the surface to assist with later processing (e.g. epitaxial wafers).

Circuit design: The circuit is designed and tested (through simulation) and printed out on large sheets. These are then decomposed into layers (up to twelve or more), each of which is transferred to a mask. The IC is constructed sequentially as each circuit layer is laid down in silicon.

Mask preparation: Masks are prepared as reticles through light processes or, as the density of ICs increases, through X-ray diffraction or even electron beam diffraction (eBeam). Wafers are cleaned and then coated with various forms of photoresist to generate an image through 'etching'. Circuit images transmitted through the mask are then printed through 'contact alignment', with circuit images repeated sequentially in a process of 'stepping' (where the aim is to pack as many ICs onto a wafer as possible).

Silicon processing/layering: Junction formation in the silicon is achieved through the diffusion of dopants and ion implantation. There is also epitaxial metal deposition where metal layers are deposited through sputtering or evaporation and multiple interconnects formed within the silicon. These are chemical and heat-related treatments.

IC assembly: The individual circuits ('dies') now printed on the wafer are first separated ('sawn'), and attached ('bonded') individually to a substrate or leadframe. Wire bonding is then effected to connect the circuit to the leadframe, ending in tapered pins that allow the finished chip to be plugged into a circuit. The assembly is then packaged within a plastic or epoxy mould to form a finished chip. More recent techniques include ball grid array, which simplifies the connections, or 'wafer bumping', which channels all the leads into a single 'bump' of gold or conductive material.

Testing: Chips are subjected to exhaustive testing before despatch to ensure that they behave as predicted by the circuit design. Testing procedures are frequently linked to the design itself (which is why 'fabless' chip producers test their own products and secure a competitive advantage by doing so).

Flexibility of fabrication Most semiconductor fabrication facilities ('fabs') are designed and built to produce a small range of similar products, such as DRAMs. The production steps are conducted within a clean-room environment. A more flexible production system has been developed that uses 'clean-room mini-environments'. This has a dual advantage: the expensive clean environment is maintained within small capsules ('pods') that can be manipulated within normal operating conditions, and different operations can be conducted alongside each other in modular fashion. This technology uses standardised interfaces between the capsules, and so is termed standard mechanical inter-face (SMIF) technology. The Taiwanese silicon foundry, TSMC, was the first semiconductor facility to install fully modularised and encapsulated (SMIF) fabrication technology, provided by the US firm Asyst Technologies. For a description of the experience of TSMC with this fabrication technology, see Shu and Tu (1992).

Hybrid ICs These mix semiconductor technology with other traditional devices within a single package.

MOS devices These operate through an arrangement of metal oxide on silicon (MOS). They can be NMOS or PMOS depending on whether they use p or n junctions; or they can use both, as in complementary MOS (CMOS) devices. CMOS has become the standard IC technology because of its low power consumption.

Optoelectronic devices These are light-sensitive semiconductor devices that either absorb light as signal (e.g. photosensors) or emit light (e.g. liquid crystal displays [LCDs], light-emitting diodes [LEDs]).

Semiconductor A material that is a partial conductor of electric current (such as silicon, gallium arsenide). By modifying its conductivity through the introduction of extraneous materials, semiconductor materials can mimic the elements of electric circuits such as switches.

Semiconductor devices Products that contain semiconductor materials and which react dynamically to an input signal, either by adding energy to it or modifying it. They are 'active' components as opposed to 'passive' elements such as capacitors and resistors. Semiconductor devices are generally classified as discrete or integrated circuits (logic devices; analog devices; memory devices; microprocessors).

> *Discretes* are single components such as transistors, diodes or thyristors. They are the least sophisticated of semiconductor products.
>
> *Integrated circuits* (ICs) are semiconductor devices in which a large number of active and passive discrete components

are integrated into single packages. If they are all on a single piece of silicon ('chip') this is called a monolithic integrated circuit. Integrated circuits are classified according to their functions as logic devices, analog devices, memory chips or processors.

Logic devices are ICs that accept binary ('digital') signals and give binary output, processed according to logic functions such as 'and', 'nor' or 'nand'. The functions can be defined by hard-wiring ('in the silicon') by mask programming or by field programming.

Analog devices are ICs that accept analog (continuously varying) inputs and give analog or binary output. They are essential in capturing real-world data (which is always analog in nature) before it can be processed in digital form by computers.

Memory devices are ICs that store and retrieve logic bits. They can be ROMs (Read Only Memories) that are pre-loaded with data or instructions; RAMs (Random Access Memories), which can be filled with data and emptied over and over again. RAMs can be dynamic (DRAMs) or static (SRAMs). EPROMs (Electrically Programmable ROMs) are ROMs whose contents can be overwritten. DRAMs can be standardised ('commodity') DRAMs or have extra sophistication, such as synchronous DRAMs (SDRAMs), which operate at the same speed as the processor. When installed in PCs, synchronous DRAMs enable the computer's memory operations to keep pace with the processing operations, rather than acting as a drag on them. Embedded DRAMs (eDRAMs) are combined memory and logic circuits on the same chip. This makes for simplification of design of PCs and other IT products using ICs.

Microprocessor devices are ICs that act as computers, applying sequences of processes to bits of data according to the programs loaded into them. Microprocessors (MPUs) process data in terms of bit sequences; the earliest were 4-bit devices, going up to 8-bit, then 16-bit, 32-bit and 64-bit, which are the most sophisticated standard devices today. Embedded microcontrollers are microprocessor ICs contained within existing electronic products, endowing them with programmability.

System on a Chip/System Integration   This is the most sophisticated semiconductor product, in which logic, memory and processor functions are all contained in a single chip. System integration is being pursued through the standardisation of interfaces between system components, such as through the virtual socket interface (VSI) worldwide consortium.

Yields/quality   The key operating parameters in wafer fabrication are yields (of 'good' dies per wafer) as well as the packing of ICs onto wafers. Yields are improved at the pilot stage of production, and can also be improved at mass production stage through 'tweaking' the production steps to eliminate sources of circuit operation error. Packing density is improved by 'shrinking' dies through improved circuit design in successive versions of a given product generation, e.g. 64M DRAM. Enhanced yields and packing densities are the sources of competitive advantage in IC fabrication.

Bibliography

Abe, E. And Fitzgerald, R. (eds) 1995. *The Origins of Japanese Industrial Power: Strategy, Institutions and the Development of Organisational Capability.* London: Frank Cass.

Abegglen, J. C. 1994. *Sea Change: Pacific Asia as the New World Industrial Centre.* New York: The Free Press.

Abernathy, W. J. and Clark, K. B. 1985. 'Innovation: Mapping the winds of creative destruction', *Research Policy*, 14: 3–22.

—— and Utterback, J. M. 1979. 'Patterns of industrial innovation', *Technology Review*, 80 (7): 41–7.

Agmon, T. and von Glinow, M. (eds) 1991. *Technology Transfer in International Business.* Oxford: Oxford University Press.

Akamatsu, K. 1962. 'A historical pattern of economic growth in developing countries', *The Developing Economies*, no. 1 (Mar–Aug): 3–25.

Ali, Anuwar 1992. *Malaysia's Industrialisation: The Quest for Technology.* Singapore: Oxford University Press.

Amsden, Alice 1989. *Asia's Next Giant: South Korea and Late Industrialisation,* New York: Oxford University Press.

—— 1997. 'Manufacturing capabilities: Hong Kong's new engine of growth?' In Suzanne Berger and Richard Lester (eds), *Made by Hong Kong.* Hong Kong: Oxford University Press.

—— and Chang, Chung-Chau 1992. *Taiwan's Enterprises in Global Perspective* (Taiwan in the Modern World). New York: M. E. Sharpe.

—— Liu, D. *et al.* 1996. 'China's macro economy, environment, and alternative transition model', *World Development*, 24 (2): 273–86.

Anchordoguy, Marie 1989. *Computers Inc: Japan's Challenge to IBM.* Cambridge, MA: Council on East Asian Studies, Harvard University (Harvard University Press).

Angel, D. 1994. *Restructuring for Innovation: The Remaking of the U.S. Semiconductor Industry.* New York: The Guilford Press.

Aoki, Masahiko, Kim, Hyung-Ki and Okuno-Fujiwara, Masahiro (eds) 1997. *The Role of Government in East Asian Economic Development: Comparative Institutional Analysis.* Oxford: Clarendon Press.

Appelbaum, R. and Henderson, J. (eds) 1992. *States and Development in the Asian Pacific Rim.* London: Sage Publications.

Argyris, Chris and Schon, Donald 1995 (1978). *Organisational Learning II: A theory of action perspective* (Second Edition). Reading, MA: Addison-Wesley.

Baba, Y. and Hatashima, H. 1995. 'Capability transfer in the Pacific Rim nations: the case of Japanese electrical and electronics firms', *International Journal of Technology Management*, 10 (7–8): 732–46.

Bae, Y. H. 1995. 'Technology absorption and R&D development in the Korean semiconductor industry: The case of Samsung'. PhD dissertation: Seoul National University.

Baranson, J. and Roark, R. 1985. 'Trends in North-South transfer of high technology'. In N. Rosenberg and C. Frischtak (eds) *International Technology Transfer: Concepts, Measures and Comparisons*. New York: Praeger.

Barney, Jay 1997. *Gaining and Sustaining Competitive Advantage*. Reading, MA: Addison-Wesley.

Battat, J., Frank, I. and Shen, X. 1996. 'Suppliers to multinationals: Linkage programs to strengthen local companies in developing countries', Foreign Investment Advisory Service Occasional Paper #6. Washington, DC: The World Bank.

Beane, D., Shukla, A. and Pecht, M. 1997. *The Singapore and Malaysia Electronics Industries*. (The Electronics Industry Research Series: World Technology Evaluation Center, University of Maryland) Boca Raton, FL: CRC Press.

Bell, Martin and Pavitt, Keith 1993. 'Technological accumulation and industrial growth: Contrasts between developed and developing countries', *Industrial and Corporate Change*, 2 (2): 157–210.

Berger, Suzanne and Lester, Richard (eds) 1997. *Made by Hong Kong*. Hong Kong: Oxford University Press.

Bernard, Mitchell and Ravenhill, John 1995. 'Beyond product cycles and flying geese: Regionalisation, hierarchy, and the industrialisation of East Asia', *World Politics*, 47 (2): 171–209.

Bloom, Martin 1992. *Technological Change in the Korean Electronics Industry*. Paris: Development Centre, OECD.

Bohn, Roger E. 1995. 'Noise and learning in semiconductor manufacturing', *Management Science*, 41 (1): 31–42.

Borrus, Michael 1988. 'Chip Wars: Can the US regain its advantage in microelectronics?', *California Management Review*, 30 (4): 64–79.

—— 1994. 'Left for dead: Asian production networks and the revival of US electronics'. In E. Doherty (ed) *Japanese Investment in Asia: International Production Strategies in a Rapidly Changing World*. Berkeley, CA: Berkeley Roundtable on the International Economy (BRIE).

—— Milstein, J. and Zysman, J. 1982. *US–Japanese Competition in the Semiconductor Industry*. Berkeley, CA: Institute of International Studies, University of California.

—— Tyson, L. and Zysman, J. 1987. 'Creating advantage: How government policies shape international trade in the semiconductor industry'. In P. Krugman (ed.) *Strategic Trade Policy and the New International Economics*. Cambridge, MA: MIT Press.

—— and Zysman, J. 1997. 'Globalisation with borders: The rise of Wintelism as the future of global competition', *Industry and Innovation*, 4 (2): 141–66.

Bowie, Alasdair 1991. *Crossing the Industrial Divide: State, Society and the Politics of Economic Transformation in Malaysia*. New York: Columbia University Press.

Burgelman, Robert 1995. *Strategic Management of Technology and Innovation*. Chicago: Irwin.

Byun, Byung-Moon and Ahn, Byong-Hun 1989. 'Growth of the Korean semiconductor industry and its competitive strategy in the world market', *Technovation*, 9: 635–56.

Callon, Scott 1995. *Divided Sun: MITI and the Breakdown of Japanese High-Tech Industrial Policy, 1975–1993.* Stanford, CA: Stanford University Press.

Castley, R. 1996. The role of Japan in Korea's acquisition of technology, *Asia Pacific Business Review,* 3 (1) (Autumn): 29–53.

Chan, Lai Ngoh 1994. *Motorola Globalisation: The Penang Journey.* Bayan Lepas, Penang: Motorola Malaysia.

Chandler, A. 1977. *The Visible Hand: The Managerial Revolution in American Business.* Cambridge, MA: Harvard University Press.

—— 1990. *Scale and Scope: The Dynamics of Industrial Capitalism.* Cambridge, MA: Harvard University Press.

—— Amatori, F. and Hikino, T. (eds) 1997. *Big Business and the Wealth of Nations.* Cambridge: Cambridge University Press.

—— Hagström, P. and Sölwell, Ö. (eds) 1998. *The Dynamic Firm: The Role of Technology, Strategy, Organization and Regions.* New York: Oxford University Press.

Chang, Ha-Joon 1994. *The Political Economy of Industrial Policy.* London: Macmillan.

Chang, Pao-Long, Shih, Chintay and Hsu, Chiung-Wen 1994. 'The formation process of Taiwan's IC industry – method of technology transfer', *Technovation,* 14 (3): 161–71.

Chaponniere, J. R. 1992. 'The newly industrialising economies of Asia: International investment and transfer of technology', *STI Review,* No. 9. Paris: OECD.

Chen, Chao-yih and Shih, Chintay (eds) 1995. *Technology Transfer: Proceedings of the APEC Technology Transfer Seminar,* December 1994. Taipei: Ministry of Economic Affairs.

Chiang, Jong-Tsong 1990. 'Management of national technology programs in a newly industrialising country – Taiwan', *Technovation,* 10 (8): 531–54.

—— 1991. 'From "mission-oriented" to "diffusion-oriented" paradigm: the new trend of US industrial technology policy', *Technovation,* 11 (6): 339–54.

Cho, Dong-Sung 1987. *The General Trading Company: Concept and Strategy.* Lexington, MA: Lexington Books.

—— 1994a. 'Determinants of bargaining power in OEM negotiations', *Industrial Marketing Management,* 23: 343–55.

—— 1994b. 'A dynamic approach to international competitiveness: The case of Korea', *Journal of Far Eastern Business,* 1 (1): 17–36.

—— 1995. *The myth of the Korean semiconductor industry: The success of Korean firms in meeting the challenge of US and Japanese competitors.* Seoul: Bi Ryong So Publishing [In Korean].

—— 1998. 'Korea's economic crisis: Causes, significance and agenda for recovery', *Korea Focus,* Jan–Feb: 15–26.

—— Kim, D. J. and Rhee, D. K. 1998. 'Latecomer strategies: Evidence from the semiconductor industry in Japan and Korea', *Organisation Science,* 9 (4): 489–505.

Cho, Soon 1994. *The Dynamics of Korean Economic Development.* Washington, DC: Institute for International Economics.

Choi, Hyung-Sup 1975. 'Adapting technology – the Korean case' in E. and V. Rabinowitch (eds), *Views of Science, Technology and Development.* New York: Pergamon Press.

Choi, Young-Rak 1996, *Dynamic Techno-Management Capability: The Case of Samsung Semiconductor Sector in Korea.* Aldershot: Avebury.

Chowdhury, A. and Islam, I. 1993. *The Newly Industrialising Economies of East Asia.* London: Routledge.

Chu, Wan-wen 1994. 'Import substitution and export-led growth: A study of Taiwan's petrochemical industry', *World Development*, 22 (5): 781–94.

Chu, Yun-Han 1995. 'The East Asian NICs: A state-led path to the developed world.' In B. Stallings (ed.) *Global Change, Regional Response: The New International Context of Development*. Cambridge: Cambridge University Press.

Cohen, Wesley M. and Levinthal, Daniel A. 1990. 'Absorptive Capacity: A New Perspective on Learning and Innovation', *Administrative Science Quarterly*, 35, March: 128–52.

Cowhey, Peter F. and Aronson, Jonathan D. 1993. *Managing the World Economy: The Consequences of Corporate Alliances*. New York: Council on Foreign Relations.

Cumings, Bruce 1984. 'The origins and development of the North East Asian political economy: Industrial sector, product cycles and political consequences', *International Organisation*, 38, 3.

—— 1997. *Korea's Place in the Sun: A Modern History*. New York: W. W. Norton.

Cusumano, Michael and Elenkov, Detelin 1994. 'Linking international technology transfer with strategy and management: A literature commentary', *Research Policy*, 23: 195–215.

Dahlman, Carl J. 1993. 'Electronics development strategy: The role of government', in B. Wellenius, A. Miller and C. J. Dahlman (eds) *Developing the Electronics Industry*. Washington, DC: World Bank.

—— and Westphal, Larry 1981. 'The meaning of technological mastery in relation to transfer of technology', *Annals of the American Academy of Political and Social Sciences*, 458: 12–26.

—— and Westphal, Larry 1982. 'Technological effort in industrial development – an interpretative survey of recent research', in F. Stewart and J. James (eds) *The Economics of New Technology in Developing Countries*. London: Frances Pinter.

—— and Westphal, Larry 1983. 'The transfer of technology: Issues in the acquisition of technological capability by developing countries', *Finance and Development*, 20, 4.

—— Ross-Larson, B. and Westphal, L. 1987. 'Managing Technological Development: Lessons from the Newly Industrialising Countries', *World Development*, 15 (6): 759–75.

Das, Dilip (ed.) 1996. *Emerging Growth Pole: The Asia-Pacific Economy*. New York: Prentice Hall.

D'Aveni, Richard 1994. *Hypercompetition: Managing the Dynamics of Strategic Maneuvring*. New York: The Free Press.

Davis, Warren and Hatano, Daryl 1985. 'The American semiconductor industry and the ascendancy of East Asia', *California Management Review*, 27 (4): 128–43.

Deyo, F. (ed.) 1987. *The Political Economy of the New Asian Industrialism*. Ithaca: Cornell University Press.

DoC 1996. *Globalising Research and Development: Methods of Technology Transfer Employed by the Korean Public and Private Sector*. Washington, DC: Office of Technology Policy, US Department of Commerce.

Dodgson, Mark and Rothwell, Roy (eds) 1994. *Handbook of Industrial Innovation*. Aldershot: Edward Elgar.

Dosi, Giovanni 1982. 'Technological paradigms and technological trajectories', *Research Policy*, 11: 147–62.

—— 1984. *Technical Change and Industrial Transformation*. New York: St Martins Press.

—— Freeman, C., Nelson, R., Silverberg, G. and Soete, L. (eds) 1988. *Technical Change and Economic Theory*. London: Pinter Publishers.

—— Teece, D. and Chytry, J. 1998. *Technology, Organisation and Competitiveness: Perspectives on Industrial and Corporate Change*. New York: Oxford University Press.

Enos, J. L. 1991 *The Creation of Technological Capability in Developing Countries*. London: Pinter Publishers.

Ernst, D. 1994. 'What are the Limits to the Korean Model? The Korean Electronics Industry Under Pressure.' Berkeley, CA: Berkeley Round Table on the International Economy.

—— and O'Connor, D. 1992. *Competing in the Electronics Industry: The Experience of Newly Industrialising Economies*. Paris: Development Centre, OECD.

—— Ganiotsos, T. and Mytelka, L. (eds) 1995. *Technological Capabilities and Export Success: Lessons from East Asia*. Cambridge: Cambridge University Press.

Evans, Peter 1995. *Embedded Autonomy: States and Industrial Transformation*. Princeton, NJ: Princeton University Press.

Evenson, R. and Ranis, G. (eds) 1990. *Science and Technology: Lessons for Development Policy*. Boulder, CO: Westview Press.

Ferguson, Charles and Morris, Charles 1993. *Computer Wars: The Fall of IBM and the Future of Global Technology*. New York: Times Books.

Flamm, Kenneth 1987. *Targeting the Computer: Government Support and International Competition*. Washington, DC: The Brookings Institution.

—— 1996. *Mismanaged Trade? Strategic Policy and the Semiconductor Industry*. Washington, DC: The Brookings Institution.

Fransman, Martin 1984. 'Promoting technological capability in the capital goods sector: The case of Singapore', *Research Policy*, 13: 33–54.

—— 1990/1993. *The Market and Beyond: Information Technology in Japan*. Cambridge: Cambridge University Press.

—— 1995. *Japan's Computer and Communications Industry: The evolution of industrial giants and global competitiveness*. Oxford: Oxford University Press.

Freeman, C. 1988. 'Japan: A new system of innovation'. In G. Dosi *et al.* (eds) *Technical Change and Economic Theory*. London: Pinter Publishers.

Fruin, Mark 1992. *The Japanese Enterprise System: Competitive Strategies and Cooperative Structures*. Oxford: Clarendon Press.

Garud, R., Nayyar, P. R. and Shapira, Z. B. (eds) 1997. *Technological Innovation: Oversights and Foresights*. Cambridge: Cambridge University Press.

Gereffi, G. 1996. 'Commodity chains and regional divisions of labor in East Asia', *Journal of Asian Business*, 12 (1): 75–112.

—— and Wyman, D. (eds) 1990. *Manufacturing Miracles: Paths of Industrialisation in Latin America and East Asia*. Princeton, NJ: Princeton University Press.

Gerlach, M. 1992. *Alliance Capitalism: The Social Organisation of Japanese Business*. Berkeley: University of California Press.

Gerschenkron, Alexander 1952. 'Economic backwardness in historical perspective'. In B. Hoselitz (ed.) *The Progress of Underdeveloped Areas*. Chicago: University of Chicago Press.

—— 1962. *Economic Backwardness in Historical Perspective*. Cambridge, MA: The Belknap Press of Harvard University Press.

Gilder, George 1989. *Microcosm: The Quantum Revolution in Physics and Technology*. New York: Touchstone Books.

Goh, Keng Swee 1972 (1995). *The Economics of Modernisation*. Singapore: Federal Publications.

—— 1977 (1995). *The Practice of Economic Growth*. Singapore: Federal Publications.

—— 1995. *The Wealth of East Asian Nations* (ed. Linda Low). Singapore: Federal Publications.

—— 1996. 'The Technology Ladder in Development: The Singapore Case', *Asian-Pacific Economic Literature*, 10 (1): 1–12.

—— and Linda Low 1996. 'Beyond "miracles" and total factor productivity: The Singapore experience', *ASEAN Economic Bulletin*, 13 (1): 1–13.

Goto, F. and Irie, K. 1990. *The Theoretical Basis of Industrial Policy*. Tokyo: Research Institute of International Trade and Industry.

Grant, Robert 1991. The resource-based theory of competitive advantage: Implications for strategy formulation, *California Management Review*, Spring 1991, pp. 114–35.

Grant, Wyn (ed.) 1995. *Industrial Policy*. The International Library of Comparative Public Policy. Aldershot, UK: Edward Elgar.

Haggard, S. 1990. *Pathways from the Periphery: The Politics of Growth in the Newly Industrialising Countries*. Ithaca: Cornell University Press.

Haley, Usha C. V., Low, Linda and Toh, Mun-Heng 1996. 'Singapore Incorporated: reinterpreting Singapore's business environments through a corporate metaphor', *Management Decision*, 34 (9): 17–28.

Hamel, Gary 1990. 'Competitive collaboration: Learning, power and dependence in international strategic alliances'. PhD Thesis, Dept of Business Administration, University of Michigan.

—— and Prahalad, C. K. 1994. *Competing for the Future*. Boston: Harvard Business School Press.

Hamilton, Gary G. (ed.) 1996. *Asian Business Networks* (Studies in Organisation, 64). Leyden: De Gruyter.

Hanna, N., Boyson, S. and Gunaratne, S. 1996. 'The East Asian Miracle and Information Technology: Strategic Management and Technological Learning', World Bank Discussion Paper #326. Washington, DC: The World Bank.

Hart, J. 1992. *Rival Capitalists: International Competitiveness in the United States, Japan and Western Europe*. Ithaca: Cornell University Press.

Hatch, W. and Yamamura, K. 1996. *Asia in Japan's Embrace: Building a Regional Production Alliance*. Cambridge: Cambridge University Press.

Hayter, R. and Han, S. S. 1998. 'Reflections on China's open policy towards foreign direct investment', *Regional Studies*, 32 (1): 1–16.

Hikino, T. and Amsden, A. 1993. 'Staying behind, stumbling back, sneaking up, soaring ahead: Late industrialisation in historical perspective'. In W. J. Baumol, Nelson, Wolff (eds), *International Convergence of Productivity*. New York: Oxford University Press.

Hill, Hal 1990. 'Foreign investment and East Asian economic development', *Asian-Pacific Economic Literature*, 4 (2): 21–58.

Hobday, Michael 1989. 'Corporate strategies in the international semiconductor industry', *Research Policy*, 18.

—— 1990. 'Trends in the diffusion of ASICs: Implications for latecomer strategies in the semi-industrialised countries'. Paris: OECD Development Centre.

—— 1994a. 'Technological learning in Singapore: A test case for leapfrogging', *Journal of Development Studies*, 30 (3): 831–58.

—— 1994b. 'Export-led technology development in the four dragons: The case of electronics', *Development and Change*, vol. 25, pp. 333–61.

—— 1995a. *Innovation in East Asia: The Challenge to Japan*. Aldershot, UK: Edward Elgar.

—— 1995b. 'East Asian latecomer firms: Learning the technology of electronics', *World Development*, 23 (7): 1171–93.

Hon, Sui Sen 1997. *Strategies of Singapore's Economic Success: Speeches and Writings* (edited by Linda Low and Lim Bee Lum). Singapore: Federal Publications.

Hong, Seok-Hyun 1987. 'The experiences and prospects of the high technology industrial development of Korea: The case of semiconductors'. Conference on Industrial Policies of the Republics of China and of Korea. Taipei: Chung-Hua Institution for Economic Research.

Hong, Sung-Gul 1992 'Paths of Glory: semiconductor leapfrogging in Taiwan and South Korea', *Pacific Focus*, 7 (1): 59–88.

—— 1997. *The Political Economy of Industrial Policy in East Asia: The Semiconductor Industry in Taiwan and South Korea*. Cheltenham, UK: Edward Elgar.

Hong, Yoo-Soo 1993. 'Leveraging technology for strategic advantage in the global market: The case of the Korean electronics industry.' KIEP Working Paper 93–07. Seoul: Korea Institute for International Economic Policy.

—— 1994. 'Technology transfer: The Korean experience'. Paper presented to APEC Technology Transfer Seminar, Taipei, Dec 6–7.

Hou, Chi-Ming and San, Gee 1993. 'National systems supporting technical advance in industry: The case of Taiwan'. In R. Nelson (ed.) *National Innovation Systems: A Comparative Analysis*. New York: Oxford University Press.

Howell, Thomas, Noellert, W. A., MacLaughlin, J. H. and Wolff, A. M. 1988. *The Microelectronics Race: The impact of government policy on international competition*. Boulder: Westview Press.

—— Bartlett, Brent and Davis, Warren 1992. *Creating Advantage: Semiconductors and Government Industrial Policy in the 1990s*. Washington: Dewey Ballantine; San Jose, CA: Semiconductor Industry Association.

Hsu, Wenbin 1994. 'IC industry development in Chinese Taipei', Paper presented to APEC seminar on *Technology Transfer*, Taipei, Dec 6–8.

Huff, W. G. 1994. *The Economic Growth of Singapore: Trade and Development in the Twentieth Century*. Cambridge: Cambridge University Press.

Hughes, H. (ed.) 1988. *Achieving Industrialisation in East Asia*. Cambridge: Cambridge University Press.

Imai, Ken-Ichi 1986. 'Japan's industrial policy for high technology industry'. In H. Patrick (ed.) *Japan's High Technology Industries: Lessons and Limitations of Industrial Policy*. Seattle: University of Washington Press.

—— and Sakuma, A. 1983. 'An industrial organisation analysis of the semiconductor industry: A US–Japan comparison'. Tokyo: Institute of Business Research, Hitotsubashi University.

Inoue, R., Kohama, H. and Urata, S. (eds) 1993. *Industrial Policy in East Asia*. Tokyo: JETRO.

Islam, I. 1992. 'Political economy and economic development', *Asian Pacific Economic Literature*, 6 (2): 69–101.

Itami, H. 1995. *Japan's Semiconductor Industry: Why three kinds of reversal were possible*. Tokyo: NTT Publishing [In Japanese].

Jegathesan, J. 1994. 'Malaysia: Status of technology development and experiences with transfer of technology', Paper presented to APEC seminar on *Technology Transfer*, Taipei, Dec 6–8.

Johnson, Chalmers 1982. *MITI and the Japanese Miracle: The Growth of Industrial Policy, 1925–75*. Stanford: Stanford University Press.

—— 1987. 'Political institutions and economic performance: The government-business relationship in Japan, South Korea and Taiwan'. In F. Deyo (ed.)

The Political Economy of the New Asian Industrialism. Ithaca: Cornell University Press.

—— 1995. *Japan: Who Governs? The Rise of the Developmental State in East Asia.* New York: Norton.

Jomo, K. S. (ed.) 1993. *Industrialising Malaysia: Policy, Performance, Prospects.* London: Routledge.

—— 1994. *U-Turn? Malaysian Economic Development Policies After 1990.* Townsville, Qld: Centre for East and South East Asian Studies, James Cook University.

—— Felker, G. and Rasiah, R. (eds) 1998. *Industrial Technology Development in Malaysia: Industry and Firm Studies.* London: Routledge.

Jones, Leroy and Sakong, Il 1980. *Government, Business and Entrepreneurship in Economic Development: The Korean Case.* Cambridge, MA: Harvard University Press.

Kajiwara, H. 1993. 'Taiwan's Electronics Industry: From an import substitution and export oriented industry to a highly advanced industry'. In R. Inoue, H. Kohama and S. Urata (eds) *Industrial Policy in East Asia.* Tokyo: JETRO.

Kang, M. H. 1996. *The Korean Business Conglomerate: Chaebol Then and Now.* Korea Research Monograph #21. Berkeley: Institute of East Asian Studies, University of California, Berkeley.

Kikuchi, M. 1983. *Japanese Electronics: A worm's eye view of its evolution.* Tokyo: The Simul Press.

Kim, Eun-Mee (ed.) 1998. *The Four Asian Tigers: Economic Development and the Global Political Economy.* New York: Academic Press.

Kim, J. I. and Lau, L. 1994. 'The sources of economic growth of the East Asian newly industrialised countries', *Journal of the Japanese and International Economies*, 8: 235–71.

Kim, Linsu 1980. 'Stages of development of industrial technology in a developing country: a model', *Research Policy*, 9 (3): 254–77.

—— 1993. 'National System of Industrial Innovation: Dynamics of Capability Building in Korea'. In R. Nelson (ed.) *National Innovation Systems: A Comparative Analysis.* New York: Oxford University Press.

—— 1995. 'Absorptive capacity and industrial growth: A conceptual framework and Korea's experience'. In Bon-Ho Koo and Dwight Perkins (eds) *Social Capability and Economic Growth.* London: Macmillan.

—— 1997a. *From Imitation to Innovation: The Dynamics of Korea's Technological Learning.* Boston: Harvard Business School Press.

—— 1997b. 'The dynamics of Samsung's technological learning in semi-conductors', *California Management Review*, 39 (3): 86–100.

—— 1998. 'Crisis construction and organisational learning: Capability building in catching-up at Hyundai Motor', *Organisation Science*, 9 (4): 506–21.

—— and Dahlman, C.J. 1992. Technology policy for industrialisation: An integrative framework and Korea's experience, *Research Policy*, 25 (5): 437–52.

—— and Utterback, J. 1983. 'The evolution of organisational structure and technology in a developing country', *Management Science*, 29 (10): 1185–97.

Kim, Ong-Giger 1996. 'The political economy of the semiconductor industry in Malaysia: The new international division of labour revisited'. PhD Thesis, Australian National University, Canberra, ACT.

Kim, S. R. (ed.) 1998. 'The Korean system of innovation and the semiconductor industry: A governance perspective', *Industrial and Corporate Change*, 7 (2): 275–310.

Kim, Young-Soo 1997. 'Technological capabilities and Samsung Electronics' international production network in Asia', BRIE Working Paper #106. Berkeley: Roundtable on the International Economy.

Kimura, Y. 1988. *The Japanese Semiconductor Industry: Structure, Competitive Strategies, and Performance*. London: JAI Press.

Kirk, Donald 1994. *Korean Dynasty: Hyundai and Chung Ju Yung*. Hong Kong: Asia 2000 Ltd.

Kobayashi, K. 1991. *The Rise of NEC: How the world's greatest C&C company is managed*. Oxford: Blackwell Business.

Kodama, Fumiyo 1991. *Analyzing Japanese High Technologies: The Techno-Paradigm Shift*. London: Pinter Publishers.

—— 1995. *Emerging Patterns of Innovation: Sources of Japan's Technological Edge*. Boston, MA: Harvard Business School Press.

Kogut, Bruce and Zander, Udo 1992. 'Knowledge of the firm, combinative capabilities, and the replication of technology', *Organisation Science*, 3 (3): 383–97.

Koh, Ai-Tee 1995. 'Technological development and technology policy in East Asia: Prospects for technological leapfrogging', *Seoul Journal of Economics*, 8 (2): 129–60.

Kohama, H. and Urata, S. 1993. 'Korea: Export promotion policies for the electronics industry'. In R. Inoue, H. Kohama and S. Urata (eds) *Industrial Policy in East Asia*. Tokyo: JETRO.

—— 1993. 'Protection and promotion of Japan's electronics industry'. In R. Inoue, H. Kohama and S. Urata (eds) *Industrial Policy in East Asia*. Tokyo: JETRO.

Kosai, Y. and Takeuchi, F. 1998. 'Japan's influence on the East Asian economies', in H. S. Rowen (ed.) *Behind East Asian Growth: The Political and Social Foundations of Prosperity*. London/New York: Routledge.

Krugman, P. 1979. 'A model of innovation, technology transfer and the world distribution of income', *Journal of Political Economy* 87: 253–66.

—— 1994b. 'The myth of Asia's miracle', *Foreign Affairs*, 73 (6): 62–78.

Kuo, Cheng-Tian 1995. *Global Competitiveness and Industrial Growth in Taiwan and the Philippines*. Pittsburgh: University of Pittsburgh Press.

Lall, S. 1990. *Building Industrial Competitiveness in Developing Countries*. Paris: Development Centre of the OECD.

—— 1992. 'Technological capabilities and industrialisation', *World Development*, 20 (2): 165–86.

—— 1997. *Learning to Industrialise: The Acquisition of Technological Capability by India*. London: Macmillan.

Langlois, R. *et al.* 1988. *Microelectronics: An Industry in Transition*. Centre for Science and Technology Policy, Rensselaer Polytechnic Institute, New York. Boston: Unwin Hyman.

Leachman, Robert 1996. 'Making the transition: Korea's manufacturing accomplishments and new requirements', Paper presented to KSIA/IQE Seminar: 'Is the Korean Semiconductor in a Trap and Can It Get Out?', Seoul, Nov 1997.

Lee, Chung H. and Yamazawa, I. (eds) 1990. *The Economic Development of Japan and Korea: A Parallel with Lessons*. New York: Praeger.

Lee, Chung-Shing and Pecht, M. 1997. *The Taiwan Electronics Industry*. (The Electronics Industry Research Series: World Technology Evaluation Centre, University of Maryland) Boca Raton, FL: CRC Press.

Lester, Richard K. 1998. *The Productive Edge: How US Industries Are Pointing the Way to a New Era of Economic Growth*. New York: W. W. Norton.

Levy, Brian 1988. 'Korean and Taiwanese firms as international competitors: The challenges ahead', *Columbia Journal of World Business,* Spring: 43–51.
—— and Kuo, W-J. 1991. 'The strategic orientations of firms and the performance of Korea and Taiwan in frontier industries: Lessons from comparative case studies of keyboard and personal computer assembly', *World Development,* 19 (4): 363–74.
Li, K. T. 1988. *The Evolution of Policy Behind Taiwan's Development Success.* New Haven: Yale University Press.
Lieberman, Martin 1987. 'The learning curve, diffusion, and competitive strategy', *Strategic Management Journal,* 8: 441–52.
Lim, Linda and Pang, Eng Fong 1991. *Foreign Direct Investment and Industrialisation in Malaysia, Singapore, Taiwan and Thailand.* Paris: OECD Development Centre.
Lim, Peggy 1991. *Steel: From Ashes Rebuilt to Manufacturing Excellence.* Petaling Jaya, Malaysia: Pelanduk Publications.
Lin, Otto 1994. 'Development and transfer of industrial technology in Taiwan, ROC', in O. Lin, C. T. Shih and J. C. Yang (eds), *Development and Transfer of Industrial Technology.* Amsterdam: Elsevier.
—— C. T. Shih and J. C. Yang (eds) 1994. *Development and Transfer of Industrial Technology.* Amsterdam: Elsevier.
Lin, Yeo 1994. 'The transfer of IC technology: Lessons and experience', Paper presented to APEC seminar on *Technology Transfer,* Taipei, Dec 6–8.
Linden, G., Hart, J., Lenway, S. and Murtha 1998. 'Flying geese as moving targets: Catching up with Japan in advanced displays', *Industry and Innovation,* 5 (1): 11–34.
Liu, Chung-Yuan 1993. 'Government's role in developing a high tech industry: The case of Taiwan's semiconductor industry', *Technovation,* 13 (5): 299–309.
Loh, L. 1997. 'Technological policy and national competitiveness', in K. Y. Tan and M. H. Toh (eds) *Competitiveness of the Singapore economy: A Strategic Perspective.* Singapore: Singapore University Press.
Low, Linda (ed.) 1995. *Wealth of East Asian Nations: Speeches and Writings by Goh Keng Swee.* Singapore: Federal Publications.
—— Heng, T. M., Wong, S. T., Yam, T. K. and Hughes, H. 1993. *Challenge and Response: Thirty Years of the Economic Development Board.* Singapore: Times Academic Press.
—— and Lim, B. L. (eds) 1997. *Strategies of Singapore's Success: Speeches and Writings of Hon Sui Sen.* Singapore: Federal Publications.
Lundvall, Bengt-Ake (ed) 1992. *National Systems of Innovation: Towards a Theory of Innovation and Interactive Learning.* London: Pinter Publishers.
—— and Johnson, Bjorn 1994. 'The learning economy', *Journal of Industry Studies,* 1 (2): pp. 23–42.
Lynn, Leonard 1982. *How Japan Innovates: A Comparison with the US in the case of Oxygen Steelmaking.* Boulder, CO: Westview Press.
McKendrick, David 1992. 'Obstacles to "catch-up": The case of the Indonesian aircraft industry', *Bulletin of Indonesian Economic Studies,* 28 (1): 39–66.
Malerba, F. 1985. *The Semiconductor Business: The Economics of Rapid Growth and Decline.* London: Frances Pinter.
Mascitelli, Ronald (1996). *The Growth Warriors: Creating Sustainable Global Advantage for America's Technology Industries.* Northridge, CA: Technology Perspectives.
Mathews, John A. 1995a. *High-technology Industrialisation in East Asia: The Case of*

the Semiconductor Industry in Taiwan and Korea. Contemporary Economic Issues Series, No. 4. Taipei: Chung-Hua Institution for Economic Research.

—— 1996a. 'Organisational foundations of economic learning', *Human Systems Management*, 15 (2): 113–24.

—— 1996b. 'High technology industrialisation in East Asia: Part 1 Industrialisation through developmental resource leverage; Part 2: The semiconductor industry; Part 3: Ten propositions', *Journal of Industry Studies*, 3 (2): 1–77.

—— 1997a. 'The competitive advantages of the latecomer firm', Paper presented to Academy of Management Annual Conference, (Organisation and Management Theory), Boston, August.

—— 1997b. 'A Silicon Valley of the East: Creating Taiwan's semiconductor industry', *California Management Review*, 39 (4): 26–54.

—— 1998a. 'Fashioning a new Korean model out of the crisis', Working Paper #46 (May 1998), University of California, San Diego: Japan Policy Research Institute.

—— 1998b. 'Jack and the Beanstalk: The creation of dynamic capabilities through knowledge leverage by latecomer firms', Paper presented to Academy of Management Annual Conference (Business Policy and Strategy), San Diego, August.

—— 1998c. 'Fashioning a new Korean model out of the crisis: The rebuilding of institutional capabilities', *Cambridge Journal of Economics*, 22 (6): 747–59.

—— 1999. 'A Silicon Island of the East: Creating a semiconductor industry in Singapore', *California Management Review*, 41 (2): 55–74.

—— and Cho, Dong-Sung 1998. 'Combinative capabilities and organisational learning: The case of the Korean semiconductor industry', *Journal of World Business* (forthcoming).

—— and Poon, T. 1995. 'Innovation alliances in Taiwan: The case of the New PC consortium', *Industry in Free China*, 84 (6): 43–58.

—— and Snow, Charles C. 1998. 'A conversation with The Acer group's Stan Shih on global strategy and management', *Organisational Dynamics*, Summer 1998: 65–74.

Mead, Carver and Conway, Lynn 1980. *Introduction to VLSI Systems*. Reading, MA: Addison-Wesley.

Meaney, Constance Squires 1994. 'State policy and the development of Taiwan's semiconductor industry'. In J. D. Aberbach, D. Dollar and K. L. Sokoloff (eds) *The Role of the State in Taiwan's Development*. Armonk, NY: M. E. Sharpe.

Meng, Khoo-Lee 1994. 'Singapore's experience in technology transfer', Paper presented to APEC seminar on *Technology Transfer*, Taipei, Dec 6–8.

Meyanathan, S. D. (ed.) 1994. 'Industrial structures and the development of small and medium enterprise linkages: Examples from East Asia.' Washington, DC: The World Bank.

Minami, R., Kim, K. S., Makino, F. and Seo, J. H. (eds) 1995. *Acquiring, Adapting and Developing Technologies: Lessons from the Japanese Experience*. London: St. Martin's Press.

Mody, Ashok 1990. 'Institutions and dynamic comparative advantage: the electronics industry in South Korea and Taiwan', *Cambridge Journal of Economics*, 14: 291–314.

Morris-Suzuki, Tessa 1994. *The Technological Transformation of Japan: From the Seventeenth to the Twenty-first Century*. Cambridge: Cambridge University Press.

Mowery, D. and Rosenberg, N. 1989. *Technology and the Pursuit of Economic Growth.* New York: Cambridge University Press.

Mueller, D. C. and Tilton, J. 1969. 'R&D costs as barrier to entry', *Canadian Journal of Economics,* 2.4 (Nov): 570–79.

Murakami, Yasusuke and Patrick, Hugh T. (eds) *The Political Economy of Japan* (in three volumes). Stanford, CA: Stanford University Press.

Muscat, R. J. 1994. *The Fifth Tiger: A Study of Thai Development Policy.* New York: M. E. Sharpe and United Nations University Press.

Myrdal, Gunnar 1968. *Asian Drama: An Inquiry into the Poverty of Nations* (in three volumes). New York: The Twentieth Century Fund.

Najmabadi, F. and Lall, S. 1995. 'Developing industrial technology: Lessons for policy and practice.' Washington, DC: The World Bank.

Natarajan, S. and Miang, T. J. 1992. *The impact of MNC investments in Malaysia, Singapore and Thailand.* Singapore: Institute of South East Asian Studies.

Nelson, Richard R. 1990. 'Acquiring technology', in H. Soesastro, and M. Pangestu (eds) 1990. *Technological Challenge in the Asia-Pacific Economy.* Sydney: Allen & Unwin.

—— (ed.) 1993. *National Innovation Systems.* New York: Oxford University Press.

—— 1998. 'The coevolution of technology, industrial structure, and supporting institutions', in G. Dosi, D. Teece and J. Chytry (eds) *Technology, Organisation, and Competitiveness: Perspectives on Industrial and Corporate Change.* New York: Oxford University Press.

—— and Sidney G. Winter 1982. *An Evolutionary Theory of Economic Change.* Cambridge, MA: The Belknap Press of Harvard University Press.

Nishi, N. 1993. 'The Japanese semiconductor industry', in B. Wellenius, A. Miller and C. J. Dahlman (eds) *Developing the Electronics Industry.* Washington, DC: World Bank.

Nonaka, Ikujiro 1994. 'A dynamic theory of organisational knowledge creation', *Organisation Science,* 5 (1): 14–37.

—— and Takeuchi, Hirotaka 1995. *The Knowledge-creating Company: How Japanese Companies Create the Dynamics of Competition.* New York: Oxford University Press.

NRC 1984. *The Competitive Status of the US Electronics Industry: A Study of the Influences of Technology in Determining International Industrial Competitive Advantage.* Washington: National Research Council/National Academy Press.

—— 1992. *U.S.–Japan Strategic Alliances in the Semiconductor Industry: Technology Transfer, Competition, and Public Policy.* Washington: National Research Council.

—— 1996. *Open Trade Policy for High-tech Industry Promotes Technological Progress.* Washington: National Research Council/National Academy Press.

O'Connor, D. 1993. 'Electronics and industrialisation: Approaching the 21st century'. In K. S. Jomo (ed.) *Industrialising Malaysia: Policy, Performance and Prospects.* London: Routledge.

Odagiri, H. and Goto, A. 1996. *Technology and Industrial Development in Japan. Building Capabilities by Learning, Innovation and Public Policy.* Oxford: Clarendon Press.

OECD 1992. *Technology and the Economy: The Key Relationships.* Paris: Organisation for Economic Cooperation and Development.

Okimoto, Daniel 1989. *Between MITI and the Market: Japanese Industrial Policy for High Technology.* Stanford: Stanford University Press.

—— Sugano, T. and Weinstein, F. (eds) 1984. *Competitive Edge: The Semiconductor Industry in the US and Japan.* Stanford: Stanford University Press.

OTA 1991. *Competing Economies: America, Europe and the Pacific Rim.* Washington, DC: Office of Technology Assessment.

Ozawa, T. 1979. *Multinationalism, Japanese Style: The Political Economy of Outward Dependency.* Princeton: Princeton University Press.

Pack, H. and Westphal, L. 1986. 'Industrial strategy and technological change: theory versus reality', *Journal of Development Economics*, 22, pp. 87–128.

Park, W. H. and Enos, J. L. 1991. *The Adoption and Diffusion of Imported Technology: The Case of Korea.* London: Routledge.

Park, Woo-Hee 1995. Technology transfer and absorption in Korea: Methodology and measurement, *Seoul Journal of Economics*, 8 (2): 195–226.

Patrick, H. (ed.) 1986. *Japan's High Technology Industry: Lessons and Limitations of Industrial Policy.* Seattle: University of Washington Press.

Pavitt, K. 1985. 'Technology transfer in the context of the newly emerging international division of labor'. In N. Rosenberg and C. Frischtak (eds) *International Technology Transfer: Concepts, Measures and Comparisons.* New York: Praeger.

Pecht, M., Bernstein, J. B., Searls, D. and Peckerar, M. 1997. *The Korean Electronics Industry.* (The Electronics Industry Research Series: World Technology Evaluation Center, University of Maryland) Boca Raton, FL: CRC Press.

Peck, M. J. and Tamura, S. 1976. 'Technology' in H. Patrick and H. Rosovsky (eds) *Asia's New Giant.* Washington, DC: The Brookings Institution.

—— and Goto, A. 1981. 'Technology and economic growth: The case of Japan', *Research Policy*, 10 (3): 222–43.

Polanyi, Michael 1967. *The Tacit Dimension.* Garden City, New York: Doubleday Anchor.

Porter, Michael 1985. *Competitive Advantage: Creating and Sustaining Superior Performance.* New York: The Free Press.

—— 1990. *The Competitive Advantage of Nations.* New York: The Free Press.

—— 1994. 'The competitive advantage of Far Eastern business: A response', *Journal of Far Eastern Business*, 1 (2): 1–12.

Prahalad, C. K. and Hamel, Gary 1990. 'The core competence of the corporation', *Harvard Business Review*, May–June: 79–91.

Quinn, J. B. 1969. Technology transfer by multinational companies, *Harvard Business Review*, 47, 6 (Nov–Dec): 147–61.

Ranis, Gustav (ed.) 1992. *Taiwan: From Developing to Mature Economy.* Boulder, CO: Westview Press.

Rao, V., Bhanoji, V. and Lee, Christopher 1995. 'Sources of growth in the Singapore economy and its manufacturing and service sectors', *Singapore Economic Review*, 40 (1): 83–115.

Rasiah, Rajah 1994. 'Flexible production systems and local machine tool subcontracting: Electronics components transnationals in Malaysia', *Cambridge Journal of Economics*, 18 (3): 279–98.

—— 1995. *Foreign Capital and Industrialisation in Malaysia* (Studies in the Economies of East and South-East Asia). London: St Martin's Press.

—— 1996. 'Innovation and institutions: Moving towards the technological frontier in the electronics industry in Malaysia', *Journal of Industry Studies*, 3 (2): 79–102.

Ravenhill, John (ed.) 1995. *The Political Economy of East Asia* (six volumes). Aldershot: Edward Elgar.

Reddy, N. M. and Zhao, L. 1990. 'International technology transfer: A review', *Research Policy*, 19: 285–307.

Rodan, G. 1989. *The Political Economy of Singapore's Industrialisation: National State and International Capital.* London: Macmillan.

Rogers, Everett 1995. *Diffusion of Innovations* (fourth edition). New York: The Free Press.

Root, H. 1996. *Small Countries, Big Lessons: Governance and the Rise of East Asia.* Report of the Asian Development Bank. Hong Kong: Oxford University Press.

Rosenberg, Nathan 1976. *Perspectives on Technology.* Cambridge: Cambridge University Press.

—— 1992. 'Joseph Schumpeter: Radical Economist', Paper presented to Schumpeter Society in Kyoto, August 1992. In N. Rosenberg 1994. *Exploring the Black Box: Technology, Economics and History.* Cambridge: Cambridge University Press.

—— and Frischtak, Claudio (eds) 1985. *The International Transfer of Technology: Concepts, Measures and Comparisons.* New York: Praeger Publishers.

—— Landau, R. and Mowery, D. (eds) 1992. *Technology and the Wealth of Nations.* Stanford, CA: Stanford University Press.

Rowen, Henry 1998 (ed.) *Behind East Asian Growth: The Social and Political Foundations of Prosperity.* London: Routledge.

Samuels, Richard J. 1994. *'Rich Nation, Strong Army': National Security and Technological Transformation of Japan.* Ithaca: Cornell University Press.

—— 1996. 'Japan as a Technological Superpower', JPRI Working Paper, no. 15. Cardiff, CA: Japan Policy Research Institute.

San, Gee and Kuo, Wen-Jeng 1993. 'Technological dynamism behind Taiwan's successful export performance: An examination of the electronics and textile industries': Report to UNCTAD. Taipei: Chung-Hua Institution for Economic Research.

Saxenian, AnnaLee 1996/1994. *Regional Advantage: Culture and Competition in Silicon Valley and Route 128.* Cambridge, MA: Harvard University Press.

Schein, Edgar 1996. *Strategic Pragmatism: The Culture of Singapore's Economic Development Board.* Cambridge, MA: The MIT Press.

Schive, Chi 1989. 'The next stage of industrialisation in Taiwan and Korea', in G. Gereffi and D. Wyman (eds) *Manufacturing Miracles: Paths of Industrialisation in Latin America and East Asia.* Princeton: Princeton University Press.

—— 1990. *The Foreign Factor: The Multinational Corporation's Contribution to the Economic Modernisation of the Republic of China.* Stanford University: Hoover Institution Press.

—— and Hsueh, Kuang-Tao 1987. 'The experiences and prospects of high-technology industrial development in Taiwan, ROC: The case of the information industry'. Conference on the Industrial Policies of the Republics of China and of Korea.Taipei: Chung-Hua Institution for Economic Research.

Schnaars, S. 1994. *Managing Imitation Strategies: How Later Entrants Seize Markets from Pioneers.* New York: The Free Press.

Schumpeter, Joseph A. 1911/1934/1961. *The Theory of Economic Development: An Inquiry into Profits, Capital, Credit, Interest and the Business Cycle.* Cambridge, MA: Harvard University Press.

—— 1928. 'The instability of capitalism', *Economic Journal*, 38 (151) Sept.: pp. 361–86. (Reproduced in U. Witt (ed.) 1993. *Evolutionary Economics.* Aldershot: Edward Elgar.)

—— 1942/1950. *Capitalism, Socialism and Democracy.* New York: Harper & Brothers. (Third edition 1950).

Shin, J. S. 1996. *The Economics of the Latecomers: Catching-up, Technology Transfer and Institutions in Germany, Japan and South Korea.* London: Routledge.

Shu, C. Y. and Tu, L. C. 1992 'Designing, operating a submicron facility with isolation technology', *Microcontamination*, March 1992.

SIA 1981. *The International Microelectronic Challenge.* Cupertino, CA: The Semiconductor Industry Association.

—— 1983. *The Effect of Government Targeting on World Semiconductor Competition.* Cupertino, CA: Semiconductor Industry Association.

Sigurdson, J. 1986. *Industry and State Partnership in Japan: The VLSI Project.* Lund: Research Policy Institute, University of Lund (edited and reproduced in *Industry and Innovation*, 5 (2) Dec. 1998).

Simon, D. F. 1992. 'Taiwan's emerging technological trajectory: Creating new forms of competitive advantage', in D. F. Simon and M. Y. M. Kau (eds) *Taiwan: Beyond the Economic Miracle.* Armonk, NY: M. E. Sharpe.

—— 1993. 'Strategic underpinnings of the electronics industry in the newly industrialised economies of Asia', in B. Wellenius, A. Miller and C. J. Dahlman (eds) *Developing the Electronics Industry.* Washington, DC: World Bank.

—— (ed.) 1995. *The Emerging Technological Trajectory of the Pacific Rim.* Armonk, NY: M. E. Sharpe.

—— and Soh, Chan-rok 1994. 'Korea's Technological Development', *Pacific Review*, 7 (1): 89–103.

Soesastro, H. and Pangestu, M. (eds) 1990. *Technological Challenge in the Asia-Pacific Economy.* Sydney: Allen & Unwin.

Soete, L. 1985. 'International diffusion of technology, industrial development and technological leapfrogging', *World Development*, 13 (3): 409–22.

Soh, Chang-Rok 1992. 'Political economy and technological innovation: Implications for development of high-tech industries in Korea', *Korean Journal of Policy Studies*, 7 (Dec): 73–97.

Song, Byung-Nak 1990. *The Rise of the Korean Economy.* New York: Oxford University Press.

Soon, Teck-Wong and Tan, C. Suan 1993. *Singapore: Public policy and economic development.* Washington, DC: World Bank.

Spencer, W. J. and Grindley, P. 1993. 'SEMATECH after five years: High-technology consortia and U.S. competitiveness', *California Management Review*, Summer: 9–32.

Steers, R., Yoo, K.S. and Ungson, G. 1989. *The Chaebol: Korea's New Industrial Might.* New York: Harper & Row.

Steinmueller, W. Edward 1993. 'The US, Japanese and global integrated circuit industry: Prospects for new entrants', in B. Wellenius, A. Miller and C. J. Dahlman (eds) *Developing the Electronics Industry.* Washington, DC: World Bank.

Stiglitz, J. 1987. 'Learning to learn, localised learning and technological progress.' In P. Dasgupta and P. Stoneman (eds), *Economic Policy and Technological Performance.* New York: Cambridge University Press.

Tan, K. Y. and Toh M. H. (eds) *Competitiveness of the Singapore Economy: A Strategic Perspective.* Singapore: Singapore University Press.

Tanaka, M. 1989. 'Japanese-style evaluation systems for R&D projects: The MITI experience, *Research Policy* 18: 361–78.

Tang, H. K. and Yeo, K. T. 1995. 'Technology, entrepreneurship and national development: lessons from Singapore', *International Journal of Technology Management*, 10 (7/8): 797–814.

Taniura, T. 1993. 'The Lucky-Goldstar Group in the Republic of Korea', *The Developing Economies*, 31 (4): 465–82.

Teece, D. 1992. 'Competition, cooperation and innovation: Organisational arrangements for regimes of rapid technological progress', *Journal of Economic Behavior and Organisation*, 18: 1–25.

—— 1997. 'Managing intellectual capital: Licensing and cross-licensing in semiconductors and electronics', *California Management Review*, 39 (2): 1–34.

—— Pisano, G. and Shuen, A. 1997. 'Dynamic capabilities and strategic management', *Strategic Management Journal*, 18 (7): 509–33.

Tsiang, S. C. 1989. *Success or Failure in Economic Take-Off*, CIER Economic Monograph Series No. 26. Taipei: Chung-Hua Institution for Economic Research.

Turpin, Tim, Lian, Yanhua, Jian Tong and Xin Fang 1995. 'Technology and innovation networks in the People's Republic of China', *Journal of Industry Studies*, 2 (2): 63–74.

Tushman, Michael L. and Anderson, Philip 1986. 'Technological discontinuities and organisational environments', *Administrative Science Quarterly*, 31: 439–56.

Tyson, Laura D'Andrea 1992. *Who's Bashing Whom? Trade Conflict in High-technology Industries*, Institute for International Economics, Washington DC.

US Congress 1984. 'Japanese technological advances and possible United States responses using research joint ventures'. Committee on Science and Technology, Washington, DC.

Utterback, James M. and Abernathy, William J. 1975. 'A dynamic model of process and product innovation', *Omega*, 6: 639–56.

—— and Suarez, F. 1993. 'Innovation, competition and industry structure', *Research Policy*, 22: 1–21.

Van de Ven, Andrew and Garud, Raghu 1989. 'A framework for understanding the emergence of new industries', *Research on Technological Innovation, Management and Policy*, 4: 195–225.

—— 1993. 'Innovation and industry development: The case of cochlear implants', *Research on Technological Innovation, Management and Policy*, 5: 1–46.

Vernon, R. 1966. 'International investment and international trade in the product cycle', *Quarterly Journal of Economics*, 80 (2): 190–207.

—— 1979. 'The product cycle hypothesis in a new economic environment', *Oxford Bulletin of Economics and Statistics*, 41, 255–67.

Vogel, E. F. 1991. *The Four Little Dragons: The Spread of Industrialisation in East Asia.* Cambridge, MA: Harvard University Press.

Wade, Robert 1990. *Governing the Market: Economic Theory and the Role of Government in East Asian Industrialisation.* Princeton, NJ: Princeton University Press.

Wang, Jiann-Chyuan 1994. Cooperative research in a newly industrialised country: Taiwan, *Research Policy*, 23: 697–711.

Weiss, Linda 1994. 'Government–business relations in East Asia: The changing basis of State capacity', *Asian Perspective*, 18 (2): 85–118.

—— 1995. 'Governed interdependence: rethinking the government-business relationship in East Asia', *Pacific Review*, 8 (4): 589–616.

—— 1998. *The Myth of the Powerless State: Governing the Economy in a Global Era.* Cambridge: Polity Press and Ithaca: Cornell University Press.

—— and Hobson, John 1995. *States and Economic Development: A Comparative Historical Analysis.* Cambridge: Polity Press.

—— and Mathews, John 1994. 'Innovation Alliances in Taiwan: A coordinated approach to developing and diffusing technology', *Journal of Industry Studies*, 1 (2): 91–101.

Wellenius, Bjorn, Miller, Arnold and Dahlman, Carl J. (eds) 1993. *Developing the Electronics Industry: A World Bank Symposium.* Washington, DC: The World Bank.

Westney, D. Eleanor 1996. 'The Japanese business system: Key features and prospects for change', *Journal of Asian Business*, vol. 12, no. 1, pp. 21–50.

Westphal, L., Kim, Linsu and Dahlman, K. 1985. 'Reflections on the Republic of Korea's acquisition of technological capability'. In N. Rosenberg and C. Frischtak (eds) *The International Transfer of Technology: Concepts, Measures and Comparisons.* New York: Praeger Publishers.

Winter, S. 1987. Knowledge and competence as strategic assets. In David Teece (ed.) *The Competitive Challenge: Strategies for Industrial Innovation and Renewal.* New York: Ballinger.

Wong, Poh-Kam 1991. 'Technological development through subcontracting linkages.' Tokyo: Asian Productivity Organisation.

—— 1995. 'Competing in the global electronics industry: A comparative study of the innovation networks of Singapore and Taiwan', *Journal of Industry Studies*, 2 (2): 35–62.

—— 1997. 'Upgrading Singapore's manufacturing industry', in M. H. Toh and K. Y. Tam (eds) *Competitiveness of the Singapore Economy.* Singapore: Singapore University Press.

—— and Mathews, John A. 1998. 'Introduction to the special issue: The global dynamics of the flat panel display industry', *Industry and Innovation*, 5 (1): 1–10.

Woo, Jung-En 1991. *Race to the Swift: State and Finance in Korean Industrialisation.* (Studies of the East Asian Institute). New York: Columbia University Press.

World Bank 1993. *The East Asian Miracle.* New York: Oxford University Press.

Wortzel, L. H. and Wortzel, H. V. 1981. 'Export marketing strategies for NIC and LDC-based firms', *Columbia Journal of World Business*, Spring 1981.

Wu, S. 1992. 'The dynamic cooperation between government and enterprise: The development of Taiwan's integrated circuit industry. In N. T. Wang (ed.) *Taiwan's Enterprises in Global Perspective.* New York: M. E. Sharpe.

Yamamura, Kozo (ed.) 1997. *The Economic Emergence of Modern Japan.* Cambridge, UK: Cambridge University Press.

—— and Hatch, Walter 1997. 'A looming entry barrier: Japan's production networks in Asia', *NBR Analysis*, 8 (1). Washington: National Bureau of Asian Research.

Yanagihara, Toru and Sambommatsu, Susumu (eds) 1997 *East Asian Development Experience: Economic System Approach and its Applicability.* Tokyo: Institute of Developing Economies.

Yeung, Henry W. C. (ed.) 1999. *The Globalisation of Business Firms from Emerging Economies.* Cheltenham, UK: Edward Elgar.

—— 1998. 'The political economy of transnational corporations: a study of the regionalisation of Singaporean firms', *Political Geography*, 17 (4): 389–416.

Yoffie, David B. 1990. *International Trade and Competition: Cases and notes in strategy and management.* New York: McGraw-Hill.

Yoon, Chang-Ho 1992. 'International competition and market penetration: A model of the growth strategy of the Korean semiconductor industry'. In G. K. Helleiner (ed.) *Trade Policy, Industrialisation and Development: New Perspectives.* Oxford: Clarendon Press.

Yoon, Jeong-Ro 1989. 'The State and Private Capital in Korea: The Political

Economy of the Semiconductor Industry, 1965–87'. PhD Thesis, Harvard University, Cambridge, MA.

Young, Alwyn 1994. 'Lessons from the East Asian NICs: A contrarian view', *European Economic Review*, 38 (3–4): 964–73.

Yu, Tzong-shian and Lee, Joseph S. (eds) 1995. *S. C. Tsiang: His Contribution to Economic Theory*. Taipei: Chung-Hua Institution for Economic Research.

Zhao, H. 1995. 'Technological imports and their impacts on the enhancement of China's indigenous technological capability', *Journal of Development Studies*, 31 (4): 585–602.

Index